ARBITRATION IN THE DIGITAL AGE

Arbitration in the Digital Age analyzes how technology can be efficiently and legitimately used to further sound arbitration proceedings. The contributions from a variety of arbitration scholars report on current developments, predict future trends and assess their impact from a practical, legal, and technical point of view. The book also discusses the relationship between arbitration and the Internet and analyzes how social media can affect arbitrators and counsel's behaviour. Furthermore, it analyzes the validity of electronic arbitration agreements and awards, as well as Online Arbitration (OArb). The volume establishes, on a very practical level, how technology could be used by arbitration institutions, arbitrators, parties to an arbitration and counsel. This book will be of special interest to arbitrators and lawyers involved in international commercial arbitration.

MAUD PIERS is Professor of Law at the University of Ghent in Belgium where she focuses her research and teaching on arbitration law, European private law and Alternative Dispute Resolution (ADR). She is also the director of the UGent's Transnational Law Center that studies the role of technology at the service or as a means to resolve transnational business disputes. She regularly acts as an arbitrator and is Vice-President of the Belgian Center of Arbitration and Mediation (Cepani). She was a founder and is currently an editor (and former editor-in-chief) of the *Belgian Review for Arbitration*; an editor for *Tijdschrift@ipr.be*; an editor of the *Nederlands-Vlaams Tijdschrift voor Mediation en Conflict Management*; and a 'korrespondierende Herausgeber' of the Zeitschrift für Europäisches Privatrecht.

CHRISTIAN ASCHAUER is professor of arbitration law and practice at the University of Graz (Austria) and Independent Arbitrator based in Vienna. His practice encompasses different industry sectors, with an emphasis on engineering, general trade, machinery and corporate disputes. He is also a member of the Arbitral Council of the Chamber of Arbitration of Milan (Camera Arbitrale di Milano). Christian Aschauer has conducted arbitrations, including arbitrations with states and state entities, under the Rules of the ICC, VIAC, DIS, Camera Arbitrale di Milano, FTCA (Belgrade) and UNCITRAL, as well as ad hoc arbitral proceedings. He is a frequent speaker at seminars and is publishing in the field of arbitration as well as mediation.

ARBITRATION IN THE DIGITAL AGE

The Brave New World of Arbitration

Edited by

MAUD PIERS

University of Ghent

CHRISTIAN ASCHAUER

University of Graz

CAMBRIDGE
UNIVERSITY PRESS

CAMBRIDGE
UNIVERSITY PRESS

University Printing House, Cambridge CB2 8BS, United Kingdom

One Liberty Plaza, 20th Floor, New York, NY 10006, USA

477 Williamstown Road, Port Melbourne, VIC 3207, Australia

314-321, 3rd Floor, Plot 3, Splendor Forum, Jasola District Centre, New Delhi - 110025, India

79 Anson Road, #06-04/06, Singapore 079906

Cambridge University Press is part of the University of Cambridge.

It furthers the University's mission by disseminating knowledge in the pursuit of education, learning and research at the highest international levels of excellence.

www.cambridge.org
Information on this title: www.cambridge.org/9781108417907
DOI: 10.1017/9781108283670

First published 2018

A catalogue record for this publication is available from the British Library

ISBN 978-1-108-41790-7 Hardback

CONTENTS

CONTRIBUTORS

MOHAMED S. ABDEL WAHAB, Partner, Zulficar & Partners (Cairo), Vice President of the ICC International Court of Arbitration

CHRISTIAN ASCHAUER, Professor at the University of Graz (Austria), Independent Arbitrator

NIUSCHA BASSIRI, Partner, Hanotiau & van den Berg (Bruxelles)

MAX BURGER-SCHEIDLIN, General Manager of ICC Austria and Consultant at ICC Commercial Crime Services

PAUL H COHEN, Barrister, 4–5 Gray's Inn Square (London) and Editor in Chief of the *Journal of Technology in International Arbitration*

TONY COLE, Of Counsel, Gentium Law Group (Geneva)

PABLO CORTÉS, Professor at the University of Leicester Law School (UK)

ANNET VAN HOOFT, Partner, Bird & Bird (Paris)

ETHAN KATSH, Director, National Center for Technology and Dispute Resolution and Professor Emeritus, University of Massachusetts Amherst

JULIA KROES-LASTOCHKINA, Associate, Clifford Chance (Amsterdam)

SOPHIE NAPPERT, Independent Arbitrator, 3 Verulam Buildings (London)

MAUD PIERS, Professor at the University of Ghent (Belgium), Independent Arbitrator

PHILIPP SCHAUMANN, Independent Security Consultant, Lecturer at the Donau University Krems (Austria)

AMY J. SCHMITZ, Professor at the University of Missouri School of Law

ERIK SCHÄFER, Partner, Cohaus & Florack (Düsseldorf) and Co-Chair of the ICC Task Force on the Use of Information Technology in International Arbitration

MARC D. VEIT, Partner, Lalive (Zurich)

REINMAR WOLFF, Assistant Professor at the University of Marburg (Germany) and Independent Arbitrator

FOREWORD

Welcome to the 'Brave New World of Arbitration'

The interaction between technology and arbitration is not something for the future – it is happening right now. The challenge that lies before us is how to integrate technology in an orderly fashion and use it in order to improve arbitration. Technology will change the way we arbitrate. It is up to the arbitration community to decide on how this happens, not when.

The international arbitration community has always been focused on improving the efficiency and overall quality of arbitration. The different stakeholders in arbitration seek to optimize such factors as the duration and costs of arbitration, as well as the transparency and predictability of these factors. The key question is now how technology can (continue to) play a role in achieving these goals.

Three ways of interaction between arbitration and technology are distinguished here.

The first one is the most comprehensible, i.e. whereby parties and arbitrators make use of technology, e.g. online and electronic tools, in support of the procedure. Costs and time are saved by communicating solely by way of email and filing submissions and exhibits on an online platform or 'drop box', the access to which is provided by the arbitral institution or the arbitrator. Moreover, over the last few years, procedural hearings have been increasingly held by telephone or video-conference. In contrast, witness hearings or hearings on the merits today largely remain physical encounters which have to be planned well in advance and which have an important impact on the arbitration costs. How much longer will it take before an arbitrator, counsel and parties, all in the comfort of their own office, log in to a virtual hearing room wearing their virtual reality glasses, instead of flying out to some major capital for a weeklong witness hearing. There can be little doubt that this evolution adds to the efficiency of the arbitral process. The question is of course whether this does not pose a threat to the principles of fairness and due process. We believe that this should not be the case, provided that the tools are available to cover the issue of security.

The second interaction is in full development: the creation and use of platforms for Online Dispute Resolution (ODR) to facilitate dispute resolution. ODR platforms exist in all shapes and sizes and can serve different purposes, but they all aim at resolving a dispute in a simple, fast, flexible and efficient way. The main question surrounding ODR is how to guarantee that the fundamental principles of dispute resolution are preserved. An ODR system should meet the principles of fairness, due process, transparency, accountability, independence, impartiality, efficiency and effectiveness. Until now, the main focus of ODR is to get disputes regarding low-value transactions away from traditional judicial systems. To that end, an ODR system will try not to impose costs, delays or burdens that are disproportionate to the economic value at stake. ODR can also be a relevant solution when traditional judicial mechanisms for legal recourse may not offer an adequate solution for cross-border e-commerce disputes. The ODR platform created by the European Union in 2015 tries to meet that goal, although it would appear it is primarily a way for consumers to (try to) interact with traders when a dispute has arisen.

One of the most interesting features of ODR platforms is that they usually offer different ways or levels to resolve a dispute. In general, an ODR process will have three stages: negotiation, facilitated settlement and a third/final stage with some kind of adjudication. An ODR process will start up with a notice of claim through an ODR platform, whereby the ODR administrator will notify the respondent. After that, a technology-enabled negotiation stage will start. Known forms are, e.g. double-blind bidding or visual-blind bidding, whereby an algorithm will either generate suggestions or automatically settle a monetary claim if the parties' proposals/offers fall within the range (zone of agreement) set or accepted by them. One could state that it is an automated, and perhaps more precise, form of baseball arbitration, whereby parties are encouraged to be reasonable.

In any case, a result should be obtained within a certain timeframe after which the ODR system will move to the next stage, the facilitated settlement. Here, the ODR administrator will appoint a neutral intermediary who will communicate with the parties in an attempt to reach a settlement. If that fails, the parties will move to the third and final stage which is a dispute resolution through arbitration, third-party binding decision, expert determination, etc. Therefore, in the end, it all comes back to classic adjudication by a judge, an arbitrator or an expert, who – as a human – will weigh the elements of the dispute at hand and make a final decision.

This brings us to the third way that technology will interact with arbitration, i.e. the ever-growing science of artificial intelligence. Data mining is gradually finding its way into the field of law. Systems exist whereby case law and doctrine are selected out of huge databases in order to generate a first opinion on a question of law. And just around the corner are systems which learn and therefore create such opinions themselves in order to solve legal issues.

We no longer ask ourselves the question how can bolts most efficiently be screwed into a car: by a robot or by a human being? Soon we may not even reflect anymore upon the question who is more efficient at coming up with relevant case law and doctrine for a certain legal issue: a paralegal or a computer? How far are we from asking the same question when it comes to suggesting a solution for a legal issue, i.e. whether it is more efficient to hire an associate at the firm or to order some form of advanced computer software? And finally, at what point in time will we rely on the decision taken by such a software as opposed to an arbitrator or state judge? When drafting an arbitral clause, will we soon make the distinction between artificial intelligence (AI) arbitration and human arbitration, instead of the choice between institutional and ad hoc arbitration as we do today?

The opportunity to ask ourselves the question whether we want this evolution to take place is long gone. The remaining question is how we want it, in order to avoid a society strictly run by logic, by ways of formulas and equations, as described in the 1921 dystopian novel *We* by Yevgeny Zamyatin. So it is time to get to work. It is time to think or rethink any and all aspects of arbitration, from the appointment of an arbitrator right up to the final award, and identify how the process can be made more efficient through interaction with technology. The field lays wide open and the academic world, the arbitral institutions and the users of arbitration all have a role to play. Undoubtedly it will be a step-by-step process, in which this book forms an important part, but we should heighten our pace.

Technology is not a menace to arbitration. It can and should be used to enhance the aspects for which arbitration is criticized today. Our strength is that dispute resolution in commercial disputes, in many jurisdictions around the world, is not and has never been the monopoly of State judicial systems. To the contrary, in international commercial relationships, alternative ways to resolve disputes remain increasingly popular. The international arbitration community has grown and is still growing in strength at a very high pace. We should use this strength to stay on top of our game and applaud any initiative taken in the direction of further increasing it, whatever angle taken.

Dispute resolution is a very serious matter and it has been so ever since the first dispute arose. Over centuries, mankind has identified the standards for fair adjudication. Technology, on the other hand, is an equally serious matter. The staggering pace of technological development causes last year's inventions to be outdated today. Justice and technology have now met; they have started to interact; and they will interact more and more, faster than we can all believe or even imagine.

This remarkable book not only identifies the different challenges before us, it also directs us to (find) the answers.

Dirk De Meulemeester
President, CEPANI

Introduction

MAUD PIERS AND CHRISTIAN ASCHAUER

Arbitration Unplugged?

Technological innovations have transformed the way in which people and businesses interact and have permeated almost every aspect of our lives. Count the number of screens that surround you and you will get only a slight idea of how 'tech-enabled' our professional and private lives have become. We have certainly not reached the technological finishing line (and probably never will). The future seems to be that of more and increasingly powerful information technology (IT) applications.

It is therefore surprising that arbitration has, in comparison, undergone only modest changes. In promoting arbitration, the mantra is that arbitration is an efficient and fair procedure that is freely tailored to specific requirements of the dispute and the needs of the parties involved, and this much more so than could be expected of a regular court proceeding. One of the main characteristics of arbitration is that it is not bound by a preconceived set of rules; eliminating unnecessary formalities saves on time and costs. This is exactly where technology can play a much greater role than it has taken up so far. The question is only how fast arbitration will adapt: Are we waiting for the generation of digital natives to modernize arbitration? Or is the generation of digital immigrants, which currently still make up the large majority of the arbitration community, ready to reinvent themselves and break free from some of the preconceived notions of what an adjudicative process should be?

Tales of Innovation and Arbitration

This book aims to explore how arbitration is catching up with the rapid changes in our electronically connected world. We are immensely grateful to our authors who undertook to establish how technology could be used to optimize efficiency and identify the most significant challenges that arbitration practitioners will encounter along the way. To that end, they report on recent developments, predict future trends and analyze their impact from a practical, a legal and a technical point of view.

Our authors will not stop at merely improving the 'efficiency' of the process. They also ponder how technology can be used in international (commercial) arbitration without jeopardizing the legitimacy and quality of the process and the parties' right of due process. They also consider potential threats to the confidentiality and security of the information stored or communicated. Finally, our authors even examine whether and in what circumstances a technology-assisted or even technology-based arbitration could outdo the traditional human-driven equivalent, thereby abolishing the system of adjudication as we know it.

Why Read This Book?

There are three main indications, from both an academic and a practical point of view, that the work of our authors is of utmost relevance for all generations of lawyers, the digital natives and the digital immigrants.

Firstly, there is a factual reality that simply cannot be ignored and that results from the immensely successful application of new information and communication technologies (ICTs). This trend has dramatically altered the ways in which people or businesses interact. Digital technology has created ubiquitous connectivity and increased the potential for business opportunities on a global scale. It has boosted virtual mobility and has reduced the practical constraints of geographic distance. One could even say that it has made national borders meaningless, though at the same time, resulting in an increasingly complex legal reality.

As the number of cross-border transactions has multiplied, this has given rise to a multitude of cross-border disputes. For a long time, this was where the 'technology push' encountered its limits: while interpersonal dealings started to occur increasingly 'online', resolving potential disputes often remained an 'offline' or face-to-face endeavour. Technology has thus for a long time been underutilized for the actual conduct of dispute resolution proceedings. This has, however, effectively changed over the last ten years, as the use of ICTs in the service of dispute resolution has become unavoidable. Businesses rightly expect that the dispute resolution mechanism which they select lives up to the standards of virtual mobility and connectivity they are used to in their day-to-day dealings.

Secondly, many legislative proposals and working groups' activities currently focus on the use of new ICTs in dispute resolution. The work of the Hague Conference on Private International Law in the context of evidence taken abroad, for instance, reveals that there is a lively debate on the use of information technology and a revision of the Evidence Convention to allow, for instance, video-conferencing in state court proceedings. The recent EU instruments resulting in the Online Dispute Resolution (ODR) Regulation are an illustration of another equally important trend, namely to refer (consumer) disputes to online dispute resolution. In this context, there is also a concern that the European legislature shows for a party's right to 'human decision-making', for instance in the context of general data protection, where one has the right to object to automated decision-making and where automated decision-making is allowed under certain circumstances. According to Article 22(3) of the General Data Protection Regulation, a party has 'at least the right to obtain human intervention on the part of the controller, to express his or her point of view and to contest the decision'. Furthermore, there is the initiative of the UNCITRAL Working Group III on Online Dispute Resolution.[1]

Similarly, several arbitration institutions have made significant efforts to modernize arbitration proceedings and to bring them up to speed with technological innovation. An example is the Netherlands Arbitration Institute, which allows and effectively promotes an e-arbitration procedure. This is in line with a trend that is now firmly anchored in the Netherlands Arbitration Law, which explicitly allows the electronic conduct of arbitration proceedings (Article 1072(b) DCCP). We also notice a revival of the ICC Commission on Arbitration and ADR's Task Force on Information Technology in Arbitration, which has presented an enlightening report on Information Technology in arbitration in light of current developments.

Thirdly, as we observe that practitioners increasingly rely (or have to rely) on technology and the Internet to optimize the efficiency of the arbitration procedure, various actors in the arbitration field have echoed the sentiment that scientific research into this development is urgently needed. That is why in October 2015 the Transnational Law Center (University of Ghent) and the Institute for Civil Procedure and Insolvency Law (University of Graz), in cooperation with the Belgian Centre for Arbitration and Mediation (CEPANI) and the Vienna International Arbitration Centre (VIAC), set up a survey on the use of technology in the context of arbitration ('the Survey'). The results of the Survey confirmed that there is indeed very strong interest in technology as a tool to optimize the arbitration procedure. However, the Survey also confirmed the hypothesis that, although most lawyers are technophiles, their use of

[1] See www.uncitral.org/uncitral/commission/working_groups/3Online_Dispute_Resolution.html.

technology is often limited to a functional integration of the most common means of technology into their law practice.

Structure and Topics

This book comprises of the presentation of the results of our survey and two main parts. Part I deals with the use of new ICTs in international arbitration. In this part, the authors discuss the online and electronic tools and services of which the main actors in arbitration (may) avail themselves, already now or in the future, in view of a more efficient and cost-effective procedure, or as a means to facilitate access to justice. They will also deal with security issues, both of a technical and a human nature. In a distinct line of arguments, our authors will analyze how arbitration institutions, legislatures and the practitioner deal with the implementation and application of new ICTs.

In Part II, our book focuses on the relationship between arbitration and the Internet. Our authors analyze the validity of electronic arbitration agreements and awards, as well as Online Arbitration (OArb). This second section also addresses two questions: how the Internet, and more particularly social media, affect arbitrators and their behaviour; and how online legal sources and the Internet of machines determine the strategy that counsel might adopt during an arbitration.

Survey on the Present Use of ICT in International Arbitration

To prepare our book, we found it necessary to go out in the field and collect data on the present use of technology in international arbitration, as this has helped us in the detection of the questions that are of real practical importance. The results of the Survey presented in Chapter 1 provide a significant justification for this book. We understood that arbitration practitioners were integrating new technologies into their practices, but in rather spontaneous and reactive ways, which leave much room for improvement. Above all, they fail to take advantage of the full potential, which new technologies are already providing to other service industries.

Part I: The Use of Technology in International Arbitration

In Chapter 2 Mohamed Wahab and Ethan Katsh provide us with an insightful perspective on what has been called the new 'growth industry' of dispute resolution. On the one hand, the implementation of new technologies leads to additional disputes and even new categories of disputes such as domain name disputes, which are settled online, through a system of non-binding 'arbitration'. On the other hand, technology is used to assist ADR, to perform ADR, and to facilitate dispute prevention. This is not a matter of mere convenience. Quite to the contrary, technology fills in the need for efficiency that, together with trust, is essential for any dispute resolution mechanism. The 'liquid expectations' paradigm compels arbitration practitioners to apply technological processes that have been seen to have value in other contexts. Laws, jurisprudence and legal systems of different countries are openly accessible online. Tablets and iPads are replacing paper-based documents. Naturally, it is easier, faster and more cost-efficient to send a 300-page document through email by a mouse click than sending it by post. Driven by the need to be at least as e-proficient as their clients, lawyers have taken arbitration proceedings online. Online platforms, chatrooms and video-conferencing technologies are increasingly used for electronic synchronous or asynchronous interaction between parties and their arbitral tribunals. One might say this is a matter of due course and simple market pressure.

However, the process will not stop at merely taking arbitration 'online'. The possibility of (partly) replacing human interaction by Artificial Intelligence (AI) in the context of arbitration might no longer be an imaginary tale. It is conceivable that more and more data will not only be submitted, but also processed, categorized and searched electronically. This may make it much easier to reconstruct historical events and may gradually diminish the relevance of oral evidence. The question of 'Who said what to whom?', which vexed generations of lawyers in arbitration and litigation, may thus be replaced by a compilation of email correspondences which is generated automatically.

At this point, two important caveats need to be made, which are information security and the human factor. This will be dealt with in Chapter 3 by Philipp Schaumann and Max Burger-Scheidlin.

We all have to live with the fact that there is no such thing as 100 per cent security. The challenge is, rather, that the measures taken be commensurate with the skills of the possible attackers. The most dangerous species among those attackers are professional players such as companies that specialize in the retrieval of sensitive information, organized crime organizations that target bank accounts of private citizens and companies alike, and governmental services of many countries that either spy on their own citizens and businesses or that engage in industrial espionage in order to help their own industries. Unfortunately, there is a large market for attack tools (programs that can perform attacks), and even attacks-as-a-service (where the whole attack is outsourced).

To protect their businesses, it is imperative for all arbitration practitioners to learn how to apply basic security hygiene. Everybody needs to learn that emails are dangerous and clicks on attachments are only to be done with considerable caution. Everybody needs to select and to protect his or her passwords carefully. Everybody needs to update his or her security software regularly. Another important aspect of basic security hygiene is regular data backup. If emails are synchronized to the smartphone, it is necessary to carefully evaluate the reliability of the provider.

Law firms face additional challenges. They need a strict and effective separation of their internal networks from the Internet through well-managed firewalls. Even within the organization, it may be advisable to secure highly sensitive information against internal attackers (e.g. the young 'intern'). Today, obtaining illicit access to internal data is basic spycraft not only for government services, but also for information-retrieval services. Other issues to be dealt with are email communications (consider digital signatures and encryption), instant messaging and telephone calls, which seem to be the weakest link as they can be intercepted at relatively low cost. US telephone companies have been giving metadata (who called whom, at what time, and how long) to US government services regularly, and the same can be expected in other countries from the local telephone companies as well. Switzerland, by contrast, seems to have strict and extensive data privacy regulations that restrict access by law enforcement or other governmental services.

As crucial as all technical safeguards may be, true security ultimately boils down to the human factor. This brings us to Max Burger-Scheidlin, who specifically asks office managers what the working environment is in their organizations: Is it heavy, emotionally dank and stagnant, or crisp, emotionally warm and invigorating? Will associates be proud of their work? Are they regularly working close to exhaustion? Are associates mature enough to keep confidential matters confidential under all circumstances? Is there a high staff turnover? Even in a digitized world, all these factors remain relevant.

Digitization, moreover, will not protect us against 'social engineering' attacks. Quite to the contrary, it will make them easier. For example, Burger-Scheidlin knows of a case where a specialized boutique law firm handling a number of major, sensitive cases experienced repeated breakdowns of its air-conditioning system during a hot summer. The maintenance engineer had to come in frequently. Later, a review by security specialists revealed that the air-conditioning system was housed in the same utility room as the firm's telephone exchange and computer servers, and that there had been no one supervising the engineer during his repairs to the air-conditioning system.

Against the background of a constantly evolving electronic environment, it is perhaps no surprise that arbitration institutions prefer to stay on the safe side and to use ICT with circumspection. This will be explained by Erik Schäfer in Chapter 4. While using ICT in their daily communications, arbitral institutions regularly notify the Request for Arbitration (or Statement of Claim) to the Claimant by courier, against written proof of receipt. The same applies to the award. This is sound practice considering that arbitration institutions are chosen by the parties over ad hoc arbitration as they are expected to provide a higher level of procedural security.

Some arbitral institutions have also extended their services by offering online file repositories that are administered under the auspices of the respective institutions. For example, WIPO maintains a facility called ECAF, The American Arbitration Association maintains a facility called AAA WebFile, and the ICC International Court of Arbitration had maintained a facility called NetCase, which is currently being relaunched. By doing so, however, arbitral institutions might become Internet Service Providers which could trigger a host of special statutory duties regarding system availability, data integrity and data authenticity. Users may not be ready to pay for this additional offer. It is also apparent that arbitral institutions (have to) take a broader view, as they are rightly concerned about the 'equality of arms'. The party disposing of more technological resources should not per se be structurally favoured by the system over a party that does not have such resources.

The cautious approach of institutions is perhaps complimentary to that of law firms which usually wholeheartedly embrace new ICT solutions. Erik Schäfer concludes that currently, it seems more likely that the usage of ICT, particularly in commercial and investment arbitration, will be driven more by the parties' representatives and less by the arbitral institutions.

In Chapter 5, we shift our focus from the arbitral institution to the legislature. Annet Van Hooft and Julia Kroes refer to the law of a technophile jurisdiction, namely the Netherlands. One of the main goals of the 2015 Arbitration Act was to create an environment where arbitration can take place electronically, from the conclusion of the arbitration agreement up until the notification of the award (Article 1072(b) of the Dutch Civil Procedure Code). This seems to be only one aspect of a much broader initiative in the Netherlands to introduce wholly digital court proceedings, which has been implemented in stages as from 1 January 2017. As of 2019, every party (other than natural persons acting in a personal capacity) will be obliged to conduct the entire civil proceeding in electronic form. This is expected to result in significant cost savings, speedier proceedings and increased accessibility to judges. Interestingly, the Dutch legislature has also simplified the substance of the Civil Procedure Code to bring it in line with the new technologies, for example by introducing more uniform and shorter time limits. The next round of revisions of the major rules of arbitration will show whether the application of ICT technologies will also impact the 'substance' of the arbitration rules. At the very least, it can be expected that arbitration proceedings regarding small claims will become entirely digitized.

In Chapter 6, Sophie Nappert and Paul Cohen examine how ICTs have been and will be affecting the processes and procedures of international arbitration, and they reflect on the (conceivably diminishing) role of the 'human mind' in arbitration. They get under the hood of the arbitration practitioner and examine, more precisely, how the technological advances affect the role of arbitrators and counsel. To examine why technology has not reached its full potential in arbitration, but is rather slowly permeating the arbitration procedure, Sophie Nappert and Paul Cohen focus on video-conferencing. They identify video-conferencing as the single one technology that has the greatest potential for cost savings, and that might have the greatest transformative impact on the arbitral process in the near future. In the past, traditionalists rightly had reservations, stating that everything that one expects from a hearing, formal decorum as well as the informality of personal interaction, is missing from a virtual hearing. As technology continues to develop, however, we will see the release of virtual reality headsets that will represent a step-change in current technology. With their three-dimensional, immersive quality, the headsets will provide a more realistic, real-time feel to a virtual meeting than even today's high-definition video-conferences. Before long, the high costs of these devices will also decrease, as it is the case with all new technologies.

Yet the impact of new technologies will not only be supportive but also transformative of the process. Technology is reaching a phase in which devices can not only compensate for human shortcomings in decision-making, but also substitute their own, more accurate evaluation of the facts. Doctors today, for instance, are increasingly beset by competition from diagnostic tools that perform better on many metrics than human physicians. If we have reached this point, then we must rightly ask ourselves what we want from the arbitral process and what it can deliver. Unimpeachable decisions by humans, or do we need appeals or reviews of computer-generated decisions? What is the place of equity and empathy in a technology-dominated arbitration world? And what will be the place of lawyers when we are increasingly dealing with machines?

Part II: Arbitration, Arbitrators, Counsel and the Internet

In Part II, we move on to the relationship between arbitration and the Internet, starting with electronic arbitration agreements and electronic arbitration awards.

In Chapter 7, Reinmar Wolff explains how electronic arbitration agreements and electronic arbitral awards test the boundaries of traditional form requirements. Arbitration agreements must typically be concluded in writing and may have to be submitted to court. Arbitral awards usually have to be rendered in writing and have to bear the arbitrators' signatures, have to be delivered to the parties, and have to be submitted to court in order to be recognized and enforced. A multitude of national laws and international treaties govern these issues, where the need for harmonization was (and is) obvious. In his analysis, Reinmar Wolff consistently takes an approach which is aiming to achieve this harmonization. This is extremely helpful. The utility of a high-speed train link (online arbitration proceedings) is greatly diminished if certain parts of the railway (arbitration agreements or arbitral awards) are not even electrified.

In Chapter 8, Amy Schmitz considers the use of OArb for resolution of disputes in business-to-consumer transactions. She does so from the perspective of the United States, where pre-dispute arbitration agreements between consumers and businesses are considered valid. As unusual as this may be for the European practitioner, one cannot deny that OArb and other forms of 'quasi online arbitration' (which do not end by a definitive and enforceable decision of the conflict) may have huge benefits for the consumer: in many cases, consumers forego their rights rather than face the costs and hassles of an in-person process. Unlike traditional in-person dispute resolution methods, online dispute resolution allows parties to communicate from anywhere, using any type of Internet access at their convenience. Consumers do not have to travel, miss work, 'dress up' or arrange for childcare to attend hearings and meetings. Using computer-mediated communications may also empower individuals by allowing them to communicate from behind the buffer of their lectronic devices. Race, gender, and disabilities play a lesser role. Thus, OArb can even expand the access to justice for the consumer. This has already become visible in the United States, where a number of quasi online arbitration sites have emerged. Sites such as BBB (Better Business Bureau), for example, offer an accreditation system for businesses that comply with their Code of Business Practice, or they offer any kind of dispute resolution services, from informal mediation to binding arbitration. Another example of growing relevance is eBay's Resolution Centre, which processes consumer claims related to website purchases free of charge. This will remain a growth sector in the United States especially for small claims, provided that the system can guarantee due process and fairness standards.

In Chapter 9, Pablo Cortés and Tony Coyle analyze the use of online arbitration and online dispute resolution in a business-to-consumer context from the very different European point of view. The regulatory framework in the European Union is set up by the Unfair Terms Directive which classifies as 'unfair' those contractual terms which 'exclude or hinder the consumer's right to take legal action . . . in particular by requiring the consumer to take disputes exclusively to arbitration not covered by legal provisions'. Furthermore, the European Court of Justice has found that consumer protection laws rank as an aspect of the 'public policy' of the EU, and thus trump enforcement of arbitration agreements between businesses and consumers.

On the other hand, the EU has passed legislation that encourages the use of high-quality consumer ADR/ODR schemes. According to the ADR Directive, all Member States must ensure the availability within their jurisdiction of ADR entities that comply with minimum legal standards when resolving disputes between traders and consumers. The hope is that this two-faceted approach will protect consumers while still encouraging high-quality consumer arbitration.

A more promising avenue may be that of 'Online Courts' as proposed by Lord Justice Briggs in the July 2016 Final Report of the Civil Courts Structure Review for the Judiciary of England of Wales, which are designed to cover civil and commercial monetary claims under £25,000. In the words of our authors, this is an 'impressively ambitious amalgam of computer technology, mediation and the traditional court system'. Another alternative to online consumer arbitration might be online adjudication in the form of the Uniform Dispute Resolution Policy (UDRP) for domain name disputes, which strongly resembles a 'documents only' arbitration.

What makes this procedure effective, despite not being binding on the parties, is that the decision issued by the Administrative Panel is binding on the domain name registrar, i.e. the entity that issued the domain name. Ombudsman schemes might complement the future European picture of online dispute resolution between consumers and business parties.

In Chapter 10, Niuscha Bassiri is dealing with an everlasting fundamental topic of international arbitration, the independence and impartiality of arbitrators, which has entered a novel dimension as a consequence of the use of new ICTs, in particular social media networks. Interacting on social media networks greatly increases the visibility of arbitrators. The professional and personal connections, relationships, and dealings of an arbitrator with other people become easily accessible and visible. Even if the information about the arbitrator is inaccessible due to his or her stringent privacy settings, the relaxed privacy settings of the arbitrator's connections enables that certain information about the arbitrator (more particularly: information pertaining to his or her online relationship with the connection) may still quite easily be obtained.

The 2014 IBA Guidelines on Conflicts of Interest in International Arbitration are already dealing with social media contacts of an arbitrator, stating an arbitrator's contact through a social media network with another arbitrator, counsel, and/or one of the parties does not have to be disclosed. However, this refers only to the limited activity of being connected on social media networks. Comments, contents and posts put on social media networks can nevertheless give rise to doubts as to the independence or impartiality of an arbitrator.

To date, there is only limited case law as to whether and under which circumstances an arbitrator's online connections may jeopardize his or her independence and impartiality. In one case, where the party's counsel was a Facebook friend with the presiding arbitrator and where party's counsel had also supported the presiding arbitrator's election to the Paris Bar by 'liking' his Facebook status, the other side sought the annulment of the award. In that case, the Court of Appeal of Paris effectively set aside the award, but this decision was subsequently quashed by the *Cour de Cassation* and remitted to the Court of Appeal of Lyon. The latter ultimately came to the conclusion that the alleged Facebook friend argument was irrelevant as the counsel in question supported the president's candidacy only *after* the award was issued. The lesson we can learn from this decision is that counsel and arbitrator should better refrain from all interaction pending the arbitration.

Naturally, the Internet can also be extremely helpful for arbitrators to promote themselves, or for parties to collect information about arbitrators. In addition to their personal websites or LinkedIn, arbitrators may use services such as OGELFORUM/OGEMID/YOUNG-OGEMID to publish their profiles. In June 2016, the ICC International Court of Arbitration started to publish the arbitrators' names and nationalities and whether the arbitration is pending or closed on its website, and the Chamber of Milan is doing the same since autumn 2016, and VIAC since autumn 2017. Tools like this will help in fostering the careers in particular of younger arbitrators.

In Chapter 11, Marc Veit deals with the potential of new ICTs for counsel strategies. He states at the outset that a good lawyer must always have the classical skills of a good lawyer (analytical skills, drafting skills, and advocacy skills), but that a good arbitration lawyer must also be able to understand and use technology.

Obviously, one source to obtain information about counterparties and witnesses is the conventional web search, which can produce surprising amounts of valuable information. The 'Surface Web', however, is only a small fraction of information and content; more is available sub-surface in the so-called 'Deep Web'. The 'Deep Web' can show, for example, government-related sites that are not indexed by search engines, or earlier versions of websites through 'way-back machines'. It may be very helpful, or even relevant for the outcome of the case, to see how a website appeared on a certain date.

Social media can also be a 'treasure trove' for counsel. It appears that nowadays, lawyers are regularly investigating counterparties and witnesses through the Internet. This poses obvious ethical questions: depending on the applicable rules, it may be ethical to retrieve publicly available information, but it may be unethical to 'friend' a witness without disclosing the purpose. In this context, reference can be made to the 2013 IBA Guidelines on Party Representation in International Arbitration which provide in Guideline 18 that a party representative should identify himself or herself before seeking any information.

An even bigger wealth of information can be drawn from the 'Internet of Things', which is the network of vehicles, buildings and other items embedded with electronics, software, sensors, actuators and network connectivity that enable these objects to collect and exchange data. In a few years, the Internet of things will include a large majority of devices or machines that are currently traded through contracts providing for arbitration as the dispute resolution mechanism. It does not take a lot of imagination to predict that key issues, the occurrence of defects, the proper use of machines, proper maintenance, can be assessed much more comprehensively if evidence is readily available in electronic format over the Internet of Things. It is presumed that the total number of arbitrations is going to increase with the advent of the Internet of things, while the costs of arbitrating these disputes are going to decrease.

Mission Statement: Navigating a Changing World

> 'The Inventions Office is stuffed with plans for labour-saving processes. Thousands of them.' Mustapha Mond made a lavish gesture. 'And why don't we put them into execution? For the sake of the labourers; it would be sheer cruelty to afflict them with excessive leisure. It's the same with agriculture. We could synthesize every morsel of food, if we wanted to. But we don't. We prefer to keep a third of the population on the land. For their own sakes – because it takes longer to get food out of the land than out of a factory. Besides, we have our stability to think of. We don't want to change. Every change is a menace to stability. That's another reason why we're so scary of applying new inventions. Every discovery in pure science is potentially subversive; even science must sometimes be treated as a possible enemy. Yes, even science.'
>
> Aldous Huxley, *Brave New World*

This book is about change. Change that technology can, could, should (or should not) bring about. Change in the way we conduct arbitration. Change in the way we think about arbitration. It dares the reader to keep an open mind about innovation, to promote change and to be 'subversive', as Aldous Huxley put it into the mouth of Mustapha Mond. Despite the risks of a potential 'Brave New World of Arbitration', this book is fuelled by optimism regarding the potential of technology. And we are not alone with this optimistic outlook, as it is largely shared by our authors. What they also make clear is that the future of digitalized arbitration is starting now, driven by today's lawyers and law firms. Thus, it is essential to learn to ride this new wave of digitization immediately for anyone who has an interest in remaining relevant in the arbitration community.

This book aims to prepare the reader for a changing world of arbitration. It contributes to a better understanding of how technology can be efficiently and legitimately used to further sound arbitration proceedings. It also identifies, on a very practical level, how technology could be used by arbitration institutions, arbitrators, and parties to an arbitration. That is why this book is of interest to lawyers involved in international commercial arbitration, as well as technical experts and staff that are called on to implement IT in a business and legal setting.

This book has the great ambition to be among the first publications on a rapidly evolving subject. Therefore, it comes with an expiration date. One of our authors rightly noted that 'the life cycle of new ICT technologies can mimic that of a dragonfly'. Nonetheless, the editors and the authors of this book hope to initialize or to contribute to an important debate. Lastly, the editors note that all contributions are up to date as per September 2017.

1

Survey on the Present Use of ICT in International Arbitration

MAUD PIERS AND CHRISTIAN ASCHAUER

Summary: To prepare our book, we found it necessary to go out in the field and collect data on the present use of technology in international arbitration. Through a Survey, we measured the extent to which arbitration practitioners avail themselves of online and electronic tools and services, in offline arbitration, in view of a more efficient and cost-effective procedure. We also examined how the Internet, and more particularly social media, affects arbitration practitioners, their strategies, and their behaviour. The results of the Survey are useful in the detection of questions that are of great practical importance, and also provide a significant justification for this book. We understood that arbitration practitioners were integrating new technologies into their practices, but in rather spontaneous and reactive ways. Also, we found that practitioners, compared to other service industries, are rather hesitant to take advantage of the new technologies. This led us to conclude that there is still much room for exploring the true potential of technologies in international arbitration.

Introduction

This first chapter discloses some of the results of a first empirical study that explores how arbitration is catching up with the fast-evolving electronically connected world, and how technology could be harnessed as a means to optimize efficiency in arbitration (hereinafter called 'Survey'). This Survey was conducted (naturally: online) among members of CEPANI and/or VIAC, who traditionally focus on business-to-business disputes. Through these institutions, we reached a group of 103[1] participants from

[1] Almost three-quarters (73.15 per cent) of the participants are men, while 24.07 per cent are women. Note that 2.78 per cent did not disclose their gender.

different age groups[2] and jurisdictions[3] who have primarily been involved in regular (thus offline) arbitration procedures, either as counsel, arbitrator, in-house counsel or secretary of the tribunal[4], and for disputes in different areas of the law[5].

The Survey was designed from a realistic perspective and the questions asked reflect a rather conservative proposition, as we focused our questionnaire on technological applications that are ordinarily used in day-to-day life and business practice (e.g. email, cloud computing, etc.), rather than on more sophisticated tools (e.g. cognitive computing and other AI applications) that require quite an investment both in capital and in special training.

This Survey focused on the following sets of issues.[6] Apart from a number of questions that allow us to form an overall view of the demographic and digital profile of the participant, the survey focused on mainly two sets of issues. First, the Survey aimed to assess how the participants manage to integrate information technology in their arbitration practice. It therefore examines how the participants communicate in an arbitration, how they manage and store arbitration-related information, and what security measures they take to do so. Secondly, the Survey explores how arbitrators, as digital citizens with an online identity, behave in the arbitration world. In what follows we will share our observations and conclusions based on a first analysis of these results.[7]

[2] The largest group of participants (35 per cent) were born between 1975 and 1984. For a more detailed division of age, see Figure 1.1 on page 22.

[3] The majority of the participants practice primarily in European jurisdictions; 14 participants indicated that the jurisdiction in which they primarily practice arbitration lies in an Asian country, while for 16 participants, this is America.

[4] The participants' primary involvement(s) in arbitration is as a counsel or as an arbitrator. See Figure 1.5 on page 24.

[5] The primary practice areas indicated by the participants are general trade, construction, and engineering, and Mergers & Acquisitions (M&A) agreements. The participants indicate that 68.25 per cent of their practice in the past five years focused on international arbitration, and 20.81 per cent on multi-party arbitration.

[6] The survey also established a number of questions that allow us to form an overall view of the demographic (Part 1) and digital (Part 2) profile of the participant. For more information on these data, see page 17 and pages 23–24.

[7] Note that, for several reasons, we did *not* examine to what extent arbitration practitioners have been involved in an online arbitration as such. Firstly, extensive research was already conducted to this effect by Pablo Cortés and Tony Cole, who surveyed 160 arbitration practitioners in Europe and Switzerland to examine their engagement with online arbitration. Secondly, online arbitration is still primarily used for resolving business-to-consumer disputes and is oftentimes conducted without the intervention of an attorney.

The Participants' Digital Profile

The findings on the participants' digital profile are in line with our expectation that arbitration practitioners adopt a rather conservative approach: We found that the overwhelming majority of our participants indeed make use of the more common technologies, such as email (99.07 per cent), telephone conferencing (98.13 per cent), electronic databases for legal research (91.59 per cent), and electronic timesheets (73.83 per cent). A large minority of the participants use voice-over-IP (voIP; such as skype) for their communication (40.19 per cent)[8], store information in the cloud (43.93 per cent)[9], or rely on technology for the automatic generation of documents (36.45 per cent). Only a few individual participants indicated using 'advanced' electronic tools such as digital identification when signing submissions, secured electronic filing platforms, real-time transcription methods (e.g. with the Live Notes app), or software that allows the setting up of a database of exhibits and the creation of e-briefs (e.g. ExhibitManager). There is no indication whatsoever that our participants make use of AI software that would take over a part of the argumentation or decision-making process. This confirms that there is only a slowly growing awareness of the huge potential that more advanced means of technology could have for boosting efficiency in their legal and arbitration practice.

It is probably in this context that we have to understand why the overwhelming majority of our participants, namely 90.65 per cent, primarily rely on self-study to keep up with the technological developments, and why only 27.10 per cent take up additional professional training courses.[10] This only proves that there is a dire need for more information about the many technological applications that may be useful for arbitration.

As conservative as the approach of arbitration practitioners may be, we noted quite a broad interest of arbitration practitioners in the use of technologies offered by the arbitration institutions.[11] There was a clear positive response to the question of whether the participants would use the

[8] See further below the rather low number of participants that indicate regular use of videoconferencing.

[9] See further below the data on the use of cloud storage in arbitration.

[10] Some 4.67 per cent of the participants indicated that they rely on other means of study, such as training, by a cloud-based practice management company that provides new technology and training and in-house training by the law firm's IT team.

[11] Note that, in fact, only 23.81 per cent of the participants indicated that they have already been involved in an arbitration with institutions, such as the ICC, ICSID, and the AAA, that have made certain Internet tools available for storage and exchange of documents.

following tools if they were offered by the arbitration institution: (1) Dropbox or other secured cloud-based file-sharing services (84.78 per cent)[12]; (2) secured means of Internet communication (92.31 per cent); (3) email communication with electronic signatures (88.17 per cent); (4) hearing rooms with tele- and video-conference facilities (97.87 per cent); and (5) hearing rooms with audio recording facilities (94.62 per cent).

Computer-Mediated Communication in Arbitration

In Part 3 of the Survey, we measured how technology is used as a tool for written and oral communication. Here, too, we departed from the hypothesis that technology is an immensely undertapped resource. Lawyers are insufficiently aware that technology could play a role beyond the support function for which it is ordinarily used.

As it became clear from our survey, in line with the general trend in professional life, email has become the most prevalent means of communication in arbitration. In fact, our participants indicated that written communication in their arbitration practice primarily occurs through email alone in the relationship between the members of the arbitral tribunal (92.14 per cent), between counsel and client (81.93 per cent), and between the arbitral tribunal and the arbitration institution (66.54 per cent). In communication between counsel and the arbitration institution, in 48.94 per cent of the times, email is followed by post or fax. Email communication between counsel and the arbitral tribunal primarily occurs through email followed by post or fax (59 per cent).

As expected, moreover, communication is practically never done solely via post or fax. None of the participants indicated to rely primarily on only post or fax in the relationship between counsel and client, while only a very small percentage conceded to do so in their communication between counsel and arbitral tribunal (1 per cent), between counsel and the arbitration institution (1.06 per cent), between members of the arbitral tribunal (1.12 per cent), and between the arbitral tribunal and the arbitration institution (2.08 per cent).

In this regard, we refer to the most recent ICC Note to Parties and Arbitral Tribunals on the conduct of the arbitration under the ICC Rules

[12] One of the participants does point out, though, that the general terms and conditions of Dropbox, which allow that information is shared with, for instance, '*others working for Dropbox*', may breach the obligations of confidentiality that bind the arbitrators, counsel and parties. See in this regard, www.dropbox.com/privacy.

of Arbitration, which states that the Secretariat will generally correspond via email and thus parties, their counsel, and prospective arbitrators must provide the Secretariat with their email addresses.[13]

Video-conferences are a less widely used means of communication in arbitration. Almost 40 per cent (38.03 per cent) of the participants reported never using video-conferences to examine witnesses that are beyond travel distance; 56.34 per cent indicate that they have done so in 25 per cent of the arbitrations. Interestingly enough, the number of counsel that never participated in witness examination through video-conferencing is still 57.14 per cent, while 38.96 per cent specify having been involved in witness examination through video-conference in about 25 per cent of the arbitrations. Even a higher percentage of the participants, namely 49.32 per cent, indicate that as arbitrators they never use video-conferencing for deliberations between members of the arbitral tribunal that are beyond travel distance. More than a quarter (35.62 per cent) answered that they do so in 25 per cent of the arbitrations, 10.96 per cent in 50 per cent of the arbitrations, and 1.37 per cent in 75 per cent of the arbitrations. Only 2.74 per cent indicate that they always discuss the case through video-conference when the arbitrators are beyond travel distance.

Highly interesting are also the numbers regarding the issuance of an electronic arbitral award. In response to the question of whether as an arbitrator, one has ever issued an award *solely* electronically, 84 per cent of the participants answer in the negative. A minority thus indicated that they have done so in 25 per cent of their arbitrations (9.33 per cent), in 50 per cent of their arbitrations (1.33 per cent), in 75 per cent of their arbitrations (2.67 per cent), or that they do so always (2.67 per cent). More than half (56 per cent) of the counsel or in-house counsel indicated never having received an award electronically. A significant percentage answered that they have received electronic awards, namely 18.67 per cent in 25 per cent of the arbitrations, 9.33 per cent in 50 per cent of the arbitrations, 5.33 per cent in 75 per cent of the arbitrations, and 10.67 per cent always.

Storage of Information Related to Arbitration

The large majority of the arbitration practitioners (86.41 per cent) keep the arbitration files stored in hard copy and electronic copy. The reasons

[13] ICC Note to Parties and Arbitral Tribunals on the conduct of the arbitration under the ICC Rules of Arbitration, 13 July 2016, para. 7.

that the participants give for storing information electronically have to do with the easy organization of e-documents, as well as the lower risk of loss or theft during, for instance, travel. A mere 11.65 per cent trust to storing their files solely on an electronic carrier; arbitration practitioners who only keep a hard copy of their files are becoming very rare (1.94 per cent). Those that store their files electronically primarily keep them on a local carrier: of those participants that indicate to keep a hard copy and electronic copy, 82.61 per cent do so on a local carrier and 17.39 per cent store this electronic copy in the cloud.[14] From those who keep only an electronic file, these percentages are 68.75 per cent and 31.25 per cent, respectively. Although apparently it seems counterintuitive for most practitioners to trust one's sensitive information to a professional cloud company, this seems to be exactly the advice that Schaumann gives in Chapter 5. A sophisticated cloud service offers the best (possible) protection against the different types of attackers.

Security Precautions in Arbitration

When using Internet-based communication, 68.42 per cent of the participants reported never using encryption systems to secure the information, while 6.32 per cent indicated they always do so. These precautions are taken in 25 per cent of the cases by 14.74 per cent of the participants, 50 per cent of the cases by 7.37 per cent of the participants, and 75 per cent of the cases by 3.16 per cent of the participants. Moreover, 71.74 per cent of the participants never use certified electronic signatures for email communication, while 2.71 per cent used it for every email. The range of participants that sometimes use certified electronic signatures range from 21.74 per cent in 25 per cent of the emails, 3.06 per cent in 50 per cent of the emails, and 1.09 per cent in 75 per cent of the emails.

From the arbitrators that store sensitive information in the cloud, 90.91 per cent do so in a secured manner, while 90 per cent work with a service provider that guarantees the security of the sensitive information stored. This is the case for 87.50 per cent of the counsel in both scenarios. Of the 63.64 per cent *arbitrators* that write down passwords, 81.82 per cent indicate keeping this information locked. Of 33.33 per cent of the *counsel* that indicate that they write down passwords, 85.71 per cent keep this information locked.

[14] Note that one of the participants indicated that they only keep information stored in the cloud when a party expressly requests them to do so.

Social Media and Defining an Arbitration Practitioner's Identity

Part 4 of the Survey focused on the arbitration practitioners' online identity and behaviour, and the extent to which they participate in social media. More specifically, we searched for indications as to how the Internet, and more particularly social media, affects arbitrators and their behaviour. The results of this research are relevant to assess how online legal sources determine the strategy that counsel adopts during an arbitration. Also, it is relevant for the question of how arbitrators may use the Internet to their advantage for promotional and networking purposes without risking their neutrality or impartiality, and to evaluate ethical standards of disclosure for an arbitrator who is active on social media.

What is clear is that arbitration practitioners are no strangers to social media. From the survey, we learnt that 77.88 per cent of the participants in the study are on LinkedIn, 54.81 per cent are on Facebook, 50.96 per cent use WhatsApp, and 22.12 per cent have a Twitter account. Some 47.61 per cent of the participants also indicated that they contribute to arbitration blogs or electronic newsletters, whereas 87.75 per cent concede to reading them.

The Internet is also used for obtaining information on the relevant parties in an arbitration. Almost 95 per cent (94.62 per cent) of the participants admitted to surfing the Internet in order to get acquainted with either a party, a counsel, an arbitrator, a case manager, or an arbitration institution. Nearly half (49.46 per cent) of the participants do this in all cases in which they are involved; 13.98 per cent in 75 per cent of the cases, 17.20 per cent in 50 per cent of the cases, and 13.98 per cent in 25 per cent of the cases. Specifically, for a conflict of interest check, the Internet is considered as a reliable tool by 74.16 per cent of the participants. Exactly 37.08 per cent concedes to always using the Internet as part of a conflict of interest check, 12.36 per cent do this in 75 per cent of the cases, 6.74 per cent in 50 per cent of the cases, and 17.98 in 25 per cent of the cases in which they are involved.

However, those surveyed indicated hesitance when it came to sharing information on their own social media status. To the question of whether one discloses or would disclose a social media account connection in a conflict of interest check, only 25.96 per cent of the participants indicated that they would or do disclose a connection to a party in the arbitration, 20.19 per cent gave a positive answer with regard to a social media connection to a counsel in an arbitration, 24.04 per cent with regard to a connection with an arbitrator, and 17.31 per cent with regard to a connection to a case manager.

Conclusion

The Survey measures to what extent arbitration practitioners are familiar with the benefits and risks of the use of information technologies and the Internet in their arbitration practice. Although only scratching the surface, this Survey gives a clear indication on the large number of issues that must be addressed. It is for instance clear that arbitration practitioners have integrated a number of common applications into their arbitration practice, though remain cautious when it comes to novel and more sophisticated information technology tools. Also, there seems to be a rather limited awareness of the security risks involved even in the technological applications that are routinely used. Finally, there is an interest in more advanced technological applications and even a demand for a broader offer by the arbitration institutions. The results of the Survey therewith only confirm that there is a need to explore and inform, about the opportunities and challenges of the use of technology in arbitration.

Appendix to the report: some demographic information

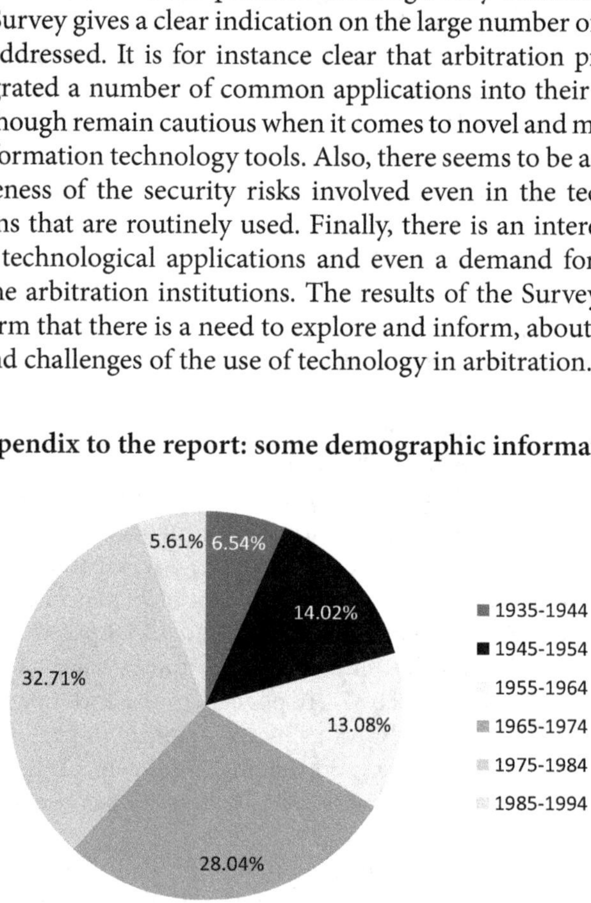

Figure 1.1 The participants' year of birth.

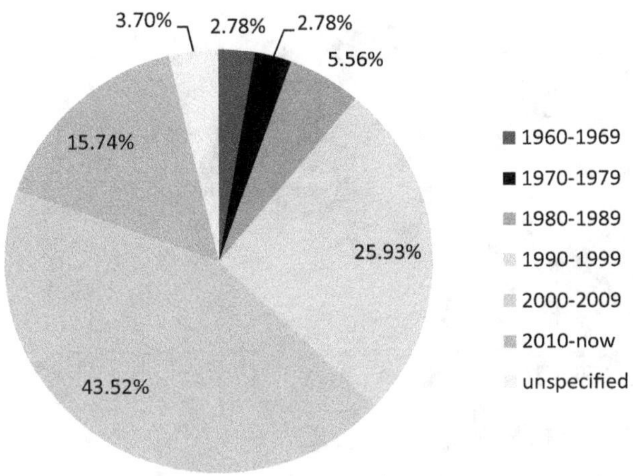

Figure 1.2 Year in which the participants became involved in arbitration.

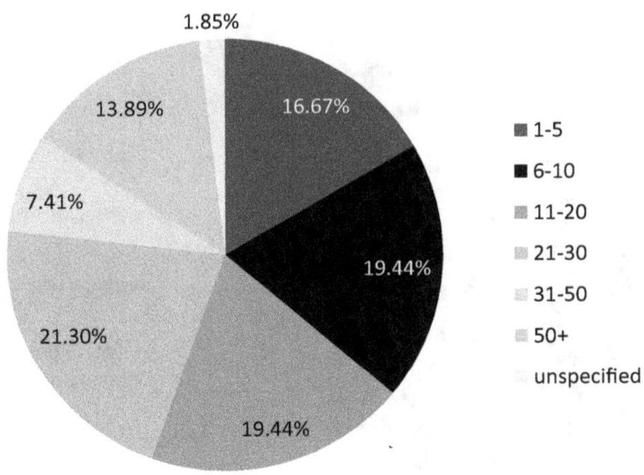

Figure 1.3 The number of arbitrations that the participants have been involved in in the past five years.

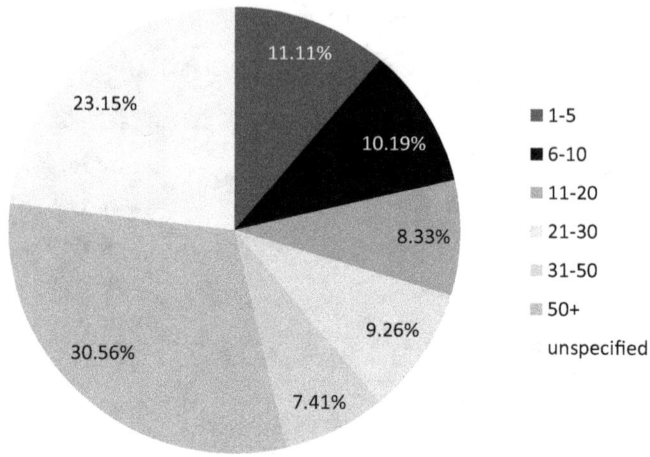

Figure 1.4 The number of legal practitioners in the law firm in which the participants work.

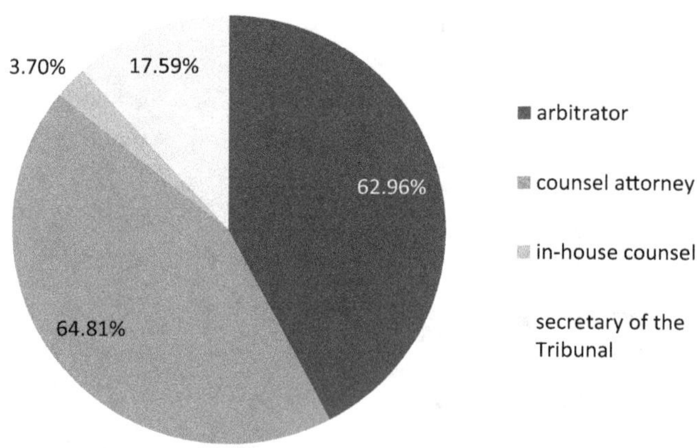

Figure 1.5 The participants' primary involvement in arbitration concerned the following functions.

PART I

The Use of Technology in International Arbitration

2

Revolutionizing Technologies and the Use of Technology in International Arbitration

Innovation, Legitimacy, Prospects and Challenges

MOHAMED S. ABDEL WAHAB AND ETHAN KATSH

Summary: Arbitration, like all forms of dispute resolution, whether formal or informal, is dependent upon the communication and processing of information. Parties communicate with the arbitrator and with each other. The arbitrator invites evidence, evaluates behaviour, and makes decisions. Various rules limit how information may be introduced and employed. This chapter explores the impact of innovative uses of new technologies on the practice and process of arbitration. More particularly, we explore the nature and implications of the shift from reliance on paper and face-to-face approaches, to processes that are technologically supported and either partly online or all-online.

'When we change the way we communicate,
we change society'.[1]

Introduction

The brave new world of arbitration, just like Aldous Huxley's novel *Brave New World*, is linked to technology. Huxley's *Brave New World* takes place six hundred years in the future and in a society where behaviour is shaped more by drugs and biological technologies than by law. Our experience, over no more than a few decades, is with information technologies, and our focus is much narrower than Huxley's, being limited to technology's impact on arbitration and dispute resolution. In spite of these differences, *Brave New World* is worthy of our attention because we share with Huxley a sense that the use of technology will greatly impact important societal institutions and values.

[1] C. Shirky, *Here Comes Everybody* (New York: Penguin Press, 2008), p. 17.

Marshall McLuhan once wrote when 'a new technology comes into a social milieu it cannot cease to permeate that milieu until every institution is saturated'.[2] This chapter analyzes the challenges and opportunities arbitrators, and the process of arbitration, will face as they adapt to the new information technologies. It begins with a consideration of the nature of the new technologies, and how they affect the emergence of conflict. It proceeds to identify areas of practice which may need to be reevaluated as the arbitration process moves online, reviews a variety of new technological tools and resources, and considers how their introduction and adaptation to traditional arbitration practice can bring efficiencies and improve 'access to justice' in an era of growing conflict.

Technology and Arbitration: An Overview

A New Environment of Disputes

A new technology almost inevitably generates disputes. That the introduction and expanded use of emerging information technologies would increase the numbers and types of disputes should not surprise us. Disputes emerge out of relationships and transactions between any and all those who are involved as businesses or consumers. It is incontrovertible that computer networks and information-processing machines increase numbers and kinds of transactions, and numbers and kinds of relationships. Some percentage of these new transactions and relationships will end up in conflict. Therefore, the increase in the number of relationships and transactions influences the likelihood of disputes.

In their well-known book *Getting to Yes*, Roger Fisher and William Ury assert on the very first page, that 'conflict is a growth industry'.[3] Although their book was published in 1981, their statement holds true in light of the astounding increase in the number of disputes during the last few decades. However, they probably would also understand that any environment experiencing the level of creativity, activity, change, and potential wealth generated by our digital lifestyles is unlikely to be harmonious or friction-free.

We can expect this new disputing environment to continue to grow and, as this occurs, increase the need for arbitration and other forms of dispute resolution. In addition, as the online environment matures, it will have an impact on the offline environment and on traditions and practices

[2] M. McLuhan, *Understanding Media* (New York: McGraw Hill, 1964), p. 161.

[3] R. Fisher, W. Ury and B. Patton, *Getting to Yes: Negotiating Agreement Without Giving In* (New York: Penguin Books, 1991), p. 1.

associated with offline approaches. Increasingly, some of what used to be handled face to face and with paper will now be communicated online. Much of what used to be physical and tangible will now be digital and virtual. There are fewer and fewer offline activities that are not touched in some way by technology, and this will continue to impact this new 'growth industry'.

What Fisher and Ury were hoping for was that conflict resolution would become a growth industry. If they had followed the trend of technological development over the last few decades, they might have understood how that adds to the need for new or revised models of dispute resolution. The following observations illustrate this trend:

1. The more novel the technological activity, the greater the likelihood of disputes. The first iteration of an innovative product or activity rarely anticipates all the disputes that it will generate.
2. As data and the application of data become more valuable, the more likely it is that a problem or grievance will turn into a dispute. This is even more compounded in the digital world with the advent of new technologies.
3. The more data that are not only collected, but also processed and communicated electronically, the more opportunities for disputes to occur. The more data that are collected, the more bad data there are.
4. Speed and time pressure lead to disputes. If value is likely to erode quickly, as is often the case with technology, the pressure to protect and aggressively extend its value increases.
5. Increased complexity in relationships and systems create more opportunities for disputes. In the words of computer scientist Peter Neumann, 'Complex systems break in complex ways'.[4] When informing shareholders about a federal investigation of problems in correcting errors, Experian stated that, 'We might fail to comply with international, federal, regional, provincial, state or other jurisdictional regulations, due to their complexity, frequent changes or inconsistent application and interpretation'.[5]
6. The easier it is to complain by filling out an online form or sending an email, the more disputes there will be.
7. If proprietary algorithms underlie the transaction or relationship, the more likely it is for misunderstandings to grow.

[4] P. Neumann, quoted in J. Markoff, 'Killing the Computer to Save It', *New York Times*, 30 October 2012.

[5] J. Horwitz, 'Alleged Abuses Put Credit Agencies on the Hot Seat,' *Boston Globe*, 17 June 2014, p. B9.

8. The less attention given to preventing disputes, the more disputes there will be.

The first large-scale, technology-generated disputing environment surfaced in the 1990s with the growth of e-commerce. eBay launched its online auction platform in September 1995 and disputes were present almost from the start. As one employee observed, it was clear that 'one thing Omidyar (eBay's founder) knew was that he did not want to arbitrate all of these disputes'.[6] When receiving email complaints, eBay's founder would write back to the buyer and seller and ask them to 'work it out'.[7] When disputes continued to increase, eBay asked the National Center for Technology and Dispute Resolution at the University of Massachusetts to conduct a pilot project to see if buyer–seller disputes could be mediated.[8] The success of the pilot project led to the development of a technology-assisted online dispute resolution process. Currently, eBay's software-based process handles more than sixty million disputes a year between buyers and sellers.[9]

Online disputes began to touch the arbitration field in the latter half of the 1990s when a process was established to resolve disputes between trademark owners and domain name holders. Domain names, such as google.com or odr.info, are essentially online addresses and each domain name must be unique if the system is to work. Just as there cannot be two Main Streets in a town, there cannot be two domains with the same name. If there were, clicking on a URL or IP address would not lead us where we wanted to go.

During the 1990s, the number of .com domain names increased from 1,151 in October 1990[10] to 1,301,000 in July 1997, and to more than twenty million in November 2000.[11] Gradually, during that period, companies realized that domain names were valuable and became worried that their trademarks would be damaged if someone registered a domain name that was the same as the trademark. In 1998, the Internet Corporation for Assigned Names and Numbers (ICANN) took over management of the domain name system. One of its first actions was to develop and

[6] A. Cohen, *The Perfect Store* (Boston: Little, Brown, 2002), p. 27. [7] Ibid.

[8] E. Katsh, J. Rifkin and A. Gaitenby, 'E-Commerce, E-Disputes, and E-Dispute Resolution: In the Shadow of "eBay Law"', (2000) 15 *Ohio State Journal on Dispute Resolution*, 705, 708–709.

[9] Conversation with Colin Rule, former Director of Online Dispute Resolution at eBay; see Chapter 8, p. 195.

[10] See www.iaps.com/internet-history-october-1990.html#email.

[11] See www.zooknic.com/Domains/counts.html.

implement a process for resolving disputes between trademark owners and domain name holders. This system, called the Uniform Dispute Resolution Policy (UDRP), is referred to as non-binding arbitration, since anyone dissatisfied with the decision of the arbitrator or arbitrators can start over again by filing a complaint in court. In practice, this happens infrequently.[12]

Arbitrators under the UDRP can order a domain name to be transferred to a trademark owner if the arbitrator finds that the domain name was registered in 'bad faith'. The policy requires several conditions that must be met in order to find 'bad faith'. There would not be 'bad faith' if the domain name holder showed 'proof of a legitimate, non-commercial or fair use of the domain name'. In such an instance, the domain name holder could keep the domain even if it appeared to be similar to the trademark.

The domain name process has been a success in terms of convenience. It is much less expensive than going to court and decisions are usually made in fewer than forty days. Questions of fairness, however, are still present. Trademark owners win approximately 85 per cent of cases. Moreover, approximately half of all respondents fail to respond. This may be because the respondent feels that its case is weak or, alternatively, that it is unlikely to receive a fair hearing. Arbitrators in such cases are still allowed to find for the domain name holder, but such an outcome is unusual.

A New Environment of Dispute Resolution: The Fourth Party Model

The new technologies provide not only a growth industry of disputes, but also new opportunities for dispute resolution. The reason for this is that all dispute resolution processes rely on communication and the management and processing of information. Arbitrators continuously pose questions and evaluate documents and other information. Computers, like arbitrators and mediators, communicate and process information. Software, by definition, manages the flow of information.

Every dispute resolution process has its own rules for managing information and communication. The challenge for software developers is to facilitate processes online without sacrificing important values that have been built into the particular process. The metaphor of the 'Fourth Party'[13] is often employed to suggest the role that technology might play. In simple

12 See Chapter 9, p. 235.

13 E. Katsh and J. Rifkin, *Online Dispute Resolution: Resolving Conflicts in Cyberspace* (San Francisco: Jossey-Bass, 2001), p. 93.

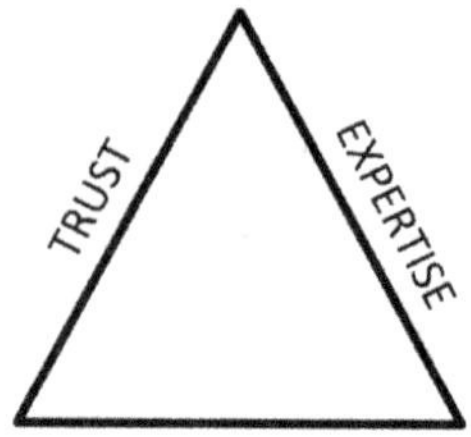

Figure 2.1 The dispute resolution triangle.

cases, software might replace a mediator or arbitrator. More commonly, however, it would assist and collaborate with the neutral third party in any kind of case. The Fourth Party is a metaphor that is intended to remind us of how important communication and information-processing tools are in arbitration, and the potential that technology provides for improving work of third parties in any dispute resolution process.

More specifically, the role of the 'Fourth Party' can be visualized as a triangle, with the three sides representing trust, convenience and expertise (see Figure 2.1). Any dispute resolution system, if it is to be used, must include all three elements, but not necessarily to the same degree. All three are needed if the system is to attract users and survive over time. The shape of the triangle, however, can change and, by doing so, emphasize visually that one element is more present than the others. Online Dispute Resolution (ODR) began with a triangle that had a much longer convenience side. The earliest ODR systems were convenient because they enabled communication at a distance, often asynchronously, so that some degree of participation was possible at any time and from any place. In so doing, communication over the network removed many long established physical constraints of time and space. However, in the early days, the expertise and trust sides of the triangle were limited, as there was no software that could aid the building of trust in the process or assist third parties in making decisions.

Over time, there has been a lengthening of the expertise side of the triangle. Expertise is now embedded in advanced software that takes advantage of the computer's processing capabilities. Increasingly speedier processors are supporting machines in becoming 'smarter'. It has been understood from the beginning that ODR was dependent upon software, but the software that tended to be employed in the earliest experiments was software that optimized convenient communication. Moreover, focusing on convenience and on disputes arising from online activities was not threatening to human mediators and arbitrators. However, as ODR software becomes more advanced and ODR expands its application to more traditional offline disputes, it will necessarily challenge some traditions and practices of third parties.

In theory, the idea of software as a 'Fourth Party' should resonate well in the arbitration context. As noted earlier, the flow of information and the evaluation of information are central to arbitration. Arbitrators communicate and process information and that is also what computers do. For instance, some of the specific informational tasks performed by third-party neutrals can include brainstorming, evaluating, explaining, discussing, identifying, defining, organizing, clarifying, caucusing, collecting, aggregating, assigning meaning, simulating, measuring, calculating, linking, proposing, arranging, creating, publishing, circulating and exchanging, charting, reminding, scheduling, monitoring, and so on. Some of these tasks are simple or clerical but others involve making decisions at appropriate times and in appropriate ways. While technology can assist with all of these efforts, software can also be disruptive, as spatial and temporal constraints are removed, and long-established rules need to be reevaluated.

Technology as a Double-Edged Sword: The Use and Abuse of Technology in International Arbitration

Approximately twenty years of experience has taught us that ODR is no more 'Online ADR' or 'Online Arbitration' than the online versions of banking, education or gaming are simply the offline versions of those systems moved online. It has often been found in other contexts that '[w]hen a new online technology is created for any process, the initial impulse is to create online mirror images of the "live" or offline process'.[14] Once a process moves online, however, its very nature begins to change. That is what has been occurring with ODR and ADR over the last two decades. Some ODR approaches may resemble face-to-face ADR processes, and ADR practitioners may employ ODR tools to supplement face-to-face meetings, but the goal of ODR is not simply to digitize inefficient offline processes. Technology changes the nature of the interaction between the parties and introduces new possibilities for helping them achieve resolution. We may

[14] E. Katsh and D. Rainey, 'ODR and Government,' in M. S. A. Wahab, E. Katsh and D. Rainy (eds.), *Online Dispute Resolution: Theory and Practice* (The Hague, Netherlands: Eleven International Publishers, 2012), p. 260, available at www.ombuds.org/odrbook/Table_of_Contents.htm.

learn from offline approaches in designing ODR systems, but the larger challenge is to take advantage of what we can do with technology that we could not do before. As a result, as the full potential of ODR is realized over time, future applications are likely to diverge more and more from how disputes were handled in the past.

The challenges to the field as this digitization occurs will be numerous. Consider the following array of questions:

1. How will new information systems impact the field of Dispute Systems Design?
2. Will technology develop new models for building trust, convenience, and expertise?
3. What new skills and training will arbitrators need?
4. How will access to data be employed to prevent disputes?
5. How will the desire for data place pressure on confidentiality practices?
6. What will happen when ODR provides much earlier access to disputants in the overall dispute lifecycle?
7. How will technology and automated processes affect the boundaries between arbitration, mediation, and negotiation?
8. Where are the areas of overlap between ODR and ADR; including the optimal use of technology inside of a face-to-face dispute resolution process?
9. Will technology and the speed of communication change the use and role of apology in dispute resolution processes?
10. How will the sense of participation and voice change in asynchronous, text-based interactions?
11. What types of technologies will be used most (i.e. video-conferencing, texting, emailing, mobile phones, chat rooms, etc.) and how will this change over time?
12. As the use of algorithms increases, who will have access to the underlying codes?
13. How will we be able to assess the fairness of algorithms?
14. How will training in virtual arbitration differ from traditional training practices?
15. What kind of training should be a prerequisite for ODR practitioners?
16. Most importantly, what limits to the use of technology should there be in arbitration?

Similar kinds of questions are surfacing in many fields, partly because of the attraction of new software tools but partly also from pressure exerted by clients and parties. What has been called 'liquid expectations' consists of a need to adopt technological processes that have been seen to have value in other contexts. The pressure for change being felt from technology is, in other words, felt directly and also indirectly as parties begin to expect dispute resolution tools and systems to be as sophisticated and powerful as the ones they use in other contexts. As Shah and Greene suggest, this pressure occurs when experiences:

> seep over from one industry into another, creating an expectations chasm. As customer experiences with any product category affect how customers experience products in other categories previously thought to be unrelated, all businesses need to add new dimensions to how they understand and define their competitive strategy . . . Increasingly, your most important competitors are those we call perceptual: those competing to shape the expectations customers have for experiences in every category. For example, Uber's checkout, which is as simple and seamless as shutting the car door, will reset consumers' expectations for how convenient checkout can be in every industry, causing consternation as they stand in a queue at a store or wait for a server to bring the check.[15]

These examples from the consumer context may not seem to be relevant to the future of arbitration, but the current use of software to accomplish transactions and build relationships in complex environments is growing. This may ultimately lead to an expectation for processes that are powerful, and support the goals of the dispute resolution triangle of trust, convenience, and expertise.

Taking Arbitration Online

In a quarter of a century, Internet and Information Technology have rapidly evolved to facilitate and emphasize globalization. The new world of technology has certainly influenced our lives on all different levels. While time is passing by, humanity becomes more and more attached to and dependent on technological advancements that have surpassed all presumptive limits. It is no coincidence that technology has affected legal frameworks and mechanisms. Laws, jurisprudence, and legal systems of different countries are openly accessible online. There are also specialized sites and databases giving access to books and online articles such as Kluwer Arbitration, ICC Library, Global Arbitration Review, LexisNexis, Dalloz, Eastlaws, and many more; the list is endless. This enables access to all necessary documentation in a faster way and without occupying

[15] B. Shah and J. Greene, 'Liquid expectations, Consumers setting a different bar for experiences', *The Economist Group*, 19 May 2015, available at www.economistgroup.com/leanback/consumers/accenture-liquid-expectations.

any space with books and journals. Usually these databases are payable services offered to practitioners. The continuous innovation of products encourages people to be more dependent on digital screens instead of using paper. Nowadays, social media has invaded our lives; smartphones are becoming indispensable for business and social conduct, while tablets and iPads are replacing paper-based documents. There is no surprise that the softcopy became the new hardcopy. For example, it is easier, faster, and more cost-efficient to send a 300-page document through email than sending it through the post: the document is sent with a click.

In principle, it is submitted that the role technology plays with respect to dispute resolution processes varies according to: (i) the degree of utilization of modern technological tools and software applications, and (ii) the balance between the human factor and the artificial intelligence 'electronic element' in the process.[16]

On a sliding scale analysis and according to the role technology plays in the process, ODR schemes could be grouped into three broad categories: (a) *Technology-assisted ODR mechanisms*, where the role of technology is restricted to the provision of an adequate and secure medium of communication and information exchange; (b) *Technology-based ODR mechanisms*, where a fully fledged application of cutting-edge technology is utilized to resolve disputes; and (c) *Technology-facilitated online dispute prevention ("ODP") guarantees*, which help reduce the risk of potential e-disputes and incontrovertibly enhances trust and security in e-business.[17]

Facing all of these technological innovations, international arbitration has also been largely affected by technology. Since the early 1990s, there has been a remarkable evolution of the digital world that has led to increasing integration of technology in arbitration. This leads to the question: to what extent has technology been integrated in arbitration? To answer this question it is crucial to differentiate between the diverse stages of the arbitral process starting with the conclusion of the arbitration agreement until the rendering of the arbitral award.

ICTs and Arbitration: Issues and Challenges

It is submitted that for a process to qualify as online arbitration, the information and communication technologies ('ICTs') employed should not

[16] See Chapter 6, p. 137.

[17] See M. A. Wahab, 'The Global Information Society and Online Dispute Resolution: A New Dawn for Dispute Resolution' (2004), 21(2), *Journal of International Arbitration*, 167–168.

be used as a simple assisting tool in the process, but should be integrated and embedded into the process itself, and should be indispensable for its proper functioning and administration.[18] Therefore, it is necessary to observe how ICTs are utilized throughout the whole arbitration process.

E-Arbitration Agreements and E-Awards

Online arbitration is suitable for both online disputes and offline disputes, yet it is more frequently used to resolve online e-commerce disputes. Nowadays, it is not anomalous to have an arbitration agreement concluded by electronic communications. However, the conclusion of arbitration agreements by electronic means may, in many jurisdictions, raise concerns as to the formal requirement of having an agreement in writing. This aspect of online arbitration will be dealt with in the following [Chapter 7, p. 151].

E-Proceedings

It is unequivocal that arbitral proceedings conducted online or electronically are less costly than traditional offline arbitral proceedings.[19]

In online arbitration, e-proceedings normally commence by filing an e-request for arbitration and would involve e-hearings (audio and/or video-conferencing), e-submissions and e-production of documents/evidence, e-deliberations, and/or e-communications (whether inter-party, inter-tribunal, and/or party-tribunal), and would normally end by an e-award.

Generally, practice has shown that email is the most commonly used means of communications, enabling parties not only to communicate swiftly and efficiently, but also to attach written texts or even audio and video files to their messages.[20] However, one of the inconveniences of emailing is that email capacity may be limited and subject to certain constraints.

Additionally, online platforms, chatrooms, and video-conferencing technologies are increasingly used as fora for electronic synchronous and asynchronous interactions including e-submissions and e-hearings by and between people located in different time zones across the globe.

[18] See M. Abdel Wahab, 'ODR and E-Arbitration' in M. S. A. Wahab, E. Katsh and D. Rainy (eds.), *Online Dispute Resolution: Theory and Practice* (The Hague, Netherlands: Eleven International Publishers, 2012), pp. 387–388.

[19] Ibid., p. 400.

[20] See S. Kallel, 'Online Arbitration' (2008) 25(3), *Journal of International Arbitration*, 347.

That said, there are two legal principles that merit due consideration in the context of e-proceedings, namely: (i) the principle of procedural autonomy, and (ii) the principle of neutrality. The principle of procedural autonomy allows the parties to agree and organize arbitral proceedings in the manner they deem appropriate and in a manner tailored to the electronic sphere. The principle of neutrality entails that the use of e-communications and the Internet as a 'stateless' tool, offers the parties a neutral space to communicate and interact. Moreover, neutrality may also imply that the use of ICTs ought not to influence the outcome of the dispute. However, given the possible transformation of the process as a result of the utilization of ICTs, it may not be inconceivable that more data and information could be submitted, processed, and ascertained in a much easier way. This may ultimately impact the decision-making process, in a manner that could distinctively differ from what would have likely ensued in a more conventional procedure.

During the arbitral proceedings, the use of ICTs also impacts the process of taking of evidence and document production, where the parties and arbitral tribunals would be able to exchange communications, documents, and information instantaneously, extensively, and in a much easier way. Gradually, this may lead to displacement, or minimal use of oral evidence. With the advent of ICTs and the proliferation of bespoke programs, reconstruction of factual and historical events would be much easier, expeditious, and more accurate and reliable, and possibly factual, and legal gaps and contradictions would be identified using artificial intelligence. Moreover, the need to hear witnesses for hours or days may become moot or less desired, especially that human memories fail to capture with specificity and accuracy all relevant factual events. It would not be surprising to witness the utilization of system- or program-generated cross-examination questions, to identify lacunas and contradictions in witness testimony.

At present, arbitrators increasingly communicate via email, and, in time, parties would also use more frequently electronic file management systems that enable parties and arbitrators to file all documentation on a web-based platform and communicate principally through such e-platform and systems.[21] This also enables the parties, if the proceedings are not document-only, to conduct hearings online via the increasingly sophisticated online systems and state-of-the-art video-conferencing applications. Nevertheless, the efficiency of e-hearings will ultimately depend on the quality of ICT applications used, including the

[21] See Chapter 1, p. 17.

strength and suitability of e-connections and the frequency of delays or interruptions that might occur.

ICT applications can also increase the opportunity to hear passive respondents, thus reducing the number of default proceedings, where one party, usually the respondent, fails to participate. Obviously, arguments of costs and cumbersome travel would be moot and excuses by delinquent respondents would be largely reduced.

On a related note, arbitral institutions are innovating and adapting their rules to cater for the possible and likely use of ICT applications in arbitral proceedings.[22] For example, Article 24(4) of the ICC Arbitration Rules (2012) permits the use of video-conferencing for the case management conference; a flexibility that is also confirmed by Appendix IV of the ICC Arbitration Rules related to case management techniques, where letter (f) provides for the use of telephone or video-conferencing for procedural and other hearings where attendance in person is not essential. Similarly, Article 4(2) of Appendix V, pertaining to the Emergency Arbitrator Rules, states that any meeting with the emergency arbitrator may be conducted through video-conference, telephone or similar means of communications, and it is the emergency arbitrator who decides on the appropriate means.

The ICC 'Note to Parties and Arbitral Tribunals on the Conduct of the Arbitration under the ICC Rules of Arbitration' dated 13 July 2016 states at margin no. 6 that the Secretariat will 'generally send correspondence by email' and make clear that prospective arbitrators 'must' provide the Secretariat with their email addresses.

The ICC's position is not exceptional, as many arbitration institutions have made references to telephone and video-conferencing in their respective arbitration rules. For example, the CRCICA Arbitration Rules (2011) provide, in Article 28(4), that witnesses may be examined by means of telecommunications that do not require physical presence at the hearing. The AAA Arbitration Rules (2013) also refer to the use of video-conferencing, where it is stated that during the conduct of proceedings, when deemed appropriate, the arbitrator(s) may also allow for the presentation of evidence by alternative means including video-conferencing, Internet communication, telephonic conferences and means other than an in-person presentation. The LCIA Arbitration Rules (2014) are flexible and encourage the parties and arbitral tribunals to conduct the

[22] See Chapter 4, p. 87.

proceedings by any means, including by a telephone conference call, a video-conference, or an exchange of e-communications.

In addition to the previously mentioned changes, some well-established arbitral institutions have even developed special e-platforms and services for e-filing and e-management of arbitral proceedings such as the AAA Webfile, the ICC NetCase, and the CIETAC Online Dispute Resolution Centre. Furthermore, some arbitral institutions have adopted online arbitration rules such as the CIETAC Online Arbitration Rules and the HKIAC Electronic Transaction Arbitration Rules.

With respect to deliberations, modern arbitration laws and rules do not preclude electronic deliberations amongst arbitrators. Arbitral practice already allows that deliberation takes place by email, telephone, and even video-conferencing, if needed.

Italian law explicitly allows for deliberation by video-conferencing.[23] Under Swiss law, the Swiss Supreme Court has held that arbitrators need not meet in person and are free to conduct deliberations by electronic means, including email, provided that suitable precautions are taken.[24] These precautions fall into four conditions under which electronic deliberations among arbitrators would be admissible. First, all the arbitrators should agree on the use of such electronic means. Second, all the arbitrators must participate in the discussion, unless an arbitrator is replaced for valid reasons such as protracted illness (inability to serve as an arbitrator) or refusal to participate in any form of deliberation. Third, the arbitrators can deliberate online, unless the parties have ruled out such electronic deliberations. Finally, the procedural basis for such electronic deliberations must be properly documented, for example in the parties' agreement or in a procedural order.[25]

An analysis of these four previously mentioned conditions demonstrates that national courts are increasingly recognizing the status quo

[23] Under the *Italian Code of Civil Procedure, Book IV, Title VIII*, Italy introduced reforms in 1994 and 2006 by virtue of Law No. 25 of the 5 January 1994 (1994 Reforms) and Legislative Decree No. 40 of the 2 February 2006 (2006 Reforms). Article 837 entitled 'Deliberation of the Award' expressly states: '*The award shall be deliberated by a majority of the votes of the arbitrators meeting in personal conference or in video conference, unless the parties have provided otherwise, and shall be subsequently set down in writing.*'

[24] See Societé S. contre Societé K., Iere Cour civile, 23 October 1985 (ATF III Ia, p. 336), p. 338, cited in R. Morek, *Online Arbitration: Admissibility within the Current Legal Framework*.

[25] See R. Hill, 'On-line Arbitration: Issues and Solutions' (1999), 15 *Arbitration International*, 199, cited in R. Morek, *Online Arbitration: Admissibility within the Current Legal Framework*, Ibid.

on the proliferating use of ICTs throughout the arbitral proceedings. However, the said conditions raise certain concerns that merit due consideration.

Firstly, it is understandable that all arbitrators need to agree on the use of electronic means for deliberations, as deliberations involve all arbitrators and the format or means thereof must be conveniently available, accessible, and welcomed. Absent such collective consent, conventional deliberations must be resorted to. That said, it appears that, at present, electronic deliberations require an *opt-in* agreement. However, it is submitted that, in the not too distant future, it is likely that the default situation would be electronic deliberations, with an opt-out agreement, if all arbitrators wish to proceed with face-to-face deliberations. In other words, with the advent of ICTs and their proliferated use in arbitration proceedings, 'conventional' deliberations would transform to be 'electronic' rather than 'physical face-to-face' meetings.

Secondly, giving the parties the authority to rule out electronic deliberations is questionable, as deliberations (and their format) are a matter for the arbitral tribunal to consider, not for the parties to impose.

Thirdly, what ought to be of concern is not the procedural basis for electronic deliberations, but rather the procedural legality thereof. This requires due consideration of any mandatory requirements under the *lex loci arbitri*; absent such overriding mandatory requirements, the arbitral tribunal retains the discretion to deliberate in the format it so prefers and desires.

The Experience with Online Support Technologies

ODR technology-assisted mechanisms offer support technologies and provide adequate and appropriate means of communication (emailing, video-conferencing...) while ensuring confidentiality and security of proceedings and information flow. Arbitration support technologies include: databases, platforms, document archiving, demonstrative technologies, and so on that can cause a paradigm shift in the way arbitral proceedings are being prosecuted and administered and in a manner that promotes efficiency and cost-effectiveness.

There are many examples illustrating these support technologies. The ICC NetCase Project is indeed one notable example that needs to be reactivated. The ICC NetCase project, launched in 2005, was a service that allowed arbitrations to be conducted in a secure online environment, offering an online case management for participants in ICC arbitration proceedings. All participants were able to communicate through a secure website hosted by ICC. This service was developed to suit specific needs of ICC arbitration users by offering advantages of instantaneous and efficient communication, round-the-clock access, security, confidentiality, and organized handling and storage of documents. NetCase could only be used if all parties and all arbitrators agreed to its use by signing a Statement of Acceptance of the Conditions of Access and Use of NetCase. Once an agreement to use NetCase was made, the parties and arbitrators received access codes and all correspondences, memoranda, and other documents were posted on NetCase.[26]

All documents posted on NetCase were made available instantaneously to recipients and remained available throughout the proceedings. NetCase permitted parties to avoid costs by providing a centralized point for the storage of all documents submitted in arbitration. It also provided an efficient system for retrieval of documents, allowing participants to sort documents by date, author, or title. Storage and retrieval were standardized for ease of use. NetCase was programmed with security features and sophisticated encryption technologies to safeguard security and confidentiality, to restrain intrusion, interception, and alteration of messages or documents. Nevertheless, NetCase should not be thought of as a fully fledged online arbitration procedure; it was an ICT support facility.[27]

Similarly, several e-platforms and e-applications and technologies are being deployed and developed across the globe to cater to the resolution of disputes and the electronic transformation of traditional arbitration proceedings. A notable example is the AAA, which does a great deal of work in the context of ODR (including online arbitration) and e-management of disputes platforms.[28] Other examples include the Financial Industry Regulatory Authority (FINRA) online arbitration platform,[29] the LCIA's online filing system, which allows parties to arbitration proceedings to file requests for arbitration, responses, applications for expedited formation of the tribunal, applications for expedited appointment of a replacement arbitrator, and applications for the appointment of an emergency

[26] See Chapter 4, p. 89.

[27] See P. Mirèze, 'NetCase: A New ICC Arbitration Facility' in (2004) *ICC Bulletin Special Supplement*, 54.

[28] See for example the AAA WebFile platform: www.adr.org/aaa/faces/services/fileacase? and also the AAA New York Insurance ADR Center for No-Fault cases available at www .nysinsurance.adr.org/public/NoFault.jsp (last accessed on 2 May 2016).

[29] See www.finra.org/arbitration-and-mediation/online-claim-filing (last accessed on 2 May 2016).

arbitrator; submit any supporting documentation electronically; pay any filing fees online; and access all filings made online, including payment history.[30] Other online arbitration providers include ODREurope, which offers web solutions to arbitration cases.[31] Moreover, in the specific context of consumer-related disputes, the EU has established an ODR platform for handling such disputes.[32] On a related note, there are also arbitration cases evaluation tools such as: CaseXplorer® Arbitration™, which is a collaboration between the AAA and DecisionQuest offering an online case evaluation tool at a lower cost and faster alternative to in-person mock arbitrations.[33]

The Coming of a New Age: A Tradition of Innovation and Revolutionary Evolution

It is incontrovertible that ICTs have revolutionized the way we live our lives, interact, do business, and resolve our disputes. This digital age powered by the tidal waves of globalization sweeping across the globe has transformed and challenged the traditional means of resolving disputes through arbitration. Innovative applications and technologies have revolutionized our world and are gradually transforming the way arbitral proceedings are being conducted.

Indeed, we are experiencing and witnessing an inevitable evolutionary process of integrating ICTs in arbitral proceedings, with a view of total demise of the traditional ways of conducting arbitration, and the likely emergence of wholly virtualized and digitized arbitral proceedings is well underway.

Nevertheless, the introduction, use, and integration of ICTs in arbitration must observe the mandatory regulation and legal requirements prevailing at the level of nation States, whether at the seat of arbitration or the place(s) of recognition and enforcement.

Whilst we have indeed addressed certain legal challenges and principles in the previous sections, there remain certain overriding legal considerations that merit due scrutiny. These are: (a) due process of law, and (b) equality of the parties and the principle of contradiction.

[30] See www.onlinefiling.lcia.org (last accessed on 2 May 2016).

[31] See www.odreurope.com/odr-services/online-arbitration (last accessed on 2 May 2016).

[32] See www.ec.europa.eu/consumers/solving_consumer_disputes/non-judicial_redress/adr-odr/index_en.htm and www.webgate.ec.europa.eu/odr/main/index.cfm?event=main.home.show&lng=EN (last accessed on 1 May 2016).

[33] See www.casexplorerarbitration.com (last accessed on 2 May 2016).

As is the case with traditional offline arbitration, digitized or online arbitration proceedings must equally observe the overriding requirements of due process, equality, and contradiction. This may present procedural challenges for the technologically disadvantaged parties. Unequal access to technology and/or e-platforms hosting the proceedings could undermine the procedural integrity of the proceedings and compromise the sacrosanct principles of due process, equality, and contradiction, as a party would have procedural and technological leverage over the other, which might prejudice the ability of the party who is technologically disadvantaged to present its case reasonably and adequately.

Due process, equality, and contradiction are essential to the fairness and integrity of the proceedings and the decision-making process. Parties should be allowed to present their case on equal grounds, present evidence and counterclaims, and be notified of the other party's submissions. Accordingly, it is essential to ascertain whether the consenting parties are content with conducting the arbitral proceedings wholly or substantially online and have been given equal access to technology to enable the efficient use of audio and visual ICT applications without leverage or prejudice.

Taking into consideration the parties' freedom to opt for e-proceedings, the parties' informed choice could either be explicit in their agreement or implicit by conducting the proceedings under the auspices of an ODR provider whose applicable rules and policy provides for the exclusive or non-exclusive use of online technologies. In the absence of such informed choice, the arbitral tribunal may conduct e-proceedings, provided that the principles of due process, equal access, and e-contradiction are observed and safeguarded. That said, e-proceedings ought not be rejected, save in the exceptional cases where the use of ICTs would substantially and adversely impact the overriding due process requirements, in a manner that creates a form of 'virtual inequality'.[34]

Nevertheless, it is worth noting that, nowadays, Internet access is generally available across the globe, and emails are easily accessible from computers, laptops, smartphones, and tablets. Moreover, as wireless connections have replaced dial-up connections, Internet speed has significantly increased, which boosted accessibility and ease of use of ICTs. Furthermore, ICTs have a potential of supporting 'inclusivity', where everyone could be connected and doing business online. As such, ICTs

[34] See M. Abdel Wahab, 'ODR and E-Arbitration' in *Online Dispute Resolution Theory and Practice*, p. 403.

have made it possible for disadvantaged and weaker parties to join the global market and remain connected round the clock, which increased the volume of international trade, cross-border transactions, and their related disputes.

On the same note, the ICT revolution has brought about a new tradition of innovation powered by the revolutionizing technologies, where well-established principles of arbitration are being reconsidered and reconfigured. Confidentiality is one example, which incentivized access to arbitration and out-of-court dispute resolution.[35] However, with the increased demands for more transparency and the dilution of the relative importance of confidentiality with the proliferation of arbitration databases, news directories, and the demise of confidentiality through subsequent judicial recourse against arbitral awards, it is submitted that confidentiality no longer offers the driving incentive to arbitration. It has even been stated that 'arbitration is rarely conducted in full secrecy and applications to vacate or confirm an award can bring the existence, subject matter, and outcome of an arbitration to the forefront of public discourse'.[36]

In the context of online arbitration, confidentiality of proceedings is inextricably linked to 'security' of proceedings. E-platforms and arbitral institutions always ring-fence their applications with state-of-the-art encryption and restricted access technologies to maintain the security and confidentiality of web-based communications, so that even if information is intercepted, it remains inaccessible and unreadable. Accordingly, Secure Sockets Layer technology (SSL) and Secure Hypertext Transfer Protocol (S-HTTP) for web-based communications are constantly updated and innovated, with new encryption and secure connection technologies being developed daily to the extent that every few months new technologies become outdated and obsolete.

[35] See C. Tautschnig, 'The Arbitration Agreement and Arbitrability, Legal Challenges and Opportunities for the Next Generation of Online Arbitration', in *Austrian Yearbook on International Arbitration*, (2015) 101.

[36] See C. Cardozo, 'New Strides in Confidentiality During Enforcement Proceedings' Kluwer Arbitration Blog, 23 June 2012, available at www.kluwerarbitrationblog.com/2014/06/23/new-strides-in-confidentiality-during-enforcement-proceedings (last accessed 2 May 2016); see also Darius Chan, 'Sealing of Court Documents Relating to an Arbitration', Kluwer Arbitration Blog, 27 June 2012, available at www.kluwerarbitrationblog.com/2012/06/27/sealing-of-court-documents-relating-to-an-arbitration (last accessed 2 May 2016), where the author states that 'users of arbitration who are concerned about confidentiality ought to consider the lex arbitri, the arbitral rules, the arbitration agreement, and whether there is any need for a specific order by the tribunal, at early stages of the arbitral proceedings, relating to confidentiality'.

It is submitted that the life cycle of new ICT technologies can mimic that of a dragonfly (i.e. four months) before newer products and technologies hit the marketplace! Thus, the world of ODR and ICTs does live on a tradition of innovation; an innovation that offers the fuel that is constantly needed to power ODR processes.

Against this short cycle for ICT products, e-arbitration is indeed destined to be faster than a traditional offline arbitration while the decision-making process is gradually infiltrated by artificial intelligence and automated decision-making applications. By integrating technology into the decision-making process, online arbitration would achieve a totally different level that would undoubtedly transmogrify the process at large. Irrespective of whether this is desired or not, the present reality shows that the future is no longer an imaginary tale of displacing human interaction, at least in part, with artificial intelligence.

It is in this context that the authors offer three provocative and innovative applications and trends that may transform online arbitration, its principles, and our collective views thereof.

Automated Agent E-Arbitration Agreements (AAEA)

Automated Agent E-Arbitration Agreement (AAEA) pertains to the conclusion of arbitration agreements. It is worth noting that arbitration agreements are subject to the interpretation of the writing requirement as set in national arbitration laws and in international treaties such as the New York Convention on the Recognition and Enforcement of Foreign Arbitral Awards (hereafter known as NYC).[37]

An AAEA is concluded without direct human intervention and, by consequence, it does threaten the validity and/or enforceability of the parties' human-oriented consent to arbitration. For further clarification, an 'automated' or an 'intelligent' agent is a form of artificial intelligence, and is generally a tool or program that gathers information or performs other service without direct human presence or intervention. The automated agent uses the parameters provided by a human, and performs depending on its complexity and advanced technology, one or more of the following functions: gathering information, personalizing information, monitoring information (i.e. specific site watchers), analyzing and construing information, and/or undertaking actions through a cognitive knowledge base and a self-sustainable experience that enables an automated agent

[37] See Chapter 7, p. 151.

to enter into dealings and agreements, which possibly include arbitration agreements.

Thus, an agreement is valid when two or more agents engage in operations or when an individual interacts with an automated agent.[38]

There is a legal distinction between two groups of automated agents:

(a) Complex autonomous automated agents; and
(b) Simple automated agents.

The complex automated agent acts on the basis of its own self-contained knowledge base and progressive experience, while the simple automated agent purely acts in application of human-based instructions and orders. Consequently, the complex automated agents face more challenges due to the non-human, self-induced actions and decisions.

It should be noted that the sole fact that automated message systems were used for purposes of contract formation will not deprive the contract of legal effectiveness, validity or enforceability.[39] Article 12 of the Electronic Communications Convention is an enabling provision and should not be misinterpreted as allowing an automated message system or a computer to be made the subject of rights and obligations. Electronic communications that are generated automatically by message systems or computers without direct human intervention should be regarded as 'originating' from the legal entity on behalf of which the message system or computer is operated.[40]

When a contract is formed by the interaction of an automated message system and a natural person, or by the interaction of automated message systems, there are several ways to indicate the contracting parties' assent. Computers may exchange messages automatically according to an agreed standard, or a person may indicate assent by touching or clicking on a designated icon or place on a computer screen. However, the general terms employed in the Electronic Communications Convention give room to be applied to technological improvements and other means of indicating assent.[41]

[38] See M. Abdel Wahab, '*Online Arbitration: Traditional Conceptions and Innovative Trends*' in ICCA Congress book (2013), pp. 3–4.

[39] United Nations, United Nations Convention on the Use of Electronic Communications in International Contracts, Explanatory Note by the UNCITRAL Secretariat (2007), para. 210, p. 69. Available at www.uncitral.org/pdf/english/texts/electcom/06-57452_Ebook.pdf (last accessed 30 April 2016).

[40] Ibid. at 70, para. 213. [41] Ibid. at 70, para. 214.

The central rule is that the validity of a contract does not require human review of each of the individual actions carried out by the automated message system or the resulting contract. As long as the automated agent does not require human 'review or intervention' to complete its task, the validity of the arbitration agreement concluded by it would not be affected.[42]

In any event, it is worth noting that Article 12 of the UNCITRAL Convention on the Use of Electronic Communications in International Contracts (2005), of which Article 20 provides for its application to the NYC, recognizes AAEA by stating that they should not be denied validity or enforceability on the sole premise that no human intervention existed.[43] Accordingly, there is a legal basis for validating and enforcing AAEA, which mandates a profound reconfiguration and reconsideration, at the national and international levels, of the traditional human-based consent needed for the conclusion of arbitration agreements.[44]

Artificial Intelligence and the E-Arbitrator

It is incontrovertible that arbitrators are indispensable to the decision-making process in arbitration. Whilst the human nature of arbitrators was never challenged or brought into question, artificial intelligence (AI) applications are now threatening this key element in the arbitral process and non-human intelligence is increasingly considered while the human nature of arbitrators is gradually transformed from an unchallenged fact to a reality that may change in the not too distant future.[45]

It is largely admitted that almost all existing rules and laws envisage arbitrators as human neutrals and thus they require arbitrators to possess the necessary capacity, impartiality, independence, and ability to decide a case. The new French law on arbitration issued by virtue of Decree No. 2011–48 of 13 January 2011, explicitly endorsed the universal presumption that an arbitrator cannot be but human.[46] Article 1450 of the

[42] Ibid. at 70 para. 215.

[43] See UNCITRAL Convention on the Use of Electronic Communications in International Contracts, New York, 23 November 2005, in force 1 March 2013; Article (12) states: 'A contract formed by the interaction of an automated message system and a natural person, or by the interaction of automated message systems, shall not be denied validity or enforceability on the sole ground that no natural person reviewed or intervened in each of the individual actions carried out by the automated message systems or the resulting contract'.

[44] See Wahab, *'Online Arbitration: Traditional Conceptions and Innovative Trends'*, p. 4.

[45] See Chapter 6, p. 140.

[46] See Wahab, *'Online Arbitration: Traditional Conceptions and Innovative Trends'*, p. 5.

French Code of civil proceedings states, 'Only a natural person having full capacity to exercise his or her rights may act as an arbitrator. If the arbitration agreement names a legal person, the latter has only the power to organize the arbitration'.

The French Arbitration Law is extremely strict with regard to the human nature of the arbitrator. It does not permit an AI to fully act as an arbitrator, and if the arbitrator designated is non-human, the authority of that non-human legal person is limited to the organization of the arbitration but not to assess the case and render the award. The French law makes it clear that the role of artificial intelligence should be limited, contained, and restrained.

This is also confirmed under many other national laws. For example, Article 16 of the Egyptian Arbitration Law No. 27 of 1994 provides that an arbitrator cannot be a minor, bankrupt, or subject to any incapacity. Similarly, the English Arbitration Act of 1996 irrefutably presupposes that an arbitrator is inherently and by default a human, as Article 26 deals with the event of the arbitrator's death. The UNCITRAL revised Model Law on International Commercial Arbitration does not explicitly provide that the arbitrator must be a natural person; however, it implicitly presumes that the arbitrator is a natural person by using human associated pronouns such as 'he/she' or 'his/her'. For example, Article 11 of the Model Law concerning disclosures by arbitrators states: 'When a person is approached in connection with **his or her** possible appointment as an arbitrator, **he or she** shall disclose any circumstances likely to give rise to justifiable doubts as to **his or her** impartiality or independence. [. . .]' (Emphasis added.)Taking into consideration the impact of the Model Law on national arbitration legislations in many countries, it is unequivocal that many countries have adopted the rules or at least the spirit of the said Model Law in their legal framework, which entails that most arbitration legislations do perceive the arbitrator as a human being. Thus, it is difficult to consider an arbitrator as an artificial being or non-human-based intelligence, even if such AI application is created by a human.

Other examples of national arbitration laws include: the US Federal Arbitration Act in Section 50 which states: '[. . .] as if **he or they** had been specifically named [. . .]' and the Swiss Private International Law in Article 180(2) which states: '[. . .] if **he** does not possess [. . .]' (Emphasis added).

It is submitted that there is a distinction between rational and logical assessment that natural and artificial intelligence are capable of achieving. It is also submitted that only humans are capable of independently demonstrating a sociological print.[47] Additionally, having a non-human-based intelligence to act as an arbitrator would not permit beauty parades of interviewing potential candidates for party-appointed arbitrator positions to select the party-appointed arbitrator corresponding to the parties' needs and expectations.[48]

The selection process is principally driven by human-based criteria, which include the following: personal competence, intelligence, diligence, availability, nationality, integrity of an individual, individual's arbitration experience, linguistic abilities, knowledge of a particular industry or type of contract, willingness to devote time and attention to the matter, legal qualifications, being effective in working with other members of the tribunal, and of course being independent and impartial. Parties also look for co-arbitrators who are more likely to be sympathetic or supportive of their position;[49] an inclination that is inherently a function of human-based life forms. Taking into consideration all of the previously mentioned qualifications, it seems unrealistic to conduct *ex-parte* interviews with non-human-based intelligence that would undoubtedly lack the emotional inclination and sociological print that are inherent functions of humans.

For the present generation, it may be a bliss that the world has not yet evolved to a stage where humans and AI forms are infused and integrated. Evidently, the reality remains that arbitrators are natural persons. However, the future beholds such possibility. Even though it is inconceivable now for an artificial intelligence application to offer the emotional intricacies of humans, the future unfolds with highly sophisticated ICT and AI applications that promise to be self-conscious, evolving, and capable of exhibiting certain human traits. This may lead to partial or total displacement of the human element in the arbitral process. For the moment, human arbitrators remain pivotal and indispensable for the success and the proper administration of arbitral proceedings. It might be just a matter of time before such statement is challenged and reconsidered.

Authentication of E-Awards

Awards are the crown jewel and ends of the arbitral process, and so the enforcement and recognition thereof remain crucial. This necessitates the

[47] See Wahab, '*Online Arbitration: Traditional Conceptions and Innovative Trends*', p. 6.

[48] See L. Steyn, 'England: The Independence and/or Impartiality of Arbitrators in International Commercial Arbitration' in (2007) 18 *ICC Bulletin Special Supplement*, p. 106.

[49] See Gary B. Born, *International Commercial Arbitration*, Second Edition (Born: Kluwer Law International, 2014), pp. 1682–1683.

authentication and certification of awards as a step towards the enforcement and recognition thereof in diverse jurisdictions.

Considering that an apostille is an additional authentication required for international acceptance of notarized documents, the e-Apostille Pilot Program (e-APP) could be used to provide a medium facilitating cross-border recognition of foreign e-awards.[50] In 2006, the e-APP was introduced as an electronic method of issuing and certifying apostilles. Designated authorities are allowed to use special software for applying an apostille, and on the receiving end, can easily check to ensure the authenticity of a foreign apostille via a special computer database.

A number of countries have incorporated this e-apostille system to legalize documents.[51] Whilst such e-APP is not dedicated or specifically tailored to e-awards, it testifies to the possibility of inclusion of e-awards therein and/or developing a parallel cross-border system for e-awards in the not too distant future.[52]

Conclusion: A Glance through the Crystal Ball – Global Efforts and Future Trends

As discussed earlier, nowadays, Internet access is generally available across the globe, and emails are easily accessible from everywhere, and wireless connections have significantly boosted Internet speed and accessibility. Accordingly, it takes a brave new world of bold and forthright souls to acknowledge that ICTs have revolutionized our world, lives, interaction, and means of resolving our disputes. The colossal wave of digitization in the age of globalization has challenged conventional arbitration proceedings and dispute resolution schemes. Technology, as the 'fourth party' has paved the way for the introduction, use, and integration of ICTs in arbitration. However, this comes at a price, where certain legal challenges have arisen.

Our brave new world of arbitration marks an unprecedented proliferation of ICTs and AI applications that are gradually being integrated into arbitration agreements, arbitral proceedings, and arbitral awards. All are being gradually permeated and transformed with cutting-edge applications on communications, security, confidentiality, authenticity, dispute

50 See www.uihj.com/en/e-apostille-first-regional-seminar-in-helsinki-finland-1019842.html.

51 See the list of the Hague Convention Countries available at: www.apostilleguide.com/apostilleglossary/?p=21 (last accessed 30 April 2016).

52 See Chapter 7, p. 172.

management, proceedings administration, and decision-making. However, maintaining procedural integrity, neutrality, equality of arms, and due process remain at the core of the arbitral process and indispensable guarantees for its success and continuation in an efficient, trusted, and cost-effective manner.

As the main role of technology is to facilitate and accelerate the arbitration process, technology-facilitated ODR schemes remain the most utilized tools in the arbitration process. Technology-based and fully integrated ODR schemes, which will ultimately transform the arbitration process into a wholly digitized electronic process, are yet to be utilized, and will likely induce a profound change in the decision-making process with a possible introduction of AI applications in partial or total displacement of the human element.

That said, the accelerated and rapid evolution of ICTs rendered technology a double-edged sword of prospects and challenges. Undoubtedly, technology has facilitated communications between the parties and the arbitrators, generated cost savings as to the proceedings and offered plausible substitutes to traditional face-to-face interaction, and expedited the decision-making process. However, the gradual total digitization of arbitration would result in some undesired ramifications. When the virtual world takes over the physical world, arbitration would become impersonal and fully automated. This would dispense with the desired human intervention and would take away the social spirit of the process and its human dimension.

As the arbitration process becomes more technology dependent and less human oriented, it will transform into a novel technology-based ODR scheme. Whether this is desired or aspired is something for the future generations to assess and consider, in light of the relative advantages and disadvantages brought about by the double-edged sword of technology.

With this background, public and private initiatives have been established and commenced at national, regional, and global levels to address and regulate the growing field of ODR inclusive of online arbitration. One such notable ODR-specific initiative is the establishment of the UNCITRAL Working Group III on ODR (the 'ODRWG').[53] The ODRWG was established in 2010. At its forty-third session (New York, 21 June–9 July 2010), the UNCITRAL agreed that the ODRWG should be established to undertake work in the field of online dispute resolution relating to

[53] See Chapter 8, p. 182.

cross-border electronic commerce transactions, including business-to-business, and business-to-consumer transactions.[54]

At its forty-eighth session (Vienna, 29 June–16 July 2015), the Commission instructed the ODRWG to continue its work towards elaborating a non-binding descriptive document reflecting elements and principles of an ODR process, on which elements the ODRWG had previously reached consensus, excluding the question of the nature of the final stage of the ODR process (arbitration/non-arbitration). It was also agreed that the ODRWG would be given a time limit of one year or no more than two Working Group sessions, after which the work of the Working Group would end, whether or not a result had been achieved.[55]

During the thirty-third session, the ODRWG continued its work on the so-called 'Technical Notes on ODR', and after six years of frequently contentious debates, the ODRWG finalized the 'Technical Notes on ODR' as a guideline document, which incorporated, by the narrowest of voting margins, references to data 'security', 'confidentiality', and 'arbitration',[56]

[54] Between 13–17 December 2010, the Commission, held its twenty-second session in Vienna, and the session was attended by representatives of: Argentina, Austria, Belarus, Bolivia (Plurinational State of), Canada, China, Colombia, Czech Republic, Egypt, El Salvador, France, Germany, Honduras, India, Iran (Islamic Republic of), Israel, Italy, Japan, Mexico, Nigeria, Philippines, Republic of Korea, Russian Federation, Spain, Thailand, Turkey, Ukraine, United States of America, and Venezuela (Bolivarian Republic of). The session was also attended by observers from the following States: Ecuador, Indonesia, Panama, Slovakia, Slovenia, Sudan, and Yemen. See Report of Working Group III (Online Dispute Resolution) on the work of its twenty-second session (Vienna, 13–17 December 2010), A/CN.9/716, available at www.documents-dds-ny.un.org/doc/UNDOC/GEN/V11/801/48/PDF/V1180148.pdf?OpenElement (last accessed 30 April 2016). Subsequently, the ODRWG convened eleven sessions between 2011 and 2016. The most recent session is the Commission's thirty-third session held in New York from 29 February – 4 March 2016. That session was attended by representatives of: Argentina, Armenia, Austria, Brazil, Bulgaria, Canada, China, Colombia, Czech Republic, Ecuador, El Salvador, Fiji, Germany, Greece, Honduras, Hungary, India, Indonesia, Israel, Italy, Japan, Mexico, Namibia, Pakistan, Philippines, Republic of Korea, Russian Federation, Singapore, Spain, Thailand, Turkey, United States of America, and Venezuela (Bolivarian Republic of). The session was also attended by observers from the following States: Egypt, Iraq, Libya, Netherlands, Romania, Saudi Arabia, and Syrian Arab Republic. See Report of Working Group III (Online Dispute Resolution) on the work of its thirty-third session, (New York, 29 February – 4 March 2016), A/CN.9/868, available at www.documents-dds-ny.un.org/doc/UNDOC/GEN/V16/014/73/PDF/V1601473.pdf?OpenElement (last accessed 30 April 2016).

[55] See Official Records of the General Assembly, Seventieth Session, Supplement No. 17 (A/70/17), para. 352.

[56] It is worth noting that during the thirty-first session held in New York 9–13 February 2015, it was agreed and confirmed that the ODR mechanism will consist of three stages: negotiation, facilitated settlement and the final stage, which could be non-binding recommendation or arbitration.

especially that the concepts of confidentiality and security were linked, and raised important issues for an ODR process.[57]

'The Technical Notes on ODR' include an express reference to the principles that underpin any ODR process, which are: fairness, transparency, due process, and accountability.[58] This is in addition to confidentiality and security. Moreover, the Technical Notes addressed the stages of the ODR process, which are three: negotiations, facilitated settlement, and a third final stage. The first stage of the proceedings is a technology-enabled negotiation where the Parties negotiate directly through the ODR platform, and then if the negotiation process fails, the ODR administrator appoints an individual that will assist the parties in settling or resolving their dispute (a 'neutral'). The individual that assists the parties in settling or resolving their dispute is the neutral. However, neutrals ought not necessarily to be lawyers, although they should be required to have relevant professional experience as well as dispute resolution skills to enable them to deal with the dispute in question. The neutral shall provide a fair and efficient process for resolving disputes. The neutral shall remain independent, impartial, and treat both parties equally throughout the proceedings. Finally, if the second stage of the proceedings fails, the third and final stage commences,[59] which could be non-binding recommendation or arbitration.

One of the main achievements of the ODRWG was the agreement that ODR, which provides a simple, fast, flexible, and effective option for the resolution of online low-value and high-volume disputes, is a process that cannot be conducted on an ad hoc basis involving only the parties to a dispute and a neutral (that is, without an administrator). Instead, and unlike offline alternative dispute resolution, to enable the use of technology to facilitate a dispute resolution process, an ODR process requires a

See Report of Working Group III (Online Dispute Resolution) on the work of its thirty-first session, (New York, 9–13 February 2015), A/CN.9/833, available at www.documents-dds-ny.un.org/doc/UNDOC/GEN/V15/014/29/PDF/V1501429.pdf?OpenElement (last accessed 30 April 2016).

57 See Report of Working Group III (Online Dispute Resolution) on the work of its thirty-third session, (New York, 29 February – 4 March 2016), A/CN.9/868, available at, www.documents-dds-ny.un.org/doc/UNDOC/GEN/V16/014/73/PDF/V1601473.pdf?OpenElement (last accessed 30 April 2016).

58 See *Draft Outcome Document Reflecting Elements and Principles of an ODR Process* (New York, 29 February – 4 March 2016), A/CN.9/WG.III/WP.140, available at www.documents-dds-ny.un.org/doc/UNDOC/LTD/V15/089/59/PDF/V1508959.pdf?OpenElement (last accessed 30 April 2016).

59 Ibid.

system for generating, sending, receiving, storing, exchanging or otherwise processing communications, which is considered as an ODR platform. Such an ODR platform must be administered and coordinated by an ODR administrator that may be separate from or part of the ODR platform. It is desirable that all communications in ODR proceedings take place via the ODR platform.[60]

It is submitted that the ODR community will soon welcome some guidelines on principles and elements of the ODR process, and it is likely that arbitration will be an option under the final stage of the process. This marks a new era and a new step towards bridging the parallel universes of traditional offline and innovative online arbitration, with a clear inclination towards favouring institutional online arbitration, and repositioning online arbitration to cater for high-value offline disputes in as much as its predestined low-value, high-volume online disputes. However, this brave new era and world of arbitration requires top institutional players to take bold steps in embracing ICTs and gradually to integrate them into their traditionally administered arbitral proceedings. It is in this respect that leading global arbitral institutions such as the AAA, ICC, and LCIA could contribute and lead by example.

[60] Ibid.

3

The Security and Reliability of Electronic Communication

With a Critical Note on the Human Factor

PHILIPP SCHAUMANN AND MAX BURGER-SCHEIDLIN

Summary: This chapter explores security in the context of electronic communication. Firstly, a definition of information security will be given. Secondly, the method of threat assessment will be introduced, which allows the determination of the level of security that is sufficient for a given application (e.g. communications between parties and the arbitral tribunal). Thirdly, specific security requirements will be provided for each type of potential attacker in a specific context. This consists of basic security hygiene measures that are necessary for individuals accessing the Internet, followed by more specific requirements for law offices. The last part of this chapter introduces a blueprint for secure infrastructure suited for e-arbitration that is defendable against the most sophisticated adversaries.[1]

Introduction

E-arbitration requires a level of security that satisfies the legal requirement to keep client correspondence confidential and the need to protect all the information that is communicated and exchanged in an arbitration proceeding. In addition to the confidentiality requirement, information security covers other aspects as well, namely data integrity, availability, and compliance with other requirements.

Data integrity means that there shall be no unauthorized changes to the documents, neither for data-in-transit (the flow of the data from one computer to another) nor for data-at-rest (data stored on a storage device, e.g.

[1] In the IT–Security literature, 'adversary' is used to describe both the attackers that actively attack an IT system and the government organizations that try to violate the confidentiality of transmissions by collecting network traffic, trying to decrypt it when necessary and analyzing the traffic content.

on hard-disk or cloud storage). This is connected to authenticity, which requires that a recipient of an electronic communication be certain of the identity of the originator of the particular communication.

The third aspect of IT security, availability, requires that data are available to authorized persons whenever needed. Availability can be endangered not only through hardware failure, but also through targeted attacks ('denial of service', DoS)[2]. Such attacks can be very detrimental, e.g. if the submission of a document at a strict deadline is in danger.

The last aspect discussed here is compliance with other requirements that arise from legal or regulatory requirements. In many circumstances, this includes the requirement of auditability, which means that access to certain aspects of data, such as data that are protected by the data protection law,[3] are securely verifiable. Such requirements can also arise from the need to deliver a proof that is accepted as evidence in the jurisdictions concerned.

Threat and Impact Assessment

'There is no 100 per cent security!' This statement is used repeatedly to defend a low level of security. Threat assessment is the methodology that is used by security professionals to determine the level of security needed, and the specific security measures to be deployed.

To perform a threat assessment, the credibility, seriousness, and likelihood of potential threats need to be evaluated together with the potential impact of these actions. To do this, first a list of the potential adversaries needs to be compiled. In the next step, the likelihood of their attack is to be evaluated based on the value that an attack could bring for adversaries. The impact assessment estimates what the possible impacts would be if one of the adversaries would succeed. Based on these evaluations and impact estimates, one can determine what level of security is needed and thus the amount of time needed for security measures.

The main question to be asked in every situation is: 'Against which type of adversaries do we have to protect ourselves?' First, we will look at amateur hackers and hacktivists; then, professional adversaries will be evaluated. Those professionals include hackers 'for rent' who might be hired

[2] DoS attacks overwhelm a service by directing too much traffic against the system. Such attacks can be done against web servers and against any other system that is publicly reachable, including telephone systems (e.g. to prevent submission of a document before a deadline).

[3] For more details about the EU data protection rules, see www.ec.europa.eu/justice/data-protection/reform/index_en.htm.

by one of the parties involved, or government intelligence services that might want to aid 'their' businesses or otherwise consider the case to be of strategic importance. To determine the likelihood of targeted attacks, three questions have to be asked:

(1) What are possible reasons as to why a given IT setup might be attacked?
(2) What can an attacker gain by attacking your IT setup?
(3) Which skill-level of attackers are we likely to encounter?

The main reason to attack a law office or law office communication is to access the sensitive data that are stored and processed there. A reason that leads to the question 'Who might be interested in obtaining those secrets?' The answer to this question depends on the type of cases that are handled, and on the amount of money at stake. If two large international companies are arguing in a case that involves tens or hundreds of millions of euros/dollars, paying a few hundred thousand euros to professional hackers in order to gain access to the preparatory material of the other party might be considered money well spent. There are also cases where the parties involved in an arbitration proceeding are considered of strategic importance for a country. Examples could include cases that involve large industrial enterprises trying to win a large proposal, or the big energy companies fighting over access to natural resources. In such cases, involvement of government intelligence services cannot be ruled out. Government organizations that have the means to control and monitor the Internet traffic in many parts of the world are called 'global attackers'.[4] It is rather difficult to protect data from global attackers. In the following sections, when defences are discussed, we will refer back to threat assessment to see what type and level of defence is needed for each attacker type.

Non-Professional Adversaries

On the Internet, there is an endless probing or testing of all systems using automatic tools to find a vulnerability that can be exploited. This data traffic is called the 'background noise' of the Internet. Often, security professionals do not refer to such scans as 'attacks', as these scans are often executed by amateur hackers ('script kiddies'). Script kiddies are mostly young people who download attack scripts and tools that allow automated

[4] The most important (and probably currently only) example of such global attacker is the NSA in combination with its Anglo-Saxon partners.

scans for vulnerabilities. When the tools find vulnerable systems, other tools are used to attack them to gain access. The main motivation for such attacks is what is called 'bragging rights' and ego. These attacks are typically non-targeted. Non-targeted attacks are the easiest to defend against due to the lack of effort by the attacker.

When non-professional attackers choose their targets for political (or pseudo-political) reasons, they are referred to as 'hacktivists'. Examples of such hacktivists include 'Anonymous' and '4chan'. Hacktivists attack their targets in coordinated attacks, sometimes even after public announcement. Their main motivation is to make a political statement. The first of the two main attack types for hacktivists aims to gain access to the data of the target to publish such data and to embarrass the targeted organization.[5] If the first type of attack fails, the denial of service (DoS) attacks are used, often in the form of dDoS (distributed Denial of Service). In the latter case, the attacker is using a large number of systems on the Internet to attack a single target in order to overwhelm the target with data traffic and to prevent the systems of the target organization from communicating over the Internet.

Professional Adversaries

Professional adversaries pose a greater threat to data security than non-professional adversaries. Professional adversaries include companies that specialize in the retrieval of sensitive information, organized crime organizations that target bank accounts of private citizens and companies alike, and governmental services of many countries that either spy on their own citizens and businesses or that engage in industrial espionage to help their own industries.

Such government services often have access to the Internet traffic in their region (or even globally) in addition to considerable resources from the state budget. The result is that those services must be considered as the adversaries that are most difficult to defend against. This includes government services of some of the less-developed countries that try to compensate for their lack of conventional military and economic power through the use of cyber-espionage and surveillance.

Unfortunately, there is a large market for attack tools (programs that can perform attacks), for attacks-as-a-service (where the whole attack is

[5] For the best and most up-to-date list of attacks by the decentralized virtual community Anonymous, see www.en.wikipedia.org/wiki/Timeline_of_events_associated_with_Anonymous.

outsourced), and for stolen sensitive data. The market demand for attack tools and attacks is fulfilled by a considerable number of players. First, there are 'black hats': individuals that are either directly attacking systems to gain access to sensitive data that they can then sell, or they work as freelancers, selling their skills to the highest bidder. This underground community is highly specialized. Some of these participants (either employed by specialist companies that are contracted by government services, or as freelancers) do basic security research to find vulnerabilities in systems that can be integrated into attack tools. These specialists also reengineer the monthly security patches from the big vendors to analyze details of those security patches. With this knowledge, attack tools can be developed that target systems where the specific patch has not yet been applied.

Other participants of this underground economy utilize these vulnerabilities to generate malware (viruses, Trojans, etc.). Again, other players oversee distributing this malware through (phishing) emails, infected advertisement on big websites, or packaged together with stolen software. A large section of the underground market is busy developing and maintaining so called 'botnets'.[6] These are PCs, Macs, tablets, and smartphones that are infected with malware and are under control of 'botnet herders'. These botnets can be used for dDoS and other illicit tasks. Botnets can consist of up to millions of infected systems and have a constant turnover in the sense that basic systems are cleaned up and other systems are newly infected.

The main business model behind dDoS is extortion, demanding payments for stopping the attacks. But dDoS can also be used for more tactical purposes, e.g. preventing the victim from accessing some resource, for instance, to prevent a lawyer from meeting a deadline for submission of a paper. Companies that supply attack tools to government services sell two types of tools. The first type is a surveillance tool that can be deployed on the network (if the government service has control over the Internet access in their respective region[7]). Where such surveillance is not possible (e.g. when the target of the surveillance is using strong encryption), tools are available to target the endpoints of the communication, which is the end user's PCs, Macs, tablets, or smartphones.

[6] More details about botnets are found at www.en.wikipedia.org/wiki/Botnet.

[7] Such control has always to be assumed for 'non-democratic' countries, but as we learned from the Snowden publication, this also applies to the Anglo-Saxon and several other countries. One needs to remember that to attack some communication, access to one of the two endpoints is often sufficient. Attackers will attack the less strongly defended side.

A large number of professional attacks are specifically targeted against a single person or company. Targeted attacks by professionals are very hard to defend against, and much harder than non-targeted attacks that go for 'low hanging fruits', such as those that target customer bank accounts and credit cards. The chances of defending against targeted attacks depend on the amount of resources that are deployed against a specific target, and the amount of resources that the defender invests. The resources of government services can be very high, as in the case of Stuxnet, where millions were spent to build a replica of the industrial systems used in Iran for uranium enrichment.[8]

However, there is still value in deploying defensive countermeasures, as a good security system makes it much more expensive for the attackers. The goal should be that the attack costs become higher than the value of the information to be gained. To perform a threat assessment for a given situation, one must determine whether the situation is likely to cause one of the opponents to hire professionals in order to get advance information or whether even a government service in one of the countries involved might be interested in this case. For example, in the wake of the Snowden publications, it was reported that such government services had been selecting communication based on keywords (selectors) that refer to European companies and their products.[9]

Security Countermeasures

Non-targeted attacks are a fact of life on the Internet and need to be defended against constantly. The following section on Basic Security Hygiene for All will explain how to achieve the previously discussed aim. The specific (and more expensive) measures that law offices (and other similar companies and organizations) need to take will be discussed under the section on Basic Security Hygiene for (Law) Offices.

Basic Security Hygiene for All

Each Internet user should follow the following basic security measures to prevent 'infections' of their devices, to avoid being defrauded, and to

[8] For the most comprehensive summary, see www.en.wikipedia.org/wiki/Stuxnet#Target_and_origin.

[9] See, 'America's Willing Helper: Intelligence Scandal Puts Merkel in Tight Place', *Spiegel*, 4 May 2015, www.spiegel.de/international/germany/bnd-intelligence-scandal-puts-merkel-in-tight-place-a-1031944.html.

protect their bank and other accounts and/or identity from theft. These measures are about the protection of users' PCs, Macs, tablets and smartphones. For each of those system types, a key fact is that (contrary to many crime novels and movies) these systems cannot be successfully attacked and 'taken over' from the Internet by a clever attacker without some activity of the user. Since some decades, internal firewalls prevent such attacks 'from the outside' (unless the user disabled those protection mechanisms). This means that for a modern system to be infected with malware, the end user needs to actively perform a given command.

There are a number of ways in which a user can cause such an infection. Everybody needs to learn that emails are dangerous and clicks on attachments are only to be done with considerable caution. When in doubt, call the alleged sender of the email. The most common manner to infect a device is by opening a cleverly disguised phishing email with an attachment and then clicking on that attachment in order to execute the malware. Unfortunately, even for people who have been trained not to open suspicious emails, the opening of a corrupt attachment is probable. Malicious emails can also contain links to websites that either distribute malware or that ask for confidential information, such as user names and passwords for bank accounts, social networking websites, or cloud-based email services.

Other forms of infections do not require the user to click on any link; visiting a website can be sufficient. Attackers include the placement of malicious Flash or Java-Code on popular websites (not just porn websites), mostly by placing a commercial ad. In these cases, there is not much the user can do to prevent an infection except to keep all his or her software up-to-date with security patches. Security patches happen to be the most important part of basic security hygiene. This is not only true for the operating system, but also for many of the other software components, including web browsers and their plug-ins, such as Flash and Java. However, not all modern systems and software solutions are configured in auto-update mode.[10]

[10] One such example is the Personal Software Inspector from Flexera (formerly known as Secunia), available at www.flexerasoftware.com/enterprise/products/software-vulnerability-management/personal-software-inspector; for another example of social engineering against cloud services, see Teen Hacker Group Targets US Spy Chief, Lifars, 13.1.2016, www.lifars.com/2016/01/teen-hacker-group-targets-us-spy-chief and Brian Krebs, Lazy Authentication Still the Norm 'Krebs on Security', 18.12.2015 www.krebsonsecurity.com/2015/12/2016-reality-lazy-authentication-still-the-norm.

The last point regarding protection against malware concerns a simple rule: never perform your daily work under the 'administrator' setting. All systems should be configured so that no changes to the system are possible in plain user mode. In other words, to add software or change configurations, the user should actively confirm the switch to administrator mode. In a business setup with IT administrators, such changes should only be possible by them.

For all mobile systems such as laptops, tablets or smartphones, there is a considerable risk that the device is stolen or lost (especially if it is known or assumed that the device contains confidential information, in fact, it is rather cheap to ask for a specific laptop to be stolen). Therefore, all systems on these devices should be set up in such a way that the difficulty to gain access to the data is disproportional (higher than) to the value of the data on the system. Minimum protection is to configure a password on the system, which might stop a non-professional thief from accessing the data. However, if the goal of the theft is to get the data, the attacker will remove the hard disk and access the data in another manner. Therefore, any device with sensitive data needs to have the data encrypted in such a way that the data are safe even if the device is stolen. For PCs and Macs, this means hard-disk encryption with boot password, and for smartphones and tablets, it means that the encryption is enabled and a password for inactivity lock is active instead of a simple PIN (personal identification number) code.

Regarding passwords, most Internet users have a large number of services where they need to use passwords. The solution for many people is to reuse their passwords. This is, however, bad practice. Many individuals have lost their online accounts and their data because of this harmful practice.[11] One possible cause for losing a web account is that the service provider is negligent and allows your data to be stolen. This is bad, but it is even worse when the password lost in such an event provides access to more than just that specific service. The first security measure is to use separate and original passwords[12] for each service. This is cumbersome, since most users have more services than they can remember complex passwords for. There are two solutions. The first one is using a scheme that

[11] A sophisticated social engineering attack against the journalist Mat Honan that wiped out his complete online presence and his local systems is described in *Wired*: 'Mat Honan, How Apple and Amazon Security Flaws Led to My Epic Hacking', 08.06.2012, www.wired.com/2012/08/apple-amazon-mat-honan-hacking/all.

[12] In no circumstance is '123456' or its competition '12345678' (two of the most popular passwords) a good password.

allows the user to memorize the different passwords, as they are all based on the same pattern (e.g. the scheme could make use of the URL of the service). The second option is to use password-store software that is suitable for managing a large number of passwords. In addition, sensible users should use the two-factor login services that are more and more offered by Internet services. This allows the use of simpler passwords because a second authentication item has to be provided, e.g. by text message.

Another aspect of security hygiene is data backup. If there is data of value (especially private photos of sentimental value), there needs to be some form of backup. There are services available that allow users to upload data to the cloud; the other simple way is to buy an external hard disk and copy all the data to the external disk (or only the changes using backup software). A major challenge in both cases is that if a backup is not automated, it requires discipline to use it consistently.

The reasons as to why data backup is needed are numerous: storage devices have a limited lifetime and can fail unexpectedly, humans make mistakes and delete data erroneously, and ransomware encryptors[13] can encrypt all data that are accessible to the infected PC and then demand payment for the decryption (which might or might not work). The next point concerns external traffic. Communication with the Internet and on the Internet should be encrypted (e.g. though HTTPS). However, this is not consistently the case. Using the threat assessment methodology again, we might feel moderately safe regarding connections from our homes (possibly with encrypted and secure wireless) to our trusted Internet provider, but this assumption of safety is definitely a mistake if we are using public Wi-Fi (e.g. in a restaurant, the airport, or the network connections in a hotel), regardless whether the connection is wireless or via cable.[14]

Regarding smartphones and tablets, the first task is to apply the threat assessment methodology to determine whether the standard configuration is sensible. If there is no sensitive data on that device, basic security setup with a PIN code might be enough to protect the system against loss. In this case, it is advisable to enable the backup-to-cloud settings on the device so that automatic backup of the data is performed. However, if syncing business emails to the smartphone is necessary, transferring the

[13] For the most comprehensive summary, see https://en.wikipedia.org/wiki/Ransomware.

[14] In fact, government services are known to make use of the insecurity of Internet access in hotels, infiltrating hotels where their targets are likely to stay.

data to one of the big providers should be carefully evaluated. Four-digit PINs are definitely not sufficient and cloud backup is only sensible if you can exclude the governmental organizations from your list of adversaries (with or without a warrant that gives them access to your data). In the case of data protected by the EU's data-protection legislation[15] additional aspects can apply. Furthermore and without any exceptions, rooting or jailbreaking[16] the phones and installing apps from untrusted sources is never a good idea. The last point in our basic security rulebook is a threat assessment regarding cloud services. The level of security expertise that those big cloud and email service providers can use to protect your data is considerably higher than alternative methods. The data in those services are protected well compared to most web shops and other Internet services, except for the cases where relevant government services have access to the data. It should be noted that cloud services are at a risk for social engineering attacks, which are arguably the weakest points of those cloud services.[17] Again, two-factor authentication helps against such attacks, but even that is not 100 per cent 'fool-proof' (although it makes those attacks considerably harder to perform).

Basic Security Hygiene for (Law) Offices

In what follows, the author has aimed to set out technical information that is specifically and directly relevant to allow the target audience of this book to set up a secure and reliable IT system in their law office. The author is aware that these sections are of a more technical nature than the other chapters in this book. The choice to include more technical terms was inspired by the idea that this chapter should be useful also for the IT department in charge of setting up of the IT systems for a company or law firm.

15 See www.ec.europa.eu/justice_home/fsj/privacy/law/index_de.htm.
Council Directive 95/46/EC of 24 October 1995, on protection of individuals with regard to the processing of personal data and on the free movement of such data, OJ 1995 No. L281, 24 October 1995.

16 Rooting (on iPhones and other iOS devices) or jailbreaking on Android refers to the removal of the limitation that a smartphone user shall not perform administrative reconfigurations on his or her device, whereby disabling some of the security features. Smartphones without this protection are considerably more vulnerable.

17 For another example of social engineering against cloud services, see www.lifars.com/2016/01/teen-hacker-group-targets-us-spy-chief.

Separation of Networks and Wi-Fi Implementation

Regarding the basic security of law and other offices, a good separation of the network from the Internet using a well-managed firewall (the challenge is the 'well-managed') is advisable. This includes the need for any Wi-Fi in the office network to allow access to the public Internet only and never to the internal network. Even within the internal network, client data and other highly sensitive information must be further secured against internal attackers (for high-value data, it might be a very reasonable cost for the attackers to 'deploy' a young intern to work within the law office in order to gain access to the internal network). Such an 'insider' can either try to copy data directly or install a back door on an office device to enable the access of the attackers online. Obtaining such illicit access is basic spycraft not only for government services, but also for information-retrieval services that one of the parties in an arbitration proceeding might have utilized against the law office. Such a back-door installation can also be achieved remotely by sending an appropriately crafted phishing email to a staff member (in most cases, many emails are sent to increase the chances of an employee falling victim to the attack). When it comes to phishing emails and social engineering, the staff is often the weakest link in the defence of an office. More details about the role of security awareness and social engineering tricks are found in the text of Max Burger-Scheidlin.[18]

Access from Home and for Service Companies

When there is a need to allow work-from-home (or remote access for the company maintaining the office IT or some other equipment), such access shall be secured by two-factor authentication (password plus a security token or text message), since such connections are a major entry point of anyone targeted.

Data Backup and the Use of Cloud Storage

The need for professionally managed data backup, either locally or in a remote location (which offers the advantage of a recovery option in cases of disasters, e.g. if the whole building is flooded due to fire brigade) is the last key basic security rule. This is related to the question of cloud storage in general. Again, big cloud storage providers likely offer more security

[18] See also the critical note by Max Burger-Scheidlin, p. 80.

than a local office can afford. However, this is not the case if your potential adversaries include the government services of your cloud provider.[19]

The Basics of Trustworthy Communication

The following section describes in more detail the specific challenges of securing electronic communications. This section will be of a more technical nature than the previous ones, because most options for secure communications are not (yet) easy to implement.

Encryption, Digital Signatures and Trusted Identities

Regrettably, trustworthy communication on the Internet is not straightforward, although the tools to do this have already been invented many decades ago.[20] Trustworthy communication has three requirements. First, the identity of the communication partner needs to be securely verified, something that is extremely challenging. Second, tampering with the content using digital signatures applied to the text must be prevented. The first and second requirements are typically combined by digitally signing a message or document. This signature guarantees that this message has not been tampered with and has been verified by the person that is described in the details of the signature. The third requirement is that the communication must be secured against eavesdropping. The countermeasure is to use public key encryption. If the sender of a message has access to the public key of the intended recipient, this key can be used to encrypt the message so that only the intended recipient can read the message.

There are two basic approaches for certification of an identity: certification authorities (CAs) and chains-of-trust. CAs are trusted institutions that are available in nearly all countries, either as private companies or government-affiliated companies. Their service consists of verifying the identity of a person through presentation of credentials, such as identity card or passport, and then transferring that identity information to a certificate that is digitally signed using the digital identity of the CA.[21] The

[19] More details of the pros and cons of cloud storage are found in www.en.wikipedia.org/wiki/Cloud_storage.

[20] Public key encryption was discovered in 1970 by James H. Ellis, a British cryptographer at the UK Government Communications Headquarters (GCHQ); however, it had been kept secret. It was rediscovered in 1976 by Whitfield Diffie and Martin Hellman, influenced by Ralph Merkle's work on public-key distribution.

[21] Technically the CA generates a key-pair, the private part of the pair is used for signing a message or document, the public part (public key) can be distributed freely, and

identity that is certified by a CA can take on various formats. Most CAs just take the name of a natural person (and potentially information such as an ID number) and include the name in the digital certificate (which is then later used for signing). However, in many cases, the role of the person might also be important to the receiver of the communication (e.g. being a certified lawyer or a company officer for a company with statutory authority). Specialist CAs could be available for such identity certifications.

In theory, each partner in a digital communication could go to the nearest CA to receive a key pair including the digital certificate to sign his or her messages, and thereby verify the authenticity of the message. Provided that the recipient of the message or data file has access to the appropriate software and CA systems, she or he could verify the details that are provided as part of the certificate. In practice, however and despite its availability, email encryption is not yet common practice.

The implementation of encrypted emails based on CA-issued certificates has been standardized under the name S/MIME.[22] It has been implemented in many popular email programs, but is not easily configurable and usable. Those programs should be able to manage the private key of the sender and conveniently obtain the public keys of the recipients; however, they fail to do so in a consistent and reliable manner when interacting between different types of email software and certificates from various CAs. Such systems, including a central system that allows trust relationships between the CAs, were planned in the 1990s; however, they were never implemented. The fact that all partners of the communication need to participate in the secure process is another reason for the low adoption rate.

Even earlier, an alternate solution had been developed in the form of Pretty Good Privacy (PGP).[23] The PGP concept is based on a chain-of-trust and works without involvement of central authorities. The chain-of-trust is established by people who know each other's respective identities, and by meeting in a room and signing the certificates of each other to confirm their identities. This is a practice suited for communities or for closed groups, such as that of the counsel and client in a specific arbitration case. The chain-aspect comes in when a new member of the community

allows other users to encrypt a message or document so that only the owner of the private key/public key pair can decrypt it.

[22] S/MIME (Secure/Multipurpose Internet Mail Extensions) is a standard for public key encryption and signing of emails.

[23] PGP was created by Phil Zimmermann in 1991; for the most comprehensive summary see www.en.wikipedia.org/wiki/Pretty_Good_Privacy.

is introduced. If this new member knows one of the existing members, she or he will trust other certificates, as they have been signed by somebody whose certificate has been signed by somebody else in the chain. Software for the generation of such key pairs and their use is available freely, and includes amongst others, the Open-Source versions OpenPGP and GnuPG. Unfortunately, the integration of PGP-based encryption into popular email programs is not better than with CA-based encryption with S/MIME. There are plug-ins available for most of the email software on MS Windows and OS X; however, the integration is not straightforward.

(In)Security of Emails

Email exchange uses two different types of components. One option is email software that is installed on a PC, a Mac, a tablet, or a smartphone to read and write messages. This software consists of either email programs such as Thunderbird or MS Outlook, or a specialized app installed on a smartphone or tablet. Another option is the simple use of a web browser (this is the case for cloud-based mail services such as Gmail). The email software connects to a server that is either a mail server or (in the case of cloud-based mail services) a web server. Mail traffic consists of traffic between the email programs to the mail or web server on the one hand, and, possibly, server-to-server traffic on the other hand, since there is typically more than one server involved.

Law offices have a number of options regarding setting up and operating email systems. They can set up and operate their own mail servers and manage the end-user programs, or they can connect their end-user email programs to one of the many external mail services. The third option is web mail where a web browser is used instead of a mail program. In all cases, private company mail domains (e.g. xxx@mycompany.com) are available (at extra cost typically). An assessment of the third option will be discussed in the section on email services in the cloud and emails on smartphones.

There are pros and cons for each of the three cases. When the office itself operates mail servers, there is full control and responsibility over the quality and security of the setup, including the storage of the mails and the logs that show when emails have been sent and received. When the mail server is outsourced, this control is delegated. When it comes to security implementations, the office depends on the willingness and skills of the operator of the systems (which can be higher than what the office could organize itself). In both cases, the office has full control over the client systems and can implement secure email based on either PGP or S/MIME.

When PGP or S/MIME are implemented and used consistently, the security features of the mail servers are of secondary importance. Messages encrypted in the above manner are not readable with the exception of the sender name, recipient name, and subject field. This provides a very high level of security even against very professional and government attackers. However, in reality, this full security is rarely used, as it requires a complicated setup, and manual interaction and intervention. It works only if the sender and the recipient can agree on the details of the setup (e.g. whether to use PGP or S/MIME and what certificates to use). Again, threat assessment tells us whether this level of security is appropriate and necessary.

A different implementation option that could make the processing of signed and encrypted emails easier for the end user is to deploy special software that automates the use of PGP or S/MIME so that a dedicated server in front of the mail server maintains a collection of the public keys of the regular communication partners, and a private key for the local law office. The server checks for each outgoing email whether the public key for the given recipient is available and then automatically applies encryption and signature. However, this setup also has its disadvantages and is not used very often.

Since the Snowden publications, a different type of automatic email encryption has gained more popularity: automatic encryption of the connection between the mail servers using TLS/SMTP ('encryption on the transport layer'). This is a standard that allows two mail servers to verify each other's identity and to negotiate a security protocol as part of their initial handshake before exchanging emails. Default is 'opportunistic TLS/SMTP', which means that if both partners are supporting TLS, TLS will be used. 'Opportunistic TLS/SMTP' should be configured on every mail server, something that has been done post-Snowden by most of the major service providers.

If the mail servers are under control of the office itself, another configuration option is available: 'mandatory TLS/SMTP'.[24] This alternative could be very appropriate for the connections between the counsel and clients. If both servers are configured as 'mandatory', the servers will only send emails to each other if the negotiation is successful. This ensures that such mail traffic is encrypted when travelling over the Internet. It is advantageous, as the encryption is transparent to the users and no interaction or

[24] For knowledgeable mail administrators, setting up mandatory TLS/SMTP should only take about 10 minutes when the administrators on each side are in contact.

inconvenience arises. However, it is disadvantageous, as the encryption is transparent to the users and thus there are no signed messages available as proof of the integrity, and the messages are stored as clear text on the mail servers. Nevertheless, TLS/SMTP is advisable, even as an addition to full encryption, as it provides extra security against potential attacks. In the case where the client software is installed in the office network, but the mail server is outsourced and neither PGP nor S/MIME are used, there is another type of traffic to worry about: the traffic between the email client and the central mail server on the Internet. There are encrypting protocols available for this traffic; however, they must be configured correctly.

Email Services in the Cloud and Emails on Smartphones

Another option for implementing email services for a law office is to skip both mail clients and mail servers and instead use one of the many web mail services that are accessible from a web browser. In this case, there is no easy way to implement PGP or S/MIME, although a few services claim to support such features. The quality and the security for the major providers is better than what a small-town IT service can offer. However, all the messages are available to the provider and potentially to government services with or without warrant.

The last email question to be discussed is the use of smartphones for email traffic. Storing company emails on private devices should be avoided. When it comes to smartphones and tablets that are centrally managed,[25] the security depends on how the configuration of the devices has been configured by the central administrator. Without central management, company emails should not be on such devices that are easily lost or stolen or that backup their data into a cloud.

(In)Security of Messaging

When it comes to non-email messaging services (also called instant messaging), there are a number of services available that offer different types of security. As a rule of thumb, the big providers of such services such as WhatsApp or Snapchat cannot be considered secure enough for business communications.[26] One basic requirement for a secure implementation is

[25] Such central management is implemented in the form of mobile device management software (MDM) that allows configuring the settings of tablets and smart phones from a central place.

[26] For more background on secure messaging, see https://en.wikipedia.org/wiki/Secure_instant_messaging and for a table of secure messengers, see https://en.wikipedia.org/wiki/Comparison_of_instant_messaging_clients.

that the text must be encrypted and only the participants can have access to the keys (called end-to-end encryption); in other words, no keys should have to be stored and maintained on a central server. A number of those services are offering end-to-end encryption, where the keys are stored and maintained in the endpoints and not on a central server. However, there is pressure on such providers, especially in the United States and the United Kingdom, not to offer any services where the content cannot be provided to the government organizations.

Even if the service is providing end-to-end encryption there are still ways for the client software to potentially 'leak' the private keys to the central service if forced by the government. Such a 'trick' has been implemented for Skype after governments insisted on the capability to intercept the communication for selected users.[27] In cases where threat assessment has determined that the risk of communication interception is high, there is always the option of buying special secure telephones that also support text messages (see next section).

(In)Security of Telephones and Video-Conferences

Telephone communication has always been relatively easy to intercept and such eavesdropping features have been standard since the invention of telephones. The introduction of mobile phones has made such interception even easier. The encryption of the wireless part of the connection is rather weak and the intercepting of calls through fake 'antennas' (base station) using an IMSI catcher[28] is relatively affordable. Even without such efforts, the telephone service provider collects call records (meta-data) that record who called whom, at what time, and for how long. American phone companies have been giving this data to US government services regularly,[29] and the same can be expected in other countries as well.

Smartphones offer even more interception options, as additional software can be installed on these devices. This is in addition to the tracking

[27] For details, see www.heise.de/newsticker/meldung/Vorsicht-beim-Skypen-Microsoft-liest-mit-1857620.html (German language).

[28] IMSI catcher is a device that is used by law enforcement, but is also available on the black market, that 'catches' the connections of nearby mobile phones and allows the user to 'listen' to the calls.

[29] Regarding phone metadata given to government, see Vodaphone Law Enforcement Disclosure Report Legal Annexe June 2014 (they report that they have to give call information to the government of 29 countries and allow direct access in 6 countries), available at www.vodafone.com/content/dam/sustainability/2014/pdf/operatingresponsibly/vodafone_law_enforcement_disclosure_report.pdf.

feature of the smartphones, which also might be helpful for an organization that wants to learn more about the movements of a counsel. This is easily done through social engineering by convincing the victim (e.g. the counsel in an important arbitration case) to install an app that accesses the location information. Secure phone calls require special devices on each end or appropriate software on smartphones.[30] Those systems do not use regular phone services, but establish encrypted Internet connections and tunnel the voice call through those connections.[31]

This is because even when the voice content is encrypted (or scrambled) but sent over regular phone connections, the fact that one person called another would still be available as part of the metadata collected by the provider of the phone service.

Video-conferences can be set up in such a way that guarantees security against most attackers. However, even reputable companies have managed to have their video-conference systems configured in such a way that the systems have been freely available on the Internet for anybody to infiltrate.[32]

Verifying a Secure Setup: Penetration Testing

How can one have assurance that any system is set up correctly? Experience proves that asking a reputable IT company is no guarantee of success. What are needed are penetration tests that are performed by specialist companies that have attack skills comparable to the professional attackers. It should be noted that the quality of those companies, and their level of professionalism, needs to be evaluated in each case. Such penetration tests should be done for every system that is directly connected to the Internet, such as the mail servers, video-conferencing systems, VoIP systems

30 For an up-to-date summary about secure telephone apps, see www.en.wikipedia.org/wiki/Open_Whisper_Systems.

31 Several brands are available, one example is Blackphones from Silent Circle; see www.silentcircle.com/products-and-solutions/devices; how difficult secure messaging is has been shown by the capture of El Chapo who has used elaborate security for this; see Bruce Schneier, El Chapo's Opsec, 21 January 2016 available at, www.schneier.com/blog/archives/2016/01/el_chapos_opsec.html.

This article explains that user errors are the most important weakness for Crypto phones: Rachel Metz, *MIT Technology Review*, Researchers Say Security of Encrypted Communications Apps Compromised by Users, 14 December 2015, www.technologyreview.com/news/544516/user-error-compromises-many-encrypted-communication-apps/.

32 For one example, see 'Cameras May Open Up the Board Room to Hackers', *New York Times*, 22 January 2012, www.nytimes.com/2012/01/23/technology/flaws-in-videoconferencing-systems-put-boardrooms-at-risk.htm.

if installed, and the web servers. Undoubtedly, these tests add to the cost. However, these costs are justifiable, as the reputation damage as a result of a breach is much higher than these costs.

Secure Research on the Internet

A considerable part of arbitration activities includes research online, which poses two challenges. The first one is that the notion of identity is vague on the Internet. What might be the official company website of the target company could very well be a fake website set up to confuse the public (and the arbitrators who might engage in private online research even if this is not permissible or not good practice). The domain name in a URL is not verified when a domain name is sold. Slightly better trust is warranted when the website is using a certificate from a well-known CA. However, such certificates can also be faked. There are 'extended certificates' available that have a more stringent checking process. Those certificates are used often by banks and are indicated by a different colour in the URL line. When it comes to social networks such as Facebook or LinkedIn, it is even easier to set up fake accounts to fool a researcher. There is no way to verify the authenticity of such a web presence except by asking the person directly regarding an existence of such account.[33] The second challenge is that it is relatively easy for global adversaries to 'track' the research activities of specific researchers or the whole 'arbitration community'. Research that might require confidentiality includes queries against legal databases, general search engines, social networks, Wikipedia, *Global Arbitration Review*, or other websites.

Some adversaries have access to the Internet traffic in certain locations. This allows them to observe the activities of the Internet users. For this tracking, the IP address of the user might play a prominent role (e.g. as selector to indicate whose traffic to observe). By using public access points (e.g. Wi-Fi) an IP address is obtained that differs from the one in the office or at home. However, other (more sophisticated) means of identifying a given device on the Internet are also available.

In cases where a website or service is offering the secure protocol HTTPS, this option should be used. If implemented correctly by the owner of the website, HTTPS hides the content of the Internet traffic to this site,

[33] Also, members of the 'arbitration community' should be prepared that they could become victims of fake profiles; somebody could be creating a fake presence on the web in order to discredit the victim. More about the vague notion of 'identity on the web' is found in Chapter 10, p. 246.

but the fact that this resource has been visited is still traceable. Whether these issues need to be of concern to the researcher depends on the outcome of the threat assessment. If the threat assessment determines that being tracked by adversaries who could obtain access to the Internet traffic is to be avoided, then anonymization services such as TOR[34] or VPN services should be used. These services hide the identity of the end point (i.e. the PC or the Mac) by routing the traffic over one or more intermediate servers that hide the true IP address of the user. However, the fact that such a service has been used is still available to such an observer.

Blueprint for a 'Secure Arbitration Network'

This section describes a concept for a system that could be used for all types of e-arbitration activities and that is defendable against all types of attackers. The proposed concept takes into account the various vulnerabilities that have been previously outlined and the theory that 'a chain is only as strong as its weakest link'. This means that the greatest challenge to the security of communication concerns the vulnerability of one participant in the chain of communication. One should also keep in mind that the attacker can choose the means of attack and the time, whereas the defender needs to protect against each possible type of attack.

How Many Baskets Shall Be Defended?

The suggested blueprint proposes a single installation to which all participants in an arbitration proceeding connect. This approach can be summarized as an 'all eggs in one (well-defended) basket' approach. There are many points as to why this approach is advantageous. Small- and medium-sized law offices and their use of traditional electronic communication between law offices do not appear to be 'defendable' against targeted attacks based on the limited resources typically available to them. Defences against government organizations by employing local IT-service companies are highly ineffective and arguably pointless. These professional and government organizations have access to endless resources and

[34] For more details, see Damon McCoy, Kevin Bauer, Dirk Grunwald, Tadayoshi Kohno, and Douglas Sicker, 'Shining Light in Dark Places: Understanding the TOR Network' in *Privacy Enhancing Technologies* pp. 63–76, Part of the Lecture Notes in Computer Science book series (LNCS, vol. 5134); www.homes.cs.washington.edu/~yoshi/papers/Tor/PETS2008_37.pdf.

can thereby succeed in bypassing most defences.[35] The skill and experience level that is necessary for defence against such type of attackers is only affordable if the resources on the side of the defenders are pooled. Of course, this design would mean that all eggs would be in a single basket and that basket would be the target of many powerful attackers with considerable resources. The large cloud services can build such defensive infrastructures utilizing the best-practice and know-how that is available in the IT industry, but which is typically not affordable for a single company or institution. Attacks against large cloud service providers have been successful in the past; however, those attacks have been based on social engineering attacks against the accounts of users. Although social engineering attacks are hard to avoid, nearly all of them would be avoidable if the users were willing to accept better-secured account access (e.g. two-factor authentication).

The Suggested Implementation: E-Arbitration in the Cloud

A securely implemented cloud service that uses state-of-the-art defences is defendable against all types of attackers except governmental services that force their way to the data through lawful or other means (such as bribes, extortion, national security letters, etc.). The blueprint proposed in this chapter is based on the concept of a collaborative environment, where sensitive documents are shared only with a carefully controlled list of communication partners and are never downloaded to potentially insecure environments such as the law office or user end points.

The users of a cloud access the shared documents through web browsers, using secure connections. These users are all communication partners in an arbitration proceeding, including the claimant and defendant, their counsels, the arbitral institution, the arbitrators and their staff, the secretary of the arbitral tribunal, tribunal-appointed experts, party-appointed experts and court reporters. Access needs to be based on a two-factor authentication, preferably based on smart cards with digital certificates. The owner/creator of a document assigns specific access rights for that document to each of the arbitral players. Typically, this will permit

[35] Why have the NSA activities not been detected by the defence community? This website tries to give an answer: Thinkst Applied Research, 'If the NSA Has Been Hacking Everything, How Has Nobody Seen Them Coming?', blog.thinkst.com/p/if-nsa-has-been-hacking-everything-how.html.

access (but can restrict download) and in some cases, collaborative editorial work.[36]

The access rights are enforced through encryption. This ensures that even technical administrators that regularly have access to everything cannot see the content of the documents. The integrity of the documents is ensured through digital signatures (tamper-proof). Whenever more than one person edits a document, version control is maintained by applying the digital signatures at various stages of the editorial work, and assigning ownership to each of the changes. Read and write access is tracked through the logging system. The logs implement the same strict access control and are only available under certain predefined circumstances based on dual (or more) control. In some instances, download will be necessary (e.g. when a document needs to be printed to be physically presented for enforcement) and the downloaded copy would be watermarked so that it would be traceable. To ease the administrative work for the document owner/creator, assigned privilege groups can be made for easy configuration of the access privileges.

Archival features would be implemented according to the given requirements and secured by the same mechanisms as the access control. Secured key escrow based on dual (or more) control can be implemented if needed so that access is possible to the archive even after document owners are no longer available to grant access. Additional features that can easily be added to such a system include the support for anonymous research on the Internet by acting as an intermediate (or proxy) system that forwards such Internet traffic to the target system. Care must be taken that logs are protected in such a way that not even the administrators have unrestricted access to those logs. Video-conference and secure messaging facilities could also be integrated in such a service based on available open source and other tools.

Cost and Hosting Considerations

The service proposed in the blueprint would be costly to set up and to operate. However, these costs should not to be compared to the setup costs for a single office, but to the sum of the costs for the multiple offices. Since

[36] Collaborative editing in-the-cloud is still not the typical way how legal documents are generated, however, such services like Google Docs and MS Office 365 are quickly gaining acceptance.

such a system is envisioned to support a much larger number of companies (for a single case, that would be at least four specific parties involved plus the 'regular' parties such as the arbitral institution, the arbitrators, and their staff), the overall cost is expected to be lower. To save cost, the system could be based on the existing implementation of a cloud service that has the base functionalities already implemented. Many additional features could be based on existing open source code. For such a shared system to gain the trust of the arbitration community, the hosting location and formal ownership of the system must be wisely chosen. The system must be located in a country with rather strict and extensive data privacy regulations (not just personal data of individuals) that restrict access by law enforcement or other governmental services.[37] Formal ownership of the system also needs to be considered. A trusted party (e.g. an arbitral institution) would need to be assigned as the owner. However, government services have previously applied pressure on companies in their respective countries to gain access to data that are hosted in another country.[38]

Vulnerability Analysis

Even if such a system has been securely developed, deployed, and administrated in a professional manner, there are still a few attack possibilities that dedicated adversaries could use against the users of that system.[39] The attack possibilities include the option to bribe or extort one of the users into providing screenshots of documents. However, due to the restrictive access possibilities, no person will have access to all documents regarding a given case or even to other cases. Alternatively, the attackers could deploy knowledgeable staff that manages to obtain a position as an assistant to one of the users of the system in order to gain access to important and protected documents. Nevertheless, download and distribution of secured documents would only be possible in very rare cases. Lastly, attackers may try to infect the device of an eligible user and perform screenshots of what

[37] Some companies with similar requirements have moved to Switzerland after evaluating their options, e.g. Silent Circle of PGP developer Phil Zimmermann. Mike Janke, 'Our Move to Switzerland', 13 May 2014, www.silentcircle.com/blog/our-move-to-switzerland.

[38] See *New York Times*, 'Microsoft Challenges Warrant for Emails Stored in Ireland', 9 September 2015, www.nytimes.com/2015/09/10/technology/microsoft-challenges-warrant-for-e-mails-stored-in-ireland.html.

[39] It can be noted that the security of the envisaged system is considerably higher than what Edward Snowden encountered at the NSA when he accessed the many documents.

the user is observing. However, this attack would be limited to what that user is viewing at a given point in time.

Conclusion

This chapter discussed how threat assessment can be used to determine the necessary security level, and thereby the security measures needed in accordance to the expected adversaries and their attack methods. Furthermore, this chapter outlined the defences against non-targeting attackers that need to be applied in order to avoid becoming one of the 'low hanging fruits' that are picked by opportunistic attackers. In addition, this chapter argued that more advanced security precautions are needed if professional and targeted attacks are expected. It has been pointed out at various instances in this chapter that the defence against government services that have a high interest in getting access to data is an even greater challenge. The last part of the chapter described a blueprint of a shared system that could survive attacks even from dedicated attackers with serious resources to deploy.

Your Associates, Staff and Partners: Friends or Foes?

A Critical Note on the Human Factor

MAX BURGER-SCHEIDLIN

Summary: This critical note deals with the human factor out of concern that, as crucial as all technical prevention is, true security ultimately boils down to the human factor. The author explores human risks, the risk of demotivation, and its consequences, how unethical behaviour might lead to security breaches, and how social engineering attacks can exploit the slightest weakness to breach what would appear to be a tight technical security system.

Introduction

Many law firms and companies are certain they possess excellent IT security systems in line with the latest technological standards. Many firms and companies also feel certain they have provided appropriate, if not in fact unassailable training to their staff, associates, and other internal and external workers regarding the technological challenges and the importance of IT security to the long-term success of their businesses. However, a chain or a system is only as strong as its weakest link. The question which thus arises is: are all the employees you have trained truly on board with your security schemes, in technical and psychological respects?

Factors which Contribute to a Safe Working Environment

Loyalty cannot be commanded. Rather, it can only be gained through trust and through the conviction of employees that they are doing the 'right thing', that their work is for a good cause. Professor Sumantra Ghoshal who taught economics at Fontainebleau near Paris stated that when he was on holiday at home in Calcutta during the summer monsoon, he usually felt sleepy in the humid atmosphere of India, where every step felt like a major effort. However, when walking in the woods in springtime, in the cool and crisp climate of Fontainebleau, he felt energized enough to break into a run. Proceeding from that observation, he went on to ask: how does the atmosphere in your company, or your law firm, feel? Thus, managers and executives might do well to ask themselves specific questions as to what business environment and work atmosphere they have created:

- Is the working environment in your firm heavy, emotionally dank and stagnant, or crisp, emotionally warm and invigorating?
- Are your employees proud to work with/for you personally? Are they proud to work with their colleagues? Proud to work with/for your firm? If not, what are the possible consequences of this for your firm's internal security?
- Will your associates be proud of you, and proud of your work product? Does your work involve ethical issues such as, for example, the (lack of) compliance with document production requests; the (lack of) value for money with regard to the services delivered by the firm to the client.
- Have you recently promoted an employee who is not qualified in the eyes of his colleagues? Perhaps that person is technically qualified but not held in high esteem in terms of his/her fairness and ethics?
- How might fellow candidates who failed to be promoted react? Will they now start to 'work to contract' and turn against you in frustration? Are there options you can apply to mitigate this, such as finding new, challenging fields of activity for those you did not promote?
- Have you dismissed a staff member unfairly or is there a perception amongst the colleagues of the staff member that his dismissal was unfair?
- In some law firms, bright young lawyers work to exhaustion, often late into the night, driven both by their own ambition and by 'polite requests' of their senior partners. At some stage, the workload might simply become too much for them to handle properly, resulting in mistakes due to overwork, disloyalty due to ever-increasing frustration, and professional burnout.
- How do you deal with inadvertent mistakes? Those who inadvertently make a mistake must have enough trust in their superiors to inform them about mistakes without hesitation.
- When hiring new staff, the key criteria one usually considers are their legal or technical qualifications, but have you given adequate consideration to soft skills and group dynamics? Is your corporate culture a

good 'fit' for the personality of the new employee and vice versa? How well will the new employee integrate into the emotional environment of your present associates and staff? What are the new employee's long-term, personal values? Are those values a good match for the firm and existing staff?

In addition, managers and executives would do well to be on the lookout for possible conflicts between the requirements of a job and the personalities and the values of those who are requested to perform it, one of them being the required confidentiality. Secrecy is relative, not absolute, in the minds of too many young professionals, because too many of them are proud to communicate their presumed achievements to their peers. Indeed, although these young associates may not name the parties involved, in informal conversations with an interested third party who happens to know what law firms have been engaged to handle what particular cases, what initially seems to be a harmless discussion of recent court cases can turn into an unintentional disclosure of client confidences. Another risk factor is the prospective duration of the working relationship. The trend today is for many bright young trainees and lawyers to seek as much diverse experience as possible, across a range of law firms or companies. How does the firm handle the tendency of bright young associates to frequently change employers? It is important to bear in mind that every time an associate leaves the firm, your law firm suffers a loss of proprietary knowledge, skills, and training. An even more sensitive point to be considered is that with each such departure, the person walking out the door is an individual who has gained insight into your firm's security systems.

Social Engineering Attacks

The following scenario is not as uncommon as one might think: a firm is about to begin work on a large and challenging case (perhaps involving a state party), and the firm then coincidentally receives applications from qualified trainees and potential assistants with qualifications (e.g. an unusual language needed for this case) which seem to be an almost miraculous fit in light of the need to handle the enormous extra workload. One should never lose sight of the possibility that some applicants might have a second job elsewhere.

Dangerous 'social engineering attacks' are a proverbial 'black box' to many. Social engineering, in the context of information security, refers to psychological manipulation of people into performing actions or divulging confidential information. It is a type of confidence trick for the purpose of information gathering, fraud, or system access. It is often one of many steps in a more complex scheme of fraud or security breaches. To demonstrate how simple but effective some 'social engineering' tricks are, we provide a few examples in the form of anecdotal evidence:

- 'Social engineering' attacks work quite easily on the frustrated and overworked. A few rounds of beer in a pub near a factory, or, for that matter, at the nightly hangout of young lawyers in a posh district, might give an attacker valuable insider knowledge. Perhaps staff members will not disclose the latest technology, but they may say things that indicate where the cracks are, who is in a dispute with whom, who is dating whom, who is going through a divorce or who desperately needs money, etc. With this kind of knowledge, it is easy for an interested third party to devise future strategies and plan his or her next steps.
- There is a new member at your tennis club who introduces himself politely to all of the members and, over time, invites various members to lunch with their families and spouses. Slowly, contacts grow closer, conversations more intimate, acquaintances tell each other about personal or professional dramas, close calls, and perhaps the one or the other 'sensitive' tidbit. Someone rails against excessive levels of taxes and talks about how one might avoid them. Knowledge of a 'sensitive story' and an awareness that someone is seeking to avoid tax might be enough for a party to start blackmailing another, perhaps very subtly at the outset. Money is rarely the issue; information is.
- A specialized boutique law firm handling a number of major, sensitive cases experienced repeated breakdowns of its air-conditioning system during a hot summer. The maintenance engineer had to come in frequently. Later, a review by security specialists revealed that the air-conditioning system was housed in the same utility room as the firm's telephone exchange and computer servers, and that there had been no one supervising the engineer during his repairs to the air-conditioning system.
- A CEO of a 'hidden champion' with a factory in the countryside was invited by an investment consultant to an evening presentation on the latest investment opportunities. The speakers came from well-known banks and investment funds. At the end of the cocktail reception that evening the investment consultant presented further lucrative opportunities and invited a few remaining guests to test them with small amounts. That CEO invested €1,000.00, enjoying good returns over the

few next months. The investment consultant paid out the profits in cash and on time. After having seen how profitable this investment turned out to be, the CEO invested more and more in subsequent months. Some two years into this profitable arrangement, the investment consultant who had become friends with this CEO started to ask some delicate questions concerning the technology of this 'hidden champion'. When the CEO refused to disclose any information, the investment consultant inquired whether the CEO had reported all of the cash distributions, which he, the investment consultant, had happened to document on video, on his tax returns over the last two years.

- The Board Member for International Sales of a world-class company in a certain technology placed a big order in Indonesia, which 'necessitated' the payment of bribes of 30 per cent to secure the order. As a 'reward' the company's manager received 10 per cent in 'kickbacks'. The machines were delivered; the start-up went well, all parties were happy. Two years later, the manager of the company was contacted by a friendly European competitor and informed that they knew about the kickbacks, asking him to 'kindly' show them a little design for a special technical part, and then another. Two years later most of the know-how of this world market leader had been lost, its competitiveness strongly eroded. The attacker then bought the former world market leader for a pittance.

Conclusion

To achieve safety to the greatest extent possible, one needs to remain legally and ethically clean. Any questionable action taken may turn into ammunition which fraudsters can use for an attack, or might turn an ethically strong-minded associate into a whistle-blower or attacker. For law firms and companies, it is crucial for the 'chief security officer' to be not only the IT manager, but somebody who understands overall management issues and overall security needs. He or she should also be entitled to delve into HR matters and the 'emotional' side of the law firm or company, and should have immediate and direct access to the CEO.

In recent years many law firms and companies have strongly increased their security, often using excellent technology, whereas others have lagged behind somewhat in installing technology appropriate to their high-profile cases. As noted earlier, the chain is only as strong as its weakest link. In many firms, more weight and attention unfortunately is given to technology and operating systems than to the many staff and associates operating these systems on a daily basis. However, the human factor is almost always the main key to security.

The solution cannot be ever-greater supervision. As noted earlier, loyalty cannot be 'commanded'. Rather, it can only be gained through trust and through the conviction of employees that they are doing the 'right thing', that their work is for a good cause. To put it negatively, loyalty can, at best, be purchased only temporarily, until a higher offer appears on the horizon. Consequently, a culture of individual responsibility, open communication, of trust, and of risk awareness is of the essence.

4

Case Study

The Institutional Perspective

ERIK SCHÄFER

Summary: Arbitration institutions focus on arbitration practice, especially their arbitration rules and the proceedings as such. ICT is only relevant for them insofar as legal procedural aspects are concerned. The actual use of ICT or ICT services are at most an added value to their core services. By doing so, arbitration institutions respond to the demand of their members and users. Notwithstanding, arbitration institutions have a position in the market and the know-how that would place them in a good position to advance standardization of ICT use in arbitration proceedings with the perspective of making 100 percent digital proceedings technically - and legally - fully viable around the globe.

'Того, кто опоздает, накажет жизнь' ('He who comes too late is punished by life' – Michail Gorbatschow on 10 June 1989)

Introduction

Arbitration under institutional rules is only the tip of the iceberg, since non-administered arbitration with its ever-changing participants is usually confidential and unreported. Accordingly, what we know about IT use in international arbitration originates from arbitration proceedings under institutional rules. Notwithstanding, institutional arbitration is also characterized by changing players in each individual case. This is different from state court litigation that relies on a stable physical and regulatory infrastructure, with attorneys who are members of the same bar, and professional judges. In such a stable environment it is simpler, but by no means easy, to implement a workable IT-based modern communication system for filings, notifications, and the court room. Whilst in institutional arbitration, the parties involved operate under the auspices of an institution that intervenes with varying degrees of intensity in the administration of the proceedings and provides a somehow stable framework these institutions still lack the coercive powers to impose IT systems. Unlike the national judiciary, and for good reason, arbitration institutions do not possess compelling powers to impose specific technical solutions on parties or to sanction noncompliance. As a result, even in institutional arbitration, a stable comprehensive (global) IT infrastructure is lacking. Any such infrastructure needs to be conceived for the individual case under the auspices of the arbitral tribunal. Moreover, the resulting technical complexity of implementing IT infrastructure ad hoc is aggravated by diverging mandatory regulations governing Information and Communication Technology (ICT)[1]. These mandatory regulations may potentially affect the legality or legal effect of an ICT service that is being used in any given case.

In this chapter, we will first endeavour to shed light on how major arbitral institutions have responded to the challenges in the past, and then move on to define the role these institutions should, in our view, play in order to meet the actual evolving needs of the arbitration community in international arbitrations.

The Current Role of Major Arbitration Institutions as of January 2016

Predominantly, arbitration institutions offer rules to administer arbitration that provide for varying degrees of institutional involvement during the arbitration proceedings. For example, the ICC oversees and intervenes at all stages of the proceedings and requires copies of all correspondence that parties and the arbitral tribunal exchange. Other institutions such as the DIS (the German Arbitration Institution) limit their intervention to institutional core tasks such as overseeing the constitution of the tribunal in accordance with the DIS Rules. Regarding IT, all major arbitration institutions have included in their current rules wording that allows for any written communication during the arbitral process to be transmitted and served by existing means of electronic transmissions such as facsimile, email, or other electronic means, if a proof of transmission (sending) is generated.[2] However, they fall short of dealing with electronic signatures

[1] See, e.g. www.en.wikipedia.org/wiki/Information_and_communications_technology.

[2] Article 3 ICC Rules of Arbitration, available at www.iccwbo.org/products-and-services/arbitration-and-adr/arbitration/icc-rules-of-arbitration; R-43 AAA Commercial Arbitration Rules and Mediation Procedures available at www.adr.org/aaa/ShowPDF?doc=ADRSTG_004130; Article 4 LCIA Arbitration Rules available at www.lcia.org/Dispute_Resolution_Services/lcia-arbitration-rules-2014.aspx; Article 2 SIAC Rules

and the requirements for such a signature to be valid. Accordingly, an award could be transmitted by electronic means, but since it must be signed by the arbitrator(s), it remains unclear under which circumstances the electronic version of the award is the original version, signed electronically by the arbitral tribunal. A digitized scan of the physical signature of the arbitrator(s) is generally not a valid (electronic) signature, but simply a copy of a signature.[3]

Within the scope defined in their respective rules, arbitration institutions such as the ICC, AAA, ICDR, LCIA, SIAC, HKIAC, ICSID, DIS, CEPANI, CIETAC, etc. have embraced ICT and use it in their daily operations. However, when setting in motion the arbitration procedure and, more importantly, when notifying awards, they will still serve physically signed, originally printed versions against proof of receipt, normally by courier service, sometimes still by registered letter. This is sound practice considering that arbitration institutions are chosen by the parties over ad hoc arbitration, as they provide a higher level of procedural security. Considering that there is no transnationally resilient legal infrastructure for issuing and serving validly signed arbitral awards in electronic format, especially in the wider international context, it is appropriate that the arbitral institutions have opted for staying on the 'safe side'. Furthermore, the technical and regulatory (transnational) infrastructure for recognizing and enforcing electronic arbitral awards appears not to exist. No sufficiently detailed answer could be provided to whether an original electronic award, issued in Hamburg in PDF file format and electronically signed by the arbitrator with a qualified electronic signature issued by the German Federal Chamber of Notaries Public, could be recognized and enforced in Anchorage (USA), Curitiba (Brazil), Dakar (Senegal), or Guadong (PRC). Even in Germany, it would be somehow unclear whether the bailiff (Gerichtsvollzieher) at the place of execution of the award could handle an electronically signed and submitted arbitral award.

Notwithstanding, some arbitral institutions have extended their services for users of their arbitration rules by offering online file repositories

available at www.siac.org.sg/our-rules/rules/siac-rules-2016#siac_rule2; Article 2 HIAC Administered Arbitration Rules available at www.hkiac.org/arbitration/rules-practice-notes/administered-arbitration-rules/hkiac-administered-2013–1#02; Article 8 CEPANI Arbitration Rules, Administered Arbitration Rules; Article 5 DIS Arbitration Rules (1998) available at www.dis-arb.de/de/16/rules/dis-arbitration-rules-98-id10; Article 4 WIPO Arbitration Rules, available at www.wipo.int/amc/en/arbitration/rules; Article 2 UNCITRAL Arbitration Rules, available at www.uncitral.org/pdf/english/texts/arbitration/arb-rules-revised/arb-rules-revised-2010-e.pdf.

[3] See Chapter 7, p. 151ss.

that are administered under the auspices of the respective institutions. For example, WIPO maintains a facility called ECAF,[4] The AAA maintains a facility called AAA WebFile[5], while the ICC International Court of Arbitration had maintained a facility called NetCase,[6] which is currently not available pending the launch of a new revamped filing portal. ICSID is also known to offer such services but relies on a third-party service provider.[7] These portals are aimed at catering to the needs of parties and arbitrators in commercial and investment treaty cases, and are in some cases integrated to a certain extent into the case management software of the respective institution. These platforms are most likely aimed at providing an added value to the institutional spectrum of services, with the aim of differentiating these services from those provided by the competition.

However, and this has not yet been publicly discussed in detail, by offering such online services, the arbitration institutions become Internet Service Providers (ISP),[8] who may have special statutory duties in regard to personal data and intellectual property, as well as contractual duties towards parties regarding 24/7 system availability, data integrity, and data authenticity. It is not unlikely that setting up and maintaining a cloud-based secure file repository and case management information system requires additional resources to be made available by the institutions, for which the parties may not be willing to pay full costs.

The picture is different in the field of domain names and the different processes dealing with various aspects thereof. However, these processes are not arbitral proceedings, but rather adjudication or third-party expert determination procedures. As such, they are subject to strict accelerated rules and terminate in a 'self-enforcing' ruling by the neutral, as the administering authorities have full control of the domain names. Accordingly, these proceedings are virtually fully digital, but at the price of a system-inherent drastic reduction in complexity and the absence of oral hearings with witnesses and experts. Thus, these systems are unfit for complex fact-driven arbitration cases. The same is true for the many existing online dispute resolution platforms for resolving issues between consumers and businesses that tend to have comparatively low stakes. Many of these are integrated into the processes of the platforms that are used for consumer transactions. Interestingly, online vendor ratings and

[4] See www.wipo.int/amc/en/ecaf. [5] See www.adr.org (file & manage a case).

[6] M Philippe, 'NetCase: A New ICC Arbitration Facility', (2004), *The ICC International Court of Arbitration Bulletin*, pp. 53–58.

[7] See www.box.com. [8] See, e.g. www.en.wikipedia.org/wiki/Internet_service_provider.

customer reviews, coupled with fierce price-based competition, seem to encourage customer-friendly behaviour and serve as means for dispute avoidance.

More than a decade ago, when ICT appeared to be a 'hot topic', some institutions promoted so-called 'protocols'[9] on ICT use, which purported to establish and promote good practice use of ICT in arbitration proceedings. However, these protocols were either too general to provide practical guidance through the details of information technology when being actually implemented, or too technically detailed for arbitration practitioners whose focus was on the legal issues and merits.[10] The ICC Commission on International Arbitration has therefore focused on general guidance covering the interface between technical processes and arbitration procedure in Task Force Reports[11] on 'Issues to be Considered when Using IT in International Arbitration', or the procedurally relevant aspects of document disclosure for electronically generated and stored documents in international arbitration[12] within the framework of both the ICC Arbitration Rules and the IBA Rules on Taking of Evidence in International Arbitration. Other reports that deal with efficient organization of arbitral proceedings tend to address IT usage as one of many topics, but in a rather general manner.[13] The latter aspect has also been covered by conferences organized by arbitral institutions.

[9] See, e.g. arbitration-related protocols, available at www.ciarb.org/docs/default-source/ciarbdocuments/international-arbitration-protocols/e-iscolusureinarbitration.pdf?sfvrsn=8; www.jamsadr.com/arbitration-discovery-protocols/; IT-related protocols available at www.searchnetworking.techtarget.com/definition/protocol; www.en.wikipedia.org/wiki/Communications_protocol.

[10] See 'Operating Standards for Using IT in International Arbitration' (2004), available at www.iccdrl.com/commissionreports.aspx.

[11] All reports accessible at www.iccdrl.com/commissionreports.aspx; see, e.g. Arbitration, Telecommunications and Electronic Commerce (1999), Issues to be Considered when Using IT in International Arbitration (2004).

[12] ICC Techniques for Managing Electronic Document Production When it is Permitted or Required in International Arbitration (2011), available at www.iccdrl.com/commissionreports.aspx.

[13] Revision work on UNCITRAL Notes on organizing arbitral proceedings, available at www.documents-dds-ny.un.org/doc/UNDOC/LTD/V15/076/17/PDF/V1507617.pdf?OpenElement; ICC Effective Management of Arbitration: A Guide for In-House Counsel and Other Party Representatives, available at www.iccwbo.org/Advocacy-Codes-and-Rules/Document-centre/2014/Effective-Management-of-Arbitration-A-Guide-for-In-House-Counsel-and-Other-Party-Representatives; ICC Arbitration Commission Report on Techniques for Controlling Time and Costs in Arbitration, available at www.iccwbo.org/Advocacy-Codes-and-Rules/Document-centre/2012/ICC-Arbitration-Commission-Report-on-Techniques-for-Controlling-Time-and-Costs-in-Arbitration.

Nonetheless, there appears to be sporadic but no systematic or intense demand by arbitration users, be these law firms with strong arbitration practices or their clients, for institutions to take a more proactive approach or to provide specific services.[14] It seems that the use of ICT in commercial and investment arbitration is more driven by the general usage of ICT by clients and their law firms in the course of their general business activities that 'spills over' into the individual arbitration case, than by a systematic analysis of the technical and legal requirements leading to a more structured development of bespoke technical solutions that match users' work habits and legal requirements. As far as ICT use is concerned, arbitration in general follows behind trends set in other arenas. One reason could be the desire for a procedural 'equality of arms' (opportunities): the party disposing of more technological resources should not per se be structurally favoured by the system over a party that does not have such resources. This is a laudable desire. However, this may result in the application of the principle 'the slowest ship sets the speed of the convoy', i.e. the party or arbitrator with the lowest level of personnel or technical ICT capability sets the standard for the others. Often, this will be the independent arbitrator of a certain age, who has no back office that could provide him or her with the required technology and technical knowledge. Another reason could be that arbitration practitioners on average are not willing to wholeheartedly embrace technical solutions that require them to adjust working habits, to technical requirements that do not match their time-proven working habits and the requirements of procedural efficiency. They simply fear that complex technical systems could trigger incidents that transform into legal procedural issues that distract from the resolution of the dispute as such.

Interestingly, this contrasts with what occurs in the law firms that handle today's major arbitration cases and their clients, as they wholeheartedly embrace new ICT solutions. In light of this finding, one may conclude that currently, it seems more likely that changes in the usage of ICT, particularly in commercial and investment arbitration, that more substantially affect the way the proceedings are conducted, are to be driven more by the parties' representatives and less by the arbitral institutions. This makes economic sense, since ICT solution providers can more easily achieve economies of scale if they cater to the needs of the many law firms rather than those of the comparatively few arbitration institutions.

[14] See Chapter 1, p. 15ss.

Insofar as so-called 'disruptive technologies' are concerned, there is a likelihood that they will transform the legal service industry, including dispute resolution. Examples of such include sophisticated assisted decision-making and information systems, automated document analysis, or even automated contracting and contract enforcement within Industry 4.0[15] supply and distribution chains, which will rely on some form of artificial intelligence or autonomous interaction between machines and devices, replacing human intervention (e.g. decision-making) is replaced. However, the implications of this transformation remain to be determined. Moreover, in this field of global economic activities, there are no indications that arbitration institutions are in a position to take any lead. Rather, they will need to adjust their business models to such changes, in particular to those of arbitration users, as they have already successfully done in the past regarding other changes.

The Role Arbitration Institutions Could Play in the Future[16]

The Sense and Nonsense of Protocols or Guidelines

Lawyers in general and arbitration institutions in particular excel in rule-making. The 'backbone' of arbitral institutions is their sets of rules that are regularly modernized in order to remain at the forefront of arbitral proceedings. This, however, somehow conflicts with an important 'selling point' of arbitration when compared to state court litigation: less procedural formality and more flexibility for bespoke proceedings. Over the past two decades, institutions have therefore opted to produce 'soft rules' in the form of guidelines and protocols that purport to cater to a need for predictability of the proceedings and to lower the barrier of entry to newcomers to the Arcanum of arbitration by making the specific procedural know-how easily accessible. Unfortunately, efforts have not yet been undertaken to evaluate the efficiency and factual impact of these documents.

[15] Industry 4.0 is a catchword for the fourth industrial revolution which is closely linked to the concept of the Internet of Things. Basically it refers to all machinery and devices in the manufacturing and supply/distribution chain having an URL and being connected to the Internet for a vast number of purposes; e.g. in these systems the machines will collect and autonomously analyze data to trigger orders or production requests; they will also automatically make available the required logistical resources, etc.; see www.en.wikipedia.org/wiki/Industry_4.0.

[16] See in this regard also Chapter 5, p. 112ss.

Insofar as ICT usage is concerned, one may conclude on the basis of the experience gathered, since telex was replaced by facsimile and facsimile by email attachments, that guides and protocols cannot provide the depth of detail that would be required to successfully implement any ICT solution that uses tools with which all users are not already familiar in their daily professional lives. Accordingly, protocols and guides appear to be less suitable, particularly when compared to empirical assessments of actual use of proven solutions, issues that have arisen with sufficient frequency, or subsequent information dissemination based on the empirical findings. This kind of effort still needs to be taken. As arbitration institutions have access to information on all cases conducted under their auspices, they are well positioned to collect and evaluate the relevant information. Moreover, since they are not likely to dedicate the necessary resources to such an endeavor themselves, they could seek cooperation with academic research including those from computer engineering departments. The research results could then lead to focused ICT projects or otherwise advance systematic conscientious ICT usage in arbitration.

Provision of Training

Many arbitration institutions[17] provide professional training with the perspective of enlarging the pool of arbitration counsel, and for arbitrators, of enhancing diversity in all facets. This training is presently focused on legal procedural aspects. However, a curriculum for a supplementary module could be developed and offered that teaches the practical aspects of using up-to-date but reliable ICT solutions in arbitration proceedings. Topics could include professional video-conferencing, secure and data-integrity-preserving communications, and the basic know-how required for so-called *eBriefs*. It could be useful to include a section dedicated to ICT product knowledge so that participants understand what is offered in the market and what each product is actually capable of. Furthermore, the curricula should be published.

'IT-Savvy' Certified Arbitrators?

These training courses could in part be tailored to the kind of ICT-related tasks that arbitrators may be required to carry out during an

[17] Examples are the ICC's PIDA programs, see www.iccwbo.org/Training-and-Events, or the training by the Chartered Institute of Arbitrators, see www.ciarb.org/training-and-development. Other institutions and associations also offer training.

arbitration. Arbitrators could then mention this technical training in their CV. Whether they would actually need to be certified as 'ICT-proficient' is doubtful. In any event, any certification would first require a standardization of the curriculum and a certification of the institutions providing the training. It is difficult to imagine such a necessity.

'IT-Savvy' Certified Counsel?

Today, there remain few counsels in arbitration who do not work within a professional structure that provides them with technical support from specialist employees of their firms. Thus, it appears to be less important to train them in ICT usage, particularly when compared to the increasingly more frequent independent arbitrators who have only a 'small bureaucratic footprint'. From a technical perspective, using the same ICT training curriculum for counsel and for arbitrators appears to be sufficiently efficient.

Standardization of Training Requirements

The standardization of training requirements would allow for more comparability among the kind of training mentioned in an arbitrator's professional CV. However, once a standard is established, it may stifle innovation. Moreover, it is not easy to conceive that institutions will readily agree on a training standard, especially if compliance with the standard will be monitored and certified by a neutral third party. For achieving transparency, it should be sufficient to publish online a detailed curriculum of each training course.

Provision of Stable and Secure ICT Services (e.g. Paperless Files and Document Services)

Arbitration institutions have considerable interest in guaranteeing the quality and security of the arbitral proceedings conducted under their auspices. They likely also have a greater caseload than any individual party and, as neutral institutions, are thus not interested in technologically 'outgunning' any party or 'overwhelming' other arbitrators. Any investment in IT infrastructure potentially benefits all the institution's future cases and, over time, lowers the IT infrastructure cost per case. Accordingly, arbitration institutions appear to be better positioned to provide the ICT tools that parties and arbitrators may jointly need for collaborating in any given case. Notwithstanding, it remains to be seen whether parties would be willing to make additional payments for using such a preconfigured ICT infrastructure.

Proprietary ICT Services by Each Institution?

As previously mentioned, and relying on the information available to the public, each arbitration institution that offers some kind of additional ICT service has done so without having regard to any common practice or shared arbitration-specific standards. This remains without consequence for well-established ICT services that are already standardized over a wide range of industries,[18] such as file formats (predominantly .PDF), email, or video-conferencing, where the shelf equipment is readily available. However, commercial and investment arbitration is document intensive, whereby any substantial ICT solution offered by an arbitration institution needs to comprise a document repository as a 'backbone' for filing and serving documents and evidence. In this regard, the underlying technologies are, of course, mature and standardized. Many private ISPs offer cloud-based[19] document (file) repository services. However, these are generic and need to be configured specifically for the needs and roles of the various participants of any arbitration. Obviously, developing a boilerplate or standard for such rights, and the configuration of the ICT tool, would spare resources and time for any new cases, as arbitrators and parties would not need to reinvent the wheel in the usual confrontational setting that prevails at the outset of an arbitration.

Standardized ICT Services by all Institutions?

However, frequent users or, more precisely, the representatives of users, have to manage arbitrations under the auspices of more than just one arbitration institution. For them, it would be easier and less time-consuming if they could access and use file repositories essentially in the same way, even if these are provided by different institutions. If the software/user interfaces were standardized, law firms could ask the providers of their case management software to develop solutions that integrate the cloud-based services offered by the institution. By agreeing and implementing joint technical standards for the interfaces, arbitral institutions could help economize resources on the technical side. Of course, this does not necessarily mean that all institutions need to provide identical cloud-based services. Only the core communication components and the user interfaces should be standardized.

Based on the non-representative experience of the authors, all online platforms for filing and serving submissions and evidence in arbitration

[18] Such as www.box.com used by ICSID.

[19] See, e.g. cloud computing available at www.en.wikipedia.org/wiki/Cloud_computing.

proceedings offered by institutions have certain weaknesses. This is particularly true where large numbers of voluminous files need to be uploaded or downloaded, because they rely on browser-based interfaces only. From a technical perspective, it would appear to be more convenient if the user had a small client program[20] or applet[21] that allows the user to assemble and prepare an upload offline and which could have built-in verification functions that help the user correctly organize the files for the system to which the upload will be made. This piece of software could also comprise functionality for qualified digital signing and encryption. Uploads and downloads could then take place 'in the background' and any party or arbitrator could be provided with a full digital copy of the online contents in a dedicated subdirectory on her or his own system. Automated hash-number[22] checks in the background could help to maintain data integrity and security. All technological components needed for such software already exist and only need to be assembled. If such a client was open-source software and its interface would be compatible with the maximum number of online arbitration file repositories, the usage of such facilities in general would be simplified and thereby become more attractive.

The previously described local software could also be combined with existing peer-to-peer file sharing[23] software solutions, so as to enable ad hoc non-institutional proceedings. A further technological field of joint or standardized activity that one arbitration institution alone cannot efficiently cover, is managing the global digital identity of arbitrators and counsel, which in the mid or long term, will be required for the secure usage of ICT tools in arbitration. This basic infrastructure would, at a minimum, consist of qualified digital signatures[24] that could be used for signing and encrypting/decrypting files, the recognition of these signatures as equivalent to handwritten signatures in as many countries as possible, and the technical infrastructure to manage and verify these signatures. An additional component could be a virtual private network (VPN[25]) within which the previously described interaction could take place. This joint inter-institutional ICT infrastructure could become the starting platform

[20] See www.en.wikipedia.org/wiki/Client_percent28computingpercent29.

[21] See www.en.wikipedia.org/wiki/Applet.

[22] See, e.g. 'Computer Systems', available at www.en.wikipedia.org/wiki/Tamper-evident_technology and www.en.wikipedia.org/wiki/Cryptographic_hash_function.

[23] See www.en.wikipedia.org/wiki/Peer-to-peer_file_sharing.

[24] See www.en.wikipedia.org/wiki/Digital_signature.

[25] See www.en.wikipedia.org/wiki/Virtual_private_network.

for moving arbitration completely into cyberspace including the arbitral awards and other documents requiring a signed original.

ICT Services by Third Parties (ISPs)?

Parties and arbitrators who presently use or want to use ICT solutions will recur to commercial ISP providers who cater to the needs of the legal industry or even providers of generic ISP services rather than any ICT solution made available by an institution. The advantage is that such third-party solutions tend to be technically more mature and convenient, since they are part of the core business of the ISP and not simply a service that is seen as subordinated added value to a different core service, as is the case for institutions. There are good reasons to prefer such third-party ISPs. However, parties and arbitrators need to find the appropriate ISP for each case. In addition, both the arbitrators and parties need to specify their needs and the required functions to get what they want. This provides distractions during the inevitably tense early stages of arbitral proceedings. Moreover, the lawyers need to educate the software engineers on the ISP's side about their procedural requirements. This does not always work out so well.

Therefore, leaving ISP activities to third-party service providers not only helps the arbitration institutions avoid investment and maintenance costs of ICT solutions, it also helps them avoid potential contractual or regulatory liability exposure. However, there is clearly a role for the arbitration institutions to use their contact with arbitration users for developing the specifications for the required software in coordination with interested third-party service providers. In this way, at least a factual standard may develop that ensures a suitable level of quality and functionality for the competing ICT services. If core functionalities were provided by open-source software, accessibility to newcomers would not confront the same high barriers to entry.

Promoting a Universal (i.e. Treaties-Based) Standard for the Recognition and Enforcement of Original Arbitral Awards in Electronic Format

For obvious reasons, one may not expect that national governments or professional organizations will take the lead in taking arbitration fully online. This process will be driven by arbitral institutions that face the corresponding demands of their membership or users. Intergovernmental organizations might play a role as well; the most probable institution offering a platform for such an initiative at present appears to be UNCITRAL. An important task will be devising a convention that provides for the requirements for electronic signatures, such that signatures embedded in an electronic file may be recognized by contracting states as legal equivalents to a handwritten signature under an arbitral award. The convention should also lay out any eventually necessary further provisions governing the details of recognition and enforcement. Of course, such a convention will be useless if courts, bailiffs, institutions, arbitrators, and parties are not technically equipped to process such electronic awards. There will be a need to concurrently offer the required software tools at least with the basic core functions. UNCITRAL or another UN body may have to become the ultimate administrator, who certifies the signatures and rule compliance of bodies that issue electronic signatures to users.

Conclusion

Arbitration institutions tend to respond to the demands of their members and users, who in great majority have a legal background. These demands have shifted the focus to different sets of arbitration rules and other ADR services, as well as to how the proceedings as such can be improved by increasing transparency. In addition, this shift has directed the focus also to providing instruments for keeping the duration or expenditure of the arbitration at bay. Thus, information and telecommunication technology comes into play only insofar as it serves any of these goals or is perceived as a topic that could be conceived as an added value to core institutional services. As a result, no arbitration institution has yet taken the bold lead in the advancement of ICT as a powerful tool for conducting commercial or investment arbitral proceedings. However, by cooperating with other institutions and technical third-party ISPs, institutions could play a crucial role in specifying, developing, and implementing the core components of a system or open source ICT platform that will better meet the requirements of users who have already taken their business into the cloud and are presently moving to implement industry 4.0.[26] The offer is still on the table.

[26] See www.en.wikipedia.org/wiki/Industry_4.0.

5

Case Study

The Legislator's Perspective

ANNET VAN HOOFT AND JULIA KROES-LASTOCHKINA[1]

Summary: In this chapter, we will discuss the legislator's perspective towards 'the Brave New World of Arbitration' and the technological revolutions that brought it about. We will take the Dutch legislator as an example and report on its various initiatives, primarily with respect to arbitration but also, where relevant, with respect to court litigation. We will conclude that, at present, the Netherlands is one of the first countries where the use of ICT in arbitral proceedings and e-arbitration obtained a legal basis. This is surprising, considering the technological developments of the last thirty years and the potential impact they have on the proceedings.

Introduction

In this chapter, we will discuss the legislator's perspective towards 'the Brave New World of Arbitration' and the technological revolutions that brought it about. We will take the Dutch legislator as an example and report on its various initiatives, first and foremost with respect to arbitration but also, where relevant, with respect to court litigation.

After several years during which the Dutch legislator only made minor patchwork amendments, such as the introduction of Article 3:15a Dutch Civil Code ('DCC') on the electronic signature, the Dutch legislator finally decided to embrace the technological revolution. It introduced an ambitious program known under the Dutch acronym KEI,[2] which will result in fully electronic civil court proceedings by 2019.[3]

[1] Annet van Hooft is a partner at Bird & Bird in Paris and Julia Kroes-Lastochkina is an associate at Clifford Chance in Amsterdam. The opinions in this chapter are those of the authors alone.

[2] KEI stands for 'Kwaliteit en Innovatie', which means 'Quality and Innovation'.

[3] See parliamentary history, 2014–2015, 34059 A, 34138 #2, 34212 #2 and 34237(R2054) #2 for the draft acts. The final acts dated 13 July 2016 were published in the *State Gazette* (*Staatscourant*) on 21 July 2016 under Nos. 288 through 291 ('KEI Legislation').

As far as arbitration is concerned, the new Arbitration Act of 1 January 2015 ('2015 Arbitration Act') includes a specific Article dealing with the use of information technology in arbitration and provides a legal basis for electronic proceedings. We will discuss what motivated the legislator to insert this article in the 2015 Arbitration Act. In addition, we will address whether the Act deals with perceived concerns of due process, security, and data protection.

In this chapter, we will first describe the historical background of Dutch arbitration law. We will then deal with the technological revolution and how the legislator and several Dutch arbitration institutions responded to these developments. This is followed by our discussion of the 2015 Arbitration Act and the possibilities it created for the use of ICT. We will then briefly describe the initiatives of the Dutch legislator with respect to the digitalization of civil court proceedings to the extent they could be relevant for arbitration. In the last section of the chapter, we will present our conclusions.

Historical Background

The Netherlands has been on the forefront of international arbitration for the last two centuries. It is home to several reputable international arbitration institutions, such as the Permanent Court of Arbitration and the Iran–US Claims Tribunal. In addition, it has numerous arbitration institutions (predominantly) serving the domestic market. In 1838, the Netherlands was among the first countries to adopt an Arbitration Act ('1838 Arbitration Act') thereby formally introducing arbitration as a dispute resolution mechanism. The 1838 Arbitration Act was not a separate piece of legislation, but formed part of the Dutch Code of Civil Procedure (DCCP). The 1838 Arbitration Act served well for almost 150 years and during its existence was amended only once.[4]

By the 1980s, it had, however, become clear that the Netherlands needed a new Arbitration Act mainly because the 1838 Arbitration Act did not

[4] This amendment concerned the abolition of the prohibition for women to act as arbitrators, which reflected the social and cultural developments of the time. See P. Sanders, 'The New Dutch Arbitration Act', (1987) 3(3), *Arbitration International*. The underrepresentation of women arbitrators is still a subject today. See, e.g. the current initiative referred to as the 'Pledge', www.arbitrationpledge.com, whereby law firms and leading practitioners undertake to systematically consider whether a suitable female candidate could also be appointed.

take into account a number of significant international developments in the field. These included the introduction of the New York Convention of 1958, the ICSID Convention of 1965, the UNCITRAL Arbitration Rules of 1976, and the UNCITRAL Model Law on International Commercial Arbitration of 1985.[5] In 1986 the Netherlands therefore enacted a new Arbitration Act ('1986 Arbitration Act'), which was drafted by among others, Professor Pieter Sanders. At the time of its enactment the 1986 Arbitration Act was one of the most modern and progressive arbitration laws, containing several innovative provisions, e.g. regarding the correction of awards and consent awards.[6]

The Technological Revolution and the Responses from the Legislator and Arbitral Institutions

The Technological Revolution

The late 1980s and early 1990s saw several important technological developments, such as the introduction of the first commercial email connection in 1989, the release of the 'www' system by CERN (first to the energy physics community in 1991, and subsequently to the public in 1993), the introduction of PDF format for electronic publishing by Adobe in 1992, and the invention of VoIP technology in 1994.[7]

For the legal world, the following developments were especially important:

- The introduction of technologies making information, such as case law and statutes, available online;
- The invention of digital search engines;
- The introduction and spread of electronic means of communication, such as email;

[5] Convention on the Recognition and Enforcement of Foreign Arbitral Awards (New York, 1958), the text is available at www.uncitral.org/pdf/english/texts/arbitration/NY-conv/New-York-Convention-E.pdf; 1965 Convention on the Settlement of Investment Disputes between States and Nationals of Other States, the text is available at www.icsid.worldbank.org/apps/ICSIDWEB/icsiddocs/Documents/ICSIDpercent20Conventionpercent20English.pdf; UNCITRAL Arbitration Rules (1976), the text is available at www.uncitral.org/pdf/english/texts/arbitration/arb-rules/arb-rules.pdf; UNCITRAL Model Law on International Commercial Arbitration (1985), the text is available at www.uncitral.org/pdf/english/texts/arbitration/ml-arb/06-54671_Ebook.pdf.

[6] P. Sanders, 'A New Arbitration Law for the Netherlands', (1984) 4(3), *Pace Law Review*.

[7] See www.dpworkshop.org/dpm-eng/timeline/viewall.html.

- The invention of (inexpensive) video-conferencing technologies, such as Skype;
- The introduction of technologies to create documents in electronic format;
- The invention of electronic means of information storage, portable (USB, CDs) and online (clouds and online platforms); and
- The introduction of technologies related to electronic signatures.

From a legal perspective, these innovations can be divided in three categories. The first category consists of the innovations that could be used without a specific legal basis in the 1986 Arbitration Act or explicit agreement between the parties. Examples hereof are the use of online storage technologies by an individual party and the use of legal search engines. A second category concerns innovations that required agreement between the parties before they could be used. Examples are email and video-conferencing. As these technologies impact both parties, and arguably also the Arbitral Tribunal, an agreement between the parties, as well as approval from the Arbitral Tribunal is required for their use. The third category concerns technologies that are incompatible with the 1986 Arbitration Act and that required an amendment of this Act. An example of such a technology would be the electronic signature of an electronic award, which under the 1986 Arbitration Act, would be impossible because Article 1057(2) DCCP required a handwritten signature.[8] The second and third categories will be further discussed later.

The Legislator's Response to the Technological Revolution

The technological revolution required certain changes that resulted in amendments of the Dutch Civil Code and Dutch Code of Civil Procedure including the 1986 Arbitration Act, which was obviously not designed to address the significant technological developments that were to take place in the decades that followed its introduction. These changes were the result of international and European initiatives rather than the initiative of the Dutch legislator.

[8] Article 1057(2) of the 1986 Dutch Code of Civil Procedure: 'The award shall be made in writing and signed by the arbitrator or arbitrators.' While the text of this article has not changed in the 2015 Arbitration Act, Article 1072(b) DCCP now adds that the award 'may also be made in electronic form by providing it with qualified signature as meant in Article 3(12) of EU Regulation 910/2014 [. . .].'

The most significant amendments concerned:

- The introduction of provisions regarding electronic signatures in 2003;
- The introduction of provisions regarding electronic agreements in 2004; and
- The introduction of provisions regarding the legal effect of electronic documents in 2010.

These developments will be discussed next.

The Introduction of Provisions Regarding Electronic Signatures

Modern technologies brought various ways of electronic signing, which differ from simple methods, such as a party sending a picture of a signed document, to sophisticated methods, including signatures based on biometric devices enabling identification by physical characteristics (e.g. fingerprints). As different electronic signatures provide different levels of certainty regarding the identity of the signatory, their legal effects were unclear, which created a hurdle for the paperless communication of legally significant information.

To end this uncertainty, in 1996, UNCITRAL introduced the UNCITRAL Model Law on Electronic Commerce, which was one of the first legislative pieces in the field of electronic signatures.[9] Article 7 of the 1996 UNCITRAL Model Law on Electronic Commerce introduced a very basic principle of recognition, whereby any electronic signature could be recognized.[10] In case of dispute, its legal effect depended on the extent to which its reliability could be demonstrated.

A few years later, in 1999, the European Parliament and Council took a step towards the recognition of electronic signatures and introduced the Electronic Signatures Directive 1999/93/EC.[11] Its main objectives were

[9] The text is available on the website of UNCITRAL at www.uncitral.org/pdf/english/texts/electcom/05-89450_Ebook.pdf.

[10] Article 7(1) of the 1996 Uncitral Model Law provides 'Where the law requires a signature of a person, that requirement is met in relation to a data message if: (a) a method is used to identify that person and to indicate that person's approval of the information contained in the data message; and (b) that method is as reliable as was appropriate for the purpose for which the data message was generated or communicated, in the light of all the circumstances, including any relevant agreement'.

[11] Council Directive 1999/93/EC of the European Parliament and of the Council of 13 December 1999 on a Community Framework for Electronic Signatures, OJ 2000 No. L 13, 19 January 2000, pp. 12–20.

the creation of a clear recognition framework and the strengthening of confidence in new technologies.[12] The Directive contains two regimes in respect of recognition of electronic signatures. The first regime is similar to the regime of Article 7 of the 1996 UNCITRAL Model Law on Electronic Commerce and allows for the recognition of any electronic signature. The second regime determines under which conditions an electronic signature is automatically recognized. Accordingly, the Directive distinguishes between (i) an 'electronic signature'[13] and an 'advanced electronic signature',[14] (ii) a 'certificate'[15] and a 'qualified certificate',[16] and (iii) a 'signature-creation device'[17] and a 'secure-signature-creation device'.[18] The advanced electronic signature, qualified certificate, and secure-signature-creation device, must meet the strict requirements of Article 2, and Annexes I, II, and III of the Directive. Pursuant to Article 5(1) of the Directive, an advanced electronic signature based on a qualified certificate and created by a secure-signature-creation device automatically has the same effect as a handwritten paper-based signature and is admissible in legal proceedings.[19]

If these requirements are not met, Article 5(2) provides that an electronic signature will not be denied legal effect and admissibility as evidence solely on the grounds that it is (i) in electronic form, (ii) not based

[12] Ibid., see 'Recital 4'.

[13] See Article 2(1), Directive 1999/93/EC: 'electronic signature' means 'data in electronic form which are attached to or logically associated with other electronic data and which serve as a method of authentication.'

[14] See Article 2(2), Directive 1999/93/EC: 'advanced electronic signature' means 'an electronic signature which meets the following requirements: (a) it is uniquely linked to the signatory; (b) it is capable of identifying the signatory; (c) it is created using means that the signatory can maintain under his sole control; and (d) it is linked to the date to which it relates in such a manner that any subsequent change of the data is detectable.'

[15] Article 2(9), Directive 1999/93/EC: 'certificate' means 'an electronic attestation that links signature-verification data to a person and confirms the identity of that person.'

[16] Article 2(10), Directive 1999/93/EC: 'qualified certificate' means 'a certificate which meets the requirements laid down in Annex I and provided by a certification-service-provider who fulfils the requirements laid down in Annex II.'

[17] Article 2(5), Directive 1999/93/EC: 'signature creation device' means 'configured software or hardware used to implement the signature-creation data.'

[18] Article 2(6), Directive 1999/93/EC: 'secure signature creation device' means 'a signature-creation device which meets the requirements laid down in Annex III.'

[19] Article 5(1) provides 'Member States shall ensure that advanced electronic signatures which are based on a qualified certificate and which are created by a secure-signature-creation device: (a) satisfy the legal requirements of a signature in relation to data in electronic form in the same manner as a handwritten signature satisfies those requirements in relation to paper-based data; and (b) are admissible as evidence in legal proceedings'.

upon a qualified certificate, (iii) not based upon a qualified certificate issued by an accredited certification service provider, or (iv) not created by a secure signature-creation device. Thus, any electronic signature can have the desired legal effect, which has to be proven by taking into account all circumstances of the case. This is comparable to the principle included in Article 7 of the 1996 UNCITRAL Model Law on Electronic Commerce.[20]

Provisions from the Electronic Signatures Directive were implemented into Dutch law in 2003 and came in the shape of the Electronic Signatures Act (*Wet Elektronische Handtekeningen*). The most important provisions relating to electronic signatures are included in Article 3:15a (1)(2)(3) DCC:

1. An electronic signature has the same legal effect as a handwritten signature if the method used for its authentication is sufficiently reliable, considering the purpose for which the electronic data were used as well as all other circumstances of the situation.
2. A method as meant in paragraph 1 is presumed to be sufficiently reliable if the electronic signature meets the following requirements:
   a. it is linked to the signatory in a unique manner;
   b. it allows for the identification of the signatory;
   c. it is created by means of resources which the signatory is able to keep under his exclusive control;
   d. it is linked to the electronic file to which it relates in such a manner that each later modification of the data can be traced;
   e. it is based on a qualified certificate as meant in Article 1.1(ss) of the Dutch Telecommunication Act, and;
   f. it has been generated by using safe equipment for producing electronic signatures as meant in Article 1.1(vv) of the Dutch Telecommunication Act.
3. A method as meant in paragraph 1 cannot be considered insufficiently reliable on the sole ground that:
   - it is not based on a qualified certificate as defined in Article 1.1(ss) of the Dutch Telecommunication Act;
   - it is not based on a certificate which is delivered by a certification service provider as defined in Article 18.16, first paragraph, of the Dutch Telecommunication Act; or

[20] The revised 2001 UNCITRAL Model Law on Electronic Signatures maintains the two different recognition regimes: one with conditions for automatic recognition and the other allowing for recognition (without conditions). See 2001 Model Law on Electronic Signatures, available at www.uncitral.org/pdf/english/texts/electcom/ml-elecsig-e.pdf.

- it is not generated using safe equipment for producing electronic signatures as defined in Article 1.1(vv) of the Dutch Telecommunication Act.

Although under Dutch law a signature does not constitute a condition for a valid agreement, signatures are important for the identification of the parties and for purposes of evidence.[21] Article 3:15a (1) DCC sets out the main rule that an electronic signature has the same legal effect as a handwritten one, if certain conditions are satisfied.

Articles 3:15a (2) and (3) DCC describe the two regimes from the Electronic Signatures Directive: compliance with the conditions from Article 3:15a (2) DCC leads to automatic recognition of an advanced electronic signature, which is based on a qualified certificate.[22] At the same time, Article 3:15a (3) DCC allows any other electronic signature to be recognized based on the circumstances of the case. An electronic signature is not denied legal effect solely because it does not fulfil the conditions for automatic recognition.

In January 2017, Article 3:15a DCC was amended to reflect EU Regulation 910/2014 of the European Parliament and Council on Electronic Identification and Trust Services for Electronic Transactions in the Internal Market, which came into effect on 1 July 2016.[23]

This Regulation introduces a comprehensive cross-border and cross-sector framework for secure and easy-to-use electronic transactions. It also aims at setting up a coherent framework of security and legal certainty of trust services. It therefore provides, among others, for mutual recognition of e-identification means and electronic trust services, such as electronic signatures, electronic seals (i.e. electronic signatures for legal persons), and electronic registered delivery services. It also provides a framework for electronic identification (eID), trust services, and infrastructure related to verifying electronic signatures and electronic seals.

[21] See Article 156 DCCP which provides that 'Deeds are signed writings, destined to serve as evidence'.

[22] Article 3:15b DCC makes a distinction between 'normal' and 'qualified' certificates. The rules regulating certificated are further set out in the following regulations: (i) Decision Electronic Signatures (*Besluit elektronische handtekeningen*), (ii) Regulation Electronic Signatures (*Regeling elektronische handtekeningen*), and (iii) Policy Rules regarding Appointment of Certificates Providers of Electronic Signatures (*Beleidsregel aanwijzing certificatieorganisaties elektronische handtekeningen*).

[23] Council Regulation 910/2014, OJ 2014, pp. 73–114. The text is available at www.eur-lex.europa.eu/legal-content/EN/TXT/?uri=uriserv:OJ.L_.2014.257.01.0073.01.ENG.

With respect to electronic signatures, the Regulation maintains the principle that an electronic signature should not be denied legal effect on the grounds that it is in electronic form or that it does not meet the requirements of the qualified electronic signature.[24] This is reflected in Article 25 of Regulation 910/2014, which provides that:

1. An electronic signature shall not be denied legal effect and admissibility as evidence in legal proceedings solely on the grounds that it is in an electronic form or that it does not meet the requirements for qualified electronic signatures.
2. A qualified electronic signature shall have the equivalent legal effect of a handwritten signature.
3. A qualified electronic signature based on a qualified certificate issued in one Member State shall be recognized as a qualified electronic signature in all other Member States.

Article 26 of Regulation 910/2014 provides the requirements for an advanced electronic signature, which are largely similar to the requirements under Directive 99/93/EC.[25]

Although the Regulation has direct effect in all the Member States and no implementation legislation is required, the Regulation resulted, among others, in amendments to the Article 3:15a DCC, which now reads as follows:

> Like a qualified electronic signature as meant in Article 3 Section 12 of Regulation 910/2014 [. . .], an advanced electronic signature as meant in Section 11, and another electronic signature as meant in Section 10 of Article 3 of this Regulation have the same legal effect as a handwritten signature, if for both of these electronic signatures the method for signing that has been used is sufficiently reliable, taking into account the purpose for which the electronic signature is used as well as all other circumstances of the case.[26]

As can be seen from this, while Article 3:15a DCC changed with a direct reference to Regulation 910/ 2014, the substance largely remained the same.

[24] Ibid., see Preamble of Regulation (EU) No 910/2014, 49.

[25] Article 26 of the Directive provides that 'an advanced electronic signature shall meet the following requirements: (a) it is uniquely linked to the signatory; (b) it is capable of identifying the signatory; (c) it is created using electronic signature creation data that the signatory can, with a high level of confidence, use under his sole control; and (d) it is linked to the data signed therewith in such a way that any subsequent change in the data is detectable'.

[26] Parliamentary History, 2015–2016, 34413 #2.

Introduction of Provisions in Respect of Electronic Agreements

In the Netherlands, the next legislative step towards embracing modern technologies is related to the conclusion of electronic agreements. Here again, the 1996 UNCITRAL Model Law on Electronic Commerce (discussed earlier) was one of the first international instruments that treated the subject. It provides in Article 11 that agreements can be validly concluded by electronic means.[27]

The most important piece of the European legislation regarding electronic agreements is the Electronic Commerce Directive 2000/31/EC, which was adopted in 2000.[28] The main objective of this Directive was to provide a general legal framework for electronic commerce. This Directive applies only to services that are 'normally provided for remuneration, at a distance, by electronic means and at the individual request of a recipient of services'.[29] Consequently, this Directive does not apply to goods. For example, the sale of music to be downloaded from a website falls within its scope, yet delivery by postal services of a book bought online does not.[30] The most important provision for conclusion of electronic contracts is Article 9(1) of the Electronic Commerce Directive, which orders the Member States to ensure that contracts can be concluded by electronic means:

> Member States shall ensure that their legal system allows contracts to be concluded by electronic means. Member States shall in particular ensure that the legal requirements applicable to the contractual process neither create obstacles for the use of electronic contracts nor result in such contracts being deprived of legal effectiveness and validity on account of there having been made by electronic means.

Article 9(1) resulted in the introduction of Article 6:227a DCC (new) in 2004:

[27] Article 11 provides: In the context of contract formation, unless otherwise agreed by the parties, an offer and the acceptance of an offer may be expressed by means of data messages. Where a data message is used in the formation of a contract, that contract shall not be denied validity or enforceability on the sole ground that a data message was used for that purpose'.

[28] Council Directive 2000/31/EC of 8 June 2000 on certain legal aspects of information society services, in particular electronic commerce, in the Internal Market ('Directive on electronic commerce'), OJ 2000 L 178, 17 July 2000, pp. 1–16. The text is available at www.eur-lex.europa.eu/legal-content/EN/ALL/?uri=CELEX:32000L0031.

[29] See Article 1(2) of Council Directive 98/34/EC of 22 June 1998 laying down a procedure for the provision of information in the field of technical standards and regulations, OJ 1998 No. L 204, 21 July 1998, pp. 37–48, as amended by Directive 98/48/ EC.

[30] Parliamentary History, 2001–2002, 28 197, #3, p. 24.

1. If a statutory provision determines that an agreement can only be validly and uncontestably formed in writing, this requirement will also be met if the agreement is entered into by electronic means and:
   a. the agreement is accessible to the parties;
   b. the authenticity of the agreement is sufficiently guaranteed;
   c. the moment of formation of the agreement can be determined with sufficient certainty; and
   d. the identity of the parties can be assessed with sufficient certainty.
2. Paragraph 1 does not apply to agreements for which the law requires the intervention of a judge, an authority or a professional who exercises a public task.

In the Netherlands, there was no need to introduce a general provision that makes the conclusion of agreements by electronic means possible. This was already possible under Dutch law, as the sole conditions for a valid agreement are an offer and its acceptance.[31] Taking into account that the form of an agreement (generally) does not constitute a condition for its validity, a valid agreement could be concluded electronically also before the introduction of Article 6:227a DCC.[32]

Dutch law, however, also has a number of *leges speciales* that require certain agreements to be in writing to have the desired legal effect, for example the sale of real estate.[33] Therefore, only when a *lex specialis* requires the agreement to be in writing for it to be valid, Article 6:227a DCC kicks in, as it allows the 'in writing' requirement to be fulfilled by electronic means.

Pursuant to Article 6:227a DCC, electronic means can only replace 'written form' if the four conditions mentioned in the Article are satisfied.[34] An electronic signature is mandatory only if the presence of a signature is explicitly required under the relevant statute.[35]

Similar to Article 9(2) Electronic Commerce Directive 2000/31/EC, Article 6:227a(2) DCC provides exceptions to the main rule and describes situations in which electronic means cannot replace the written form, e.g. agreements for which the law requires the intervention of a court, a public

[31] See Article 6:217(1) DCC which determines that 'an agreement is formed through an offer and its acceptance'.

[32] For purposes of evidence, it does matter whether or not an agreement is in writing and signed, cf. Article 156(1) DCCP which provides 'Deeds are signed written documents destined to serve as evidence'.

[33] Parliamentary History, 2007–2008, 31 358, #3, p. 8.

[34] Parliamentary History, 2001–2002, 28 197, #3, pp. 52–54.

[35] Certain authors suggest that non-compliance with one of the conditions of Article 6:227a DCC might be disregarded by the courts. See, J. H. Nieuwenhuis, *Tekst & Commentaar by Article 6:227a DCC* (Deventer: Wolters Kluwer, 2013), p. 3271.

authority, or a notary. Further to an amendment of Article 6:227a DCC in 2010, the number of exceptions was reduced. As a result, it is now possible to enter into an agreement for the sale of real estate by email.

The implementation of the Electronic Commerce Directive 2000/31/EC and introduction of the Article 6:227a DCC also resulted in an amendment of Article 1021 DCCP:

> The agreement to arbitrate is evidenced by an instrument in writing. For this purpose an instrument in writing that provides for arbitration or refers to standard terms and conditions that provides for arbitration is sufficient and that has been implicitly or explicitly accepted by or on behalf of the other party.

This provision concerned evidence, and strictly speaking constituted neither a requirement for the existence nor for the validity of an arbitration agreement. If the existence of an agreement is timely disputed and has to be proven, pursuant to Dutch procedural law the parties are free to provide evidence by all possible means, unless the law stipulates otherwise.[36] Article 1021 DCCP is an example of an exception to the main rule.[37] This Article restricts the means of providing evidence by stipulating that only a document in writing can serve as such. As a result, the existence of an arbitration agreement could not be proven without written evidence.

Although this requirement is not uncommon in arbitration, since a similar provision is contained in the New York Convention 1958, this Article was considered a hindrance for digitalization. Despite the fact that the Electronic Commerce Directive 2000/31/EC applies to the conclusion of agreements by electronic means and not to the provision of evidence, the Dutch legislator decided to implement a clarification. Accordingly, the legislator declared Article 6:227a DCC applicable to arbitration and in 2004, amended Article 1021 DCCP by adding the following two sentences:

> The agreement to arbitrate may also be proven by electronic data. Article 227a(1) of Book 6 of the Civil Code shall apply *mutatis mutandis.*

Consequently, an arbitration agreement could now also be evidenced by electronic means. This provision now answers the modern technological needs better than Article II of the New York Convention and Article 7(2) of the UNCITRAL Model Law on Arbitration (as amended in 2006),

[36] See Article 152 DCCP.

[37] M. van Hooidonk, *Litigation in the Netherlands* (Den Haag: Kluwer Law International, 2009), p. 18.

which imposes that the arbitration agreement is 'in writing', and have been subject to criticism.[38]

Introduction of Provisions Regarding the Legal Effects of Electronic Documents

The next legislative step concerned the establishment of rules regarding the legal effect and evidentiary value of electronic documents. The trigger for the introduction of a new provision regarding the legal effects of electronic documents was a motion from Dutch Parliament requesting the possibility of electronic creation of insurance policies.[39] Subsequent legal research revealed that many other documents could also benefit from conclusion by electronic means.[40]

Accordingly, in 2010, the legislator introduced Article 156a(1) DCCP. This Article sets out under which conditions electronic documents can have the same legal effect and evidentiary value as documents in writing. It reads as follows:

> Private deeds can be made other than in writing in such a manner that the person for whom the document constitutes evidence, is able to save the content of the document in a manner that makes the content accessible for future use during a period adequate to serve the objectives for which the deed is made, and which makes unmodified reproduction of the content of the deed possible.

Dutch procedural law makes a distinction between the evidentiary value of private (*onderhandse akte*) and public (*authentieke akte*) deeds, whereby public deeds are those made by officials (e.g. notaries, court bailiffs), while all non-public deed are private deeds.[41]

This difference is important because Article 156(1) DCCP stipulates that only private deeds can be made by electronic means.[42] Since

[38] N. Kaplan, 'Is the Need for Writing as Expressed in the New York Convention and the Model Law Out of Step with Commercial Practice?' (1996) 5(1), *Asia Pacific Law Review*, pp. 27–46.

[39] Parliamentary History, 2005–2006, 30 137, #17.

[40] Parliamentary History, 2005–2006, 30 137, #18, p. 1.

[41] While both types of documents provide conclusive evidence in respect of the content of an agreement between the parties, public documents also provide conclusive evidence about the statements made by officials. Furthermore, the content of the officials' statements is conclusive evidence *erga omnes* and not only in relation to the parties.

[42] Article 156(1) DCCP provides that 'Deeds are signed writings, destined to serve as evidence'. Hence it appears that at present a recording of a legally relevant declaration would not have the same evidentiary value as a private deed as a signature would be lacking.

arbitration agreements are generally included in private documents, this amendment is relevant to arbitration.

The conditions that have to be satisfied are as follows: (i) it should be possible to save the content of the electronic document, (ii) the electronic document should be accessible for future reference, (iii) 'future reference' relates to a period adequate for the purpose of the document, and (iv) it should be possible to save the document in a way that allows its unmodified reproduction.

Response of Arbitral Institutions to the Technological Revolution

Given that the 1986 Dutch Arbitration Act did *not* prohibit electronic communications, various Dutch dispute-resolution institutions embraced modern technologies even before the legislator took steps in that direction. These initiatives vary from allowing communication by email, to providing advanced online case management platforms for encrypted document exchange, and offering secure video-conferencing services. Dutch arbitration institutions mostly appear to have proposed these innovations to increase efficiency and reduce costs.

The first initiative was taken by the *Stichting Geschillenoplossing Automatisering* (SGOA; Foundation for the Resolution of ICT Disputes).[43] As SGOA was focusing on ICT disputes, it was well positioned to implement the first technological innovations. Already in 1998, SGOA introduced 'MeetingWorks', an electronic platform for case management. In 2003, SGOA started exploring options for implementing modern technologies and subsequently introduced 'e-ADR' mediation proceedings. As the name suggests, the e-ADR proceedings take place by electronic means with the use of MeetingWorks, secured emails, and encryption of provided information. As early as 2005, SGOA administered its first online e-ADR proceedings, which were held exclusively via Internet, email, and telephone. When the dispute was settled, the parties signed the settlement agreement electronically.[44]

As of 2008, the arbitration institute for maritime disputes, *Stichting Transport and Maritime Arbitration Rotterdam-Amsterdam* (TAMARA), started offering an online arbitration platform.[45] The online platform

[43] See for more information, www.sgoa.eu/English/.

[44] J. B. F. Mulder and J. J. Borking, 'De eerste praktische ervaringen met elektronische geschillenoplossing in Nederland', *Computerrecht*, (Wolter Kluwer, 2006), p. 135.

[45] See for more information, www.tamara-arbitration.nl.

allows the parties to file their submissions electronically and to upload new documents or submissions. Moreover, the platform sends relevant notifications to the parties.[46]

One year later, in 2009, the eCourt was established.[47] The eCourt is an arbitration institution for the online resolution of disputes related to the online purchase of goods. In 2010, it introduced an online platform for administration of arbitration disputes and documents exchange, which is comparable to the online platform offered by TAMARA.[48]

The Foundation for Internet Registration of Domain Names (*Stichting Internet Domeinregistratie Nederland* or SIDN), also deserves attention. This independent foundation manages the registration of .nl domain names and offers a proceeding for non-binding advice under auspices of the World Intellectual Property Organization (WIPO) Arbitration and Mediation Centre.[49] The procedure at the WIPO Arbitration and Mediation Centre is fully electronic. WIPO also has an online platform for case management, where all submissions and other documents can be exchanged and parties communicate by electronic means.[50] The examples show that the most important innovations concerned possibilities of communication by email, creation of secured and encrypted online case management platforms for document exchange, as well as video-conferencing services. Currently, all leading Dutch arbitration institutions make use of advantages offered by modern technologies. For example, the primary way of communication with the Netherlands Arbitration Institute is now by electronic means.[51]

Implementation of modern technologies was possible in the Netherlands to the extent that the Arbitration Act did not contain prohibitions. However, after Article 1021 DCCP was amended in 2004 (allowing

[46] See for more information, www.tamara-arbitration.nl/arbitrage/e-arbitrage.

[47] See for more information, www.e-court.nl.

[48] H. W. Wefers Bettink, 'Online arbitrage in de nieuwe arbitragewet' (Wolters Kluwer, 2013), *TvA* 2013/32.

[49] Accredited domain name registrars, which have agreed to abide by the UDRP, implement the non-binding decision after a period of ten days, unless one of the parties appeals the decision within that time. In practice, this is a relatively rare occurrence. See www.wipo.int/amc/en/center/faq/domains.html.

[50] Ibid.

[51] See Article 3 of the 2015 Netherlands Arbitration Institute, Arbitration Rules, which states 'Unless the sender is unable to do so, all requests, communications and other documents to the administrator, the Committee, the third person as referred to in Article 39 and/or the NAI shall only be sent electronically by email to the address secretariaat@nai-nl.org or to any other address to be specified by the NAI'. The 2015 NAI Rules entered into force at the same time as the 2015 Arbitration Act, i.e. 1 January 2015.

electronic evidence of the existence of an arbitration agreement), there were still certain obstacles to the complete digitalization of the proceedings. For example, Article 1057(2) DCCP imposed an obligation on arbitrators to sign the arbitral award. Only a handwritten signature could satisfy this requirement. This was an important validity requirement, as the absence of a handwritten signature constituted a ground for the setting aside of an arbitral award under Article 1065(1)(d) DCCP.[52] Therefore, despite the availability of the electronic signature technologies in the Netherlands, electronic signatures could not be used in arbitration. Besides, since there was no possibility to sign the arbitral awards electronically, it was also impossible to issue electronic awards.

The 2015 Arbitration Act

Reasons for the Introduction of the 2015 Arbitration Act: Limited Role of Modern Technologies

Technological progress and innovations were not the main reasons for replacing the 1986 Arbitration Act. The real trigger for the introduction of the 2015 Arbitration Act was a desire to improve the attractiveness of the Netherlands as an arbitration venue, which was necessary given that competing jurisdictions had significantly revised their arbitration laws in the meantime.[53] In addition, there was also a wish to bring the Arbitration Act more in line with the UNCITRAL Model Law as revised in 2006.

Proposals of Professor Van den Berg on Use of ICT in Arbitration: New Article 1072 BB

In 2005, Professor Van den Berg organized a Working Group for the revision of the 1986 Arbitration Act, which drafted 'The Proposals for Changes to Book Four (Arbitration), Articles 1020–1076 DCCP' ('Proposals'). After consultation with the arbitration community, the

[52] Dutch Supreme Court, 21 January 1966, NJ 1966/214. If one or more arbitrators refuse or are unable to sign the arbitral award, this must be mentioned in the arbitral award. The absence of a dissenting arbitrator's signature without mention in the arbitral award may lead to the setting aside (see Dutch Supreme Court, 5 December 2008, NJ 2009/6).

[53] England came with a revised Arbitration Act in 1996, Germany in 1998, Sweden in 1999, France in 2011, and Belgium in 2013. None of these acts contain any provisions on electronic proceedings.

Proposals were submitted to the Ministry of Security and Justice in 2006. The Proposals consisted of a draft Act, and a detailed Explanatory Memorandum.[54]

With respect to modern technologies and innovations, the Proposals contained a new Article 1072 BB DCCP. This Article included both provisions codifying existing practice, and provisions removing obstacles to the use of modern technologies from Dutch law. The proposed Article mentioned the possibility of making submissions, and providing notices and other documents by electronic means. The Explanatory Memorandum motivated this amendment by stating that in arbitration, and in particular, international arbitration, the use of electronic means had increased considerably.[55] Submissions are therefore made in electronic form and sent by email or uploaded on a secured website that is accessible only to the parties and the arbitrators, and in certain cases, also the relevant arbitration institute. Professor Van den Berg noted in this respect that most international arbitrations concerning domain names are administrated solely electronically.[56]

The proposed provision is thus a mere codification of the existing practice already adopted by many arbitration institutions. Furthermore, according to the Explanatory Memorandum, the only exception to this rule should be made for proceedings before the state courts so long as the court system is not capable of processing documents electronically.[57]

Another step taken in the direction of full digitalization of the arbitral proceedings concerns the extension of the meaning of the word 'documents'. The proposed new Article 1072 BB stipulates in this respect that 'documents' also include data on data carriers as well as data presented by electronic means. Moreover, the Explanatory Memorandum clarifies that the concept of 'data carriers' should be broadly interpreted and includes electronic storage of tapes, floppy disks, and hard disks, as well as audio and videotapes, and data available on the Internet.[58]

Furthermore, the proposed Article made it possible to issue electronic arbitral awards, whereby an electronic arbitral award is treated as an authentic copy. For an electronic award to be valid, it has to be signed by an advanced electronic signature within the meaning of Article 3:15a(2)

[54] A. J. Van den Berg, 'Tekst van de Voorstellen tot wijziging van het Vierde boek (Arbitrage) Artikelen 1020–1076 Rv', *TvA*, 2005.

[55] G. J. Meijer, '*Parlementaire geschiedenis Arbitragewet*', (Wolters Kluwer Nederland B.V., 2014), p. 540.

[56] Ibid. [57] Ibid. [58] Ibid.

DCC, i.e. a signature based on a qualified certificate. The Explanatory Memorandum states that an electronic signature should inseparably connect the text of an arbitral award with the arbitrators' signatures, so that each subsequent modification makes the text of an award illegible.[59] The legislator made an interesting clarification in this respect, which will be discussed in the following subchapter.

Video-conferencing is another subject dealt with by the proposed Article 1072 BB. According to the new provision, the arbitral tribunal may determine that a witness, an expert, or a party may be heard by the Arbitral Tribunal by electronic means instead of through appearance in person. The Arbitral Tribunal, in consultation with the parties, determines which electronic means would be appropriate for this purpose. The Explanatory Memorandum notes that it should be possible to hold a hearing by means of video-conferencing. Furthermore, the Explanatory Memorandum points out that this is an attractive option to the parties from a cost-saving perspective.[60]

Taking into account that a mailbox can be 'full', and modern technologies can be unreliable, the last important issue addressed by draft Article 1072 BB concerns the moment of receipt of electronic documents. In this respect, Article 1072 BB introduced a rule, according to which, a document submitted electronically is deemed to have been received on the day that it was sent. Because the legislator ultimately adopted a different approach, this topic will not be discussed any further in this chapter.

The 2015 Arbitration Act: Article 1072(b) on the Use of ICT in Arbitration

After the Proposals were presented to the Ministry of Security and Justice in 2006, no noticeable actions were taken for the next four years. The first concrete results came in 2011, when the Ministry of Security and Justice announced its Innovation Agenda for the Legal Sector. Among its main objectives were modernization, simplification, and an increase of attractiveness of the Netherlands as a place of arbitration.[61] Shortly thereafter, the legislator presented a draft Act that it published in March 2012 for online consultation. Many interested parties, such as the

[59] Ibid.

[60] A. J. van den Berg, 'Tekst van de Voorstellen tot wijziging van het Vierde boek (Arbitrage) Artikelen.

[61] Ministry of Security and Justice, Innovation Agenda for the Legal Sector, 31 October 2011.

Nederlandse Vereniging voor Rechtspraak (Dutch Association for the Judiciary), *Adviescommissie burgerlijk procesrecht* (Advisory Commission on Civil Procedure), and arbitration institutions such as the NAI, ICC, and PCA, participated in this consultation. Further to some additional amendments, a final version of the Act was approved in 2014. The Arbitration Act entered into force on 1 January 2015.

Article 1072(b) DCCP regulates the use of modern technologies:

(1) If the addressee has communicated that it may be reached in this manner for these purposes and the arbitral tribunal agrees thereto, insofar as any provision of this Title requires an agreement, a submission, a notice, a request or an action to be made in written form, these may also be made electronically except insofar as it concerns an action which takes place in court proceedings, unless this is allowed in the latter proceedings. The availability by such means shall be valid for the duration of the arbitral proceedings, unless the addressee communicates that it modifies, or, insofar as the parties have agreed to this possibility, withdraws this possibility.
(2) Documents as referred to in this Title shall also include data on a data carrier as well as data filed by electronic means.
(3) The award referred to in Article 1057(2) may also be made in electronic form by providing it with an electronic signature that complies with the provisions of Article 15a (1) and (2) of Book 3 of the Civil Code.[62]
(4) Instead of a personal appearance of a witness, an expert or a party, the arbitral tribunal may determine that the relevant person has direct contact with the arbitral tribunal by electronic means and, insofar as applicable, with others. The arbitral tribunal determines, in consultation with those concerned, which electronic means shall be used to this end and in which manner this shall occur.
(5) A notice or action that occurs by electronic means or a procedural document which is presented by electronic means is deemed to have been sent at the time at which the message has reached a data-processing system for which the sender is not responsible.

This Article is not very different from Article 1072 BB that was included in the Proposals. In fact, the legislator followed most of Professor Van den

[62] The reference to 'an electronic signature which complies with the provisions of Article 3:15a (1) and (2)' in Article 1072b will be replaced with a reference to 'a qualified electronic signature as referred to in Article 3(12) of Regulation (910/2014)' in the near future.

Berg's Proposals relating to the use of ICT in arbitration. The most important differences between Article 1072(b) DCCP and Article 1072 BB Proposals concern the following.

While Article 1072 BB stated that electronic means can be used 'unless the parties agree otherwise', Article 1072(b) provides some important clarifications in this respect. It stipulates that if one of the parties consents to the use of the electronic means, this party will stay available by electronic means for 'the duration of the arbitral proceedings' unless the parties agree otherwise. The 'availability by electronic means' refers to electronic communication. The new Article sets out rules in respect of changes in the availability by electronic means and withdrawal from it. It states that although it is possible to modify electronic availability by, for example, submitting a new email address, withdrawal from electronic availability during the course of the proceeding is an option only if the parties 'have agreed to this possibility'. This prevents that the counterparty and the arbitral tribunal suddenly face communication difficulties over the course of the arbitral proceedings

Under Article 1072(b) DCCP, the arbitral tribunal also must consent to the use of electronic means. This consent can be implicit or derived from the use of the applicable Arbitration Rules, if these contain provisions for the use of electronic means, such as the 2015 NAI Rules. While the Proposals suggested that because of an electronic signature each subsequent modification of an arbitral award should make its text illegible, the legislator stated in the Explanatory Memorandum that the electronic signature needs to make it impossible to modify the text of an award.[63] This is an important clarification, since it allows keeping the arbitral award, while under the Proposals, the award could be lost.

With respect to the use of electronic awards in state court proceedings (e.g. setting aside and *exequatur* proceedings), the Explanatory Memorandum explains that only a printed version of an electronic award can be submitted to the court.[64] Practice will show whether a printed version of an electronic award will be sufficient or whether its content would have to be additionally verified or authenticated in one way or another. This situation should change rather soon, given that civil court proceedings will become fully electronic by 2019. The same is likely to apply to enforcement of arbitral awards outside of the Netherlands, at least in so far as the court proceedings of the country where execution is requested are not yet fully electronic.

[63] Ibid. [64] Ibid.

To limit discussions about technical problems because of which electronic messages are not delivered or not delivered on time, and to divide risks and responsibilities for these technical problems between the parties, the new Article contains a provision regulating the moment when the documents are considered to have been sent. This moment is 'the time at which the message has reached a data-processing system for which the sender is not responsible'. The Explanatory Memorandum states that this provision prevents that a mistake in the system of a sender, as a result of which a message never leaves the sender's computer and consequently never reaches the addressee, is attributed to the addressee. Therefore, only from the moment that the message has left the data-processing system of the sender, and reached the data-processing system of the addressee, the addressee is responsible for collection of the message.[65]

Lastly, it should be noted that the 2015 Arbitration Act abolished the requirement of Article 1058 DCCP relating to the deposition of arbitral awards with the district court, unless the parties agree otherwise. While this change was predominantly introduced to align the 2015 Arbitration Act with international practice, it does make the use of electronic awards easier.

Issues Not Addressed by the 2015 Arbitration Act

By enacting the 2015 Arbitration Act, the Dutch legislator made significant progress regarding the use of ICT in arbitration. Some issues, however, remained unaddressed, such as the potential impact of the use of ICT on due process, protection of privacy, confidentiality, applicable data protection rules, and the prevention of cyber-attacks.

During the legislative process, some members of Parliament put forward concerns regarding the protection of privacy, security, as well as concerns in relation to security breaches.[66]

The legislator responded to the security concerns by stating that the 2015 Arbitration Act does not oblige the parties to use electronic means, but only offers them the option.[67] According to the legislator, it is the task of arbitral institutions to choose appropriate electronic means and to

[65] Ibid.

[66] Parliamentary History, 2013–2014, 33 611, #5, p. 19. For a discussion of security breaches, see Chapter 3, p. 69 of Philipp Schaumann.

[67] In practice *not* using electronic means, in particular in international arbitration, may not be a realistic option.

protect the parties' privacy.[68] In this respect, the legislator also noted that the Dutch Data Protection Act (*Wet bescherming persoonsgegevens*) regulates issues such as data and privacy protection.[69] Cyber-attacks and hacking are prohibited by the Dutch Criminal Code (*Wetboek van strafrecht*), and victims of these crimes can file charges with the police.[70] Hence, according to the legislator, the existing legal framework is sufficient and the 2015 Arbitration Act itself did not need to offer any additional protection. This means that these important issues will have to be addressed and resolved by the parties together with the arbitration institutions.

Digital Court Proceedings

While the 2015 Arbitration Act fully enabled electronic arbitration, Dutch court proceedings were far from electronic. This may seem surprising as modern technologies have the capacity to change both arbitral and state court proceedings in a similar manner.

For the Netherlands, this discrepancy is now changing. In July 2016, the legislator published four related acts introducing digital civil court proceedings.[71] To not disrupt the existing (paper) practice, digital civil court proceedings are introduced in stages starting in 2017.

Until early 2017, court proceedings in the Netherlands were hardly electronic. While in 2008, the legislator introduced the electronic docket ('*rol*'), it could only be used if (i) the parties were represented by counsel, and (ii) the procedural rules of the court in question allowed for it.[72] In 2012, it became possible to electronically file writs of summons (*dagvaardingen*).[73] In practice, however, these options were not frequently used.[74]

With the introduction of the new acts, this changed, and as of 2019, everyone (other than natural persons acting in a personal capacity), will be obliged to conduct the entire civil proceeding in electronic form. In this

[68] Parliamentary History, 2013–2014, 33 611, #5, pp. 19–20. For a discussion of the role of arbitral institutions, see Chapter 4, p. 86.

[69] Parliamentary History, 2013–2014, 33 611, #5, pp. 19–20.

[70] Parliamentary History, 2013–2014, 33 611, #5, pp. 19–20. See also, Article 138ab of the Dutch Criminal Code.

[71] The final acts dated 13 July 2016 were published in the State Gazette (*Staatscourant*) on 21 July 2016 under Nos. 288 through 291, respectively.

[72] Act of 20 March 2008 abandoning *procuraat* and introducing electronic docket (*rol*) introducing Article 33 DCCP.

[73] Ibid.; see also, Decision electronic filing writ of summons, Staatsblad 2012, 292.

[74] H. W. Wefers Bettink, 'Digitalisering van de civiele procedure: gevolgen voor de procespraktijk', *Tijdschrift voor Civiele Rechtspleging*, 2015/1, 1.

regard, the Netherlands is not unique. In many European countries, digital civil proceedings are either considered or have already been introduced. Indeed, it is fair to note that the differences between various European countries are considerable. On the one hand, countries such as Austria, Estonia, Latvia and Lithuania have fully electronic proceedings. On the other hand, countries such as Belgium, Bulgaria and Greece have a very low level of digitalization.[75] The Netherlands appear to be somewhere in the middle.

What sets the Dutch approach apart is the sheer ambition of the project. The purpose of the new Acts is more than a simple digitalization of the existing practice. Digitalization is also supposed to result in (1) significant cost savings, (2) speedier proceedings, and (3) increased accessibility to judges.

To enable the introduction of electronic proceedings, it was necessary to extensively simplify the existing civil procedural rules. This was done, among others, by abolishing the difference between requests and writs (claims). As a result, all proceedings now start with one single electronic document, called 'introduction of process.'[76] Professional parties must electronically file the introduction of process as well as any other documents they wish to file over the course of the proceedings, e.g. submissions and documentary evidence.[77] The claimant is obliged to notify the defendant within two weeks following the filing of the introduction of process, and may do so by email, simple letter, or by bailiff.[78] The defendant must then appear in the proceedings at the latest on, or before, the date indicated in the introduction of process. This date is at least four weeks, and at most six months, after the date of notification.[79]

The new Acts also introduce more uniform and shorter time limits, and emphasize the importance of the hearing and a proactive judge. Hence, after appearing in the proceedings, a defendant will have a maximum of four weeks to file a defence for matters treated by the small claims court, and six weeks for matters treated by the District Court.[80] As soon as possible after the defendant has appeared in the proceedings, or after the introduction of process has been filed, the judge determines the hour and date of the oral hearing.[81] The notice period must at least be three weeks, and

[75] CEPEJ Report on European Judicial Systems, Edition 2014 (2012 data): Efficiency and Quality of Justice, p. 124, available at www.coe.int/t/dghl/cooperation/cepej/evaluation/2014/Rapport_2014_en.pdf.

[76] Article 30 (a) DCCP. [77] Article 30(c) DCCP. [78] Article 112 DCCP.

[79] Article 30(a)(c) DCCP. [80] Article 111(2)(c) DCCP. [81] Article 30(j) DCCP.

take into account the date by which the defendant may file its defence at the latest. According to the Parliamentary History, it is expected that hearings in proceedings related to claims (as opposed to requests) will take place approximately nine weeks after the appearance of the defendant.[82]

During the hearing, the judge may request further information from the parties; offer parties the opportunity to further develop their position; try a settlement; or discuss case management with the parties.[83] Instead of a written summary of the hearing (*proces verbaal*), sound or video recordings may be made.[84] Unless the judge provides his or her judgment orally at the hearing, or extends the applicable deadline, judgments are rendered within four weeks of the oral hearing in matters dealt with by the small claims court, and six weeks in matters treated by the District Court.[85]

Thus, it is fair to say that the KEI Legislation does much more than just allowing the use of electronic means in court proceedings. The push for digitalization is transformative of the litigation process itself.

The KEI Legislation contains separate provisions regarding electronic signatures, the receipt of digital messages, and the effects of technical problems.

With respect to electronic signatures, Article 30(c)(3) DCCP determines:

> An electronic signature means a signature consisting of electronic data that are linked to or have a logical connection with other electronic data and that are being used by the signatory to sign. Where in this Code signing has been prescribed, this requirement is met if the document is signed with an electronic signature that fulfils the requirements imposed by governmental decree. A document that has been filed electronically in the digital system for data processing of the courts is considered to be signed. This provision does not apply to documents as meant in Article 156 and to the signing of documents in arbitral proceedings within the meaning of Book Four.

This Article does not refer to the definition of a (qualified) electronic signature included in Regulation 910/2014, although according to Parliamentary History, the description of Article 30(c)(3) is based on this Regulation.[86]Requirements will be laid down in regulations that are easier to amend, rather than in the DCCP itself, which should allow legislative bodies to keep up with relevant technological developments.

[82] T&C, p. 163. [83] Article 30(k) DCCP.

[84] Article 30n(7) DCCP. [85] Article 30(q) DCCP.

[86] Parliamentary History 2014/2015, 34059 #3, p. 64. These requirements have been criticized as not meaning anything as any email will comply. See R. Jacobs, 'Een verslag van de expertmeeting over E-arbitration (en breder)', TVA 2016/66, p. 73.

Article 30(c)(3) does not apply to public deeds as mentioned in Article 156 DCCP. It does not apply to electronic signatures in arbitration either, which as far as Arbitral Tribunals are concerned, are governed by the relevant provisions of Article 1072b and Regulation 910/2014.

With respect to deadlines, Article 30(d) contains very specific provisions regarding the receipt of documents:

1. A message is considered electronically received by the judge, at the moment when the message has reached the digital system for data processing of the courts. After every electronic filing, the filer will receive a confirmation of receipt in the digital system for data processing of the courts.
2. A message placed by the judge in the digital system for data processing will be considered received by the addressee at the moment when the judge has informed the addressee about this through a notification sent outside the digital system for data processing of the courts.

This Article contains a deviation of the general modified theory of receipt as practiced in the Netherlands (Article 3:37 DCC). Not with respect to any filings by parties, but with respect to judges, who only need to inform an addressee by way of notification (which may be automatically generated) that a message has been placed on the system. A party is deemed to have received a document if the court made a digital notice that a document has been placed. The risk that a document is not received is then for receiver.

This Article also differs from Article 1072(b) DCCP, which requires that the message has left the systems of the sender, at least with respect to the sending of documents to an arbitral tribunal compared to a judge.

We also refer to Article 30(f) DCCP, which provides, among others that governmental regulations may set out further rules on when the failure to meet a deadline is excused because of technical malfunctions.

It is interesting to note that several of the important practical 'details' still have to be arranged in further regulations. This is despite of the fact that some of these 'details' could have a significant impact on due process.

Finally, while the legislator has paid a lot of attention to the expected increase in celerity, as well as accessibility and decrease of costs, less attention seems to have been paid to due process, security (cyber-attacks), data protection, and privacy. While the question of the impact of digitalization on due process has received virtually no attention, the legislator considered that data protection and security are sufficiently addressed by the overall legal framework. With respect to data protection, the courts will be subject to the obligation to comply with relevant rules. It is therefore to be expected that we may, in the coming years, witness a number of incidents, e.g. the impossibility to file while a part of the system is down, hacking and publication of sensitive information, or unintentional data leaks that will require attention from the courts and the legislator.

Conclusion

With the introduction of 1072(b) DCCP, the use of ICT in arbitral proceedings having their seat in the Netherlands obtained a legal basis. At present, the Netherlands is one of the first countries to have done so. This is surprising, taking into account the technological developments of the last thirty years and the potential impact they have on the proceedings. This impact not only relates to the celerity of the proceedings and the costs, but also to matters of due process.

The Netherlands introduced fully electronic court proceedings. It is far from the first country to do so; many other countries, in particular in Europe, have already done so. The introduction of fully electronic court proceedings will lead to profound changes to civil court proceedings, among others because of simplified proceedings and shortened deadlines. The aim of the Dutch legislator is not only to make legal proceedings faster, but also less expensive. It remains to be seen whether this will indeed be the case. In the meantime, it is clear that the introduction of ICT in Dutch court proceedings is not just a 'neutral' technological change, but also has an impact on the manner in which parties resolve their disputes.

With respect to the protection of data, and security in general, both in the case of arbitration and court litigation, the legislator considered that the current legal framework was sufficient. The obligation to comply with existing data protection rules lies with arbitral institutions and the courts, respectively. Breaches of security (hacking) may, however, lead to criminal prosecution.

This approach appears to be fairly light. Dealing with data protection rules these days is no simple matter. While breaches of security may in theory lead to criminal prosecution, in practice this is hardly the case. Moreover, once certain confidential information relating to a litigation or arbitration is 'out', the damage may already have been done. In the coming years, we may therefore expect a number of incidents, which may require a change to the current approach.

Hopefully, arbitral tribunals and courts will thereby learn from their mutual experiences, instead of each advancing in separate tracks, as appears to have been the case to date. One thing is clear however: we are at the threshold of profound changes in the practice of litigation and arbitration.

6

Case Study

The Practitioner's Perspective

SOPHIE NAPPERT AND PAUL COHEN

Summary: This chapter, written by practising lawyers who serve as counsel and arbitrator in international arbitrations, examines how technology has affected the processes and procedures of international arbitration, and how current and future technological developments might fundamentally alter those processes and procedures. The authors discuss in particular: the elements of human decision-making that might be affected by the onset of sophisticated diagnostic programs and artificial intelligence; the kinds of technology that might affect arbitration; whether a technologically driven decision-making process would represent a step forward for the arbitral process, or whether a program- and machine-based process would deprive arbitration of its fundamental qualities as a form of human dispute resolution.

Introduction

Internal office communication in the twenty-first century is light years away from the days of *Mad Men*:[1] you type and read emails; you listen to voicemail; you receive few if any handwritten notes from personal assistants saying, 'while you were out, Mr. Jones called'; you participate in video-conferences. Arbitration proceedings, by contrast, are conducted in substantially the same way as they were 50 years ago. Everyone shows up in one place at an appointed time, for in-person hearings before a panel reading hard-copy documents from A5 bundles. This scenario, however, is about to become obsolete, even as virtual technology, Facebook's Oculus Rift,[2] Magic Leap,[3] Star VR (formerly Infiniteye),[4] provides a startling replication of interpersonal interaction.

[1] See www.en.wikipedia.org/wiki/Mad_Men. [2] See www.oculus.com/en-us.
[3] See www.www.magicleap.com/#/home. [4] See www.starvr.com.

This chapter aims at taking a forward look, from a practitioner's standpoint, at the place and role of the human mind, and more specifically its decision-making capabilities and limitations, alongside technology in the arbitration process. A "forward" look, because whilst it is undisputed that technology until now has been at the service of the arbitral process, assisting with the accuracy and speed of procedurally repetitive or voluminous tasks, we are reaching a stage where technological development enters the realm of the substantive, hitherto the preserve of the decision-makers. It may for instance allow assessing the truth of a witness's testimony based on an analysis of her voice intonations and facial micro-expressions. Human shortcomings such as fallibility in recollection, memory gaps and cognitive bias could thus be assisted/corrected by technology. Also, technology could assist to generate in record time a reasoned decision that takes into account and cross-references each and every document, fact, witness and all applicable law.

Beyond the gadgetry, it is not a far-fetched proposition to say that technological advances entail paradigm-shifting consequences that affect the very core of arbitration as a dispute resolution mechanism and the role of the (human) counsel and arbitrator.

From these examples and proposition, the following questions arise:

1. Will technology step in to assist the decision-making process?
2. Will technology take the process over and, by shepherding the human participant(s) through those areas where s/he is eminently fallible, make that process fundamentally different from what we know now?
3. Does this amount to a better arbitration process in the end?

Such questions on the role of technology in professional services are not mere science fiction. Doctors today, for instance, are increasingly beset by competition from diagnostic tools that perform better on many metrics than human physicians. In the medical sector, this evolution has stirred up quite some debate: on the one hand, the advocates of diagnostic technology rightfully argue that several programmes have proved themselves consistently more adept than doctors at recognising symptoms of illness and properly treating disease. There is, by definition, no human error in such programming. On the other hand, it is hard to see how a machine or computer can replace a physician's ability to empathise with a patient, to treat the patient holistically rather than according to a discrete set of symptoms, or (where necessary) to break hard truths about a patient's condition as gently as possible. Computers, after all, are not known for their bedside manner.

Returning to arbitration, the previously mentioned questions lead to more core questions. First of all, what do we want from the arbitral process and what can it deliver? Do we want a flawlessly logical, entirely dispassionate outcome? Unimpeachable legal reasoning (and if so, would we need appeals or reviews of arbitral decisions in tomorrow's dispute resolution world)? Or are we, through arbitration, seeking the truth? What is the place of equity in a world where technology dominates arbitration and what is the place, if any, of empathy in arbitral decision-making?

Secondly, technology also causes us to rethink the tenet of the *intuitu personae* nature of the arbitrator's mandate, and how much of it can be relinquished without delegating the function altogether. If writing one's own awards is the safeguard of intellectual integrity, then what happens if technology gets ahead of you, leads you by the hand through true or false witness testimony and presents you with an inevitable conclusion? These are questions for the arbitrator(s).

A parallel set of questions presents itself to advocates in arbitrations. The use of technology presents potential advantages to tech-savvy counsel. For example, shrewd and suitably sophisticated advocates can use modern media to augment the appeal of their evidence. An interactive video of a defective manufacturing plant will likely carry home the message of the plant's failings more effectively than would a dry, oral recitation of how the construction went wrong. Similarly, a video of the devastation wrought by a natural disaster might carry more visceral weight in a dispute about insurance coverage than a mere spreadsheet with the facts summarising the damage. Conversely, the advanced predictive and analytic power of artificial intelligence stands to strip advocates of their ability to use these kinds of non-rational shortcuts to appeal to arbitrators. A computer is not susceptible to emotion and will not be any more impressed with a video than with a spreadsheet. There is no sense playing to a machine's 'System 1' biases,[5] because of course it has none.

The next generation of advocates in arbitration therefore faces potential ups and downs with technology. Today and for the coming years, counsel can make the most of technology to sway arbitrators by the slickness of their presentation; however, it is inevitable that technological progress may work to neutralise these kinds of tools aimed more at the arbitrators' visceral feelings about a case than at their rational faculties.

[5] The terms 'System 1' and 'System 2' refer, respectively, to the unconscious and conscious decision-making and operating processes of the brain, per Daniel Kahneman, *Thinking, Fast and Slow* (London: Penguin Books Ltd, 2011).

Whether or not that proves in the best interests of the arbitral process once again depends on what we ultimately believe arbitration should provide as a form of dispute resolution.

In this chapter, we first assess the current state of technology in international arbitration. We next explore how current and coming technologies stand to change the role and strategies of arbitrators and counsel alike. During that discussion, we examine the issue of human cognitive bias, and how such bias might be affected by the onset of more sophisticated machine technology in arbitration. Finally, we examine how the arbitral process, in decades to come, might ultimately be able to cut out human arbitrators and counsel altogether. We then pose the question whether such a process could ultimately be acceptable to the human stakeholders who profit or lose from decisions made in arbitral awards.

The Current State of Affairs: Same As It Ever Was?

One would have expected that by now technology would have had a real, positive impact on the time and costs of arbitration. The reality, however, is that time and costs of arbitration are on the rise. One reason for this apparent mismatch might be that, in attempting to connect the use of technology in proceedings and the time and costs of those proceedings, we are drawing the wrong parallel. The right parallel to draw is between the use of technology and instantaneous information. In doing so, we must not confuse the immediacy of acquiring information with our capacity to sift through that information, digest it, and use it to inform our decision-making. There is no technology to accelerate that latter process. Immediacy of communication and information does not necessarily translate into faster, more accurate decision-making. This may explain why international arbitration has been slow to embrace technology.[6]

The current state of affairs, as pointed out in the informative 2012 ICC Report on Managing Electronic Document Production,[7] is that technology for the time being is largely confined to document management and presentation. The NetCase initiative at the ICC is a virtual case room.[8] The immediate, live transcription of the record of hearings is another

[6] We leave aside for these purposes the phenomenon of documents-only arbitration, such as domain name disputes under the auspices of ICANN, and the like.

[7] See www.iccwbo.org/Advocacy-Codes-and-Rules/Document-centre/2012/ICC-Arbitration-Commission-Report-on-Managing-E-Document-Production.

[8] See Thomas Schultz, *Information Technology and Arbitration: A Practitioner's Guide* (The Netherlands: Kluwer Law International, 2006), p. 93.

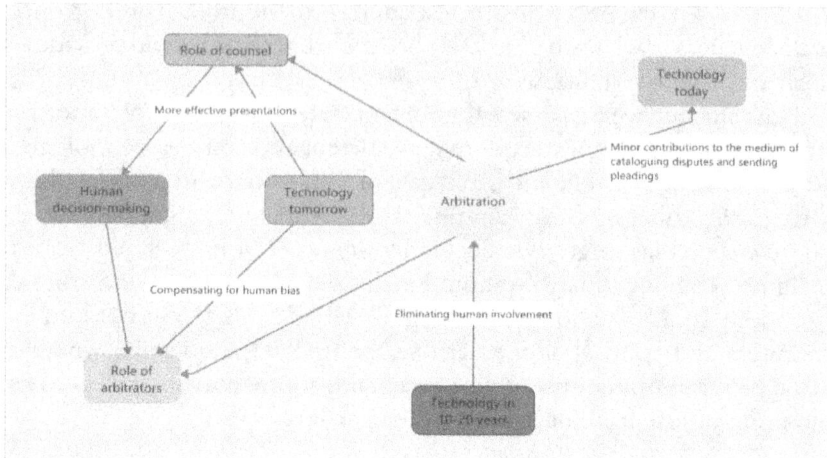

Figure 6.1 An illustration of the effects of technology upon arbitration, using the Mindjet software.

instance of technological advance, but it remains pages and pages of transcript in long hand. Moreover, memorials with hyperlinks to the exhibits, a wonderful invention, are still hundreds of pages long. We are still one step away from routine use of opening statements on animated slides, and the use of software such as Mindjet[9] to illustrate one's arguments by way of a mind map and other visual pyrotechnics with an immediate impact on the brain. If we did, presentations in hearings, lectures about arbitration, and even book chapters might more frequently look something like Figure 6.1.

Technology, Time Lapses and Transformation

Broadly speaking, we can divide technological innovations into those that have not affected the practice of arbitration, and those that have, or at some point will, affect it. For example, the advent of solar technology has not fundamentally altered the arbitral process (though it has contributed its fair share of arbitral disputes). By contrast, the spread of email has changed the method of delivery for the bulk of documents and pleadings exchanged during arbitrations (albeit not yet as much as one might expect

[9] Mindjet is a software company that permits interactive commentary on projects through a visual interface.

for so transformative a medium of communication). This chapter focuses on the latter category.

It is nonetheless difficult to predict exactly how, and when, a new technology will affect the practice of arbitration. This is because there is usually a lag time between when a technology is introduced and when it becomes widely used. Most technology thus takes a considerable amount of time to penetrate the popular consciousness and to permeate the workplace. For instance, the mobile phone was invented in 1973[10]; the first videoconference technology was shown at the 1964 World's Fair[11]; email was created in 1969 (granted, under the auspices of the US Department of Defence, so it was not widely available at first)[12]; the first mass-produced personal computer, the IBM PC, was released in 1981.[13] In all these examples, the new technology took several decades to become widely used. The reasons are many, but one common factor has been the declining cost and rising efficiency of each new technology.

There are exceptions to this slow pace of permeation. Some technological innovations have transformed the commercial and business landscape with remarkable speed. Hypertext Transfer Protocol, the backbone of the World Wide Web, was created in 1991. The Internet exploded soon thereafter. Apple released the iPhone, the first touchscreen smartphone, in 2007 and has since sold hundreds of millions of iPhones.

These examples are exceptions to the rule. Most technology, for reasons of cost or unfamiliarity, has taken its time to penetrate the legal market and the arbitral process. One reason for this state of affairs might be the legal field's conservative nature. The international arbitration community, stitching together a hybrid series of procedures from disparate traditions, is perhaps even less likely to embrace technological advance for fear of later challenges in the local courts at the enforcement stage. Nowadays parties exchange pleadings via email, and most communications from arbitrators are electronic. Testimony and argument in a hearing are routinely tracked via software that instantaneously transcribes what counsel, witness, and arbitrator(s) are saying – although until recently such technology still depended on a court reporter to feed in the transcription to the computer screen through an old-fashioned stenography machine. Despite

10 See www.cnn.com/2010/TECH/mobile/07/09/cooper.cell.phone.inventor.

11 See www.wired.com/2012/04/april-20–1964-picturephone-dials-up-first-transcontinental-video-call.

12 See www.inventorofemail.com/history_of_email.asp.

13 See www.wired.com/2011/08/0812ibm-5150-personal-computer-pc.

the slow move towards the use of technology, we are at a defining point when technology in arbitration may go from merely utilitarian to truly transformative. The issue is how arbitrators and counsel will cope with these transformations, and whether we ought to welcome them or to resist them.

The Virtual Tribunal

We can see where the fault lines of a progressive versus conservative legal landscape will lie with one piece of technology whose use straddles the boundary between the traditional and the transformative. That technology is video-conferencing. As noted earlier, video-conferencing has been technically feasible since 1964, but became commonplace only after the turn of the millennium. As the technology has improved and spread, it has increasingly been offered in arbitration as the mode for examination and cross-examination of witnesses who have difficulty appearing in person at hearings.

The use of video technology has provoked an interesting split in the opinions of arbitrators and counsel alike. On one side stand traditionalists who believe that it is fundamentally unsound to question a witness from a remote location. On the other side stand enthusiasts who believe that video technology will help eliminate much of the time and expense that bedevils arbitration hearings. And of course, several practitioners stand somewhere in between those two poles.

In the past, the traditionalists undoubtedly had a strong argument to make. The video technology then in use was relatively primitive, prone to breakdown and delay, and hardly an ideal medium for the art of cross-examination. From about 2010, however, newer and better video technology has enabled multiple users from disparate locations to meet and confer by video, in high definition and with no appreciable time lag. This newer generation of video technology largely eliminates the objections that many arbitrators and counsel had initially advanced against the use of video-conferencing in arbitral hearings. Furthermore, it makes feasible the possibility of not only examining witnesses remotely, but also conducting arbitrations with several of the participants and stakeholders in different locations.

Nonetheless, there remains a sizeable portion of practitioners who remain uncomfortable with the prospect of conducting all or part of an arbitral hearing by video. These objections all boil down, one way or another, to the loss of in-person contact that follows from a virtual proceeding. For example, video technology can be isolating, and isolation is unlikely to be conducive to the effective conduct of a hearing – especially where an arbitral tribunal consists of three members. Even though modern video technology can accommodate multiple video streams, with different video "chat rooms" for arbitrators and each side's counsel, these chat rooms cannot completely replicate the back-and-forth sidebars, comments, and attendant camaraderie that accompany a fully in-person hearing.

An arbitrator stuck in a room with a video remains stuck in that room at the end of the day, no matter how high-quality and high-tech that video link might be. Everything that one expects of a hearing – the formality and decorum of a quasi-judicial proceeding, as well as the informality of interpersonal interaction – is missing from a virtual proceeding. The loss of that formal and informal sense of participating in the ritual of a hearing should not be underestimated.[14] In many ways, that ritual provides the glue that binds and legitimises arbitration as a mode of dispute resolution. Hence, although the occasional witness may testify remotely, the advent of an entirely remote hearing, with all the stakeholders participating from different locations, raises concerns among arbitrators that the essence of the arbitral process will be missing.

From the perspective of counsel in arbitrations, the concern about video-conferencing is slightly different. When they object to video-conferencing, counsel do so because they fear that the reactions of a remote witness will not be sufficiently clear to counsel (or to the tribunal) for them to form an opinion about the strength and veracity of the witness's testimony. It is much easier to know when a witness is misremembering – or quite simply lying – if he or she is present in the room. However, it is at this juncture in the development of technology in arbitration that this sort of view exposes a deeper underlying belief. As noted earlier, the newest wave of high-definition video-conferencing provides as clear a picture of a participant on the screen as we would get if we were sitting right next to him or her in the room. The participant's facial expressions, body language, and voice tone are, if anything, magnified by the medium of the video-conference. It is no longer tenable with this kind of video to object that one cannot process a witness's non-verbal and subliminal cues.

[14] For one examination of the ritual aspects of arbitration, see generally Emmanuel Gaillard, *Sociology of Arbitration*, available at www.shearman.com/en/newsinsights/events/2014/11/gaillard-lectures-on-sociology-of-arbitration.

As technology continues to develop, we moreover face the prospect of even more immersive and realistic technology to simulate in-person interaction. As we write [2017], we stand on the verge of a revolution in virtual reality technology. Some of technology's titans, such as Google, Facebook, and Microsoft have recently released virtual reality headsets that will represent a step-change in current technology. These companies are vying with independent outfits such as Magic Leap to develop the cheapest and most realistic devices. The first such headsets have proved more useful for video games than for virtual hearings. Nevertheless, it is unlikely to take long before virtual reality headsets can effectively replace video-conferences as proxies for in-person meetings. With their three-dimensional, immersive quality, the headsets will provide a more realistic, real-time feel to a virtual meeting than even today's high-definition video-conferences.

The cost of such meetings over the next few years will be quite high and is thus unlikely to compete with the price of simply flying witnesses, arbitrators, and counsel to a single hearing location. However, that calculus will rapidly change, as it has done with all such technology. At that point, any objection about the immediacy of the medium and the difficulty of interacting with others in a hearing will be gone, although the reality will remain that a person might find him or herself in an empty room once he or she takes off the headset. All that would be left, then, as a potential objection to virtual hearings, is an indescribable preference for the 'feel' of dealing with a witness in person rather than remotely. The notion behind the 'feel' is that there is an ineffable component to in-person human contact, in which the participants are afforded a better chance to evaluate and assess the qualities of their interlocutors than they would be by phone, video, or hologram. The question remains whether any weight ought to be accorded to the consideration of something as unscientific and unspecific as an advocate's or an arbitrator's 'gut feeling'.

Is Human Decision-Making Flawed?

Not every case depends on whether a witness is telling the truth. Often arbitrators need to decide between two competing legal theories when facts are not in dispute, or to arrive at a result from evidence on both sides that is equally accurate and believable. Nonetheless, the issue of witness credibility, in one form or another, is central to the concept of an arbitral hearing. Likewise, the idea that an advocate's role is to persuade the arbitrator(s) of the rightness of his or her party's case underlies the role of counsel in hearings. If neither premise were true, we would not bother with hearings at all. Hence, it is necessary to examine what factors determine how an arbitrator decides a case.

At the sentimental level (for want of a better term), the fundamental issue is simply whether a witness is credible to the arbitrators. The witness's credibility will influence the arbitrators' assessment of the witness's evidence. If the arbitrators, for reasons articulated or unspoken (and perhaps felt only unconsciously), prefer the testimony of live witnesses, the appearance of those witnesses will carry greater weight. At the scientific level, however, there appears to be a disconnect between what the 'gut' feeling of arbitrators may be telling them about witnesses and the quality of the witnesses' evidence. Most people consider themselves good judges of character and able to distinguish a truthful witness from an untruthful or evasive one. Certain classes of occupation – police officers, intelligence professionals, and (to a lesser extent) litigation and arbitration specialists – are adjudged to be more competent than the norm in sifting out salient and truthful details in a complex fact pattern. However, studies have shown that most people perform no better than chance in distinguishing accurate testimony from the untruthful variety.[15] Therefore, lawyers, police, intelligence officers and other professionals have the same abilities as the proverbial man in assessing the truthfulness of testimonies.[16]

The cues that we take to be indications of false or misleading testimony – visible nervousness, failure to make eye contact, frequent blinking, fidgeting – often signify something else. Nevertheless, some people exhibit these signs when they lie. Sometimes a witness is nervous simply because he or she finds it stressful to testify; however, because we take such cues as proxies for the pattern we are looking for (in this case, untruthfulness), we associate the symptom with the wrong cause. What, then, motivates us to make decisions about the merits of testimony or a case? According to modern social and scientific research discussed later, our unconscious preferences and prejudices often pull us in a direction of which we are not consciously aware, and for reasons of which our conscious brains would greatly disapprove.

[15] Michael G. Aamodt and Heather Custer, 'Who Can Best Catch a Liar? A Meta-Analysis of Individual Differences in Detecting Deception', (2006) 15(1), *The Forensic Examiner*, 6–11.

[16] See, e.g. Rachel Adelson, 'Detecting Deception', (2004) 35(7), *Monitor on Psychology* 70; Paul Ekman and Maureen O'Sullivan, 'Who Can Catch a Liar', (1991) 46 (9), *American Psychologist*, 913–920 (September 1991).

We can see the effects of the pull that our unconscious brain exerts in a number of experiments that social psychologists have performed over the past two decades. For example, one American study sought to test out subconscious prejudices in hiring practices by sending out thousands of fictitious resumes to potential employers. For each position, the study designers provided at least two sets of resumes: the qualifications on each resume were identical, but the name of the applicant on one resume was stereotypically white, while the name on the other was stereotypically African-American. The study found that the white applicants were 50 per cent more likely to receive callbacks for interviews across all sectors of the job market.[17] Furthermore, a Canadian study in 2011 showed a similar preference for job applicants with English-sounding names over those with Chinese- or Indian-sounding names.[18]

The same pattern has been identified for unconscious gender bias. Researchers took the resume of a female psychologist and reproduced it hundreds of times, affixing a female name to some copies and a male name to others. The researchers then sent out the resume to psychology departments, asking them to rate the applicants' qualifications for an academic position. Even though the resumes contained identical qualifications from the same real-world psychologist, both male and female academics rated the qualifications of a 'male' applicant more highly than a female one.[19] The biases that these studies appear to demonstrate clearly operate on elite and sophisticated populations that, in a sense, 'ought to know better'. We therefore should not be filled with confidence that arbitrators and other lawyers are immune to these kinds of subconscious influences in their decision-making.

This is not to imply that arbitrators decide cases on the basis of racist, sexist, or overtly biased beliefs. Almost all arbitrators would find these beliefs repugnant; and in any event, the question of race, gender, religion, and other sociocultural flashpoints are rarely at the heart of

[17] Marianne Bertrand and Sendhil Mullainathan, *Are Emily and Greg More Employable than Lakisha and Jamal? A Field Experiment on Labor Market Discrimination*, MIT Department of Economics Working Paper No. 03–22 (2003).

[18] Philip Oreopoulos and Diane Dechief, *Why Do Some Employers Prefer to Interview Matthew, But Not Samir?* Metropolis British Columbia Centre of Excellence for Research on Immigration and Diversity Working Paper Series, No. 11–13 (September 2011).

[19] R. E. Steinpreis, K. A. Anders and D. Ritzke, 'The Impact of Gender on the Review of Curricula Vitae of Job Applicants and Tenure Candidates: A National Empirical Study', (1999) 41 (718), *Sex Roles*, 509–528; see also C. A. Moss-Racusin, J. F. Dovidio, et al., 'Science Faculty's Subtle Gender Biases Favor Male Students', (2012) 109(41), *Proceedings of the National Academy of Sciences of the United States of America*, 16474–16479.

international arbitrations. The issue, rather, is whether arbitrators *unconsciously* attribute greater weight to, say, the testimony of the white witness, the advocacy of the male counsel, and the opinion of the co-religionist co-arbitrator. We also are not exclusively referring to the cultural bias as a factor in subconsciously influencing arbitrators. Subconscious influence in judicial and quasi-judicial decision-making can take many forms.

Perhaps the most notorious example is the study of Israeli parole judges. When surveyed over an eight-month period, the percentage of parole grants that the judges made followed a predictable pattern: they would start their work in the morning and grant parole at an average rate of 65 per cent. As the day progressed, the number of grants decreased until lunchtime. Immediately after lunchtime, an applicant's chance of parole rose again to 65 per cent before steadily falling again. The severity of the applicants' crimes bore no relation to the order in which they came before the judges. The logical and inescapable conclusion of the study was that the judges were more likely to grant parole when they were well-fed and alert than when they became tired and hungry.[20]

Technology to the Rescue?

What do all of these studies about unconscious bias and human behaviour have to do with technology? The answer is that technology is reaching a phase in which devices can not only compensate for human shortcomings in decision-making, but also substitute their own, more accurate evaluation of the facts. The question then arises: would we want to use this kind of technology to determine the outcome of arbitration? In order to address this question, we firstly analyse the state of technology for the evaluation of testimony.

Technology today is capable of detecting minute changes in a witness's voice, mannerism, gaze, heart rate, and skin temperature. Detection of these changes may signal evidence of a change in the witness's credibility, from testimony that is accurate to testimony about which he is unclear, or about which he is simply prevaricating. However, such changes might also signal something else – a heart might start to beat faster for any number of reasons, and sometimes a higher skin temperature is just a higher skin temperature. Thus, the technology is simply a more powerful version of

[20] S. Danziger, J. Levav and L. Avnaim-Pesso, 'Extraneous Factors in Judicial Decisions', (2011) 108(17) *Proceedings of the National Academy of the Sciences in the United States of America*, 6889–6892.

the same human amateur lie detector apparatus that we use to evaluate witness credibility with our own eyes and ears. Just as we can misinterpret symptoms that sometimes accompany lying as proof positive of a lie, a machine measuring a suite of these symptoms (more than we detect with our eyes and ears) can still end up jumping to the wrong conclusion. That is one reason as to why the results of polygraph machines have never been deemed admissible as evidence in US courts, despite decades of improvement and refinement.

Recently, however, the state of technology has turned a corner: using functional magnetic resonance imaging (fMRI) machines, scientists have been able to identify regions of the brain that are involved in creating and processing a lie. The fMRI can detect when those regions are activated, and therefore, can – in theory – distinguish a truthful answer from a lie. Companies such as Cephos[21] and No Lie MRI[22] have marketed this technology as a reliable alternative to polygraph machines. Lawyers and scientists alike have questioned the accuracy of fMRIs and courts have yet to admit its results into evidence.[23]

In addition, fMRIs currently have physical limitations, as the subjects must lie still inside a large tube while answering questions, which makes it impractical for witness testimony. However, like almost all other technology, fMRIs are likely to become more accurate, practical, and affordable in the near future. Assuming that this kind of technology follows that common trajectory, we will soon be presented with machines that can reliably assess the quality of a witness's evidence. This evolution may lead to a number of new questions that, today, still remain hypothetical. Examples of such questions that are also illuminating for arbitration are the following:

1. If technology could determine a witness's veracity with virtually unerring accuracy, would we be forced to use it?
2. Would arbitrators face a challenge from a party for using that technology because the party felt that the arbitrators were abdicating their responsibility to adjudicate the case to a machine?
3. Would arbitrators face a challenge for *not* using technology when the party felt that arbitrators ought to use every tool at their disposal to determine the truth?

[21] See, e.g. www.brainsontrial.com/tag/cephos. [22] See www.noliemri.com.

[23] See G. Miller, 'fMRI Detection Fails a Legal Test', *Science*, 11 June 2010, available at www.science.sciencemag.org/content/328/5984/1336.1.

4. Would counsel hesitate to advance certain witnesses on the basis that they might not survive the scrutiny of such a machine (and would that be a bad thing)?
5. Would arbitrators draw an adverse inference from a witness willing to testify but unwilling to use the machine?

Technology and Advocacy[24]

To comprehend the complexity of high-tech arbitration, we must first consider the issues of manipulation, fairness, and a level playing field. Tribunals are mindful that the technologically advanced party might have the upper hand over an opponent who is less familiar with, or has less ready access to, technology. For instance, a case can be made much 'sexier' with clever use of visuals. A party with slick technological shortcuts to facilitate the tribunal's navigation might harbour the hope that this papers over (note the anachronistic metaphor) a comparatively weak case on the merits. Thus, on the part of tribunals there may be an added element of working backwards to avoid being dazzled or blinded by technology, so to speak, and to ensure that the parties are on common ground. Although one might disagree that tribunals ought to make such an effort to ensure equality of arms between the parties, this is not as straightforward as it might seem.

First of all, in order to compensate for the effect of technology, one has to perceive and acknowledge that one is being manipulated. It is easy in the abstract to note that one party uses interactive video during its presentation and another uses a flipchart and a marker. It is more difficult for an arbitrator to point to specific portions of a presentation that were stylistically effective but substantively lacking. In addition, it is difficult to think through the effects of these phenomena in real time. That is the very reason as to why appeals to the non-rational can be extremely effective.

Secondly, one must note that unconscious appeals to arbitrators can be counterintuitive. The party allegedly deprived of its sole asset by the expropriation of a powerful state may want to project a lack of means as a message about its plight to the tribunal. The absence of technological 'bells and whistles' might be a conscious ploy in that vein. In much the same way, the lawyers for wealthy white-collar defendants in American jury trials often deliberately wear shabby suits to convey the (subliminal) message that their client cannot afford to pay them a fortune.

[24] See in this regard also, Chapter 11, p. 272.

Thirdly, it should be considered that technology provides only one means for unbalancing the equilibrium between parties. There are other scenarios that may lead to an unlevel playing field and that may raise the question whether arbitrators should intervene to restore the parties' equality. One could wonder, for instance, whether arbitrators exercise a similar compensating function, for example, when one side's advocates consist of seasoned and accomplished veterans, and the other sides are new to arbitration and unknown to the tribunal. Also, the question arises whether arbitrators should go an extra distance crediting – or at least trying to unpack – an advocate's argument when that advocate is less fluent in the language of the arbitration than his or her opposing counsel. These questions address the core of what it means to be an advocate in an international arbitration. If an advocate is not there to persuade a tribunal, what purpose does he or she serve? A sufficiently well-prepared tribunal will be interested in the advocates' opinions of the facts and the law, but it will not need their help coming to its own conclusions. Likewise, a tribunal able to be on guard against appeals to subconscious mechanisms of persuasion will not be swayed by the 'Jedi Mind Tricks' of even the most accomplished advocates. What, then, are advocates for? In the future, they might well serve no purpose at all- and the same might be true for arbitrators.

Robot Justice?

The phenomena described in the previous sections concern whether and how arbitrators should use technology to aid in the process of their decision-making. Looming not much further on the horizon is a more sophisticated category of technology that raises an even more difficult issue: whether at some point, computers can and ought to substitute for humans as arbitrators. Let us again clarify that this is not the idle speculation of arbitral science fiction. Read the following newspaper snippet that appeared on the *Los Angeles Times* website on 18 March 2014:

> A shallow magnitude 4.7 earthquake was reported Monday morning five miles from Westwood, California, according to the U.S. Geological Survey. The temblor occurred at 6:25 a.m. Pacific time at a depth of 5.0 miles.
>
> According to the USGS, the epicenter was six miles from Beverly Hills, California, seven miles from Universal City, California, seven miles from Santa Monica, California, and 348 miles from Sacramento, California. In the past ten days, there have been no earthquakes magnitude 3.0 and greater centered nearby.

This article appeared a mere three minutes after the earthquake hit – impressive journalistic speed. In addition, while the prose will not win any Pulitzer Prizes, it is both grammatically coherent and perfectly readable. Why wouldn't it be? Because it was written by a computer programme.

As we already previously mentioned, journalism is hardly the only human redoubt to come under assault from the machines. Over the past five years, computers have begun to do the jobs of white-collar professionals with notable distinction. IBM's ground-breaking Watson computer, which beat a series of champions in a popular American game show in 2011, is now being used to diagnose medical conditions.[25] IBM and New York's Memorial Sloan-Kettering Cancer Centre have teamed up to improve Sloan-Kettering's diagnostic capabilities. In addition to the baseline information that it has been given, Watson absorbs all the information on new trials from peer-reviewed medical journals, information that it would take each doctor some 160 hours of reading weekly to maintain progress. Watson is now estimated to diagnose cancers with an accuracy rate of 90 per cent, as opposed to the 50 per cent rate for human doctors.[26]

The implications for lawyers should be obvious. As with medicine, law relies upon a vast trove of written knowledge that no single person can review and retain. Furthermore, as with medicine, there are differing and competing interpretations of data, coming from multiple sources and pointing to different conclusions. In addition, and again as with medicine, different stakeholders will favour different options, with substantial costs, and expenses accruing to some stakeholders, and a substantial financial windfall to others. It is important to mention that computers are not limited to the tasks of logical inference and calculation with which we habitually associate them. Take Figures 6.2–6.5 and the art associated with them.

As you may have guessed, these artistic renditions were created from the images by computer programs, under the auspices of Google.[27] These computer-generated images show that artificial intelligence is now capable of generating results that show, for want of a better word, imagination. A mere few years ago, no one would have credited computers with the ability to improvise in this way on a picture or image. Likewise, with the progress of artificial intelligence programmes such as Watson, it is

25 See www.businessinsider.com/ibms-watson-may-soon-be-the-best-doctor-in-the-world-2014–4.

26 See www.wired.co.uk/news/archive/2013–02/11/ibm-watson-medical-doctor/viewall.

27 See www.recode.net/2015/06/20/google-trained-computers-to-make-their-own-trippy-art.

Figure 6.2 An unaltered image of clouds.

conceivable that on the current trajectory, a computer would be able to serve as a fact-finder and arbitrator on its own within the next two decades, if not much sooner. Again, that is a conclusion that would have seemed inconceivable until very recently. But there is little doubt that such a computer would sift through the applicable law more thoroughly, assess the credibility of witness evidence more accurately, and deliberate more

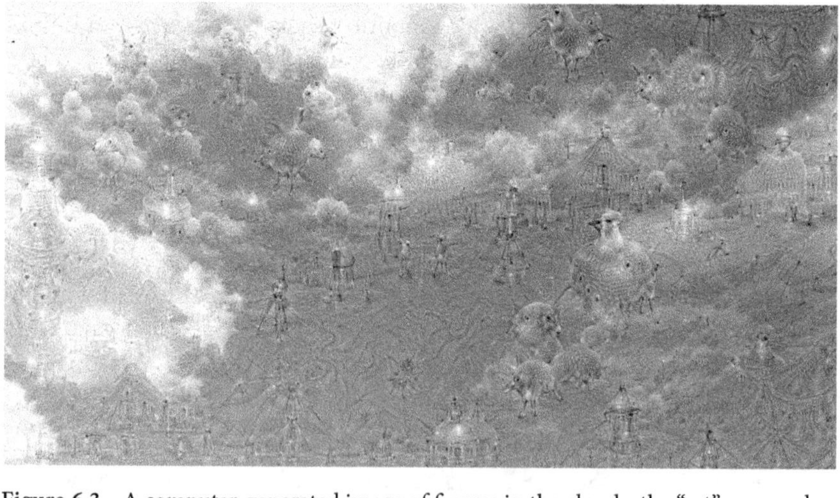

Figure 6.3 A computer-generated image of figures in the clouds; the "art" was made by a computer programme without human intervention.

Figure 6.4 An unaltered image of a tree in a field.

quickly than human arbitrators. Why, then, might parties object to the use of such a machine to decide their disputes?

One answer is that we have a reflexive preference for human control, irrespective of the knowledge that such control is limited and fallible. We

Figure 6.5 A computer-generated piece of artistic whimsy, again with no human intervention.

can see this preference in the substantial percentage of people with a fear of flying. Even though, statistically, their chance of dying in a plane is vanishingly small,[28] the notion of being at the mercy of a pilot and his or her onboard machinery stokes the fear of helplessness. By contrast, the chances of dying in a car accident (though still small) are approximately 500 times greater than that of dying in a plane; however, the fact that one is the driver provides a comfort that is in no way rational, but that nonetheless eliminates fear of travelling by car as a phobia worth noting. This same misperception of risk when one operates the controls feeds into an illusion of competence. Thus, the study showing that 88 per cent of American drivers (and, again, lest we think this an American phenomenon, 77 per cent of Swedish drivers) thought themselves above average in safety.[29] Incredibly, a more recent survey, albeit an unscientific one, showed that 80 per cent of drivers considered themselves average or above average even when texting or emailing while driving.[30]

The phenomenon of believing one is better at something than one actually is goes by the name 'illusory superiority'.[31] It is a form of cognitive bias. It may well be that our sense that technology cannot usurp the province of arbitral decision-makers is another form of illusory superiority. We know that computers until recently have been glorified calculating machines, able to process mind-numbing quantities of data, but otherwise only as useful as the programming in their software. We thus fail to acknowledge that computers have become capable of greatly more sophisticated tasks; and even if we do grudgingly acknowledge that fact, we find it hard to believe that a computer could perform typically human tasks as well as humans.

The advent of a potentially computerised arbitral process also presents challenges for counsel. The (human) arbitrator knows that he or she is a complex being, subconscious currents vying with his or her conscious thought processes as he or she grapples with the nuances of a case. The savvy counsel knows that he or she ought to engage with both the arbitrator's head and heart and must construct a narrative that is not only

[28] One recent study showed that the chances of dying in a car crash were about one in 36,000, whereas the chances of dying in a plane crash were one in 3.5 million; see www.economist.com/blogs/gulliver/2015/01/air-safety.

[29] Ola Svenson, 'Are We All Less Risky and More Skillful Than Our Fellow Drivers?' (1981) 47(2) *Acta Psychologica* 143–148.

[30] See www.cheapcarinsurance.net/24-of-drivers-admit-to-coming-close-to-causing-an-accident-while-texting.

[31] See www.en.wikipedia.org/wiki/Illusory_superiority.

logically persuasive, but also emotionally appealing. These considerations lose all relevance if one is arguing before a machine. Counsel's presentation style before a computer would, by any standard, be less flamboyant than before a human panel.

Indeed, the presence of a machine arbitrator raises the question of why counsel would be needed at all. Leaving aside the form and style of advocacy that may be designed to appeal to an arbitrator's sympathies and (unconscious) biases; the role of counsel is to draw the arbitrators' attention to the facts and law of the case that are in his or her client's favour. However, a computer presumably could know and process facts without the benefit of pointers from counsel. A computerised arbitral process therefore might mean a process not only without human arbitrators, but also without human counsel. Of course, it would remain the parties' choice whether to use a non-human arbitrator when one becomes feasible. Given our predilection and preference for human interaction, parties may decline the opportunity to have their dispute decided by a computer programme, even at the risk of having humans that are more fallible decide the case, and potentially decide it 'wrongly'.

An interesting scenario might present itself if one party is willing to use a machine as an arbitrator, but another is not. Would the arbitral institution be able to impose a non-human arbitrator on an objecting party, or would that constitute an abuse of process? It might be that parties and institutions adopt a hybrid approach, with parties appointing human and computer arbitrators. Perhaps the parties would appoint machine arbitrators, with a human chair; or vice versa.

Less radically, a human tribunal might consult with a computer programme as a supplement to, or check on, their decisions. The computer might therefore perform a role similar to that for which the tribunals use (and occasionally abuse) tribunal secretaries. This kind of approach might provide a happy medium between those who insist on human interaction in an arbitral proceeding and those willing to place their faith in the less fallible, but less palatable, prospect of 'robot justice'.

Conclusion

In 1986, one of the authors of this chapter took a seminar in university about Soviet politics. At the time, the Soviet Union was embarking on the risky (for the Soviet system) political experiment of 'Glasnost' (openness), even as it was embroiled in a ruinous war in Afghanistan. The price of oil, the Soviet Union's most valuable export commodity, dropped precipitously, and it suffered the catastrophic meltdown of a nuclear reactor at Chernobyl. Despite this confluence of circumstances, the seminar's instructor – a noted expert in Soviet studies – confidently assured us that the Soviet Union's political system would remain intact for the foreseeable future.

If by 'foreseeable future' the instructor meant the rest of the 1980s, then he was right. Nevertheless, one has to question, with hindsight, how this expert could have been so incorrect in the face of overwhelming evidence that the Soviet Union was on the verge of collapse. There is arguably similarly strong evidence to indicate that the way we conduct international arbitrations may be on the verge of fundamental transformation. There is widespread dissatisfaction among arbitration's users with the time and cost of proceedings and the 'business-as-usual' indifference of the arbitral community; at the same time, technology is becoming available and affordable to address users' grievances about the process. Despite this confluence of circumstances, arbitration's cognoscenti focus on every conceivable issue; the potential role of investment courts in lieu of tribunals; the problem of arbitrator selection; third-party funding; *except* the impending transformation in the way technology will mediate disputes.

If we are right that the arbitral community's complacency about the role of technology is ill-advised, then we must prepare to answer some concluding questions about how (if at all) the community might remain relevant in a technology-driven arbitral process. The first such question must be the extent to which a human appellate or review procedure remains suited, and relevant, as a check on a decision-making process largely influenced, or driven, by technology. However superior, or more accurate, or closer to the truth, a computer-led decision may prove to be, those affected by these decisions are still humans, and humans hold a reflexive preference for human oversight, even if it serves no rational purpose. Moreover, qualified experts may for some time dispute any consensus that computers provide "better" outcomes in arbitrations. All of this suggests that a computer-driven arbitral process will be subject to the oversight of a human arbitrator. The savings in time and cost generated by a technological dispute-resolution process would likely justify the additional human review. Whether that review would be *de novo* or more perfunctory might depend on the level of computerisation in the underlying arbitration itself.

A second, related question is how relevant the New York Convention would remain in the wake of a computer-driven arbitral process.[32] The

[32] See Chapter 7, p. 151.

justifications for refusing to enforce an arbitral award set forth in Article V of the New York Convention largely focus on phenomena that occur as a result of human error, chief amongst which is non-compliance with public policy under Article V(2)(b). Thirdly, one wonders what stage of computerisation that domestic courts may have reached by the time that computer programmes have become commonplace in international arbitration. The human reviewers of judicial and arbitral decision-making may therefore have to be computer scientists first, and jurists second.

Yogi Berra,[33] the baseball player and inadvertent apostle of the statement of the obvious, once allegedly quipped, 'Predictions are hard to make, especially about the future'. This chapter has attempted to trace the likely path of technology in arbitral proceedings from today until the next generation of arbitrators (if there is a next generation). Future generations will determine how accurate or inaccurate we were about the prevalence of technology in arbitral procedure and decision-making. The one certainty to which we can point is that, as arbitration is increasingly criticised for getting slower and more expensive than users expect and want, technology that could be used in arbitration is becoming cheaper and more sophisticated. The economics of dispute resolution thus suggest an inflexion point somewhere in the next decade, when the benefits of technology are brought to improve the arbitration process that we know today. O brave new world, that has such programmes in it . . .

[33] www.en.wikipedia.org/wiki/Yogi_Berra.

PART II

Arbitration, Arbitrators, Counsel and the Internet

7

E-Arbitration Agreements and E-Awards: Arbitration Agreements Concluded in an Electronic Environment and Digital Arbitral Awards

REINMAR WOLFF

Summary: Electronic arbitration agreements and electronic arbitral awards test the boundaries of traditional form provisions. Arbitration agreements must typically be concluded in writing and may need to be submitted to court. Arbitral awards usually have to be rendered in writing and have to bear the arbitrators' signatures, have to be delivered to the parties and have to be submitted to court in order to be recognized and enforced. A multitude of national laws, which are harmonized only in part, govern these issues. If arbitration agreements or arbitral awards are invoked before foreign courts, the same issues of form are even governed by another legal regime. This contribution undertakes to distinguish the relevant scenarios and to identify the applicable rules in each case.

Introduction

Technology promises a brave new world for international arbitration: a paperless, cost-efficient and fast alternative for some or all stages of international arbitral proceedings. The potential for technology in international arbitration does, however, end where key legal instruments are denied legal recognition. The most important of these legal instruments are arbitration agreements and arbitral awards. Both of these instruments are commonly subject to specific form requirements: arbitration agreements are often to be concluded in writing and arbitral awards usually are to be made in writing and to be signed by the arbitrators. Some of these form requirements date back to the times when the exchange of telegrams reflected the most modern technology to conclude arbitration agreements (see Article II(2) of the New York Convention [NYC][1]). The more technology progressed, the more pressing the question became of whether these old provisions evolve with technology or whether they effectively bar the use of digital means for the conclusion of arbitration agreements and the making of arbitral awards. This is particularly relevant since the New York Convention has proven to be too successful to be amended[2] so that, for the time being, solutions have to be provided under the current law.

I. Digital Arbitration Agreements

Arbitration agreements concluded in an electronic environment raise specific issues in terms of form and other prerequisites for validity. In order to illuminate the factual background, the relevant scenarios will be identified in a first step (see section A). As the validity of domestic arbitration agreements (see section B) and the recognition of foreign arbitration agreements (see section C) follow different rules, both have to be dealt with separately.

A. Relevant Fact Situations

The electronic conclusion of arbitration agreements can assume various shapes that mainly include declarations by email or through a web application, either of which may be complemented by a declaration by conduct, e.g. by delivery of the goods ordered. Declarations through a web application in particular include 'click-wrap' declarations for which the user clicks an 'ok' or 'agree' button. The web application will technically not permit to proceed further and complete the declaration without such click. Web-based declarations may also assume the form of 'browse-wrap' declarations for which the user does not click a button but simply downloads a file or otherwise accesses a website under the terms displayed thereon.

B. Domestic Arbitration Agreements

Domestic arbitration agreements that have been concluded in an electronic environment raise issues of contract conclusion (see section 1) and, more importantly, of validity in terms of form (see section 2). A last issue

1 Convention on the Recognition and Enforcement of Foreign Arbitral Awards, New York, 10 June 1958, 330 UNTS 38 (1959).

2 See Report of the Working Group on Arbitration on the work of its thirty-third session, A/CN.9/485, paras. 60 *et seq.*

at the interface between law and practice is the submission of an electronic arbitration agreement to court where it is legally required (see section 3).

1. Contract Conclusion

If the parties did not agree otherwise, the conclusion of an arbitration agreement is governed by the contract law at the place of arbitration.[3] This follows from Article 34(2)(a)(i) of the UNCITRAL Model Law on International Commercial Arbitration (ICA-ML), which on its face only provides for a conflict of law rule for the agreement's validity. Since formation of contracts and their validity may be difficult to distinguish and not properly concluded contracts have the same effect as invalid contracts, this rule is to be applied also to the law governing the arbitration agreement's conclusion.[4]

As the general rules for the conclusion of contracts are not harmonized, no general determination may be made as to how agreements are concluded in a digital environment. Generally, however, contracts may be concluded by email.[5] The same conclusion can be drawn regarding contracts concluded through web applications as long as the statement or conduct indicates an acceptance of an offer that has been made on the website.[6] While click-wrap declarations usually express consent,[7] the mere

[3] For the controversy whether the choice of a law governing the main contract also constitutes an implied agreement on the choice of the law governing the arbitration agreement, see P. Nacimiento, in H. Kronke, P. Nacimiento, D. Otto and N. C. Port (eds.), *Recognition and Enforcement of Foreign Arbitral Awards, A Global Commentary on the New York Convention* (Alphen aan den Rijn: Kluwer Law International, 2010), pp. 224 *et seq.*; S. Wilske and T. J. Fox, in R. Wolff (ed.), *New York Convention, Convention on the Recognition and Enforcement of Foreign Arbitral Awards of 10 June 1958, Commentary* (Munich, Oxford, and Baden-Baden: C. H. Beck, Hart Publishing and Nomos, 2012), Article II paras. 232 *et seq.*

[4] Kammergericht, KGR 1996, 68, 70 (Article V NYC); A. J. van den Berg, *The New York Arbitration Convention of 1958: Towards a Uniform Judicial Interpretation* (Deventer etc.: Kluwer Law and Taxation, 1981), pp. 290 *et seq.*; P. Schlosser, in F. Stein and M. Jonas (eds.), *Kommentar zur Zivilprozessordnung*, vol. X: sects. 1025–1066, 23rd ed. (Tübingen: Mohr Siebeck, 2014), annex to section 1061 para. 68.

[5] See, e.g. C. v. Bar, E. Clive, H. Schulte-Nölke et al., *Principles, Definitions and Model Rules of European Private Law Draft Common Frame of Reference (DCFR)* (available at http://ec.europa.eu/justice/contract/files/european-private-law_en.pdf, last visited 10 September 2017), II.4:204 comment A, p. 335; for the legal situation in the Netherlands, see Chapter 5, p. 109.

[6] See, e.g. II.–4:204 *DCFR*.

[7] Not even broadly discussed e.g. by European Court of Justice, *Jaouad El Majdoub* v. *CarsOnTheWeb.Deutschland GmbH*, C-322/14 para. 39 (choice of forum clause under the Brussels I Regulation); *Lieschke, Jackson & Simon* v. *Realnetworks Inc.*, 2000 WL 631341 (E.D. Ill.) = XXV Y.B. Com. Arb. 530 (2000).

use of a website (browse-wrap) expresses consent only if such a meaning was made sufficiently clear on the website so that the other party could reasonably understand the use of the website as conduct indicating consent.[8] This is usually not the case if the relevant information is hidden somewhere below the 'download' button on the website.[9]

The law governing the conclusion of contracts is also called upon to determine the criteria for the inclusion of general terms and conditions in a contract. This is particularly relevant since contracts concluded through web applications rarely rely on individually negotiated contracts, but usually employ general terms and conditions. The national laws on general terms and conditions, at least if the United Nations Convention on Contracts for the International Sale of Goods (CISG) does not apply,[10] are not harmonized just as other rules on the conclusion of contracts are not.

National laws will typically provide for rules on arbitration agreements in general terms and conditions to the following effect:[11] if the arbitration agreement is contained in a document that is separate from the main contract, it must be referenced (by general reference to the terms and conditions or, depending on the applicable law, by specific reference to the arbitration clause contained therein), either implicitly or explicitly. The customer must be provided with a reasonable opportunity to take note of the general terms and conditions' content, usually by transmission of the general terms and conditions (including the arbitration clause) to the other party at the latest at the time of the conclusion of the contract. Finally, the general terms and conditions must be drafted in the language of the contract or in a global language and must be sufficiently transparent. Precise determinations are, again, subject to the applicable national law.

2. Form Requirements for Validity

Unlike its conclusion, the form of the arbitration agreement raises specific issues. The specific treatment of form requirements already starts with the applicable law. While the law governing the conclusion of an

[8] Cf. II.–4:102 *DCFR*.

[9] *Specht* v. *Netscape Communications Corp.*, 306 F.3d 17 (2002).

[10] Prevailing view, see U. Schroeter, in P. Schlechtriem and I. Schwenzer (eds.), *Commentary on the UN Convention on the International Sale of Goods (CISG)*, 4th ed. (Oxford: Oxford University Press, 2016), Article 14 para. 40.

[11] Such rules are time and again (but incorrectly, see section C 1) assumed to be part of the autonomous rules under Article II NYC; for details on and references for the following criteria see Wolff, in Wolff (ed.), *NYC* (fn 3), Article II paras. 132 *et seq.*, 137 *et seq.*; Schramm, Geisinger and Pinsolle, in Kronke, Nacimiento, Otto and Port (eds.), *NYC* (fn 3), p. 62.

arbitration agreement is determined by the parties' choice or, in absence of such choice, by the law at the place of arbitration, the arbitration agreement's form is governed by the *lex arbitri*, i.e. by the applicable arbitration law (cf. Articles 1(2), 7 ICA-ML). Traditionally, most national arbitration laws entail form requirements for arbitration agreements, in particular various requirements for written form. Unlike the rules on contract conclusion, the form of arbitration agreements has been subject to repeated attempts of harmonization. A lack of the prescribed form is mostly considered to invalidate arbitration agreements, although a number of common law jurisdictions accept the validity of arbitration agreements under general contract law (e.g. section 81(1)(b) of the English Arbitration Act 1996).

a) Requirement of Written Form Provisions under national law that demand written form for arbitration agreements without providing further detail shall serve as a starting point for the discussion. Section 2 of the US Federal Arbitration Act which simply requires a 'written provision' may serve as an example for such provision. The interpretation of such lean wording, however, is always embedded in its national context. In fact, national laws have defined 'in writing' requirements inconsistently.[12]

aa) *Lack of Complementary Legislation on Electronic Communication* If the national law (unlike US law) does not contain specific provisions on electronic communication, two general approaches can be distinguished. Under the first approach, electronic communication does not qualify as being in writing. In favour of this approach, the traditional understanding of writing, namely fixing characters readable for humans on paper or other surfaces, may be invoked. From that perspective, an email (and even more so communication through web forms) cannot be considered to be in writing, as it does not fix characters but only displays them on a computer screen. Emails do not necessarily materialize and the fulfilment of the form requirement cannot depend on whether or not the email is subsequently printed. Given that electronic communication was unavailable at the time most of these provisions were enacted, a narrow understanding of written form can also rely on a historic argument to the extent the

[12] T. Landau, 'The Requirement of a Written Form for an Arbitration Agreement When "Written" Means "Oral"', in A. J. van den Berg (ed.), *International Commercial Arbitration: Important Contemporary Questions*, ICCA Congress Series, vol. XI (Alphen aan den Rijn: Kluwer Law International, 2003), pp. 19, 20.

historic legislator's understanding is relevant under the applicable rules of interpretation.

The counter-position recognizes electronic form as also being in writing. This position can rely on the plain contemporary meaning of the term, which is not restricted to materialized characters, but also comprises emails that have been 'written'. Moreover, the purpose of written form will usually be to provide evidence for the conclusion of the arbitration agreement or its content.[13] This purpose can equally be met by electronic communication, which has widely substituted formerly paper-based communication. Given the business need for electronic communications and its common use in everyday business, the better reasons militate for an extensive interpretation of 'in writing'.

Similar arguments can be made if the *lex arbitri* requires the parties' signatures as part of the written form requirement. The inherited meaning of the term 'signature' and the fact that historically no other signatures but handwritten signatures were imaginable may be invoked in favour of a restrictive interpretation. Again, the modern use of the term 'signature', which may also comprise electronic signatures, allows for an interpretation that accommodates today's business needs. It will, however, be intricate to determine, on an abstract level, the precise specifications for such electronic signatures.[14]

bb) *Complementary Legislation on Electronic Communication is in Place*

While both the requirements of written form and of signatures can reasonably be interpreted in a way that also captures electronic form equivalents, a considerable risk remains that the courts do not follow this route and deny recognition of electronically concluded arbitration agreements. In light of this risk, parties will often refrain from using electronic communication for the conclusion of contracts including arbitration agreements.[15]

This risk, which is not limited to arbitration agreements but also encompasses other declarations that require written form or signatures by law, often gives rise to complementary legislation that sets out the conditions under which traditional form requirements can be met by electronic

[13] Traditionally, the form requirement has often been assigned the purpose of providing a warning, see G. A. Alvarez, 'Article II(2) of the New York Convention and the Courts' in A. J. van den Berg (ed.), *Improving the Efficiency of Arbitration Agreements and Awards: 40 Years of Application of the New York Convention*, ICCA Congress Series, vol. IX (Alphen aan den Rijn: Kluwer Law International, 1999), pp. 67, 73; van den Berg, *NYC* (fn 4), p. 173.

[14] For details, see below bb(ii).

[15] See Otto, in Kronke, Nacimiento, Otto and Port (eds.), *NYC* (fn 3), p. 176.

communication. In fact, states have frequently enacted such complementary legislation, which usually is detached from their arbitration law and contained in separate laws. For this reason, examples of complementary legislation shall be discussed here regardless of the precise form requirements that the arbitration law of that state sets out.

(i) 'In Writing' Requirement

Jurisdictions usually entail detailed definitions of the traditional requirements for written form. These definitions vary depending on the form requirement's purpose and complementary legislation also ties in with the specific requirements. German law may serve as an example for a national law in which written form does not only require legible information, but also pursues additional purposes such as warning of the parties or protection against forgery. Consequently, written form prescribed by German law generally requires the issuer's personal signature (section 126(1) of the German Civil Code). In order to comply with the electronic equivalent of this written form requirement, the issuer must add its name to the declaration and provide the electronic document with a qualified electronic signature (section 126a(1) of the German Civil Code).[16]

The proper electronic equivalence for written form becomes clearer if the purposes of the particular form requirement are distinguished. This is the approach chosen by Article 6(1) of the 1996 UNCITRAL Model Law on Electronic Commerce (EC-ML) and by Article 9(2) of the 2005 UN Convention on the Use of Electronic Communications in International Contracts (Electronic Communications Convention). Under these provisions, a requirement of written form set out by law is met by a data message if the information contained therein is accessible so as to be usable for subsequent reference. These provisions focus on the basic purpose of any 'in writing' requirement, namely to produce legible information.[17] Consequently, they do not require a handwritten signature or its electronic equivalent for written form.

(ii) Signature Requirement

If the applicable *lex arbitri* requires the arbitration agreement to bear the parties' signatures (be it as part of a requirement of written form, be it as an additional requirement), national legislation often provides for electronic

[16] For the approach of the Dutch legislature, see Chapter 5, p. 109 *et seq.*

[17] UNCITRAL Model Law on Electronic Commerce, Guide to Enactment, para. 50; Explanatory note by the UNCITRAL secretariat on the United Nations Convention on the Use of Electronic Communications in International Contracts, paras. 143 *et seq.*

equivalents. Although the rationale underlying signature requirements is clearer as compared to that of written form requirements, national legislation still provides for regulations that differ significantly.

Most commonly, signatures are understood to identify the creator of a declaration, to document its consent and to provide a high degree of reliability for both. Based on these purposes of a handwritten signature, Article 7(1) EC-ML follows a flexible approach in determining its electronic equivalent. The provision reads: 'Where the law requires a signature of a person, that requirement be met in relation to a data message if (a) a method is used to identify that person and to indicate that person's approval of the information contained in the data message; and (b) that method is as reliable as was appropriate for the purpose for which the data message was generated or communicated, in the light of all the circumstances, including any relevant agreement.' This approach was influential – the Model Law on Electronic Commerce has been adopted in 69 states and in a total of 145 jurisdictions worldwide.[18] It has successfully implemented inter alia the principles of technological neutrality (i.e. the rules do not relate to a specific technology so that they do not need to be revised if technology progresses, cf. Article 2 lit. a) and functional equivalence (i.e. the purposes and functions of the traditional requirements are analyzed and their electronic counterparts are determined based on these purposes and functions; see inter alia Articles 6(1) and 7(1)). Such technologically neutral approach, however, comes at the price of diminished legal certainty and predictability: the parties bear the risk whether the competent court or arbitral tribunal will hold their electronic signature's reliability 'appropriate . . . in the light of all the circumstances' as required by Article 7(1)(b) EC-ML. As mentioned earlier (section bb), diminishing such uncertainty is one of the grounds for complementary legislation to define electronic equivalents to traditional form requirements.

Two subsequent harmonizing instruments drafted under UNCITRAL's auspices undertook to remedy this shortcoming. The 2001 UNCITRAL Model Law on Electronic Signatures (ES-ML) maintains a broad concept of electronic signatures (Article 2(a)), reiterates Article 7(1)(b) EC-ML's reliability test (Article 6(1)) and establishes the (elsewhere) so-called digital signature by adding criteria for an electronic signature to be considered reliable in its Article 6(3) (namely unique link, sole control and detectability of alterations). If the parties use electronic signatures that

[18] See www.uncitral.org/uncitral/en/uncitral_texts/electronic_commerce/1996Model_status.html (last visited 10 September 2017).

meet these criteria, the signatures' effectiveness can reliably be determined before the signature is actually supplied; this resolves the uncertainty that always accompanies the application of Article 6(1) ES-ML's reliability test by a future court or arbitral tribunal.[19] Article 12(2) ES-ML allows for cross-border recognition by recognizing underlying foreign certificates if they offer a substantially equivalent level of reliability. This provision intends to alleviate the otherwise unreasonable burden on suppliers of certification services to obtain licences in multiple jurisdictions.[20]

The 2005 Electronic Communications Convention, which entered into force in 2013, adds to Article 7(1)(b) EC-ML's reliability test (Article 9(3)(b)(i)) an exception, namely that the electronic signature does not need to pass the reliability test if both the identity of the party and its intention are proven in fact (Article 9(3)(b)(ii)). Therefore, under the Convention, no party can invoke the reliability test to repudiate its signature where both its identity and intent can be proven otherwise.[21] Under this concept, the signature requirement becomes evidentiary in nature.

National laws often deviate from the approach taken by UNCITRAL's harmonizing instruments. In the European Union (EU), Article 25(2) eIDAS Regulation[22] provides for full legal equivalence of qualified electronic signatures and handwritten signatures. Qualified electronic signatures have to meet certain requirements, have to be created by a qualified electronic signature creation device and have to be based on a qualified certificate for electronic signatures (Article 3(12) eIDAS Regulation). The validity of a qualified electronic signature requires that the qualified certificate supporting the signature be issued by a qualified trust service provider (Article 32(1)(b) eIDAS Regulation); such qualified status is granted by a supervisory body. Mutual recognition within the EU Member States is safeguarded inter alia by Articles 4 and 6 eIDAS Regulation; trust service providers in non-EU states are to be recognized only on the basis of bilateral treaties (Article 14 eIDAS Regulation).

The United States pursues a concept of electronic signatures that differs significantly from the detailed reliability criteria set out in the UNCITRAL Model Law on Electronic Signatures and in the EU eIDAS Regulation.

19 UNCITRAL Model Law on Electronic Signatures, Guide to Enactment, paras. 4, 76.

20 UNCITRAL Model Law on Electronic Signatures, Guide to Enactment, para. 153.

21 Explanatory note by the UNCITRAL secretariat on the United Nations Convention on the Use of Electronic Communications in International Contracts, para. 164.

22 Regulation (EU) No. 910/2014 of the European Parliament and of the Council of 23 July 2014 on electronic identification and trust services for electronic transactions in the internal market and repealing Directive 1999/93/EC, OJ 2014 No. L 257, p. 73.

The 2000 Electronic Signatures in Global and National Commerce Act (E-SIGN) sets out as a general rule that a signature may not be denied legal effect, validity or enforceability solely because it is in electronic form (15 U.S.C. § 7001(a)(1)). 15 U.S.C. § 7006(5) defines 'electronic signature' broadly as 'an electronic sound, symbol, or process, attached to or logically associated with a contract or other record and executed or adopted by a person with the intent to sign the record'. As a result, a party's qualified electronic signature, its scanned handwritten signature and even its typewritten name under an email all meet a signature requirement in law including if such requirement is set out for arbitration agreements. The waiver of any reliability test is substituted by an evidentiary concept: whoever relies on an electronic signature bears the burden of proof if the identity of the signature's holder or its consent is disputed. The electronic signature's reliability remains relevant only for meeting that burden. The 1999 Uniform Electronic Transactions Act (UETA), which is more comprehensive than E-SIGN, follows the same approach. Under this Act, if a law requires a signature, an electronic signature satisfies the law (section 7(d) UETA). Section 9(a) UETA explicitly sets out the evidentiary approach: 'An . . . electronic signature is attributable to a person if it was the act of the person. The act of the person may be shown in any manner, including a showing of the efficacy of any security procedure applied to determine the person to which the electronic record or electronic signature was attributable.' Similar to the UNCITRAL instruments, the US legislation easily allows for the recognition of foreign signatures.

As an interim result, the electronic equivalences for written form and signatures are as diverse as the form provisions for arbitration agreements under national law.

b) Harmonized Form Requirements In light of the variety of form requirements for arbitration agreements under national law and the relevance of this issue in international trade, the need for harmonization was (and is) obvious. Some states have adopted the form standard for recognition of foreign arbitration agreements under Article II(2) NYC (see section C 2) as the form requirement for arbitration agreements under their national *lex arbitri*.[23] By setting out an autonomous standard for the recognition of foreign arbitration agreements, the New York Convention, however, never intended such *de facto* harmonization.

[23] G. B. Born, *International Commercial Arbitration*, 2nd ed., 3 vols. (Alphen aan den Rijn: Kluwer Law International, 2014), p. 694.

aa) *Contained in Means of Telecommunication which Provide a Record of the Agreement, Article 7(2)(2) ICA-ML 1985* The earliest attempt to create unified form requirements for arbitration agreements under national law was undertaken by the UNCITRAL Model Law on International Commercial Arbitration 1985. Legislation based on this model law has been adopted in 57 states (and 80 jurisdictions in total)[24] and has served as a blueprint for other states. Under Article 7(2)(2) ICA-ML 1985, an agreement is in writing if it is contained in a document signed by the parties – details of this option have been previously discussed in section a – or in an exchange of letters, telex, telegrams or other means of telecommunication which provide a record of the agreement.

This definition clearly covers arbitration agreements that have been concluded by exchange of emails.[25] Arbitration agreements concluded as click-wrap contracts likewise meet these requirements:[26] the relevant text of the declaration is transferred from the website operator to the customer on whose screen it is displayed. By pressing the 'ok' button or otherwise accepting the offer, the customer's declaration is transferred back to the website that completes the exchange of declarations. Within this exchange, either the wording of the arbitration agreement or a link or other reference to a separate document, website or other source containing such an arbitration agreement may be transferred. To meet the form requirement, such link or reference suffices as confirmed by Article 7(2)(3) ICA-ML 1985, provided that the reference to the arbitration clause is sufficient to incorporate the arbitration clause according to the law applicable to the formation of the arbitration agreement (see previous section 1).

Browse-wrap agreements comply with Article 7(2)(2) ICA-ML 1985 only if the customer's acceptance is transferred back to the website

24 See www.uncitral.org/uncitral/en/uncitral_texts/arbitration/1985Model_arbitration_status.html (last visited 10 September 2017). A further 17 states (and 28 jurisdictions in total) have adopted the 2006 UNCITRAL Model Law on International Commercial Arbitration, taking the total of adopting states to 74 (and 108 jurisdictions).

25 C. Tautschnig, 'Legal Challenges and Opportunities for the Next Generation of Online Arbitration' in C. Klausegger et al. (eds.), *Austrian Yearbook on International Arbitration 2015* (Vienna, Munich and Bern: Manz, C. H. Beck and Stämpfli, 2015), pp. 87, 92 *et seq.*; W. Voit, in H.-J. Musielak and W. Voit (eds.), *Zivilprozessordnung mit Gerichtsverfassungsgesetz*, 14th ed. (Munich: Vahlen, 2017), section 1031 para. 4 (on section 1031(1) of the German Code for Civil Procedure, an adoption of Article 7(2)(1) ICA-ML 1985).

26 M. A. Alqudah, 'Enforceability of Arbitration Clauses in Online Business-to-Consumer Contracts', (2011) 28 *J. Int. Arb.* 67, 72.

operator – otherwise no exchange takes place.[27] Whether such back transfer occurs depends on the means by which the customer expresses its consent: simply reading does not transfer the acceptance (which, if any, can only be one by conduct) back to the website operator while the download of a file does if such a download includes the customer's acceptance.

bb) *Recorded in Any Form, Option I Article 7(3), (4) ICA-ML 2006* Following discussions within UNCITRAL's Working Group II, the ICA-ML 2006 offers two alternative options for Article 7. The first option in its Article 7(4) defines 'in writing' for a digital environment as follows: 'The requirement that an arbitration agreement be in writing is met by an electronic communication if the information contained therein is accessible so as to be useable for subsequent reference; "electronic communication" means any communication that the parties make by means of data messages; "data message" means information generated, sent, received or stored by electronic, magnetic, optical or similar means, including, but not limited to, electronic data interchange (EDI), electronic mail, telegram, telex or telecopy.' This wording literally transformed Articles 9(2), 4(b) and (c) of the Electronic Communications Convention (see section a bb). Email, click-wrap and browse-wrap all comply with this form requirement.[28]

cc) *Liberty of Form, Option II Article 7 ICA-ML 2006* Option II Article 7 ICA-ML 2006 entirely abolishes the 'in writing' requirement. Under national laws that have adopted this provision, digitally concluded arbitration agreements cannot be invalid for a lack of form.

c) Other Form Requirements Under the *Lex Arbitri*, in Particular for Consumer Contracts Some jurisdictions entail specific form provisions for non-standard cases, an example being section 1031(5) of the German Code of Civil Procedure. Under this provision, arbitration agreements to which a consumer is a party must be contained in a document that has been personally signed by the parties and must not contain agreements other than those referring to the arbitral proceedings. As with other form provisions under national law (see section a), first the existence of provisions defining form standards for electronic communication must be

[27] Dissenting Alqudah, 'Enforceability of Arbitration Clauses' (fn 26), 72 (always compliance).

[28] Cf. Tautschnig, 'Legal Challenges' (fn 25), 92.

determined (which indeed exist in section 1031(5) of the German Code of Civil Procedure). Absent such provisions, the applicable standards must be developed by interpretation of the form provision (see section a aa).

3. *Submission to Court* Typically, arbitration agreements are to be submitted to court if their existence or content is disputed in court proceedings or if such submission is specifically required by law. The Model Law on International Commercial Arbitration orders submission of domestic arbitration agreements for the recognition and enforcement of a subsequent arbitral award. While Article 35(2)(1) ICA-ML 1985 requires supply of 'the original arbitration agreement…or a duly certified copy thereof', this requirement has been abandoned in the Model Law's 2006 revision in order to reflect Article 7's modified understanding of 'in writing' in Article 35.[29] It is acknowledged that, contrary to its at least ambiguous wording, Article 35(2)(1) ICA-ML 1985 stipulates nothing but an evidentiary requirement.[30]

The procedure for the introduction of electronic communication in litigation is generally subject to the national law on civil procedure, which is not harmonized and differs largely. For instance, while emails qualify as documentary evidence under the law of England and Wales, German law classifies emails as evidence by inspection.[31] Unsurprisingly, the means of evidencing electronic communication (as a hard copy, by transmission to court, by transmission to an expert or by other means) differ from state to state as much as the courts' technical equipment does.

Legislation implementing Article 35(2)(1) ICA-ML 1985 raises additional questions as the notions of 'original arbitration agreement' and 'duly certified copy thereof' are difficult to reconcile with electronic communication. Electronic communication may easily be (re-)produced in an unlimited number of indistinguishable copies. Moreover, if the original was understood as the message originally fixed by the sender, the addressee would never receive the original.[32] These notional challenges

29 Note by the Secretariat, A/CN.9/606, para. 22; Report of the United Nations Commission on International Trade Law on the work of its thirty-ninth session, A/61/17, para. 171.

30 J. Münch, in W. Krüger and T. Rauscher (eds.), *Münchener Kommentar zur Zivilprozessordnung mit Gerichtsverfassungsgesetz und Nebengesetzen*, vol. III: sects. 1025–1109, EGZPO, GVG, EGGVG, UKlaG, Internationales und Europäisches Zivilprozessrecht, 4th ed. (Munich: C. H. Beck, 2014), section 1064 para. 4 (on section 1064(1) of the German Code for Civil Procedure, an adoption of Article 35(2)(2) ICA-ML 1985).

31 Huber, in Musielak and Voit (eds.), *ZPO* (fn 25), section 371 para. 12.

32 Explanatory note by the UNCITRAL secretariat on the United Nations Convention on the Use of Electronic Communications in International Contracts, para. 166; H. A. Haloush,

are mastered by harmonizing instruments: under Article 8(1) EC-ML, a data message qualifies as an original if its integrity is reliably assured and if it can be displayed. The same solution has been implemented in Article 9(4) of the Electronic Communications Convention. Since any copy amounts to an original if it passes this test, the definition of a (certified or simple) copy becomes meaningless. If such legislation equating electronic communications is not in place, the national law on submission requirements is subject to interpretation. In particular if such requirements trace back to Article 35(2)(1) ICA-ML 1985, the Model Law on Electronic Commerce should be taken into account for the proper understanding of what an original is. In any event, it would be formalistic and inconsistent to legally grant validity to electronically concluded arbitration agreements but to deny subsequently their enforceability on grounds that no original can be submitted to court.

C. **Foreign Arbitration Agreements** A partially different legal framework applies to foreign arbitration agreements, i.e. to arbitration agreements that form the basis of an award that will possibly qualify as foreign under Article I(1) NYC.[33] Recognition of foreign arbitration agreements is governed by Article II NYC. Again, contract conclusion (see following section 1), form requirements (see following section 2) and submission to court (see following section 3) have to be distinguished.

1. Contract Conclusion

The rules governing the conclusion of contracts are generally the same as for domestic arbitration agreements. Although Article V(1)(a) NYC contains a ground for the denial of recognition and enforcement of an arbitral award, the conflict of law rule enshrined in this provision likewise applies in the context of Article II NYC.[34] Similar to Article 34(2)(a)(i) ICA-ML, the law at the place of arbitration governs the conclusion and validity of

'The Authenticity of Online Alternative Dispute Resolution Proceedings', (2008) 25 *J. Int. Arb.* 355, 359; Otto, in Kronke, Nacimiento, Otto and Port (eds.), *NYC* (fn 3), pp. 175 *et seq.*

33 Lively disputed, see Schramm, Geisinger and Pinsolle, in Kronke, Nacimiento, Otto and Port (eds.), *NYC* (fn 3), pp. 41 *et seq.*; Wolff, in Wolff (ed.), *NYC* (fn 3), Article II paras. 26 *et seq.*, 35.

34 Bundesgericht, 14(2) ASA Bull. 255, 259 *et seq.* (1996) = XXII Y.B. Com. Arb. 800, 804 *et seq.* (1997); J. M. Lew, L. A. Mistelis and S. M. Kröll, *Comparative International Commercial Arbitration* (The Hague, London and New York: Kluwer Law International, 2003), paras. 6–54 *et seq.*

the arbitration agreement unless the parties have chosen another law. Reference can therefore be made to the assessment of electronic declarations under that law (section B 1).

The law thus determined also governs the inclusion of an arbitration agreement contained in general terms and conditions (as it will often be the case in web-based communications). While this result is undisputed under the Model Law, some advocate that rules on the inclusion of general terms and conditions in a contract are part of Article II NYC's autonomous law[35] – not convincingly, however, as the New York Convention does not set out rules on contract conclusion.[36] Article II(2) NYC only ousts provisions under national law that share its purpose, i.e. providing evidence, while national provisions on general terms and conditions pursue another purpose, namely to limit the imparity between the parties.[37] Any other understanding would also increase the risk that a domestic court's assessment falls apart from a foreign court's assessment of the same clause. Therefore, issues like the necessity of a specific (as opposed to a general) reference to the arbitration agreement, the need for an explicit reference to the arbitration agreement and for a reasonable opportunity to take note of the general terms' and conditions' content are to be determined under the national law governing the conclusion of the arbitration agreement.

2. Form Requirements for Validity and for Recognition

Unlike rules on contract conclusion, Article II NYC imposes rules on form on the recognition of foreign arbitration agreements that differ from the regime governing domestic arbitration agreements. Under Article II(1) NYC, arbitration agreements in writing are to be recognized; the term 'agreement in writing' shall include an arbitral clause in a contract or an arbitration agreement, signed by the parties or contained in an exchange of letters or telegrams (Article II(2) NYC). The 'in writing' requirement (including its definition) belongs to the Convention's autonomous law.[38]

35 Van den Berg, *NYC* (fn 4), p. 209; R. Hausmann, in C. Reithmann and D. Martiny (eds.), *Internationales Vertragsrecht, Das internationale Privatrecht der Schuldverträge*, 8th ed. (Cologne: Otto Schmidt, 2015), paras. 8.267, 8.292; Schramm, Geisinger and Pinsolle, in Kronke, Nacimiento, Otto and Port (eds.), *NYC* (fn 3), p. 89.

36 Wolff, in Wolff (ed.), *NYC* (fn 3), Article II para. 135 with further references.

37 Wolff, in Wolff (ed.), *NYC* (fn 3), Article II para. 135.

38 Oberster Gerichtshof, XXI Y.B. Com. Arb. 521, 522 para. 4 (1996); Cour d'appel Paris, Rev. arb. 1987, 482, 485 = XIII Y.B. Com. Arb. 466, 469 para. 15 (1988); Bundesgericht, BGE 111 Ib 253 = XII Y.B. Com. Arb. 511 para. 2 (1987); van den Berg, *NYC* (fn 4), pp. 173 *et*

Article II(1), (2) NYC is concerned only with the recognition of arbitration agreements and not with their validity in terms of form, which solely is to be determined under the *lex arbitri* (see previous section B 2). Even if an arbitration agreement fails to meet the form requirements under Article II(2) NYC, its validity remains untouched.[39]

a) Irrelevance of Form Requirements for Validity Article II(2) NYC's autonomous form requirement for the recognition of foreign arbitration agreements ousts all form provisions under domestic law that share the form requirement's purpose[40] to preserve evidence, in particular form requirements under the *lex arbitri* that pursue that purpose.

b) Signed by the Parties, Article II(2) Option 1 NYC Under the first option of Article II(2) NYC, an arbitration agreement is in writing (and thus to be recognized) if it is signed by the parties. The provision does not specify its underlying rationale, which impedes identification of proper electronic equivalents. A systematic reading, however, reveals that Article II(2) NYC requires the parties' signatures only for its first and not for its second option.[41] Since an 'exchange of letters or telegrams' in option 2 similarly requires the identity of the parties and their intent to be apparent, the purpose of option 1's signature requirement must go beyond that. In fact, the signature requirement under Article II(2) option 1 NYC also pursues the purpose of attributing the declaration's creatorship to the party with an increased degree of reliability. This is in line with the fact that facsimiles[42] or copies of signatures given elsewhere[43] do not suffice. Given this rationale, a simple electronic signature that merely reflects the party's

seq.; Schramm, Geisinger and Pinsolle, in Kronke, Nacimiento, Otto and Port (eds.), *NYC* (fn 3), pp. 73 *et seq.*

39 Wolff, in Wolff (ed.), *NYC* (fn 3), Article II para. 181.

40 Hausmann, in Reithmann and Martiny (eds.), *Internationales Vertragsrecht* (fn 35), para. 8.267; K. H. Schwab and G. Walter, *Schiedsgerichtsbarkeit*, 7th ed. (Munich: C. H. Beck and Helbing & Lichtenhahn, 2005), ch. 44 para. 9.

41 Born, *International Commercial Arbitration* (fn 23), p. 680.

42 D. Czernich, *New Yorker Schiedsübereinkommen – UN-Übereinkommen über die Anerkennung und Vollstreckung ausländischer Schiedssprüche – Kurzkommentar* (Vienna: LexisNexis, 2008), Article II para. 29; Hausmann, in Reithmann and Martiny (eds.), *Internationales Vertragsrecht* (fn 35), para. 8.302; Schlosser, in Stein and Jonas (eds.), *ZPO* (fn 4), annex to section 1061 para. 96.

43 Bayerisches Oberstes Landesgericht, NJW-RR 2003, 719 = XXIX Y.B. Com. Arb. 761, 764 *et seq.* para. 7 (2004); Hausmann, in Reithmann and Martiny (eds.), *Internationales Vertragsrecht* (fn 33), para. 8.303.

name (as standard emails or web-based declarations do) does not qualify as in writing under this option.

Emails or web-based declarations with digital signatures could, however, meet this standard. Since the 'in writing' requirement including the notion of signatures belongs to the Convention's autonomous law, it is to be interpreted irrespective of any view that a national law (including the *lex fori*, i.e. the law of the court where recognition and enforcement is sought) takes. In this context, it is particularly irrelevant whether a state has adopted the Model Law on Electronic Commerce or has enacted provisions to a similar effect.

Unlike provisions under national law (including implementations of model laws), other conventions can determine the interpretation of 'signature'. If the Electronic Communications Convention applies, its Article 9(3) broadens the definition of a signature to include digital signatures that meet the specific criteria.[44] Article 20(1) of the Electronic Communications Convention explicitly applies to the use of electronic communications in connection with the formation of contracts (namely arbitration agreements)[45] under the New York Convention. It is, however, unclear whether Article 20(1) of the Electronic Communications Convention broadens the Convention's scope of application as defined in its Article 1(1). Under the latter provision, the Convention applies to contracts between parties whose places of business are in different states. The New York Convention, conversely, ties in with the foreign nature of the arbitral award that is fully detached from the parties' places of business.[46] The better grounds militate in favour of applying the Electronic Communications Convention to any arbitration agreement under the New York Convention regardless of the parties' places of business. Article 20(1) of the Electronic Communications Convention aims to offer substantive rules that allow the New York Convention and others to operate effectively in an electronic environment[47] while obviating the need to

[44] It does not, however, create an alternative enforcement regime that could apply under Article VII(1) NYC (dissenting I. Amro, 'Enforcement of Cross-Border Online Arbitral Awards and Online Arbitration Agreements in National Courts', (2016) 5(2) *Slovenska arbitražna praksa* 17, 25).

[45] Explanatory note by the UNCITRAL secretariat on the United Nations Convention on the Use of Electronic Communications in International Contracts, para. 5; Otto, in Kronke, Nacimiento, Otto and Port (eds.), *NYC* (fn 3), p. 175.

[46] Oberster Gerichtshof, XXII Y.B. Com. Arb. 619, 625 para. 11 (1997); Ehle, in Wolff (ed.), *NYC* (fn 3), Article I para. 95.

[47] Explanatory note by the UNCITRAL secretariat on the United Nations Convention on the Use of Electronic Communications in International Contracts, para. 289; Report of

amend individual international conventions.[48] Effective operation with a similar effect as an amendment of Article II NYC can only be achieved if the Electronic Communications Convention applies to any arbitration agreement under Article II NYC. Otherwise, different legal regimes would be created for foreign arbitration agreements depending on the parties' places of business. This would be irreconcilable with the Electronic Communications Convention's approach of avoiding such parallel regimes in other cases: it is precisely for this reason that the Convention does not require the parties' places of business to be in contracting states.[49]

When applying Article II(2) NYC, a state is bound to implement the signature definition under Article 9(3) of the Electronic Communications Convention once this Convention has entered into force for that state. For such a duty to apply, neither the seat of the parties (as demonstrated earlier) nor whether the Electronic Communications Convention has likewise entered into force for the state in which an arbitral award will be made based on the arbitration agreement examined under Article II(2) NYC have any bearing. While conventions have legal effect only between contracting states, the Electronic Communications Convention aims to adapt Article II(2) NYC to modern means of communication. The New York Convention, in turn, obliges its contracting states to recognize foreign arbitration agreements (above C) regardless of whether or not the arbitration agreement determines another contracting state as the place of arbitration. This effect benefiting arbitration agreements from non-contracting states is evidenced by the wording of Article I(1)(1) NYC and by the reciprocity reservation under Article I(3)(1) NYC. Since the Electronic Communications Convention, according to its Article 20(1), applies to agreements under the New York Convention, it would make little sense to leave the comprehensive approach set out by Article I NYC and to restrict the application of the Electronic Communications Convention to agreements from other contracting states. Such understanding would also find no support in the Electronic Communications Convention's wording. To the contrary, the reciprocity declaration in

the Working Group on Electronic Commerce on the work of its forty-third session, A/CN.9/548, para. 51.

[48] Explanatory note by the UNCITRAL secretariat on the United Nations Convention on the Use of Electronic Communications in International Contracts, para. 288.

[49] Explanatory note by the UNCITRAL secretariat on the United Nations Convention on the Use of Electronic Communications in International Contracts, para. 63; Report of the Working Group on Electronic Commerce on the work of its forty-third session, A/CN.9/548, para. 87.

Article 19(1)(a) of the Electronic Communications Convention demonstrates a broad understanding. Although this reciprocity declaration relates to the Convention's scope of application under its Article 1 which does not (as demonstrated earlier) govern the conclusion of arbitration agreements under Article II(2) NYC, it indicates that without such declaration the Convention extends to any cross-border setting regardless of whether other contracting states are involved.

Not least in light of the currently limited number of parties to the Electronic Communications Convention,[50] the question remains whether the term 'signed by the parties' in Article II(2) NYC also comprises digital signatures if the Electronic Communications Convention does not apply. The answer is subject to Article II NYC's autonomous interpretation. It is clear that the drafters of the Convention, at a time when the German delegation travelled to the 1958 conference in New York by freighter,[51] could not imagine electronic communication including digital signatures. However, the Convention was open to modern technologies that facilitate international trade as demonstrated by the inclusion of telegrams as the then-current technology in the wording of Article II(2) NYC.[52] This historic technology-friendliness (as part of the Convention's rationale to accommodate business needs) advocates in favour of an extensive interpretation of the 'signature' requirement as long as the object and purpose of the requirement is equally met by electronic communication.[53] In this regard, Article II(2) NYC's interpretation should be guided by the requirements set out in Article 9(3) of the Electronic Communications Convention even where these criteria are not legally binding. Since the effect of the Electronic Communications Convention on the signature

[50] Currently eight: Congo, the Dominican Republic, Fiji, Honduras, Montenegro, the Russian Federation, Singapore and Sri Lanka (see www.uncitral.org/uncitral/en/uncitral_texts/electronic_commerce/2005Convention_status.html, last visited 10 September 2017); the US has, under its previous administration, been in the course of ratification (see www.whitehouse.gov/the-press-office/2016/02/10/message-senate-un-convention-use-electronic-communications-international, last visited 10 September 2017).

[51] O. Glossner, 'Das Übereinkommen über die Anerkennung und Vollstreckung von ausländischen Schiedssprüchen vom 10. Juni 1958, New York', *SchiedsVZ* 2009, 39.

[52] J. Arsic, 'International Commercial Arbitration on the Internet – Has the Future Come Too Early?', (1997) 14 *J. Int. Arb.* 209, 216; F. G. Mazzotta, 'The Written Form Requirement of an Arbitration Agreement in Light of New Means of Communication' in C. B. Andersen and U. G. Schroeter (eds.), *Sharing International Commercial Law Across National Boundaries: Festschrift for Albert H. Kritzer on the Occasion of his Eightieth Birthday* (London, Wildy, Simmonds & Hill Pub., 2008), pp. 326, 329; van den Berg, *NYC* (fn 4), p. 191; see also Denkschrift der Bundesregierung, BT-Drucks. 3/2160, p. 24.

[53] Concurring Arsic, 'International Commercial Arbitration on the Internet' (fn 52), 217.

requirement in Article II(2) NYC is not based on its binding force under international treaty law but on the NYC's autonomous interpretation, it even remains unaffected by a state's declaration limiting the Convention's scope of application (Article 19 of the Electronic Communications Convention), by a state's opt-out declaration under Article 20(4) of the Electronic Communications Convention or by its inapplicability to electronic communications made before it entered into force (Article 24 of the Electronic Communications Convention).

The reason for interpreting Article II(2) NYC in light of the Electronic Communications Convention is that, even if it has not spread widely, was drafted under the auspices of UNCITRAL, the same international body in whose field of activity the New York Convention falls. The Electronic Communications Convention has been adopted by the UN General Assembly[54] and thus reflects a broad consensus amongst nations. Moreover, the 2006 UNCITRAL Recommendation,[55] which suggests a broad interpretation of Article II(2) NYC's 'in writing' requirement, expressly references in its recitals UNCITRAL's texts on electronic commerce. Finally, effective operation of the New York Convention is a sensible aim to be pursued by its autonomous interpretation. If the Electronic Communications Convention can enable the New York Convention to operate effectively in an electronic environment,[56] an autonomous interpretation should adopt these rules even if they are not legally binding. Conversely, a restrictive interpretation would calcify the signature requirement and cut it off from technological development. Such interpretation would contravene the Convention's aim to facilitate international commerce.

The arbitration agreement is therefore also considered 'signed by the parties' within the meaning of Article II(2) NYC if the parties have signed it with a digital signature that meets the requirements of Article 9(3) of the Electronic Communications Convention.

c) Contained in an Exchange of Letters or Telegrams, Article II(2) Option 2 NYC Under Article II(2) NYC's second option, which does

[54] Resolution adopted by the General Assembly on 23 November 2005, A/RES/60/21.

[55] Recommendation regarding the interpretation of article II, paragraph 2, and article VII, paragraph 1, of the Convention on the Recognition and Enforcement of Foreign Arbitral Awards, done in New York, 10 June 1958, adopted by the United Nations Commission on International Trade Law on 7 July 2006 at its thirty-ninth session, issued in Official Records of the General Assembly, Sixty-first Session, Supplement No. 17 (A/61/17), annex II.

[56] See fn 47.

not require signatures,[57] an arbitration agreement is in writing if it is contained in an exchange of letters or telegrams. Emails and web-based declarations are apparently neither letters nor telegrams, but the provision applies to emails by way of analogy: emails share the main characteristics of telegrams, as they are not physically transmitted and do not authenticate the sender's identity.[58] The mere fact that telegrams necessarily materialize before they reach the recipient while emails materialize only if printed cannot be decisive in light of Article II NYC's aim to provide evidence for the conclusion of the arbitration agreement.[59]

Article II(2) option 2 NYC likewise includes click-wrap and browse-wrap declarations regardless of whether they employ means of encryption or authentication. It has to be noted, however, that Article II(2) option 2 NYC always requires an exchange of declarations. Such exchange exists if the website operator makes an offer that the customer accepts by clicking a button (click-wrap) or downloading a file (browse-wrap) or through similar means that are reported back to the website operator.[60] Declarations are not exchanged if the website operator does not yet make a binding offer but only invites the customer to submit an offer that the website operator accepts by delivery of the goods or other conduct. Likewise, no declarations are exchanged if, in case of browse-wrap, no message is returned to the website operator.

d) Non-Exhaustive Character of Article II(2) NYC In line with No. 1 of UNCITRAL's 2006 Recommendation,[61] Article II(2) NYC should be understood as providing a non-exhaustive list of options for meeting the form requirement.[62] Due to the term 'include' in the provision's

57 Schramm, Geisinger and Pinsolle, in Kronke, Nacimiento, Otto and Port (eds.), *NYC* (fn 3), p. 81 and Wolff, in Wolff (ed.), *NYC* (fn 3), Article II para. 102 with further references.

58 *Chloe Z Fishing Co., Inc. v. Odyssey Re (London) Ltd.*, 109 F. Supp. 2d 1236, 1250 (S.D. Cal. 2000) = XXVI Y.B. Com. Arb. 910, 923 para. 32 (2001); Tautschnig, 'Legal Challenges' (fn 25), 90 *et seq.*; Wolff, in Wolff (ed.), *NYC* (fn 3), Article II para. 130 with further references; similarly, N. Horn, 'Arbitration and Electronic Communications: Public Policy', 12 *Int. A.L.R.* 107, 108 (2009).

59 R. Hill, 'On-Line Arbitration: Issues and Solutions', (1999) 15 *Arb. Int'l* 199, 201 *et seq.*; Wolff, in Wolff (ed.), *NYC* (fn 3), Article II para. 130.

60 Haloush, 'Authenticity of Online ADR' (fn 32), 363 *et seq*; dissenting Alqudah, 'Enforceability of Arbitration Clauses' (fn 26), 71.

61 See fn 55.

62 Tautschnig, 'Legal Challenges' (fn 25), 90; Wolff, in Wolff (ed.), *NYC* (fn 3), Article II paras. 104 *et seq.* with further references.

English-language version, the wording allows for such reading[63] and in light of the provision's spirit to accommodate business needs and its openness for (then-)modern technologies ('telegram') (see previous section c),[64] it should be understood that way.

The unlisted options under Article II(2) NYC are to be detailed by taking recourse to Option I Article 7 ICA-ML 2006.[65] Although the 2006 Model Law cannot be legally binding for the interpretation of the 1958 New York Convention, its stipulations can be relied on for similar reasons as the inclusion of Article 9(3) of the Electronic Communications Convention in Article II(2) option 1 NYC (see previous section b).[66] Reference can therefore be made to Option I Article 7(3) and (4) ICA-ML 2006 (see previous section B 2 b bb). This recourse is, however, limited by the broadest meaning of 'in writing'. For example, while video recording through the customer's computer camera would meet the requirements under Option I Article 7(3) and 7(4) ICA-ML 2006, it cannot be understood as being 'in writing' under Article II(2) NYC.[67] Applying Article 9(2) of the Electronic Communications Convention leads to the same result, be it directly (if the enforcement state is a party to that Convention) or within the autonomous interpretation of Article II(2) NYC (above b). These approaches are not mutually exclusive,[68] as is highlighted by the fact that the 2006 UNCITRAL Recommendation[69] references both Article 7 ICA-ML 2006 and the Electronic Communications Convention in its recitals.[70]

e) More Favourable National Law, Article VII(1) NYC Finally, the form requirements under Article II(2) NYC are alleviated by reliance on more favourable domestic law on the form of arbitration agreements under Article VII(1) NYC. While Article VII(1) NYC's original scope of application is restricted to the recognition and enforcement of foreign

[63] Report of the Working Group on Arbitration and Conciliation on the work of its forty-fourth session, A/CN.9/592, para. 87; Note by the Secretariat, A/CN.9/607, para. 7; G. Herrmann, 'The Arbitration Agreement as the Foundation of Arbitration and Its Recognition by the Courts' in A. J. van den Berg (ed.), *International Arbitration in a Changing World*, ICCA Congress Series, vol. VI (Alphen aan den Rijn: Kluwer Law International, 1994), pp. 41, 45; Landau, 'Requirement of a Written Form' (fn 12), 68 *et seq.*

[64] Mazzotta, 'Written Form Requirement' (fn 49), 329; Tautschnig, 'Legal Challenges' (fn 25), 91.

[65] Wolff, in Wolff (ed.), *NYC* (fn 3), Article II paras. 114; irresolute Schramm, Geisinger and Pinsolle, in Kronke, Nacimiento, Otto and Port (eds.), *NYC* (fn 3), pp. 78 *et seq.*

[66] For details, see Wolff, in Wolff (ed.), *NYC* (fn 3), Article II para. 114.

[67] Wolff, in Wolff (ed.), *NYC* (fn 3), Article II paras. 113, 114.

[68] Mazzotta, 'Written Form Requirement' (fn 49), 334.

[69] See fn 55.

[70] Mazzotta, 'Written Form Requirement' (fn 49), 340.

arbitral awards, the provision applies by way of analogy – and in line with No. 2 of UNCITRAL's 2006 Recommendation – to arbitration agreements.[71] The provision's limited wording is owed to the last-minute introduction of Article II NYC, which was not properly reflected in other articles (as Articles I or VII NYC).[72] The more favourable domestic law applicable by virtue of Article VII(1) NYC is understood to be the law of the enforcement state or the law applicable by virtue of the enforcement state's conflict of law rules (see previous section B 2).[73]

3. Submission to Court, Article IV(1)(b) NYC

The submission of electronically concluded foreign arbitration agreements to court raises similar issues as that of their domestic counterparts (see previous section B 3). A specific submission requirement is set out by Article IV(1)(b) NYC under which the recognition and enforcement of a foreign arbitral award requires supply of the 'original agreement referred to in article II or a duly certified copy thereof'. Like Article 35(2)(1) ICA-ML, this provision is of merely evidentiary nature and requires supply of documents only in case their existence or content is in dispute.[74] By virtue of Article VII(1) NYC, more favourable national law can be relied on, in particular law that abstains from requiring submission of any arbitration agreement as suggested by Article 35(2)(1) ICA-ML 2006 (see previous section B 3).[75]

Article IV(1)(b) NYC's interpretation becomes decisive only in the remaining cases. Then the first question is that of the provision's autonomous understanding of 'original' and 'copy', the subsequent question is that of technical implementation. It is clear from the explicit reference to Article II NYC and from the fact that a proper reading of that

[71] Cour d'appel Paris, XXIX Y.B. Com. Arb. 657, 660 para. 2 (2004), confirmed by Cour de Cassation, XXXII Y.B. Com. Arb. 290, 292 *et seq.* (2007); Arrondissementsrechtbank Rotterdam, XXII Y.B. Com. Arb. 762, 764 para. 6 (1997); Rechtbank Rotterdam, XXXIV Y.B. Com. Arb. 722, 725 para. 3 (2009); Tribunal Supremo, XXXIII Y.B. Com. Arb. 703, 706 para. 5 (2008); van den Berg, *NYC* (fn 4), pp. 86 *et seq.*

[72] Van den Berg, *NYC* (fn 4), p. 86; Quinke, in Wolff (ed.), *NYC* (fn 3), Article VII para. 45.

[73] Bundesgerichtshof, SchiedsVZ 2005, 306, 307 = XXXI Y.B. Com. Arb. 679, 683 (2006); Quinke, in Wolff (ed.), *NYC* (fn 3), Article VII para. 58.

[74] Bundesgerichtshof, NJW-RR 2001, 1059 = XXIX Y.B. Com. Arb. 700, 710 para. 26 (2004); NJW 2001, 1730 = XXIX Y.B. Com. Arb. 724, 726 *et seq.* para. 4 (2004).

[75] Bundesgerichtshof, SchiedsVZ 2003, 281, 282 = XXIX Y.B. Com. Arb. 767, 769 paras. 5 *et seq.* (2004); Oberlandesgericht Munich, SchiedsVZ 2012, 156, 158 = XXXIX Y.B. Com. Arb. 389, 392 para. 4 (2014); SchiedsVZ 2012, 339, 341 = XXXIX Y.B. Com. Arb. 394, 396 (2014).

provision allows for electronically concluded arbitration agreements (see previous sections 2 b and 2 c) that the procedural provision of Article IV NYC cannot thwart recognition based on an arbitration agreement that is to be recognized under Article II NYC.

If the Electronic Communications Convention applies (see previous section 2 b), its Article 9(4) clarifies what an 'original' of electronic communications is for purposes of Article IV NYC (see previous section B 3). This definition is likewise to be adopted as the proper autonomous interpretation of Article IV NYC if the Electronic Communications Convention does not apply (see previous section 2 b).

The legal and technical channel through which such electronic original is to be introduced in court proceedings for the recognition and enforcement of a foreign arbitral award is not governed by Article IV NYC but subject to the (non-harmonized) national law on civil procedure (Article III cl. 1 NYC).[76]

II. Digital Arbitral Awards

According to standard practice, arbitral awards (or their signature pages) are sent by courier from one arbitrator to the other and, in institutional arbitration, to the institution, which forwards copies to the parties. This procedure could effectively be streamlined if an arbitral award was rendered digitally, which may particularly be of interest in light of the ongoing efforts to shorten arbitral proceedings.

A. Relevant Fact Situations

Two types of digital awards shall be discussed: digital awards that contain the names of the concluding arbitrators or their digitalized handwritten signatures ('simple' electronic signatures) and digital awards with advanced digital signatures.

B. Domestic Awards

Digital arbitral awards raise issues with the form requirements applicable to them, with their delivery to the parties and with their submission to court.

[76] See Amro, 'Enforcement of Cross-Border Online Arbitral Awards' (fn 44), 22 *et seq.* (with reference to Brazil and Greece); apparently dissenting Otto, in Kronke, Nacimiento, Otto and Port (eds.), *NYC* (fn 3), p. 175 ('sufficient to submit a printout of the electronic communication').

1. Form Requirements

The form requirements for arbitral awards are governed by the *lex arbitri*. Most arbitration laws require a written award plus the signatures of all arbitrators; this is also the rule that Article 31(1)(1) ICA-ML disseminates as harmonized arbitration law. Some laws only require signatures, but therewith imply that the award must be in writing (example: Article 1480(2) of the French Code of Civil Procedure). While most laws demand that all arbitrators sign (example: Article 31(1)(1) ICA-ML with an option to replace signatures with the reason for their omission), others deem the signatures of the majority of the arbitrators (examples: section 52(3) of the English Arbitration Act 1996 and section 19(a)(1) of the US Uniform Arbitration Act 2000) or of the chairman alone (example: Article 189(2)(3) of the Swiss Private International Law Act as a default rule) sufficient. Domestic arbitration laws also differ as to the consequences of a lack of form. While some (such as the German law) then deny the existence of an arbitral award,[77] others (like Article 1065(1)(d) of the Dutch Code of Civil Procedure) assume a ground for setting aside the award.[78]

Some arbitration laws hand over the rules of form for arbitral awards to the parties; examples include section 52(1) of the English Arbitration Act 1996 and Article 189(1) of the Swiss Private International Law Act. Under these laws, digital awards raise no issues of form if the award complies with the relevant requirements set out by the parties.[79] However, if the parties have failed to allow for digital awards in their agreement, these arbitration laws face the same interpretation issues as other laws. Regardless of whether they let party agreements on form prevail, almost all arbitration laws require the award to be in writing and to bear at least one signature. The decisive question is whether a digital award meets these requirements.

Some jurisdictions answer this question in the affirmative, either directly in their arbitration law or within their general rules on form. Section 19(a)(1) of the US Uniform Arbitration Act 2000, for example, requires that the award 'must be signed or otherwise authenticated by any arbitrator'. The 'other authentication' refers to the E-SIGN Act under which an arbitrator can sign an award with an electronic signature

[77] R. Wolff, 'The Arbitral Award' in R. Kreindler, R. Wolff and M. S. Rieder (eds.), *Commercial Arbitration in Germany* (Oxford: Oxford University Press, 2016), para. 6.92.

[78] Born, *International Commercial Arbitration* (fn 23), p. 3037.

[79] Amro, 'Enforcement of Cross-Border Online Arbitral Awards' (fn 44), 21.

(15 U.S.C. § 7001, § 7006(5)). The German provision on delivery of the award to the parties was amended in 2005 in order to allow for electronic transmission of awards,[80] which implies that the award can also be made as an electronic document. Here again, written form can be substituted by electronic form for which a qualified electronic signature under the German Signature Act is needed (sections 126(3), 126a of the German Civil Code).[81] Under Article 1072b(3) of the Dutch Code of Civil Procedure, an award can also be made electronically and can bear electronic signatures.[82] More generally, the adoption of the UNCITRAL Model Law on Electronic Commerce paves the way for the substitution of written form by data messages (Article 6) and of signatures by electronic signatures (Article 7). The Electronic Communications Convention does not apply to arbitral awards, since its scope of application is limited to 'electronic communications in connection with the formation or performance of a contract' by virtue of its Article 1(1).[83]

The applicable law that allows for electronic arbitral awards likewise determines their form. German law, for example, requires the arbitrators' qualified electronic signatures (section 126a(1) of the German Civil Code), while under US law, a simple reproduction of the names of the arbitrators suffices[84]. Dutch law requires the method used for authentication of the electronic signature to be sufficiently reliable; that is presumed if a qualified electronic signature is used (Article 3:15a of the Dutch Civil Code).[85] The electronic equivalents for written form and signatures have already been discussed in the context of arbitration agreements (see previous section I B 2 a). If the applicable law remains silent on electronic equivalents, the national law is preferably to be interpreted in a technology-friendly manner (see previous section I B 2 a aa);

[80] Government bill, BT-Drucks. 15/4067, p. 36.

[81] Wolff, 'The Arbitral Award' (fn 77), para. 6.93; dissenting Münch, in Krüger and Rauscher (eds.), *ZPO* (fn 30), section 1054 para. 5. Under the prior version of section 1054(4) of the German Code for Civil Procedure, qualified electronic signatures did not suffice (OLG Oldenburg, order of 30 May 2006, 9 SchH 03/05, available at www.disarb.org, last visited 10 September 2017).

[82] For details, see Chapter 5, pp. 116 *et seq*.

[83] Note by the Secretariat, A/CN.9/WG.II/WP.132, para. 9; Otto, in Kronke, Nacimiento, Otto and Port (eds.), *NYC* (fn 3), p. 177; partially dissenting Mazzotta, 'Written Form Requirement' (fn 49), 329 ('under certain circumstances, an award can also be an agreement').

[84] National Conference of Commissioners on Uniform State Laws, Uniform Electronic Transactions Act (1999), section 2, comment 7 (available at www.uniformlaws.org/shared/docs/electronic% 20transactions/ueta_final_99.pdf, last visited 10 September 2017).

[85] For details and forthcoming amendments, see Chapter 5, pp. 105 *et seq*.

national adoptions of Article 31 ICA-ML should be interpreted in light of UNCITRAL's instruments on electronic commerce.

2. Delivery to the Parties

Compared to the form requirements for awards, their delivery to the parties is a minor challenge for digital awards.[86] If the *lex arbitri* allows for electronic awards, it will not render their delivery to the parties impossible.

In fact, most provisions on the delivery of the award to the parties are sufficiently flexible in their wording to accommodate digital delivery, be it via email or on data carrier. Article 31(4) ICA-ML, under which the signed award 'shall be delivered to each party', serves as a typical example. Likewise, under section 19(a)(3) of the US Uniform Arbitration Act 2000, '[t]he arbitrator or the arbitration organization shall give notice of the award, including a copy of the award'. In 2005, the German legislature replaced in section 1054(4) of the German Code of Civil Procedure the term 'transmit' ('übersenden') – which would already have covered digital delivery easily – by 'transfer' ('übermitteln') in order to also allow for digital delivery.[87]

3. Submission to Court

A domestic award is usually to be submitted to court if its recognition and enforcement is sought. While Article 35(2)(1) ICA-ML 1985 required 'the duly authenticated original award or a duly certified copy thereof' to be supplied, the provision's 2006 version has abandoned the authentication and certification requirements. This was, however, not done to promote digital awards, but to eliminate problems in practice due to different interpretations of authentication[88] and certification.[89]

These requirements raise similar issues for digital awards as for digital arbitration agreements (see previous section I B 3): the distinction between original and copy does not make sense for digital documents. If the applicable law does not provide for further guidance, the term

[86] See Horn, 'Public policy' (fn 58), 113 for a general statement that notification of the award can be carried out by secure email that automatically is timed and dated and is accompanied by secured electronic signatures of the arbitrators.

[87] Government bill, BT-Drucks. 15/4067, p. 36.

[88] Report of the Working Group on Arbitration and Conciliation on the work of its forty-fourth session, A/CN.9/592, para. 79.

[89] Report of the United Nations Commission on International Trade Law on the work of its thirty-ninth session, A/61/17, para. 172.

'original' may be interpreted in light of Article 8(1) EC-ML. To the extent that the award must be authenticated as under Article 35(2)(1) ICA-ML 1985, the applicable law determines both the competent authority and the procedure for authentication of a digital award.[90] Since Article 35(2)(1) ICA-ML 1985 was modelled on Article IV NYC,[91] reference can be made to the interpretation of that provision (see section C 3).

C. *Foreign Awards*

Recognition and enforcement of a foreign arbitral award raise similar issues as that of a domestic award (see previous section B). As the recognition and enforcement of foreign awards, however, is typically governed by the New York Convention, the legal regime differs.

1. Form Requirements

The New York Convention does not expressly set out form requirements for arbitral awards. Such form requirements may come into play at two stages.[92] First, they could already be included in the notion of an arbitral award; a lack of form would then result in the entire New York Convention becoming inapplicable (Article I(1) NYC). Second, the form of an arbitral award could also be a factor that bars the arbitral award from becoming binding on the parties; in that case a lack of form constitutes a ground for denying recognition and enforcement under Article V(1)(e) NYC.

The notion of an arbitral award under Article I(1) NYC is a highly debated topic. In this debate, mainly three main positions can be identified:[93] some assume that the New York Convention relies on an autonomous notion of arbitral awards, others find that no autonomous definition of arbitral awards is enshrined in the Convention but that national law governs this notion (be it by virtue of an autonomous conflict of law rule or of a conflict of law rule under the *lex fori*), namely the *lex arbitri* or the *lex fori*, or, last, that these standards are to be combined

[90] Cf. Report of the Secretary-General (Analytical Commentary), A/CN.9/264, Article 35 para. 5.

[91] Report of the Secretary-General (Analytical Commentary), A/CN.9/264, Article 35 para. 5.

[92] For a third option, namely a violation of public policy under Article V(2)(b) NYC, see Horn, 'Public policy' (fn 58), 112 (without further details).

[93] For details on and references for the following views see Ehle, in Wolff (ed.), *NYC* (fn 3), Article I paras. 14 *et seq.*

alternatively or cumulatively. The Convention's aim to facilitate recognition and enforcement of foreign arbitral awards speaks in favour of an alternative combination of an autonomous standard and the *lex fori*. This understanding extends the recognition-friendly, minimum-standard approach of Article VII(1) NYC to the Convention's applicability. It goes hand in hand with a low-key autonomous standard under the Convention, in particular in terms of form requirements. When the Convention was concluded, form requirements for arbitral awards under national law differed (and still differ today, see previous section B 1). It cannot be assumed that the Convention intended to exclude entire groups of arbitral awards that fully complied with the form requirements under their applicable *lex arbitri*. No contracting state with liberal form requirements would have ratified the Convention and excluded arbitral awards rendered under its law from recognition and enforcement abroad. Specifically on electronic form, the Convention demonstrated openness for modern technologies (see previous section I C 2 b). At the same time, the commonly accepted standard for form requirements has evolved to also allow for digital awards (see previous section B 1). It would run counter to these developments if the Convention's autonomous standard for awards stayed behind the form standard recognized by UNCITRAL's harmonizing instruments. Therefore, an autonomous interpretation results in the same standard as under the UNCITRAL Model Law on International Commercial Arbitration (see previous section B 1).[94]

The second option, denial of recognition and enforcement under Article V(1)(e) NYC, refers to the *lex arbitri*. If the law under which the arbitral award was made does not deprive an award that fails to meet its form requirements of its classification as an award and, at the same time, considers it not yet binding, Article V(1)(e) NYC can be invoked. In these cases, the award is in existence as such, but is not yet binding pending the repair of the formal defect and thus subject to denial of recognition and enforcement.

2. Delivery to the Parties

The New York Convention is likewise silent on the delivery of the award to the parties. However, the award's delivery to the parties is a typical element under arbitration laws for the award's binding effect on the parties. A lack of proper delivery under the *lex arbitri* (see previous section B 2)

[94] Concurring Otto, in Kronke, Nacimiento, Otto and Port (eds.), *NYC* (fn 3), p. 177 ('Arbitration awards might also be issued in electronic form.').

therefore constitutes a ground for denying recognition and enforcement of the award under Article V(1)(e) NYC.[95] Once the delivery of an electronic award complies with the *lex arbitri* (see previous section B 2), the award's recognition and enforcement cannot be denied under Article V(1)(e) NYC.

3. Submission to Court, Article IV(1)(a) NYC

Finally, Article IV(1)(a) NYC requires that '[t]he duly authenticated original award or a duly certified copy thereof' be supplied to court with the application for its recognition and enforcement. This provision applies if the party seeking recognition and enforcement cannot rely on a more recognition-friendly national law such as Article 35(2)(1) ICA-ML 2006 (see previous section B 3).

As in Article IV(1)(b) NYC (see previous section I C 3), the term 'original' in Article IV(1)(a) NYC is to be interpreted along the definition of Article 9(4) of the Electronic Communications Convention.[96] The New York Convention, however, does not entail autonomous law on authentication; authentication is rather governed by national laws (either the *lex arbitri* or the *lex fori* or a combination of both).[97] These laws are to be consulted for the proper form of authentication of a digital arbitral award.[98] German law, for example, allows notaries public to electronically authenticate documents by adding their qualified electronic signature under the German Signature Act and a confirmation of the competent authority that the signature's user is a notary public (section 39a of the German Authentication Act). In the cross-border context, an undertaking to establish an 'electronic apostille' has been underway since 2006.[99]

[95] Liebscher, in Wolff (ed.), *NYC* (fn 3), Article V para. 359; see also Oberlandesgericht Celle, XXXII Y.B. Com. Arb. 322, 325 para. 7 (2007).

[96] Or under the equivalent definition in Article 8(1) EC-ML, as the Electronic Communications Convention does not apply to arbitral awards (fn 83 above). See also Tautschnig, 'Legal Challenges' (fn 25), 110; M. S. A. Wahab, 'Online Arbitration: Tradition Conceptions and Innovative Trends' in A. J. van den Berg (ed.), *International Arbitration: The Coming of a New Age?*, ICCA Congress Series, vol. XVII (Alphen aan den Rijn: Kluwer Law International, 2013), pp. 654, 660 *et seq.*

[97] For details see Otto, in Kronke, Nacimiento, Otto and Port (eds.), *NYC* (fn 3), pp. 178 *et seq.*; Scherer, in Wolff (ed.), *NYC* (fn 3), Article IV paras. 9 *et seq.*

[98] See also Horn, 'Public policy' (fn 58), 112 (in favour of an extensive functional (autonomous?) understanding of authentication under Article IV(1)(a) NYC).

[99] See www.hcch.net/en/publications-and-studies/details4/?pid=4945 (last visited 10 September 2017).

Conclusion

Digital arbitration agreements and digital arbitral awards appear attractive for international arbitration, as they promise to replace anachronistic transmission of paper documents by speedy and convenient alternatives. Gains in speed and convenience are, however, to be weighed against the risk that electronic instruments will not be legally recognized and thus fail to meet their objectives.

In many instances, the pertinent form requirements are governed by national laws. This is obvious not only for the arbitration law at the place of arbitration, but also within the New York Convention's autonomous law framework where recourse is often made to the *lex arbitri*. While the Model Law on International Commercial Arbitration has achieved a great deal of harmonization, its acceptance is by far not as comprehensive as that of the New York Convention. Moreover, even the Model Law requires complementary legislation to fully open up to modern technologies. While harmonizing instruments to that effect exist, their acceptance thus far leaves much to be desired.

The remaining risks are lower for digital arbitration agreements than for digital arbitral awards. At a first glance, this is because the electronic equivalent to signatures gives rise to particular difficulties and that only the form requirements for arbitration agreements allow for alternative options to signatures. What is more, speed and convenience are of greater importance for arbitration agreements: arbitration agreements are concluded day-to-day in large number by business people who are used to employ modern means of communication. The distinctive business need for the use of electronic means has been accommodated by more advanced harmonizing instruments. Such business need is lower for digital arbitral awards which are concurrently smaller in number than arbitration agreements. At the same time, the tolerance for form risks is significantly lower for arbitral awards than for arbitration agreements, not least considering the time and efforts spent on the arbitral proceedings. If the arbitral tribunal makes every effort to make sure that the award is enforceable at law (as prominently required by Article 42 ICC Rules 2017), it will often refrain from rendering a digital arbitral award.[100]

[100] Cf. Amro, 'Enforcement of Cross-Border Online Arbitral Awards' (fn 44), 29 ('desirable') and 30 ('advisable'); Hill, 'On-Line Arbitration' (fn 59), 207 ('wise'); Horn, 'Public policy' (fn 58), 113 ('advisable'); Otto, in Kronke, Nacimiento, Otto and Port (eds.), *NYC* (fn 3), p. 177 ('unwise'). In practice, however, digital arbitral awards are not as uncommon as the risks that they face at the enforcement stage may imply (see Chapter 1, p. 19).

8

Building on OArb Attributes in Pursuit of Justice

AMY J. SCHMITZ*

Summary: This chapter will consider the use of online arbitration (OArb) for resolution of disputes, especially those in business-to-consumer (B2C) transactions. First, it will provide background on arbitration law and explain the impetus for moving arbitration from face-to-face (F2F) to online procedures in order to augment the efficiency and fairness of these processes. Next, the chapter will discuss the development of quasi-OArb and OArb programs already in existence that may serve as models for OArb aimed to benefit both businesses and consumers. The chapter will conclude by acknowledging hurdles and drawbacks to OArb programs, and suggest ideas for fostering global development of OArb that expand individuals' access to justice.

Introduction

Traditional face-to-face (F2F) arbitration has earned a bad reputation for resolution of consumers' claims against businesses with respect to purchases of goods and services (business-to-consumer, or B2C transactions). This is especially true with the proliferation of arbitration clauses in United States' consumer contracts. For example, cellular phone customers in the United States who disputed charges related to their wireless phone data plans were dismayed to learn that their contracts contained arbitration clauses that precluded class relief and imposed prohibitive costs. These hurdles led many cellular phone customers to withdraw their complaints before arbitration began.[1] These

* Amy J. Schmitz, Professor of Law, University of Missouri School of Law. I thank Danielle Lineman, Alex Gano and Jasmine Rodenburg for their research assistance. I also thank Maud Piers, Christian Aschauer and other participants in the conference at University of Ghent for their insightful comments.

[1] *In re Sprint Premium Data Plan Marketing and Sales Practices Litigation* [2014] WestLaw 202621 (US District Court of New Jersey) 5–10. Sprint's current terms and conditions contain the same clause. Sprint, 'Dispute Resolution and Arbitration, Terms &

consumers therefore claimed their access to justice was denied in practice, regardless of any F2F arbitration rights stated in contract terms.[2] They argued that arbitrating F2F was not feasible in light of expected recovery.[3]

These consumers may have had greater access to justice even without class relief if they could have asserted their claims through online arbitration (OArb).[4] Instead of having to each pay separate filing fees and costs of representation in individual F2F proceedings, OArb would allow for each consumer to quickly and cheaply file his or her claims online. The OArb portal also could have eased complexities and time of F2F proceedings by allowing consumers to upload and submit all supporting documentation to support their claims. This could be done at individuals' convenience, thus eliminating need for travel, arranging childcare or missing work. The online neutral could then make determinations based on each consumer's case. Such an OArb system could provide more accurate and complete redress for each consumer, perhaps to an extent greater than that achieved through class actions – which have been criticized for providing insufficient and inequitably distributed relief.

Such considerations regarding the potential of online remedy systems have inspired the growth of online dispute resolution (ODR), covering any computer mediated process for resolving claims. The prime example of ODR's growing popularity is the European Union's Directive on Alternative Dispute Resolution for Consumer Disputes (the 'ADR Directive')[5] and a Regulation on Online Dispute Resolution for Consumer Disputes (the 'ODR Regulation').[6] These provisions work in tandem to require Member States to implement ODR systems for consumer claims. Furthermore, the United Nations Commission on International Trade Law (UNCITRAL)

Conditions', available at www.shop2.sprint.com/en/legal/os_general_terms_conditions_popup.shtml; last visited 16 July 2017.

[2] Ibid., p. 2–4.

[3] American Arbitration Association, 'Costs of Arbitration (Including AAA Administrative Fees)', https://www.adr.org/sites/default/files/Employment%20Fee%20Schedule.pdf Amended and Effective July 1, 2016 (last visited 17 July 2017). The notice states that there are additional fees for an in-person hearing ($500 + room rental), but the AAA says these fees are to be paid by the business.

[4] A. J. Schmitz, '"Drive-Thru" Arbitration in the Digital Age: Empowering Consumers through Regulated ODR', *Baylor Law Review* 62 (2010), 178–244, proposing OArb as a distinct type of online dispute resolution.

[5] Council Directive 2013/11/EU on Alternative Dispute Resolution for Consumer Disputes, OJ 2013 No. L165/63; see also in Chapter 9, p. 228.

[6] Council Regulation 2013/524/EU on Online Dispute Resolution for Consumer Disputes OJ 2013 No. L 165/1.

had advanced guidelines on ODR for cross-border e-commerce through its Working Group III on Online Dispute Resolution.[7]

It is nonetheless unclear whether these international ODR initiatives advance OArb per se. OArb is distinguishable from other ODR because it provides evaluations that lead to final resolutions.[8] In contrast, ODR more generally encompasses all forms of online dispute resolution – including online mediation, negotiation and other facilitative processes that do not necessarily involve a third-party determination of case merits. Furthermore, most ODR initiatives promote online mediation and negotiation, or automated systems that rely on algorithms to suggest settlements that parties may reject. They are not OArb in that they do not rely on a third-party neutral's determination of disputes.

Furthermore, the EU ADR Directive has been faulted for inadequacies with respect to ensuring transparency, fair processes and uniform implementation.[9] The Directive also creates choice of law complexities, and possible contradictions with Brussels I's jurisdictional requirement for the customer's country of domicile.[10] Moreover, EU Member States have largely refused to enforce pre-dispute agreements requiring F2F arbitration in B2C contexts, while the United States has been perhaps overly ambitious in advancing arbitration even when it inhibits consumers' access to remedies.

That said, there is a growing movement toward OArb because of its business efficiencies and potential for expanding access to justice. As noted earlier, OArb provides cheap or free means for consumers to obtain speedy determinations on B2C claims without need for class relief. In this way, OArb benefits both consumers and companies: consumers obtain economical remedies while companies garner goodwill and avoid costs and publicity of class actions. These benefits have led businesses to become the forerunners in creating OArb systems in the United States, even without government mandates or support.

[7] UN Commission on International Trade Law Working Group III, 29th Session, 'Online Dispute Resolution for Cross-Border Electronic Commerce Transactions: Draft Guidelines' (24–28 March 2014) UN Doc A/CN.9/WG.III/WP.128.

[8] See also the definition proposed in Chapter 9, p. 211.

[9] Joasia A. Luzak, 'The New ADR Directive: Designed to Fail? A Short but Hole-Ridden Stairway to Consumer Justice' (Amsterdam Law School Legal Studies Research Paper No. 2015–43; Ctr. for the Study of European Contract Law Working Paper No 2015–12, 2015).

[10] Marco B. M. Loos, 'Consumer ADR After Implementation of the ADR Directive: Enforcing European Consumer Rights at the Detriment of European Consumer Law', 1–15 (Amsterdam Law School Legal Studies Research Paper No. 2015–42; Ctr. for the Study of European Contract Law Working Paper No 2015–11, 2015).

This chapter will therefore consider OArb for resolution of B2C disputes, and suggest ideas for best practices in aiming to expand consumers' access to justice. Specifically, Part II will create context by explaining law that has developed for the enforcement of F2F arbitration and how strict enforcement in the United States has arguably curbed consumers' access to justice with respect to many B2C claims. Part III will then describe the evolution of OArb, including online complaints processes such as that provided by the Consumer Financial Protection Bureau (CFPB) in the United States.[11] It also will discuss OArb programs created by merchants such as eBay and ODR providers including Modria, which has been acquired by Tyler Technologies, that may serve as models for further OArb development.[12] This leads to Part IV, which will offer suggestions for best practices to overcome OArb obstacles and provide greater efficiency and fairness for all parties. Part V will conclude.

Arbitration in Context of US Law

Unlike the European Union, the United States generally insists on strict enforcement of pre-dispute arbitration clauses in B2C contexts. Although the CFPB has issued regulations to limit this enforcement of pre-dispute arbitration clauses in consumer financial products transactions, US enforcement of F2F arbitration to date has greatly limited consumer class actions. This has left US consumers to pursue individual F2F arbitration proceedings,[13] which are usually too costly and thus impractical for small dollar claims. Most US consumers therefore never utilize F2F arbitration rights.

Enforcement of Pre-Dispute Arbitration Contracts

Neither Directive 93/13 nor the Court of Justice of the EU strictly forbids enforcement of pre-dispute agreements requiring binding arbitral

[11] The US government established the CFPB to regulate consumer financial products per the Dodd-Frank Wall Street Reform and Consumer Protection Act. 12 United States Code section 5531 (2012).

[12] This author has proposed global development of an ODR system to promote consumer protection, while assisting businesses in boosting their bottom lines with returns on resolutions. See *The New Handshake: Online Dispute Resolution and the Future of Consumer Protection* (with Colin Rule) (American Bar Association 2017) (proposing an online remedy system to expand consumers' access to remedies and to revive corporate responsibility in consumer contracting).

[13] The CFPB's new regulation will stop predispute arbitration clauses from barring class actions with respect to consumer financial product contracts. 12 Code of Fed. Regs. § 1040 (2017).

awards in B2C transactions.[14] Nonetheless, the EU ADR Directive states that nationally certified ADR/ODR entities cannot use pre-dispute arbitration clauses and allows Member States to deny certification of arbitration schemes altogether, as seen in Germany.[15] Additionally, the Court of Justice of the EU ruled in *Mostaza Claro* v. *Centro Movil Milenium* that courts should examine arbitration clauses in B2C contracts, even at the enforcement stage.[16]

In contrast, the US Supreme Court has fortified strict enforcement of arbitration in consumer cases under the Federal Arbitration Act (FAA).[17] This was solidified in recent decisions including *American Express* v. *Italian Colors Restaurant*, *Stolt-Nielsen SA* v. *Animalfeeds Int'l Corp*, *AT&T Mobility, LLC* v. *Concepcion*, and *Rent-A-Center* v. *Jackson*.[18] The Court condoned class waivers with respect to statutory rights in *American Express*, significantly narrowed arbitrators' power to order class arbitration in *Stolt-Nielsen SA*, greatly limited application of contract defences to void arbitration clauses in *AT&T Mobility, LLC*, and confirmed arbitrators' power to determine the scope of their own jurisdiction in *Rent-A-Center*.[19] These decisions have allowed businesses to use arbitration and class waiver provisions to privatize consumers' access to remedies and potentially escape legal reforms.[20]

[14] Council Directive 93/13/EEC of 5 April 1993 on unfair terms in consumer contracts, OJ 1993 No. L95, p. 29, 21 April 1993.

[15] Council Directive 2013/11/EU of 21 May 2013 on alternate dispute resolution for consumer disputes and amending regulation (EC) No. 2006/2004 and Directive 2009/22/EC, OJ 2013 No. L165, p. 63.

[16] Case C-168/05 *Mostaza Claro* v. *Centro Movil Milenium* (2006) ECLI I-10421.

[17] Federal Arbitration Act (FAA), 9 United States Code section 201–08, 301–07 (2012) implements the New York Convention under section 201–208 and the Panama Convention under ss 301–307.

[18] *AT&T Mobility, LLC* v. *Concepcion* (2011) 131 Supreme Court Reporter 1740, 1743–56; *Stolt-Nielsen SA* v. *AnimalFeeds International Corp* (2010) 130 Supreme Court Reporter 1758; *Rent-A-Center, W, Inc* v. *Jackson* (2010) 130 Supreme Court Reporter 2772, 2777–80.

[19] See *American Express* v. *Italian Colors Restaurants* (2013) 133 Supreme Court Reporter 230, which enforces a class waiver in arbitration clauses with respect to anti-trust claims; *AT&T Mobility* (2011) 131 Supreme Court Reporter 1740, 1748–53 also states that classwide arbitration is inconsistent with the FAA; *Stolt-Nielsen SA* (2010) 130 Supreme Court Reporter 1758, 1773–76 holds that a party cannot be compelled to class arbitration unless there is a clear contractual basis for it; *Rent-A-Center, W, Inc* [2010] 130 Supreme Court Reporter at 2777–80 holds that a clause in employment contract delegating to the arbitrator exclusive authority to decide enforceability of the arbitration agreement was a valid delegation under the FAA.

[20] Jean R. Sternlight, 'Mandatory Binding Arbitration Clauses Prevent Consumers from Presenting Procedurally Difficult Claims' [2012] 42 *Southwestern Law Review* 87, 94–98.

The United States especially diverges from the EU in its enforcement of B2C arbitration when statutory claims are at stake.[21] US courts have uniformly held that arbitration is not subject to constitutional due process requirements and construe arbitration clauses broadly to cover tort and statutory claims.[22] In addition, arbitrators in the United States rarely order class arbitration in the wake of the US Supreme Court's ruling in *Stolt-Nielsen SA* v. *Animalfeeds Int'l Corp.*[23] In that case, the Court held that arbitrators exceeded their authority in ordering class arbitration where the contract between shipping companies and their customers was silent on class relief.[24]

Additionally, most B2C contracts expressly preclude class proceedings since *AT&T Mobility LLC* v. *Concepcion*, which narrowed consumers' power to challenge class waivers based on traditional contract defences.[25] The Supreme Court in *AT&T* held that the FAA preempts a court from using state contract law to condition enforcement of an arbitration clause on preserving consumers' ability to bring class-wide arbitration.[26] Consumers in that case filed a class action in contravention of the arbitration clause in AT&T's contract, alleging that the clause's class waiver effectively precluded vindication of their rights.[27] The California court agreed, but the US Supreme Court reversed and enforced the class waiver. It held that the FAA preempted California's use of unconscionability to strike the clause because the contract allowed for small claims court actions, the recovery of double attorney fees if an award exceeded the company's settlement offer, and the company's payment of arbitration costs.[28]

21 See *Green Tree Financial Corp* v. *Randolph* [2000] 531 United States Reporter 79, 89–92, which found TILA claims arbitrable.

22 Ibid., 91–92; *American Express* v. *Italian Colors Restaurant* [2013] 133 Supreme Court Reporter 2304 emphasized that there is no right to economical means for asserting anti-trust claims.

23 *Stolt-Nielsen SA* v. *AnimalFeeds International Corp* [2010] 130 Supreme Court Reporter 17.

24 Ibid. at 1769–77. But see *Oxford Health Plans LLC* v. *Sutter* [2013] 133 Supreme Court Reporter 2064, 2065–75, where the Supreme Court refused to void class arbitration order.

25 Peter B. Rutledge and Christopher R. Drahozal 'Contract and Choice' [2013] *Brigham Young University Law Review* 1, 38, finding that 93.6 per cent of the agreements studied waived any right to class arbitration.

26 *AT&T Mobility, LLC* v. *Concepcion* [2011] 131 Supreme Court Reporter 1740, 1743–56.

27 Ibid.

28 Ibid. at 1748–55, which emphasized that class action arbitration sacrifices informality; Sarah Rudolph Cole, 'On Babies and Bathwater: The Arbitration Fairness Act and the Supreme Court's Recent Arbitration Jurisprudence' [2011] 48 *Houston Law Review* 457, 481–91 highlighted how recent Supreme Court opinions curtail class action relief.

This jurisprudence is problematic to the extent that it hinders public litigation, which brings light to policy issues and aids the development of the law.[29] With the growth of mandatory arbitration clauses, businesses have gained quasi law-making powers that significantly decrease the compensatory and public deterrent objectives of consumer protection laws.[30] Accordingly, the CFPB has issued a regulation precluding enforcement of arbitration clauses in consumer financial product transactions where the clauses would effectively bar consumers from bringing class actions.[31] Although this regulation does not impact all B2C contracts, it signals concerns regarding equitable access to remedies for small-dollar B2C claims. Moreover, it opens doors to class actions with respect to consumer financial product claims, such as credit card claims.

Lack of Access to Remedies via F2F Arbitration

Group processes often make it possible for consumers to assert their claims. These processes also help uncover product defects, initiate recalls, and inform other consumers about business practices.[32] Nonetheless, F2F class proceedings have been criticized for failing to adequately and efficiently compensate victims.[33] Class action attorney's fees and litigation costs have been known to nearly deplete class awards and settlements.[34]

Nonetheless, consumers very rarely vindicate their rights via F2F arbitration in the United States, largely because they preclude class relief.[35] Indeed, many businesses use arbitration clauses to stop consumers from asserting their claims as a group in court or in arbitration.[36] Consumers

29 J. Maria Glover, 'Disappearing Claims and the Erosion of Substantive Law' [2015] 125 *Yale Law Journal* 3052.

30 Ibid.

31 See Consumer Financial Protection Bureau, 'Arbitration Study: Report to Congress' [2015], which lays the groundwork for rule-making to restrict class waivers in contracts for financial services. Dodd-Frank Act Wall Street Reform and Consumer Protection Act of 2010, section 1028, authorizes the Study and provides that the CFPB may regulate arbitration clauses. The regulation appears at 12 Code of Fed. Regs. § 1040 (2017).

32 See Amy J. Schmitz, 'Curing Consumers' Warranty Woes Through Regulated Arbitration' (2008) 23 *Ohio State Journal on Dispute Resolution* 627, 635–45, which discusses functions of class actions.

33 Linda S. Mullenix, 'Ending Class Actions As We Know Them: Rethinking the American Class Action' (2014) 64 *Emory Law Journal* 399, 400–430.

34 Geroge Rutherglen, 'Wal-Mart, AT&T Mobility, and the Decline of the Deterrent Class Action' (2012) 98 *Virginia Law Review in Brief* 24–27.

35 Brian T. Fitzpatrick, 'The End of Class Actions?' (2015) 57 *Arizona Law Review* 161.

36 (n 26) 164–97.

then forego claims rather than file individual arbitration claims.[37] For example, the CFPB found that US bank customers who complained about their bank's overdraft fees forewent their rights rather than filing individual arbitration claims in accordance with their bank contracts.[38]

This is unsurprising. Commonsense consumers will forego their rights, rather than face the costs and hassles of an in-person process. Furthermore, consumers from vulnerable communities may fear the explicit or implicit biases of those determining their disputes in F2F processes.[39] Even when consumers have some say in selecting an arbitrator, the merchant generally has greater power and dictates the administering institution. Accordingly, consumers and policymakers have looked to ODR as means for expanding access to remedies – especially for small dollar purchase problems.

Evolution of OArb Processes

ODR in general provides convenience, speed, low-cost, and travel and bookkeeping savings. Furthermore, OArb in particular offers enhanced potential for providing these benefits due to its binding nature, reliance on documentary evidence, and allowance for increased access to information and remedies. This is especially true with respect to B2C claims because they often involve relatively low damage claims that require fairly simple factual presentations. OArb thus may assist consumers in obtaining remedies, while generating cost savings for companies that they may pass on through lower prices and better quality goods and services. Such benefits help explain why businesses and ODR providers have already established OArb programs that may serve as models for further developments.

Impetus for OArb's Development

Convenience and Cost Savings

Many have promoted ODR generally for its convenience, stress reduction and cost savings. Unlike traditional in-person dispute resolution methods, ODR allows parties to communicate from anywhere using any type of

37 Aaron Blumenthall, 'Circumventing Concepcion: Conceptualizing Innovative Strategies to Ensure the Enforcement of Consumer Protection Laws in the Age of the Inviolable Class Action Waiver' (2015) 103 *California Law Review* 699, 700–714.

38 Ibid.

39 Elayne E. Greenberg, 'Fitting the Forum to the Pernicious Fuss: A Dispute System Design to Address Implicit Bias and 'isms in the Workplace' (2015) 17 *Cardozo Journal of Conflict Resolution* 75, 75–110.

Internet access at their convenience. This also allows consumers to forego having to travel, miss work, 'dress up' or arrange for childcare to attend F2F hearings and meetings. For example, ODR would allow consumers in the middle of the United States to assert claims they would forego if required to attend proceedings on the east or west coast under a typical venue provision.[40,41]

Furthermore, OArb is especially efficient. It is fit for asynchronous communication because it mainly involves parties' exchange of documents. It does not require the same degree of interaction and F2F contact, as more facilitative non-binding dispute resolution methods such as mediation. Instead, asynchronous postings and communications in OArb allow parties to post and carefully review briefs, affidavits, and other evidentiary submissions on their own schedules. This also leads to inexpensive and convenient preservation of case submissions and records in one virtual location.[42] Arbitrators and parties can then access the materials and carefully review them at convenient times, thereby eliminating or minimizing the monetary and environmental costs of copying and sending paper records.

Buffering Bias

Skilled arbitrators may do well managing biases and anger-driven communications in F2F arbitration. However, arbitrators are people and may harbour implicit biases that may cloud F2F interactions. This often makes it especially difficult for minorities and other vulnerable individuals to achieve justice though F2F judicial or ADR processes.[43,44]

In contrast to F2F processes, use of computer-mediated communications (CMC) in OArb empowers individuals by allowing them to submit and respond to evidentiary submissions from behind the buffer of

[40] Theodore Eisenberg and Geoffrey R. Miller, 'The Flight to New York: An Empirical Study of Choice of Law and Choice of Forum Clauses in Publicly-Held Companies' Contracts' (2009) 30 *Cardozo Law Review* 1475, 1486–92, found that New York is often the designated venue for litigation due to its history and importance as the financial centre of the United States.

[41] Regarding the increase of 'inclusivity' offered by ICT, see also Chapter 2, p. 44.

[42] See Philippe Gilliéron, 'From Face-to-Face to Screen-to-Screen: Real Hope or True Fallacy?' (2007) available at http://works.bepress.com/cgi/viewcontent.cgi?article=1000&context=philippe_gillieron, accessed 16 July 2017 ('For the consumers, ODR is not only cheaper, it is often the single method of dispute resolution available, as one is unlikely to be willing to bring a costly action into court for a small value at stake . . . ').

[43] Greenberg, 'Fitting the Forum to the Pernicious Fuss', 75–110.

[44] Regarding the possible flaws of human decision-making, see also Chapter 6, p. 134.

their electronic devices.[45] Race, gender, and disabilities remain unknown through CMC. Furthermore, CMC provides time and space for tempers to cool, often leading to more reasoned communications. It is often assumed that individuals are prone to send communications through digital devices. However, this is becoming less common as individuals are increasingly aware that their online communications are nearly impossible to erase.

OArb processes also may be more automated and form-driven, making it easier for those with limited education or linguistic skills to state their claims. These processes may utilize forms that guide consumers through the claims process in a way similar to common tax-filing programs such as TurboTax. This also eases or eliminates costs of hiring attorneys.

Evaluations Leading to Resolutions

Again, OArb is distinguishable from other ODR because it provides evaluations that lead to final resolutions, which are often essential for obtaining remedies. OArb usually leads to a final resolution more definitively than online mediation, negotiation, and other facilitative processes because OArb ends the disputes according to a neutral third parties' evaluation of the parties' cases. This is especially true for binding OArb because it precludes the parties from simultaneously or later asserting their claims in court. Nonetheless, even evaluative ODR that is not binding usually prompts parties to quickly end their disputes based on claims evaluations.

OArb awards also can be efficiently communicated to parties and preserved online so parties may take the awards and immediately have them enforced.[46] This cuts out the time and confusion regarding intermittent steps that often stall consumers' access to remedies through F2F court and arbitration processes. In the case of binding OArb, the FAA extends the same special enforcement as it provides for F2F arbitration. This enforcement includes liberal venue provisions,[47] immediate

[45] See Aashit Shah, 'Using ADR to Resolve Online Disputes' (2004) 10 *Richmond Journal of Law and Technology* 25 proposes that anonymity of CMC may help ease distrust and anger.

[46] For the notification of digital awards to the parties, see Chapter 7, p. 177 and 179.

[47] See 9 US Code section 9 2006, which supplements general venue options; *Cortez Byrd Chips, Inc* v. *Bill Harbert Construction Co* (2000) 529 United States Reporter 193, 195, which held FAA venue provisions are permissive and therefore expand possible sites for federal motions to confirm, vacate, or modify an arbitration award.

appeal from orders adverse to arbitration,[48] and arbitral immunity.[49] The FAA also directs courts to strictly enforce arbitration awards with very limited review.[50] FAA enforcement would not apply to non-binding ODR.

Again, FAA enforcement of F2F arbitration in a B2C context has been perceived as problematic. However, such enforcement may be less concerning with respect to OArb because unlike F2F Arbitration, OArb may be free or very low cost for consumers. Furthermore, OArb does not require the travel and legal costs of F2F arbitration. OArb creates a win-win for consumers and businesses: consumers gain easy and cheap access to remedies while businesses gain customer goodwill and avoid class actions.

Emergence of Quasi OArb

Online review sites such as Yelp and CFPB's complaint portals have become easy avenues for consumers to assert their complaints. These venues allow consumers to vent online and share information about product and service problems. However, they are not OArb per se in that they do not provide an evaluative determination that brings clear finality to the dispute. Additionally, the questionable quality and unmanageable quantity of reviews online is daunting.[51] Companies also may ignore complaints on third-party review sites. Furthermore, businesses may ignore or send unhelpful replies to complaints asserted to them directly via email.[52]

[48] See 9 US Code section 16 2006 specifying appeal provisions.

[49] See *Austern* v. *Chicago Board Options Exchange, Inc* (1990) 898 Federal Reporter 2d ed 882, 886, writ of certiorari denied, 498 United States Reporter 850, which held arbitrators absolutely immune from liability in damages for all acts within the scope of the arbitral process.

[50] 9 US Code section 10 prescribes limited grounds for judicial review focused on preservation of basic procedural fairness and section 11 allows for judicial modification or correction of certain apparent errors in an award. The FAA does not permit a court to question the merits of an arbitration award.

[51] Adi Ayal and Uri Benoliel, '*Revitalizing the Case for Good Cause Statutes: The Role of Review Sites*' (2014) 19 *Stanford Journal of Law Business and Finance* 331, 332–347.

[52] Queensland Government, 'Customer Complaint Behaviour', available at www.business.qld.gov.au/business/running/customer-service/managing-customer-complaints/customer-complaint-behaviour (last accessed 16 July 2017).

In the United States, the Better Business Bureau (BBB) is one of the most formidable consumer websites because it offers an accreditation, or 'trustmark,' to businesses that pay a fee and abide by the BBB Code of Business Practices.[53] Although the BBB is private, it has gained a strong reputation for its trustmark system based on consumers' feedback regarding their experiences with listed businesses.[54] Furthermore, the BBB offers a mixture of online and F2F dispute-resolution processes, ranging from informal mediation to binding arbitration with its panel of approximately 1,000 arbitrators.[55] For example, a consumer may submit a complaint through the BBB's website, but ultimately resolve his or her complaint with a business through follow-up phone calls or emails.[56] BBBs permit the delivery of [dispute resolution] services at convenient locations whether programs are national, regional or local.[57]

Similarly, consumers may submit complaints regarding financial products and services through the CFPB's public Consumer Complaint Database.[58] Although the CFPB urges companies to respond to complaints, it promises no legally enforceable ODR or follow-up on individual complaints.[59] In addition, the database of complaints is difficult to

53 'Dispute Resolution Processes and Guides', *The Better Business Bureau*, available at www.bbb.org/council/programs-services/dispute-handling-and-resolution/dispute-resolution-rules-and-brochures/dispute-resolution-processes-and-guides (last visited 17 July 2017).

54 The BBB disclaims responsibility for making a determination as to the business's product quality or competency. 'Get Accredited', *The Better Business Bureau*, www.bbb.org/council/for-businesses/about-bbb-accreditation (last accessed 17 July 2017); Steven J. Cole and Charles I. Underhill, 'Fifteen Years of ODR Experience: The BBB Online Reliability Trust Mark Program' (2010) 43(1) *Uniform Commercial Code L J* Article 2, 443, 446–445.

55 'Dispute Handling and Resolution', *The Better Business Bureau*, available at www.bbb.org/council/programs-services/dispute-handling-and-resolution (last visited 17 July 2017).

56 To the extent practical, BBB will arrange for the hearing to be held at a location convenient to the customer. 'Rules for Informal Dispute Settlement', *The Better Business Bureau*, available at www.bbb.org/council/programs-services/dispute-handling-and-resolution/dispute-resolution-rules-and-brochures/rules-for-informal-dispute-settlement/#13 (last visited 17 July 2017).

57 BBB, at https://www.bbb.org/bbb-dispute-handling-and-resolution/ last visited 17 July 2017.

58 Richard Cordray, 'Disclosure of Consumer Complaint Narrative Data', *Consumer Financial Protection Bureau* (Doc No CFPB-2014-0016, 12 March 2015) 2–3 available at http://files.consumerfinance.gov/f/201503_cfpb_disclosure-of-consumer-complaint-narrative-data.pdf.

59 The CFPB provides procedures for screening complaints and relaying them to the businesses. Consumer Financial Protection Bureau, 'Consumer Response to Annual Report' (2014) 11–12, available at http://files.consumerfinance.gov/f/201503_cfpb_consumer-response-annual-report-2014.pdf.

navigate, especially with the addition of consumers' narratives regarding their experiences.[60] Even law professors and news reporters have had difficulty using the database.[61]

Uniform Dispute Resolution Procedures (UDRP) is another non-final online administrative resolution process emerging through Internet Corporation for Assigned Names and Numbers (ICANN).[62] Domain name registrants must affirm that their selected name will not infringe others' rights, and agree to participate in the UDRP's arbitration-like proceedings should a third party assert a claim.[63] The United Nations World Intellectual Property Organization creates guidelines for these proceedings with an aim for advancing fairness and efficiency.[64] Those filing claims under the UDRP must show that the contested domain name is identical or confusingly similar to their own, and that the registrant has no legitimate interests in the domain name.[65] If ICANN finds that a complainant has made this showing, then it will cause the domain name to be transferred to the claimant within ten days. These rulings are nonbinding, leaving parties free to challenge them under the Anti-Cybersquatting Consumer Protection Act (ACPA).[66] Although the UDRP process often ends disputes, some trademark owners prefer to bring ACPA claims because the Act offers more extensive remedies, i.e. damages, whereas the

[60] A business has fifteen calendar days to provide an initial response and up to sixty calendar days to provide a final response. The Bureau then invites the consumer to review the response and provide feedback. The CFPB's further investigation is purely at the CFPB's option. Cordray, 'Disclosure of Consumer Complaint Narrative Data', Consumer Financial Protection Bureau, 'CFPB Publishes Over 7,700 Consumer Complaint Narratives About Financial Companies' (25 June 2015); see www.consumerfinance.gov/newsroom/cfpb-publishes-over-7700-consumer-complaint-narratives-about-financial-companies.

[61] See email from Pamela Foohey, Associate Professor at Indiana University Maurer School of Law, to Amy J. Schmitz, Professor of Law, 3 August 2015 (on file with author).

[62] See Jason M. Osborn, 'Effective and Complementary Solutions to Domain Name Disputes: ICANN'S Uniform Domain Name Dispute Resolution Policy and the Federal Anti-Cybersquatting Consumer Protection Act of 1999' (2000) 76 *Notre Dame Law Review* 209, 214; Internet Corp for Assigned Names and Numbers (ICANN), 'Rules for Uniform Domain Name Dispute Resolution Policy' (2000) 39 ILM 952, hereinafter 'UDRP Rules'; World Intellectual Property Org, *WIPO Arbitration Rules*, www.wipo.int/amc/en/arbitration/rules/newrules.html (current rules effective from 1 June 2014).

[63] 'Uniform Domain Name Dispute Resolution', *Internet Corp. for Assigned Names and Numbers*, www.icann.org/resources/pages/policy-2012–02–25-en (as approved 24 October 1999).

[64] World Intellectual Property, Org. Final Report of the WIPO Internet Domain Name Process (1999), www.wipo.int/export/sites/www/amc/en/docs/report-final1.pdf.

[65] See above, Internet Corp. for Assigned Names and Numbers.

[66] 15 U.S.C. § 1125(d) (2012).

ICANN proceedings are limited to cancellation and transfer of a domain name.[67]

Current Growth of OArb

The prime example of private ODR in the United States is eBay's Resolution Center, which processes consumer claims related to website purchases free of charge.[68] The eBay Money Back Guarantee that applies when a buyer does not receive an item or the item is not as promised gives the buyer the right to file an online complaint within 30 days after the latest estimated delivery date. The seller then has three business days to respond in the Resolution Center.[69] If the seller does not respond or provide an adequate remedy, the buyer may ask eBay to assign an online neutral to arbitrate.[70] If necessary, eBay may enforce these essentially OArb determinations via PayPal, eBay's payment system provider, by setting aside a seller's funds.[71]

eBay also provides what amounts to OArb in other contexts because the final determinations are effectively binding. Under its Unpaid Item Policy, eBay allows sellers to submit claims online against buyers who do not pay for purchased items within two days.[72] If a buyer fails to provide proof of payment or a valid reason for not paying, eBay may grant the seller a final credit and refund the fee for relisting the item.[73] eBay's Verified Rights Owner Program (VeRO) similarly allows intellectual property rights holders to submit a Notice of Claimed Infringement online with respect to items sold on eBay. Such Notice prompts eBay to remove a listing that arguably infringes intellectual property rights. The seller then has ten days to seek item reinstatement unless the holder of the intellectual property rights informs eBay that it is seeking a court order to restrain the relisting under the Digital Millennium Copyright Act.[74]

67 See Cybertelecom, Anti-Cybersquatting Consumer Protection Act, www.cybertelecom.org/dns/acpa.htm (last updated 28 April 2015). See also Chapter 9, p. 235.

68 Colin Rule, 'Making Peace on eBay: Resolving Disputes in the World's Largest Marketplace', (2008) *ACResolution: The Quarterly Mag. of the Ass'n for Conflict Resolution* 1–10.

69 'Ebay Money Back Guarantee', *Ebay*, http://pages.ebay.com/help/policies/money-back-guarantee.html (last visited 16 July 2017).

70 Ibid.

71 Ibid. (Also giving both parties 30 days to appeal any determinations).

72 'Unpaid Item Policy', eBay, www.pages.ebay.com/help/policies/unpaid-item.html (last visited 16 July 2017).

73 Ibid.

74 'How eBay protects intellectual property (VeRO)', *Ebay*, www.pages.ebay.com/help/policies/programs-vero-ov.html (last visited 16 July 2017). (Noting how the right for an

Under eBay's Independent Feedback Review policy, a seller may challenge a review posting within 30 days. eBay will then enlist an online neutral from a professional dispute resolution service to examine the challenged posting and determine whether to affirm, withdraw, or take no action regarding the review.[75] Similarly, under eBay's Vehicle Purchase Protection program, eBay offers up to US $50,000 with respect to vehicles purchased on eBay to cover payment for a vehicle never received or not as promised if the parties are unable to resolve their disputes through direct discussions.[76]

The online payment system, PayPal, also offers OArb for claims related to unreceived or nonconforming items.[77] PayPal's policy largely mimics eBay's, and allows for a third party's determination. PayPal then enforces these determinations by issuing refunds or imposing other consequences.[78] PayPal also may investigate and determine sellers' online submissions regarding billing errors, which may lead to PayPal crediting the seller's account.

Nonetheless, both PayPal and eBay have clauses in their user agreements that require F2F arbitration of any claims parties do not resolve online.[79] Customers may avoid this arbitration policy by filing a written opt-out form within thirty days of accepting the user agreement. Few consumers, however, are aware or take advantage of this option.[80]

Merchants outside of the United States also have embraced ODR for its ability to transcend borders and lower dispute resolution costs. For example, the online retailer Alibaba uses an ODR mechanism for resolution of buyer and seller disputes.[81] It allows parties to submit a dispute to Alibaba's online Dispute Resolution Team if they cannot resolve a complaint after ten days. The Team will make a determination based

eBay member to file a counter notice to reinstate a listing after a notice of claims infringement is rooted in the DMCA.)

75 'Independent Feedback Review', eBay, www.pages.ebay.com/help/feedback/feedback-review.html (last visited 17 July 2017).

76 If the buyer cannot resolve the issue with the seller, it must request reimbursement no later than 45 days after the listing end date. 'Vehicle Purchase Protection', eBay, www.pages.motors.ebay.com/buy/purchase-protection.

77 'PayPal User Agreement', *PayPal* (1 July 2017), Section 14, available at www.paypal.com/us/webapps/mpp/ua/useragreement-full#14.

78 Ibid.

79 'eBay User Agreement', eBay (15 June 2017), www.pages.ebay.com/help/policies/user-agreement.html?rt=nc#17.

80 Ibid.

81 'Alibaba.com', *ALIBABA*, www.rule.alibaba.com/rule/detail/2060.htm (last visited 26 July 2017).

on evidence provided. If a party does not comply with a determination, Alibaba may terminate the party from the site on claims more than $300. For claims of less than $300, Alibaba publishes a complaint case record on the recalcitrant party's web page on Alibaba.com for 90 days.[82]

Along with merchant-provided ODR, there are also outside ODR providers. For example, Modria spun-off from eBay and PayPal in 2011, and was recently acquired by Tyler Technologies.[83] Modria handled cases ranging from B2C e-commerce to divorce, landlord-tenant, insurance, and tax disputes. It offered a wide range of ODR process, including OArb, problem diagnosis, online negotiation, and case management.

Now as part of Tyler Technologies, Modria continues to provide users with numerous communication tools to help them build a resolution to any problem they may face, ranging from simple debt disputes to complex domestic cases. The online program is designed to guide users through a step-by-step process that offers a quick diagnosis of their situation, and helps them assess what will work best to resolve their problem. Through Modria, the parties may also request assistance from a mediator or negotiator if they are unable to reach a solution on their own. Although www.tylertech.com collects some general information such as a Modria user's name, email address, IP address, and access times, Tyler Technologies never sells, rents, or releases its customer lists to third parties.[84]

Smartsettle is another ODR provider.[85] It allows parties to exchange information online (sometimes including telephone or F2F meetings) and generates suggested settlements based on each party's preferences and concessions. It allows parties to asynchronously negotiate (logging in and out at their convenience); along with Visual Blind Bidding (parties indicate what they are willing to accept and a deal is declared if both parties have accepted at least one of the same values). If no agreement is reached through these processes, Dampened Pendulum Arbitration guarantees a settlement by using an expert neutral to favour the party

[82] Ibid.

[83] Aled Davies, 'Modria – The Operating System for ODR Mediator – Colin Rule', *mediatoracademy.com* (2015), www.judiciary.gov.uk/wpcontent/uploads/2015/02/colin_rule_modria_os_for_odr.pdf. Information regarding the acquisition is available at https://www.lawsitesblog.com/2017/06/modria-innovator-online-dispute-resolution-acquired-tyler-technologies.html (last visited 17 July 2017).

[84] 'All the Tools You Need for Online Dispute Resolution', *Tyler Technologies*, https://www.tylertech.com/solutions-products/modria/odr (last accessed 6 September 2017).

[85] 'Smartsettle: Changing the Way the World Negotiates', Smartsettle, www.smartsettle.com (last accessed 2 October 2015).

whose last accepted value is deemed most equitable.[86] Typical disputes include a variety of issues, including family, insurance, workplace, community, real estate, e-commerce, and more.[87]

In the insurance industry, CyberSettle[88] launched PayMD in 2012 to assist healthcare providers and patients seeking resolution of healthcare bills.[89] The service no longer exists, but it demonstrated how ODR could be used for helping providers to obtain some payment on bills that often go unpaid, while patients gain the autonomy and flexibility in paying their healthcare bills.[90] ODR programs may be contextualized to address particular issues, thus adding to the efficiency and efficacy of ODR over F2F resolution systems.

VirtualCourthouse.com (VCH) offers ODR for neutrals and disputants, as well as means for parties to resolve their disputes through CMC (including F2F hearings as necessary).[91] These ODR services may include facilitated negotiation, mediation, neutral case evaluation, or OArb.[92] If parties agree to OArb, they use the site to electronically file claims, choose a neutral to resolve their disputes, and submit exhibits and supporting materials for their cases to the assigned neutral in a secure online environment.[93] The neutral then reviews the presentations and renders a binding decision.[94] VCH's OArb process uses a 'middleware' to connect the parties regardless of whether they have disparate operating systems, and incorporates a combination of multimedia technologies and business processes with a user-friendly interface.[95] This OArb process has been used to settle hundreds of personal injury, real estate, construction, and

[86] Ibid.

[87] Ibid. *See also* www.smartsettle.com/home/products/ (gives a cost breakdown).

[88] Sung Choi, 'A Simple Walkthrough of the Cybersettle System', *LinkedIn* www.slideshare.net/cybersettle/cybersettle-walkthrough (26 February 2012).

[89] Robert Glatter, MD, PayMD: An Online Solution to Settling Your Medical Bills, Forbes, 6 December 2013, https://www.forbes.com/sites/robertglatter/2013/12/06/paymd-an-online-solution-to-your-settling-your-medical-bills/#15a78198419a.

[90] Id.

[91] 'Who We Are', *VirtualCourthouse.com*, www.virtualcourthouse.com/index.cfm/category/9/who-we-are.cfm.

[92] Ibid.

[93] Ibid. The parties select a neutral through an online negotiation, and case presentations typically include supporting medical bills, doctor reports, and pictures.

[94] The parties may complete case presentations in a few hours or days, and usually less than thirty days. 'How It Works', *VirtualCourthouse.com*, www.virtualcourthouse.com/index.cfm/category/1/how-it-works.cfm.

[95] Ibid.

contract disputes. The fee for this process is usually $400, which includes the $300 neutral fee and $50 filing fee per party.[96] Parties can therefore use this OArb process to resolve their claims for $200 each, but their costs go up for more complicated cases and those that require F2F hearings.[97] Nonetheless, the process may not be appropriate in multi-party disputes, cases involving emotional issues, or conflicts over large amounts of money.

Net-ARB provides a similar OArb process, but it is conducted purely through email instead of using a central portal for sharing case presentations.[98] Disputants using this process present their cases in emails to the arbitrator who renders a binding award.[99] net-ARB's website indicates that its awards are binding and subject to limited review (thus assuming FAA enforcement), but allows for non-binding or semi-binding awards per the parties' express agreement.[100] Net-ARB is different from VirtualCourthouse.com in that it uses a trustmark 'Consumer Confidence Program' that online merchants can join in order to post the 'Verified Trust Seal' on their websites.[101] This seal certifies that the company has agreed to 'uphold principles of net-honesty', arbitrate any customer disputes using net-ARB and abide by all net-ARB determinations.[102] Customers of that company then have the option to pay a $199 filing fee to arbitrate using this OArb process.[103]

96 'Pricing', *VirtualCourthouse.com*, www.virtualcourthouse.com/index.cfm/category/30/pricing.cfm, (last visited 15 July 2017).

97 Ibid.

98 'The Anatomy of a net-ARB Hearing', *net-ARB*, www.net-arb.com/how_arbitration_works.php (last visited 15 July 2017).

99 Ibid.

100 'Frequently Asked Questions', *net-ARB*, www.net-arb.com/FAQ.php (last visited 15 July 2017).

The site states that its awards are binding like court decisions but 'only better' because they 'cannot be appealed,' thus seemingly assuming the FAA would apply to their enforcement, unless parties expressly agree otherwise. Ibid. If parties need to have an award enforced as a judgment in court, they must get a copy of an Affidavit of Arbitration from net-ARB for a $35 processing fee. Ibid.

101 'Consumer Confidence Program', *net-ARB*, www.net-arb.com/consumer_confidence (last visited 15 July 2017).

102 The program is discussed on several pages of the company's website, advertising the program as a beneficial process for individuals and companies. Ibid.

103 The customer pays the fee, but it may be reallocated to the company in the award. 'What Will Arbitration Cost?', *net-ARB*, www.net-arb.com/what_will_arbitration_cost.php (last visited 15 July 2017). No fee is assessed, however, until an arbitration agreement is signed by both parties. 'How it Works', *net-ARB*, www.net-arb.com/how_arbitration_works.php (last visited 15 July 2017).

Arbitration Resolution Services (ARS) provides an ODR process that begins when the customer files a complaint.[104] Both parties then receive passwords that provide them with access to ARS's secure ARB-IT portal, where all communications are posted.[105] The parties communicate asynchronously through ARB-IT to ARS's emails alerting them when others post communications on the site.[106] The ARS ODR process is stepped in that parties first attempt to settle through online negotiations, then mediation, and finally binding arbitration of any remaining disputes they could not settle through the prior facilitative processes. In the OArb phase, the neutral that facilitated the parties' mediation serves as the arbitrator and issues the Certificate of Binding Settlement.[107]

In Mexico, Concilianet is an online dispute resolution process managed by Mexico's Federal Consumer Protection Agency (PROFECO) that began operation in June 2008.[108] The service is free, and the Agency receives complaints electronically and carries out conciliation telephonically and over the Internet.[109] Concilianet only resolves disputes with merchants that have concluded a 'cooperation agreement' with the Agency.[110] Recent numbers show that more than 90 companies have now registered. Furthermore, from June 2008 to August 2012, the system has resolved 96 per cent of the 7,000 filed complaints, and it was accomplished in an average of 25 days (as compared with 92 days). Moreover, 93 per cent of the consumers who have used the system report that they trust the system.[111]

Overcoming Obstacles to Achieve Best Practices

The benefits of OArb are great, but obstacles to its development remain. Along with usual concerns regarding ODR's security and provider neutrality, OArb raises special enforcement and due-process concerns. Some also have voiced concerns with respect to technological and other resource imbalances. While these concerns are noteworthy, they are not unsurmountable. Policymakers, OArb providers and other

[104] *ARS*, available at www.arbresolutions.com (last visited 5 September 2017); 'How It Works', *ARS* available at www.arbresolutions.com/how-it-works (last visited 5 September 2017).
[105] Ibid. [106] Ibid. [107] Ibid.
[108] New Developments in Civil and Commercial Mediation: Global Comparative Perspectives 503 (Carlos Esplugues & Louis Marquis eds. 2015).
[109] Ibid.
[110] Mex. Gobierno Mexicano, *Proveedores participantes*, GOB.mx, https://concilianet.profeco.gob.mx/Concilianet/proveedores_que_concilian.jsp (last visited 21 August 2017).
[111] Sergio Daniel Michel Cháves. *Memoria Documental: Conciliación através de medios electrónicos: Concilianet – 2008 a 2012*, 23–4 (2012).

stakeholders have opportunity to work together to overcome the obstacles in establishing best practices.[112]

Security of ODR Systems

Commentators voice concerns regarding the safety, reliability and privacy of ODR due to its reliance on the Internet and software programs.[113] Computers crash, hackers hone their abilities to tap into private systems, and viruses infect digital programs and files. OArb can only succeed if participants trust that their submissions and communications will be safely received by their intended recipients, and remain securely stored on a dedicated case site or portal. Privacy remains a key benefit of arbitration and ADR in general.

Nonetheless, Internet reliability and security are continually improving. Furthermore, privacy and reliability can be addressed in implementing OArb privacy protocols and using encryption and security devices.[114] Anti-virus and anti-malware programs have become commonplace, and are freely or cheaply available for computer programs and operating systems.[115] Furthermore, ODR providers often take special measures to ensure the security of their programs and incorporate their own Internet security measures in their systems. For example, the ODR provider Modria uses sophisticated encryption and other data safety mechanisms to ensure the safety of its services.[116]

Nonetheless, private entities must work in collaboration with government regulators and other public entities to ensure system security. ODR providers could be linked with a trustmark, such as that of the BBB noted earlier, allowing consumers to seek out or stay with companies that they trust for privacy and security. Such an OArb trustmark also could be used in conjunction with other measures that would address institutional

[112] See, e.g. *Parisi* v. *Netlearning, Inc.*, 139 F. Supp. 2d 745, 751 (E.D. Va. 2001) (holding that certain aspects of UDRP render the FAA provisions for judicial review of arbitration award inapplicable).

[113] Parliamentary History, see Chapter 3, p. 56, of Philipp Schaumann.

[114] Thomas D. Halket, 'The Use of Technology in Arbitration: Ensuring the Future is Available to Both Parties', (2007) 81 *St. John's Law Review*. 269, 304–305 (noting how the technology exists for protecting security, although policymakers must take care to ensure some level of equality with respect to its use in dispute resolution).

[115] See for e.g. 'Virus, Spam, Spyware Protection', *Mcafee.com*, www.home.mcafee.com/Store (last visited 1 January 2015) (providing a virus-scanning program).

[116] 'All the Tools You Need for Online Dispute Resolution', *Tyler Technologies*, https://www.tylertech.com/solutions-products/modria/odr (last visited 14 July 2017).

shortcomings in the EU ADR Directive.[117] For example, OArb providers that benefit from the trustmark could be required to educate consumers about the system and direct consumers to the OArb mechanism once they have raised a complaint.[118] Additionally, the trustmark would help fill a gap in the Directive by offering a concrete evaluative tool for ensuring compliance with safety and due process standards.[119]

Neutral and Accredited OArb Providers

Consumers may fear the unseen nature of online arbitrators, and question the neutrality and training of online arbitrators supplied through ODR providers. This is especially true for OArb provided directly by the merchant, such as eBay's ODR program. However, these concerns may be overstated, in that eBay is not a party in these disputes and has incentive to ensure fairness to maintain a good reputation.

Again, a trustmark also would boost confidence in OArb. Through these trustmark programs, online merchants may subscribe to use a provider's OArb services for customer complaints to augment consumers' confidence in Internet transactions. Adopting merchants may then post the associated trustmark logo on their sites to indicate their commitments to fair consumer dealings and using ODR to resolve consumers' claims. They hope that this will bolster their credibility and consumer trust in their websites.[120]

Moreover, policymakers are already establishing accreditation and due process standards for ODR providers.[121] For example, the EU's ADR Directive requires the Commission to establish a list of 'competent [ADR] authorities' in the Member States and the States shall ensure that ADR entities publicly post information on their compliance with Directive standards.[122] These standards include 'a set of quality requirements which apply to all ADR procedures carried out by an ADR entity which has been

[117] Joasia A. Luzak, 'The New ADR Directive: Designed to Fail? A Short but Hole-Ridden Stairway to Consumer Justice', (Amsterdam Law School Legal Studies Research Paper No. 2015–43; Ctr. for the Study of European Contract Law Working Paper No 2015–12, 2015).

[118] Ibid. [119] Ibid. at 12.

[120] Lan Q. Hang, 'Online Dispute Resolution Systems: The Future of Cyberspace Law', (2001) 41 *Santa Clara Law Review* 837, 849 (discussing the BBB's seal program for boosting consumer confidence and merchants' commitment to consumer protection).

[121] Ibid.

[122] Directive 2013/11/EU of the European Parliament and of the Council of 21 May 2013 on Alternative Dispute Resolution for Consumer Disputes, 2013 O.J. (L 165/73) Article 7, 1(b).

notified to the Commission'.[123] Furthermore, the Directive requires that designated competent authorities monitor these ADR procedures in order to advance consumers' access to high-quality, transparent, effective and fair out-of-court redress mechanisms no matter where they reside in the Union.[124]

Although this Directive does not establish a trustmark system, it does safeguard some level of due process. A trustmark could thus bolster evaluation of compliance with due process standards.[125] Furthermore, OArb practitioners should create and follow ethical standards regarding confidentiality, impartiality, competence and quality of process.[126] Practitioners must understand confidentiality risks and communicate those risks to clients. They also must ensure that all parties have an adequate opportunity to participate in the process and that parties can make voluntary and informed choices surrounding the procedures and outcome.[127]

Enforcement of OArb Agreements and Awards

Facilitative and optional ODR processes are different from OArb because they are not binding and thus do not produce binding awards that are enforceable under the FAA. This is why courts have concluded that the non-final dispute resolution procedure prescribed by the ICANN UDRP discussed earlier is not arbitration governed by the FAA.[128] Merchants and ODR providers have nonetheless created some hybrid OArb programs that often end disputes without being the type that end with final awards that are enforceable under the FAA.[129]

123 Directive 2013/11/EU of the European Parliament and of the Council of 21 May 2013 on Alternative Dispute Resolution for Consumer Disputes, 2013 O.J. (L 165/67) 37.

124 Directive 2013/11/EU of the European Parliament and of the Council of 21 May 2013 on Alternative Dispute Resolution for Consumer Disputes, 2013 O.J. (L 165/70) Chapter 1, Article 2 "Scope".

125 Luzak, Ibid. at 4–15.

126 Daniel Rainey, 'Third-Party Ethics in the Age of the Fourth Party', (2014).1 *International Journal of Dispute Resolution* 37, 56.

127 Ibid. at 45–46; for further discussion of the EU ARD Directive, see Chapter 9, p. 228.

128 *Parisi*, 139 F. Supp. 2d at 751; *see also Lockheed Martin Corp.* v. *Network Solutions, Inc.*, 141 F. Supp. 2d 648, 651–52 (N.D. Tex. 2001) (explaining UDRP's purpose and process, and noting that the average time from filing to decision is fifty-two days); *Virtual Countries, Inc.* v. *Republic of South Africa*, 148 F. Supp. 2d 256, 259–61, 265 n.10 (S.D.N.Y. 2001) (explaining UDRP's development, and doubting that ICAAN would amend the UDRP's non-binding administrative procedure to provide for binding arbitration).

129 *See supra* notes 22–29 and accompanying text.

Such non-binding ODR is not OArb per se, but it may be particularly attractive in jurisdictions that refuse to enforce pre-dispute arbitration agreements in consumer contexts. In the European Union, for example, e-merchants generally may not include pre-dispute arbitration clauses in their contracts that require consumers to resolve disputes through binding OArb, although they may offer arbitration as an option post-dispute.[130] The European Council Directive on Unfair Terms in Consumer Contracts also limits any OArb requirements that would hinder consumers' rights to legal action.[131]

Likewise, pre-dispute arbitration clauses in consumer, employment, franchise and civil rights cases would become unenforceable in the United States if the proposed Arbitration Fairness Act (AFA) is enacted.[132] Furthermore, the CFPB in the United States issued final regulations precluding enforcement of pre-dispute arbitration agreements that hinder class relief in sales of consumer financial products.[133] Although such legal reforms do not bar all arbitration they signal growing distaste for pre-dispute arbitration agreements in B2C contexts, thereby suggesting that it may be best to require post-dispute arbitration agreements for OArb awards to be universally enforceable.[134]

Additionally, non-legal forces fostered by registration requirements and reputation systems may serve as de facto enforcement mechanisms for OArb agreements and awards.[135] For example, Internet Service

[130] Gilliéron, 'From Face-to-Face to Screen-to-Screen', at 322; *see also* Haitham A. Haloush & Bashar H. Malkawi, 'The Liberty of Participation in Online Alternative Dispute Resolution Schemes', 11 *SMU Science and Technology Law Review* 119, 119, 124–31 (2007) (urging that 'consent should be at the forefront' of an ODR scheme); E.g. the special form requirement for pre-dispute arbitration agreements to which consumers are parties in Section 1031(5) of the German Civil Code, discussed in Chapter 7, p. 162.

[131] *See* Haloush & Malkawi, Ibid. at 129–131.

[132] Arbitration Fairness Act of 2009, H.R. 1020, 111th Cong. (2009) (bill barring enforcement of pre-dispute arbitration agreements in these typically uneven bargaining contexts).

[133] 12 C.F.R. § 1040 (2017). 'CFPB Considers Proposal to Ban Arbitration Clauses that Allow Companies to Avoid Accountability to Their Customers', *Consumer Financial Protection Bureau*, www.consumerfinance.gov/newsroom/cfpb-considers-proposal-to-ban-arbitration-clauses-that-allow-companies-to-avoid-accountability-to-their-customers (last visited 7 October 2015).

[134] *See* Llewellyn Joseph Gibbons, 'Creating a Market for Justice; a Market Incentive Solution to Regulating the Playing Field: Judicial Deference, Judicial Review, Due Process, and Fair Play in Online Consumer Arbitration', (2002) 23 *Nw. Journal of International Law & Business* 1, 15–18 (noting model is in place although questions remain regarding the applicable law).

[135] *See* Gilliéron, 'From Face-to-Face to Screen-to-Screen', at 324 (noting non-legal enforcement).

Providers (ISPs) may disconnect consumers that do not abide by OArb requirements.[136] Sellers also rely on buyer reviews, which could be linked with compliance reports for OArb awards. E-merchants like Amazon also may refuse to do further business with those who do not comply with OArb agreements and determinations.[137] Moreover, reputation incentives and the previously suggested OArb trustmark could effectuate compliance.[138] Indeed, individuals and merchants seeking efficient resolutions will most likely comply with online determinations due to desire to avoid courts.[139]

Nonetheless, international OArb raises additional choice of law and jurisdiction issues. It is difficult to define the 'seat of the arbitration' for OArb, as is often required to determine the jurisdiction and law applicable for enforcement of any arbitration agreements and awards.[140] Accordingly, protocols could be developed for a *lex mercatoria*, or delocalized 'law' incorporating general contract principles and e-commerce norms.[141] This could include consumer protections based on internationally accepted due process standards.

Such best practices would augment compliance, and consumer satisfaction with OArb processes. At the same time, businesses and consumers would jointly enjoy the time and cost savings of online resolutions. These are all considerations for consumers, businesses and other stakeholders in developing protocols for OArb with an aim toward providing viable means for resolution of small claims on e-contracts.

Overcoming Technological and Resource Imbalances

OArb, and ODR more generally, empowers marginalized groups by easing some of the social and power pressures of F2F communications, especially

136 Ibid. at 323–324.

137 Ibid. at 324 (citing a theory where 'e-merchants and their consumers could be seen as a close-knit community where the bad behaviour [sic] of one would quickly lead to exclusion from the community').

138 *See* Rafal Morek, 'The Regulatory Framework for Online Dispute Resolution: A Critical View', (2006) 38 *University of Toledo Law Review* 163, 167 (noting that 'although they are not law, norms can mirror, supplement, and even replace law in regulating ODR').

139 Mirèze Philippe, 'ODR Redress System for Consumer Disputes: Clarifications, UNCITRAL Works & EU Regulation on ODR', (2014) 1 *International Journal of Online Dispute Resolution* 57, 60–67 (noting that parties are not as interested in enforceability in B2C disputes due to desire to avoid courts in the first place).

140 *See* Gilliéron, 'From Face-to-Face to Screen-to-Screen', at 321–324 (highlighting jurisdiction issues).

141 Ibid. at 323 (noting arguments for delocalized law in OArb).

for consumers who fear stereotypes or biases based on appearance, voice or accent.[142] Additionally, some individuals are less adversarial online than in person because asynchronous communications give them time to digest thoughts and dissipate anger before replying.[143] Nonetheless, a 'digital divide' persists in terms of consumers' differential access to technology and the Internet.[144] Income, age and educational attainment remain considerable barriers to the use of technology, although smartphones have narrowed the divide with respect to race and ethnicity.[145]

For example, Pew Research Center (PRC) found in its 2013 study of adults in the United States that 74 per cent of white consumers had broadband Internet access, while that percentage fell to 64 per cent for blacks and 53 per cent for Hispanics.[146] However, smartphones have helped narrow the digital divide among races and ethnicities, suggesting need to create OArb applications for such smaller devices. Furthermore, policymakers and businesses must continue to work together to address the continuing divide based on age and education.[147]

Additionally, policymakers and businesses must consider ways to expand Internet access and education programs for vulnerable groups.[148] For example, senior centres in the United States usually offer educational access programs to assist those over age 65 and those with lower education in adopting and using the Internet.[149] Best practices for OArb also could

[142] See Paul Stylianou, 'Online Dispute Resolution: The Case for a Treaty Between the United States and the European Union in Resolving Cross-Border E-Commerce Disputes' (2008) 36 *Syracuse Journal of International Law and Communication* 117, 125.

[143] See Susan C Herring, 'Computer-Mediated Communication on the Internet' (2002) 36 *Annual Review of Information Science and Technology* 109, 144–145; David Allen Larson & Paula Gajewski Mickelson, 'Technology Mediated Dispute Resolution Can Improve the Registry of Interpreters for the Deaf Ethical Practices System: The Deaf Community Is Well Prepared and Can Lead by Example' (2008) 10 *Cardozo Journal of Conflict Resolution* 131, 140–141 explains evidence that less bullying occurs through online communication than F2F.

[144] Thom File, 'Computer and Internet Use in the United States' (US Census Bureau 2013) Current Population Survery Reports, pp. 20–568.

[145] Kathryn Zickuhr & Aaron Smith, 'Home Broadband 2013' *Pew Research Center*, available at www.pewinternet.org/files/old-media//Files/Reports/2013/PIP_Broadband%202013_082613.pdf, (last visited 26 August 2013).

[146] Ibid., pp. 1–5. [147] Ibid., pp. 4–5.

[148] See, e.g. Rebecca R Ruiz, 'FCC Chief Seeks Broadband Plan to Aid the Poor' *The New York Times*, 28 May 2015, available at www.nytimes.com/2015/05/28/business/fcc-chief-seeks-broadband-plan-to-aid-the-poor.html?_r=0, discusses plans to expand access to the Internet for the poor.

[149] Bob L Burger Recreation Center, 'Adult Programs: Technology Classes' available at www.cityoflafayette.com/index.aspx?NID=8, discusses the various classes and computer labs, including classes on using Google, smartphones, etc.

mimic the EU in requiring businesses to inform consumers about ODR options, and go further than the EU to require greater access to free Wi-Fi for filing OArb claims online.

Due Process Protection

As noted earlier, dissention remains regarding the binding nature of any ODR for resolution of B2C claims. OArb, however, holds special promise for quickly resolving B2C claims because it provides an evaluative determination on the merits of the parties' claims. Furthermore, parties gain assured access to remedies from final determinations. This gives parties incentive to put forth all their evidence, not holding facts back for future litigation, as may occur in non-binding facilitative processes.

That said, binding arbitration in F2F venues has garnered criticism for undermining the enforcement of statutory consumer protections and other public rights. For example, enforcement of arbitration clauses has stopped class actions on consumer claims under the Truth in Lending Act in the United States.[150] Accordingly, a trustmark-supported OArb system should incorporate due process and consumer protection measures, as noted earlier. Of course, it will require cooperation among businesses, consumers and policymakers to determine such fairness standards.

Furthermore, an OArb system could include a 'trigger mechanism' that would alert regulators about recurring claims regarding a particular product, especially where health or safety are at risk. This could 'trigger' public alerts and promote public awareness about a danger that may otherwise remain private without public action in the courts. The trigger mechanism also would benefit regulators by helping them determine when to pursue enforcement actions, thus addressing under-enforcement of statutory and other public policy claims like that which has arguably occurred in the United States. It also would augment efficiency by saving regulators the time and costs of launching broad investigations to learn about issues that may otherwise remain secret due to privatized processes.

Additionally, due process and fairness standards would develop through reporting and other transparency measures. For example, OArb determinations should be published on a central portal after appropriate redaction of private information. This portal could be easily searchable, and allow consumers to learn about consumer protection violations.

[150] *Green Tree Fin. Corp.* v. *Randolph*, 531 US 79, 91–92 (2000) (finding that although Randolph had provided information regarding high AAA arbitration fees and costs, it was not clear that she could not pay them).

Although some companies would shun such transparency, others would welcome opportunity to garner goodwill by complying with consumer protections and providing remedies to deserving consumers. Indeed, wise businesses eager to attract and retain customers rely on such public information regarding their performance to garner goodwill.

Conclusion

F2F processes have not provided consumers with adequate redress on claims against businesses regarding common purchases. It is rarely worth the cost and stress of pursuing these processes when the expected recovery is low. Nonetheless, there is growing interest in development of ODR systems, as evidenced by the EU ADR/ODR Directive and Regulation. Additionally, OArb in particular holds special promise for resolution of small dollar claims where the parties seek speedy resolutions based on evaluative determinations. Again, such third-party determinations separate OArb from other ODR, thereby paving the way to remedies. Moreover, the growth of judicial ODR programs evidences robust interest in essentially OArb administered by the courts.

That said, any OArb systems must incorporate due process and fairness standards to address the problematic aspects of F2F arbitration. Member states of the EU have mostly refused to enforce pre-dispute arbitration agreements in B2C exchanges due to arbitration's reputation for cutting off consumer protections to the advantage of repeat-player businesses. Accordingly, best practices for OArb should insist on compliance with consumer protections and address power imbalances. Of course, it will not be easy to establish what is 'fair' in the eyes of all parties. However, it is certainly a worthy goal to establish a protocol that could be backed by a global OArb trustmark. Indeed, the time is ripe for stakeholders to collaborate toward this goal to foster OArb as means for creating an online justice system.

9

Legislating for an Effective and Legitimate System of Online Consumer Arbitration

PABLO CORTÉS AND TONY COLE

Summary: This chapter addresses the conflict between the restrictive and negative view often taken towards consumer arbitration and the supportive and positive view often taken towards ODR by arguing that a properly designed system of online consumer arbitration can fulfil the promise of consumer arbitration while avoiding its greatest risks. After clarifying what is meant by the term 'online arbitration' and addressing the important differences that exist between commercial arbitration and consumer arbitration, this chapter examines the current regulatory framework applicable to consumer arbitration, contrasting the two dominant regulatory approaches found in the European Union and the United States. Moreover, this chapter discusses the distinctive and problematic features of consumer arbitration and addresses the additional problems that can develop when consumer arbitration is undertaken in the ODR context. Lastly, this chapter considers current alternatives to online consumer arbitration and concludes by proposing four guarantees that legislators should include to ensure a fair and effective system of online consumer arbitration.

Introduction

Arbitration has come to achieve a dominant position in the resolution of international commercial disputes due largely to a combination of the enforceability of arbitral awards and the ability of the parties in an arbitration to craft a procedure that matches their preferences and dispute. In many ways arbitration should also be ideal for the resolution of consumer disputes, as arbitration's flexibility allows a consumer arbitration process to be designed to match both the low amounts of money often at stake in consumer disputes and the limited periods of time consumers are usually willing to wait for redress. That is, arbitration can be designed to be fast and inexpensive in a way that more formal dispute resolution systems simply cannot match, which is essential for the effective resolution of consumer disputes.

Nonetheless, despite this promise, consumer arbitration has become a highly problematic field of legal practice, with critics in some jurisdictions alleging that it primarily provides a mechanism through which businesses can seek to contain court litigation and potentially even entirely avoid legal liability.[1] Criticisms of this type have triggered responses in a number of jurisdictions, both by governments[2] and by arbitration providers,[3] often significantly restricting the use of consumer arbitration.

In contrast to these criticisms of consumer arbitration, online dispute resolution (ODR) has been widely hailed as presenting a major opportunity for the fair and effective resolution of consumer disputes.[4] While the main attraction of ODR mechanisms is that they can provide a low-cost and speedy option for consumer dispute resolution, they are also seen as potentially offering parties a more user-friendly and informal procedure than either litigation or arbitration, and in particular one that is not constrained by the formalities, costs and delays that can often characterise both of these processes.

This chapter addresses the conflict between the restrictive and negative view often taken toward consumer arbitration and the supportive and positive view often taken toward ODR, by arguing that a properly designed

[1] See, e.g. J. Silver-Greenberg and R. Gebeloff, 'Arbitration Everywhere, Stacking the Deck of Justice', *New York Times*, 31 October 2015. See generally P. Cortés 'The Consumer Arbitration Conundrum: A Matter of Statutory Interpretation or Time for Reform?' in P. Cortés (ed), *The New Regulatory Framework for Consumer Dispute Resolution* (Oxford University Press, 2016); A. Schmitz, 'American Exceptionalism in Consumer Arbitration' (2012) 10 *Loyola University Chicago International Law Review* 81; J. Sternlight, 'Mandatory Binding Arbitration Clauses Prevent Consumers from Presenting Procedurally Difficult Claims' (2012) 42 *Southwestern Law Review* 87; T. Burch, 'Regulating Mandatory Arbitration' (2011) 4 *Utah Law Review* 1309; C. Drahozal and R. Friel 'Consumer Arbitration in the European Union and the United States' (2003) 18 *North Carolina Journal of International Law and Commercial Regulation* 357.

[2] See, e.g. Consumer Financial Protection Bureau, 'CFPB Proposes Prohibiting Mandatory Arbitration Clauses that Deny Groups of Consumers their Day in Court', 5 May 2016. Available at www.consumerfinance.gov/about-us/newsroom/consumer-financial-protection-bureau-proposes-prohibiting-mandatory-arbitration-clauses-deny-groups-consumers-their-day-court (hereinafter, last accessed 4 September 2017).

[3] C. Drahozal and S. Zyontz, 'Private Regulation of Consumer Arbitration' (2012) 79 *Tennessee Law Review* 289.

[4] See, e.g. P. Cortés and F. Esteban de la Rosa 'Building a Global Redress System for Low-Value Cross-Border Disputes' (2013) 62 *International and Comparative Law Quarterly* 407.

system of online consumer arbitration can fulfil the promise of consumer arbitration while avoiding its greatest risks. The discussion then clarifies what is meant by the term 'online arbitration' as it is used in this chapter. The next section addresses the important differences that exist between commercial arbitration and consumer arbitration. The chapter then turns to the existing regulatory framework applicable to consumer arbitration, contrasting the two dominant regulatory approaches found in the European Union and the United States. Next, the chapter establishes the distinctive and problematic features of consumer arbitration, and addresses the additional problems that can develop when consumer arbitration is undertaken in the ODR context. The discussion then considers current alternatives to online consumer arbitration. Lastly, the chapter concludes by proposing four guarantees that legislators should include in order to ensure a fair and effective system of online consumer arbitration.

What Is Online Arbitration?

A significant difficulty with any attempt to discuss 'online arbitration' is the large degree of vagueness inherent in the term itself. 'Arbitration', after all, is a loosely defined dispute resolution procedure, requiring that a third party deliver a decision binding on two or more disputing parties, but not including any further formal requirements as to the procedure involved. Furthermore, the term 'online' is itself also significantly vague, clearly referring to the use of the Internet in some form, but usable both in situations in which an entire dispute resolution process is undertaken online, and in those situations in which online and offline procedures are intertwined.[5] The combination of these two terms, therefore, cannot help but be uncertain.

As a result of this inherent ambiguity, online arbitration can potentially be understood to refer to a substantial range of activities, from arbitration procedures in which all aspects of the proceedings are conducted online, including hearings; to simpler dispute resolution schemes in which

[5] See, e.g. the description of online dispute resolution provided by the American Bar Association's Task Force on Electronic Commerce and Alternative Dispute Resolution Task Force: 'Online Dispute Resolution can be done entirely on the Internet, or "online", through email, videoconferencing, or both. The parties can also meet in person, or "offline". Sometimes, combinations of "online" and "off-line" methods are used in Online Dispute Resolution'. 'What is Online Dispute Resolution? A Guide for Consumers' (March 2012). Available at www.americanbar.org/content/dam/aba/migrated/2011_build/dispute_resolution/consumerodr.authcheckdam.pdf.

the disputing parties merely upload documents onto a website and then receive a decision from an arbitrator they have never met; to the mere use of online technology to facilitate a traditional offline arbitration. Indeed, as law-related technology improves, it becomes increasingly likely that in some instances the role of technology in specific arbitrations will be so great that it will effectively displace (though not necessarily replace) the role of the arbitrator, thereby substantially changing the entire dynamics of the dispute resolution process.[6]

For the purposes of a discussion of possible legislative activities, however, a broad understanding of the term online arbitration is appropriate, to ensure that a sufficiently broad range of activities is included that any legislation adopted can be expected to be effective. Accordingly, the term 'online arbitration' as used in this chapter refers to an arbitration in which the central elements of the arbitral procedure are handled online. This latter limitation is important, as the centrality of the Internet to contemporary life and business ensures that almost every arbitration will involve some online activity. Carving out a separate category of online arbitration, therefore, requires restricting the designation to those arbitrations in which the online element is central to the procedure as a whole, rather than merely peripheral.[7]

In other words, an online arbitration, as the term is used in this chapter, would include a documents-only process in which the disputing parties merely upload documents onto a website, that are then distributed to an arbitrator they never meet, who delivers a decision to the parties through email. It would also include a procedure in which the disputing parties participated in a more traditional arbitration procedure, including hearings, but undertook all those elements of the procedure online through the use of video-conferencing and other software. Conversely, it would not, for example, include an arbitration conducted offline, but in which documents were distributed via email, or even when an online repository was used for purposes of party disclosure of evidence. Similarly, it would not include an arbitration conducted overwhelmingly offline, but in which key witnesses or experts presented their testimony online through video-conferencing. In such cases, online technology is used in the arbitration, but it is merely used to facilitate a traditional offline arbitration.

6 This is why Katsh and Rifkin labelled the role of technology in the online dispute resolution process the 'fourth party' in the dispute. E. Katsh and J. Rifkin, *Online Dispute Resolution* (Jossey-Bass, 2001), pp. 93–116; see also Chapter 2 in this book.

7 For the difference between Online Arbitration and other forms of ODR, see also Chapter 8.

The Need for Distinct Regulation of Online Arbitration

There is no question that the dividing line between offline and online arbitrations is vague; however, effective legislation unavoidably requires line-drawing. Thus, there is a need to know where the line should be drawn. This raises the question of why particular attention needs to be paid to online arbitration, rather than leaving online arbitrations to be addressed solely by the standard rules applicable to arbitration generally.[8]

There are two aspects to the response to this question. One is simply that the incorporation of online technologies into an arbitration raises new questions that are not adequately dealt with in arbitration laws as they are currently constructed. For example, where no agreement has been reached on the seat of an arbitration, one traditional mechanism used for determining the seat has been the physical location of any hearings. Where an arbitration is held online, this option may no longer be available, as the parties and tribunal may never have come together in a single physical location, but may instead have only interacted online. Similarly, enforcement of an arbitral award under the New York Convention requires that the party seeking enforcement provide '[t]he duly authenticated original award or a duly certified copy thereof.'[9] However, where an award has been provided in an online procedure, such as by being emailed to the parties or by being read on a website, questions may arise as to what constitutes the 'original' of the award, or indeed whether there is an 'original' award.[10]

Online arbitration, that is, simply raises issues not adequately addressed by legislation focused solely on offline arbitration. As a result, adjustments to existing legislation will need to be made if online arbitration is to be regulated effectively.

The second aspect of the response, however, addresses far more fundamental issues regarding the nature of online arbitration and raises questions regarding the ability of legislation aimed at offline arbitration to effectively regulate online arbitration at all. In other words, it brings into question whether online arbitration is indeed merely a form of traditional offline arbitration, but adopting new technologies, or if instead it must be

[8] Indeed, one prominent article has expressly defined online arbitration as merely 'an electronic version of offline arbitration.' See also J. Betancourt and E. Zlatanska, 'Online Dispute Resolution (ODR): What Is It, and Is It the Way Forward?' (2013) 79 *Arbitration* 262 (quoting C. Liyanage, 'Online Arbitration Compares to Offline Arbitration and the Reception of Online Consumer Arbitration: An Overview of the Literature' (2010) 22 *Sri Lanka Journal of International Law* 175.

[9] The New York Convention, Article 4(1)(a). [10] See Chapter 7.

understood as an entirely separate form of dispute resolution, requiring its own regulations matched to its specific character.

One indication of the potentially *sui generis* nature of online arbitration comes from what has been called the 'asynchronous' nature of many online arbitration proceedings. An offline arbitration can be referred to as a 'synchronous' proceeding, in that interactions between the parties require coordinated and often simultaneous actions. Hearings, for example, require the parties and the arbitrator(s) to arrange a mutually convenient time and place for a hearing to be held. Similarly, even activities not requiring physical presence, such as the exchange of documents during the disclosure process, require coordination of schedules for the controlled handover of physical materials.

An online arbitration, by contrast, can operate as an asynchronous procedure, in the sense that typically all three actors (the arbitrator and the two parties) need not participate in the steps of the arbitration (e.g. hearings, discovery) simultaneously or in a coordinated manner. For example, documents can be uploaded to a website unilaterally, to be examined by the other party when convenient. Similarly, hearings can be operated sequentially, through unilateral uploading of presentations, instead of requiring the contemporaneous engagement of all three actors.

One obvious benefit of the asynchronous nature of online arbitration is that it can significantly lower the cost of a proceeding, both through the reduction of direct costs (airfare, hotel rooms, etc.) and through lower indirect costs (delays in the process resulting in delayed compensation and thus foregone opportunities, the need to pay higher travel costs because of inflexibility of time, etc.). Additionally, the asynchronous nature of online arbitration also creates benefits in that parties can adapt their involvement in the dispute resolution process around their regular lives or business operations, such as by focusing on their case outside their regular business hours or working time, or when no other pressing activities need attention. An asynchronous process, that is, creates indirect benefits simply by reducing the impact of the arbitral process on the ordinary activities of the disputing parties.

Nonetheless, while the potentially asynchronous nature of online arbitration can create significant benefits, and be desirable for that reason, it is important also to recognise its impact on the nature of the arbitral process. Arbitration, after all, has fundamentally evolved as an alternative to traditional court-based dispute resolution mechanisms, and so as a forum in which disputing parties can face one another before a neutral adjudicator and receive a binding resolution of their dispute. The procedural freedom of arbitration entails that face-to-face engagement between the parties and the arbitrator was never essential for a procedure to qualify as an arbitration. Nonetheless, this is the model that has guided both formal and informal regulation of arbitration around the world. Indeed, the notion of 'party autonomy', which is so central to arbitration and so routinely invoked in discussions of arbitration's regulation, is built precisely on this image of directly engaged parties who are mutually involved in the arbitral process.

An asynchronous online arbitration, however, unavoidably detaches the parties from the dispute resolution process in which they are engaged, as it deprives them of the many opportunities for direct interaction with both the arbitrator(s) and the other party that characterise traditional arbitration. Such interactions, though, provide the foundation for party engagement with the arbitral process and the ability of parties to feel that the arbitral process is one that they control. As a result, while online arbitrations remain formally party controlled, in practice they can be expected to lack the types of party engagement that give sensible meaning to the notion of party autonomy that has so prominently directed the regulation of arbitration.[11]

In addition to questions regarding the degree to which party autonomy legitimately characterises much online arbitration, the centrality of technology to online arbitration means that it can be expected to develop significantly around forms of technology that will fundamentally change the relationship between arbitrators and the case that they are resolving. As already noted, regulation of arbitration has traditionally centred on the image of arbitration as a less formal variant of court litigation, with an independent decision-maker engaging directly with the substance of the dispute to deliver a fair and just decision. The increasing sophistication of computer reasoning software, however, raises the likelihood that computers will, before long, be able to act as either a substitute for, or at least a complement to, human arbitrators, creating a dispute resolution process radically different from the traditional model on which the current regulation of arbitration is based.[12]

Arbitrations involving claims of significant value are, for the foreseeable future, likely to remain the realm of human arbitrators, even when they are conducted entirely online. Yet, not all arbitrations are of this variety, and indeed online arbitration processes already exist in which disputing

[11] For the asynchronous nature of online arbitration see also Chapter 8.

[12] As for the use of artificial intelligence for decision-making, see also Chapter 6.

parties merely upload documents onto a website, have an arbitral procedure that involves simply typing responses to questions from the arbitrator, and then receive a decision from an arbitrator they have never met. Processes of this type, however, that require no evaluation of witness testimony or direction of hearings, rely upon precisely the sort of case law analysis and formal decision-making that computer software can be designed to mimic, and software capable of making legal evaluations of this nature at a competent level can reasonably be expected to be developed in the near future.[13] Given the likelihood that computers will be able to undertake such arbitrations much more quickly and cheaply than human arbitrators, they can be expected to rapidly dominate this market.

However, this is not simply a matter of the creation of a refined and improved arbitral procedure, able to deliver faster and cheaper decisions than traditional human-centric arbitration. Rather, parties engaged in such arbitrations will be engaged in a fundamentally different type of dispute resolution process than the human-centric process on which the contemporary regulation of arbitration has been based, requiring different regulatory treatment. To give just one example, it might be questioned whether the traditional deference to arbitrators shown in the contemporary unwillingness of courts to review arbitral awards for substantive errors is appropriate where the decision is made purely by algorithm rather than by a human being.

The technology that can be expected to be central to online arbitrations raises significant issues even beyond this realm of quick and cheap arbitrations. After all, even if human arbitrators are never fully replaced by computers in more complex and higher value disputes, sophisticated evaluative computer software is likely to become important in such arbitrations because of its ability to provide human arbitrators with a neutral and thorough evaluation of the dispute.[14] Moreover, as software of this type is unlikely to be subject to the well-known flaws and biases in human reasoning, its use is likely to be encouraged as a means of improving the quality of arbitral decision-making. As a result, the use of such software by arbitrators can be expected to become standard, even for the most elite arbitrators.

Serious reliance upon such technology impacts on the relationship between the arbitrator and the resolution of the dispute, as significant

[13] See Ross Intelligence at www.rossintelligence.com; C. Schoenberger, 'Computers' Reasoning Skills to Equal Humans by 2029' (26 June 2012). Available at www.wsj.com/articles/SB10001424052702303640804577490681107864926.

[14] See Cognicor, available at www.cognicor.com; see Chapter 6.

aspects of the reasoning underlying the final decision are undertaken by the computer programme, rather than by the arbitrator. That is, an arbitrator may reach a different conclusion when using such a programme than he or she would have reached when not doing so, not solely because errors of reasoning have been eliminated, but because the computer programme's design has led it to categorise information, weigh information, and reason in ways different than the arbitrator would do. As a result, although the arbitrator has still made the final decision, that decision can no longer be accurately described as the decision of the arbitrator alone, but is instead more accurately described as a decision generated by a combination of the mind of the arbitrator and that of the software programme the arbitrator was using.

There are, then, significant ways in which online arbitration can be a fundamentally different type of dispute resolution procedure than traditional arbitration. While in some instances these differences result from the mere fact of the incorporation of online elements into the arbitral process, in others they arise from the unavoidably intimate connection between online arbitration and ongoing developments in computing technology. The existence of these differences means that even though much, and perhaps often all, of the contemporary regulation applicable to arbitration can also be applied to online arbitrations, additional and distinct regulation of online arbitration is necessary.

Commercial vs. Consumer Arbitration

It is, though, not only the online element of online consumer arbitration that creates the need for special regulatory attention. Further complications arise because contemporary arbitration regulation has overwhelmingly been constructed in response to the needs of commercial arbitration and not consumer arbitration. Consumer and commercial arbitration are, despite their substantial surface similarities, very different types of dispute resolution procedure. These differences mean that regulation that works fairly and efficiently for one of these processes may lead to unjust or undesirable results when applied to the other. A clear understanding of their differences is, therefore, essential for understanding how online consumer arbitration should be regulated.

Contemporary commercial arbitration is a highly developed and professionalised form of practice. While it is overwhelmingly left unregulated or very lightly regulated around the world, this light touch approach to regulation occurs in a context of voluntary arbitration involving largely sophisticated parties represented by lawyers, and of arbitrators who operate in a professional context in which their reputation is paramount. In other words, while in commercial arbitration formal regulation by governments is largely minimal, informal controls are strong. Parties are, in broad terms, usually evenly matched, thus ensuring the fairness of the process through 'equality of arms', while the importance of reputation to the career of an arbitrator provides a level of insurance against biased or incompetent arbitrators. Importantly, however, each of these elements, whether the foundation of arbitration on the consent of the parties, the 'equality of arms' of the parties, or the reputation and networking constraints that ensure the honesty of arbitrators, is far more tenuous in the context of consumer arbitration.

With respect to the voluntary nature of arbitration, for example, this becomes problematic in consumer arbitration because consumer contracts are overwhelmingly contracts of adhesion, with the consumer simply presented with the terms of an agreement, which he or she may accept or reject, but may not negotiate. If adhesion contracts are only used occasionally in an industry, or vary in their contents between competing businesses, then consumers have a realistic option of rejecting the proposed contract and finding better terms elsewhere. However, when any industry adopts adhesion contracts as a standard means of doing business, and where those contracts contain identical or near-identical provisions, consumer choice becomes illusory, and justifying light touch regulation based on the existence of party consent to arbitration is implausible.[15]

At least as problematically, it has been clearly established that not only do consumers usually not read the terms of the contracts they sign,[16] but that even if they do, they rarely understand their implications. In a recent US study, for example, 95 per cent of respondents to a survey reported not reading all the terms in contracts required to download software, 89 per cent stated that they did not read all the terms in contracts relating to packaged goods, and 43 per cent reported that they did not read

[15] For consumer arbitration in the United States, see Chapter 8.

[16] See, e.g. '7,500 Online Shoppers Unknowingly Sold Their Souls', *FoxNews*, 15 April 2010. Available at www.foxnews.com/tech/2010/04/15/online-shoppers-unknowingly-sold-souls.html (last visited 19 July 2016) (to demonstrate how nobody reads the terms and conditions, a game provider (Gamestation.co.uk) put in their contracts for one day (April 1) that those consumers who entered into the contract and did not opt out by clicking a link would forfeit their immortal soul to the seller).

all the terms in their apartment rental agreement.[17] Similarly, in another US study, 87 per cent of surveyed consumers stated that they had never entered into an arbitration clause, even though they also reported entering into contracts with businesses known to include arbitration clauses in their consumer contracts.[18] Moreover, the same study reported that when respondents were asked to review a sample consumer contract, only 43 per cent of respondents recognised that the agreement contained an arbitration clause, and of those who did notice the clause, 61 per cent believed that they could nonetheless still bring a claim in court regarding matters covered by the arbitration clause.[19]

Importantly, these two aspects of consumer contracting interact to effectively eliminate the role of party autonomy in consumer arbitration. An arbitration agreement, after all, will usually not only commit the parties to resolve disputes through arbitration, but will also standardly require that a particular arbitral forum be used and can further mandate that certain procedures be adopted during the arbitration. As a result, the failure of consumers to recognise that they are entering into an arbitration agreement, or to understand the consequences of such an agreement, when combined with their inability to negotiate the terms of the adhesion contract in which the arbitration clause is included, creates a situation in which one of the two parties to the contract (the business) is able to insist upon the use of a dispute resolution mechanism over which it has total control. Given the central role of 'equality of arms' in ensuring the fairness of arbitration in a context of light touch regulation, the risk this situation creates for the fairness of consumer arbitration is clear.

In addition, this foundational problem with the existence of party autonomy in consumer arbitration is enhanced by the fundamentally different professional contexts in which commercial arbitrators and consumer arbitrators work. The centrality of an arbitrator to the arbitration process, after all, means that even when an imbalance exists between the parties, an effective arbitrator can nonetheless ensure that the arbitral process proceeds fairly. The professional world of consumer arbitrators, however, is far less professionalised and controlled than that of commercial

[17] D. Pogrund Stark and J. Choplin 'A License to Deceive: Enforcing Contractual Myths Despite Consumer Psychological Realities' (2009) 5 *N.Y.U. J.L. & Bus.* 617.

[18] J. Sovern, E. Greenberg and P. Kirgis, Y. Liu, '"Whimsy Little Contracts" with Unexpected Consequences: An Empirical Analysis of Consumer Understanding of Arbitration Agreements' (2015) 75 *Maryland Law Review* 1.

[19] Ibid.; see Chapter 8

arbitrators, and is thus unavoidably less effective at providing the social sanctions that play a central role in the regulation of commercial arbitration. This creates particular risks of systematic bias in a field in which businesses alone often select the private arbitration provider, which in turn selects the arbitrators, creating a significant economic incentive for both provider and arbitrator to favour businesses.

On a purely practical level, for example, while commercial arbitrators standardly receive large fees for individual appointments, and so are expected to devote significant time and effort to the performance of their role, the small amounts at stake in individual consumer arbitrations mean that consumer arbitrators receive small payments for each arbitration and must therefore undertake a much larger number of arbitrations to generate a reasonable income. Consequently, arbitrators involved in consumer arbitrations can lack both the financial incentive and the practical ability to spend the time necessary to ensure the fundamental fairness of an arbitral proceeding.[20] In addition, while commercial arbitrators operate in a highly networked and professionalised field, in which reputational concerns operate to encourage professionalism, consumer arbitration lacks this professional context. As a result, while most consumer arbitrators undoubtedly approach their work fairly and professionally, there are no mechanisms, either formal or informal, for addressing those individuals who do not.[21]

The next section of this chapter addresses the two dominant approaches that have been adopted for the regulation of consumer arbitration, labelled here 'regulatory freedom' and 'regulatory control'. It argues that while the

[20] See, e.g. a webpage comment by a consumer arbitrator to the *New York Times* article 'Arbitration Everywhere, Stacking the Deck of Justice', *New York Times*, 31 October 2015, available at www.nytimes.com/2015/.../arbitration-everywhere-stacking-the-deck-of-justice.html. 'One part is left out, though: if you do decide to fight Amex over a bad late charge and you do go to arbitration, there is no day in court. No testimony, no witnesses. What happens? You get to file some papers, they file some papers and all the papers are shipped to someone you never get to talk to in a box full of other cases and the arbitrator spends maybe 10 minutes on your case. Why? Because they get paid almost nothing for each case'.

[21] See, e.g. D. Cassens Weiss, 'Minn. AG Sues Credit Card Arbitration Company, Claims Hidden Industry Ties', *ABA Journal*, 15 July 2009. Available at www.abajournal.com/news/article/minn._ag_sues_credit_card_arbitration_company_claims_hidden_industry_ties (referring to 'a study by Public Citizen that found businesses won 94 per cent of 19,000 cases handled by an arbitrator from the National Arbitration Forum', and that allegedly 'a group of hedge funds with ties to a large debt-collection agency called Axiant owns a stake in the forum through an entity created to hide the connection . . . Nearly 60 per cent of the debt collection claims handled in 2006 by the National Arbitration Forum had been filed by an Axiant predecessor').

model of 'regulatory freedom' matches the traditional approach to the regulation of arbitration, it has created significant problems where it has been adopted in the context of consumer arbitration. Conversely, 'regulatory control', when practiced effectively, has appropriately recognises the fundamentally different characters of consumer and non-consumer arbitration, and therefore provides an appropriate model for the regulation of online consumer arbitration.

The Regulatory Framework of Consumer Arbitration

Regulatory Freedom: Consumer Arbitration under the UNCITRAL Model Law, the New York Convention, and US Law

The 'regulatory freedom' approach to the regulation of consumer arbitration consists in the application of the standard approach to the regulation of commercial arbitration in the very different context of consumer arbitration. It focuses on an ideal of party autonomy imported from commercial arbitration, justifying light touch regulation on the basis that parties will only be compelled to participate in arbitration when they have freely consented to do so, and that parties ultimately retain control over both the identity of the arbitrator(s) and the procedural rules to be used in any arbitration. Consequently, this approach holds, it is appropriate to compel arbitration in accordance with the parties' agreement despite the concerns addressed in the earlier section of this chapter regarding consumer arbitration agreements, and deference is due to any arbitral award as reflecting the result of the dispute resolution process mutually agreed between the parties.[22]

As has already been noted, this model of regulatory freedom represents the traditional approach to the regulation of arbitration, and so is tailored to meet the needs of commercial arbitration. It is, therefore, unsurprisingly the model reflected in both the Model Law on International Commercial Arbitration adopted by the United Nations Commission on International Trade Law (UNCITRAL), and the 1958 Convention on the Recognition and Enforcement of Foreign Arbitral Awards ('New York Convention'). What receives little attention, however, is that either or both of these legal regimes, designed expressly for the facilitation of international commerce, can nonetheless end up being applied in the consumer arbitration context.

[22] See the approach taken in the United States in Chapter 8.

For example, although the UNCITRAL Model Law is according to its terms applicable only to 'international commercial arbitration', it expressly states that '[t]he term "commercial" should be given a wide interpretation so as to cover matters arising from all relationships of a commercial nature, whether contractual or not', giving as an example 'any trade transaction for the supply or exchange of goods or services'.[23] This is, though, clearly a description that would apply to most consumer transactions, and the Model Law nowhere excludes consumer arbitrations from its coverage.

In addition, while the Model Law is expressly restricted to arbitrations between parties located in different States,[24] the reality of much contemporary consumer contracting is indeed cross-border. Moreover, although as a 'model law' the Model Law is not itself binding in any jurisdiction, many of the States that have adopted arbitration legislation based on the Model Law have elided this distinction between domestic and international arbitration, and apply the same Model Law-based arbitration law to both domestic and international arbitrations.[25] As a result, in a significant number of States consumer arbitration is potentially subject to a legal regime expressly designed for a very different form of arbitration, and that exhibits a light touch approach to regulation that risks failing to protect consumers.

A similar situation exists regarding the 1958 Convention on the Recognition and Enforcement of Foreign Arbitral Awards (the 'New York Convention'). Also created in order to facilitate international commerce, the Convention establishes a mechanism for the quasi-automatic enforcement of arbitral awards in more than 150 jurisdictions, thereby making arbitral awards more easily enforceable internationally than foreign court judgments. Reflecting the deferential approach to arbitration characteristic of commercial arbitration, under the standards incorporated into both the Convention and the enforcement provisions of the Model Law, the enforcement of arbitral awards can only be prevented in very limited circumstances. These include situations such as when an arbitration clause is deemed invalid, or when there has been an important procedural breach that deprived a party of a fair opportunity to present its case (including

[23] UNCITRAL Model Law on International Commercial Arbitration (United Nations Documents A/40/17, annex I and A/61/17, annex I).

[24] Ibid. at Article 1(3)–(4).

[25] See, e.g. Australia, Austria, Denmark, Egypt, Germany, Hong Kong, Hungary, India, Ireland, Japan, Lithuania, Malaysia, Mexico, New Zealand, Peru, Poland, Portugal, Spain, Thailand and Venezuela.

when an arbitrator was not independent and impartial), or on grounds of public policy. Because of these restrictions, substantive review of awards by enforcing courts is precluded by the Convention, meaning that awards will be enforced even if the court believes that the arbitrator(s) applied the law to the case incorrectly.

Importantly for the present context, rather than being restricted to the enforcement of international arbitration awards, or even commercial arbitration awards, the enforcement provisions of the New York Convention apply to all awards 'made in the territory of a State other than the State where the recognition and enforcement of such awards are sought'.[26] Consequently, the highly deferential approach to the enforcement of arbitral awards enshrined in the Convention will also be applicable to any consumer arbitral awards being enforced in a State other than the State in which the consumer resides. When joining the Convention, States are permitted to declare that they will only apply its provisions to awards arising out of relationships 'considered as commercial under the national law of the State making such declaration'.[27] However, the term 'commercial' is left to be defined by each State independently, providing no assurance as to whether it will cover consumer transactions. Moreover, only 48 of 156 Contracting States have made this reservation.[28]

There remains, though, one prominent avenue for consumer protection under the New York Convention, namely the inclusion in Article V of the Convention of permission for courts to refuse enforcement where enforcement 'would be contrary to the public policy' of the enforcing State.[29] Nonetheless, while this provision would on its face allow courts to refuse enforcement of consumer arbitration awards in appropriate circumstances, because each State is left free to determine its own 'public policy', it is not possible to determine the degree to which this provision would operate in this way. Moreover, many States have adopted different standards for public policy in New York Convention cases than are applicable under domestic law, thereby restricting the public policy exception under the Convention to situations that would violate internationally

[26] Convention on the Recognition and Enforcement of Foreign Arbitral Awards, Article 1(1). In addition, it also applies to awards 'not considered as domestic awards in the State where their recognition and enforcement are sought'. Ibid.

[27] Ibid. at Article 1(3).

[28] See www.uncitral.org/uncitral/en/uncitral_texts/arbitration/NYConvention_status.html.

[29] Convention on the Recognition and Enforcement of Foreign Arbitral Awards, Article 5(2)(b).

accepted standards, rather than more stringent domestic public policy standards.[30]

Thus, while both the UNCITRAL Model Law and the New York Convention have played central roles in the contemporary growth of commercial arbitration, their broad applicability in many legal systems means that absent additional legislation expressly protecting consumers in arbitration, the light touch approach to the regulation of arbitration enshrined in these documents will also be applicable in the very different context of consumer arbitration. In some jurisdictions, of course, such additional legislation has been adopted, and the restrictions applied to consumer arbitration in the EU will be discussed in the next section of this chapter. However, this is not universally true, and the consequences of applying light touch regulation in the consumer arbitration context are well exhibited by the difficulties currently faced by consumer arbitration in the United States.[31]

In general, the regulation of consumer arbitration in the United States falls under two separate regimes, namely federal law and the law of each US state. However, the principle of the supremacy of federal law means that whenever federal and state law conflict, federal law will prevail. This principle has taken on a particular importance in the context of consumer arbitration, as the US Supreme Court has adopted a very expansive interpretation of the Federal Arbitration Act (FAA),[32] the Federal law applicable to arbitration. Moreover, this interpretation does not distinguish between consumer and commercial arbitration. In particular, the Court has held that state laws are inconsistent with the FAA, and thus invalid, if they impose more onerous restrictions on arbitration clauses than on other contractual clauses.[33] This is the case even if the relevant state law does not directly conflict with the FAA, but only conflicts more broadly with the 'goals and policies' of the FAA, as interpreted by the Supreme Court.[34] According to the Court, however, the very broad goal of the FAA is to 'ensure the enforcement of arbitration agreements according to their terms so as to facilitate streamlined proceedings'.[35] Therefore, any

[30] See, e.g. IBA Subcommittee on Enforcement of Arbitral Awards, 'Report on the Public Policy Exception in the New York Convention' (October 2015) at 4–5.

[31] See Chapter 8. [32] 9 U.S.C. § 1 *et seq.*

[33] *Scherk* v. *Alberto-Culver Co.* 417 U.S. 506, 511 (1974), citing 9 U.S.C. § 2. See also *Stolt-Nielsen, S.A.* v. *AnimalFeeds, Inc.*, 130 S. Ct. 1758, 1773 (2010).

[34] *Volt Info. Sciences, Inc.* v. *Board of Trustees of Leland Stanford Univ.*, 489 U.S. 468, 477–78 (1990).

[35] *AT&T Mobility LLC* v. *Concepcion*, 131 S. Ct. 1740, 1748 (2011).

state legislation that impedes the enforcement of arbitration agreements 'according to their terms', even if adopted to protect consumers from adhesion contracts or the other problematic aspects of consumer contracting discussed in the preceding section, is pre-empted by the FAA.

The consequence of this situation is that although many US states have enacted laws regulating the use of arbitration in the consumer context, these laws have consistently been held to have been pre-empted by the FAA, as opposing the FAA's goal of enforcing arbitration agreements 'according to their terms'.[36] As a result, while the FAA itself does not explicitly restrict states from protecting consumers, the Supreme Court's wide and controversial interpretation of the FAA has trumped state consumer protection laws. The predictable result has been a steadily growing recognition of the injustices such a highly deferential attitude toward arbitration can create when adopted in the consumer context, and an increasing hostility in the United States to consumer arbitration. This is witnessed not only by a large scholarly literature on this issue,[37] but also by repeated attempted legislative action[38] and most recently and prominently by a Pulitzer Prize-nominated series of articles published by the *New York Times*.[39]

[36] See, e.g. *DIRECTV, Inc.* v. *Imburgia*, 2015 WL 8546242 (2015); *AT&T Mobility LLC* v. *Concepcion*, 131 S. Ct. 1740 (2011); *Buckeye Check Cashing Inc.* v. *Cardegna*, 546 U.S. 440 (2006).

[37] See generally J. W. Hamilton, 'Pre-Dispute Consumer Arbitration Clauses: Denying Access to Justice?' (2006) 51 *McGill Law Journal* 693; J. M. Matthews, 'Consumer Arbitration: Is it Working Now and Will it Work in the Future?' (2005) 79 *The Florida Bar Journal* 1; J. Sternlight, and E. Jensen, 'Using Economic Arbitration to Eliminate Consumer Class Actions: Efficient Business Practice or Unconscionable Abuse?' (2004) 67 *Law and Contemporary Problems* 75; J. Sternlight, 'Is Alternative Dispute Resolution Consistent With the Rule of Law' (2006) 56 *DePaul Law Review* 569; J. Sternlight, 'In Defense of Mandatory Arbitration (If Imposed on the Company)' (2007) 8 *Nevada Law Journal* 82; K. Stewart and J. Matthews 'Online Arbitration of Cross-Border, Business to Consumer Disputes' (2002) 56 *University of Miami Law Review* 1119; T. Stipanowich 'The Arbitration Penumbra: Arbitration Law and the Rapidly Changing Landscape of Dispute Resolution' (2007) 8 *Nevada Law Journal* 427.

[38] Most prominently, the Arbitration Fairness Act, originally introduced in 2007. Most recently, an updated version of the Act, the Arbitration Fairness Act 2015, was introduced on 29 April 2015. See www.congress.gov/bill/114th-congress/senate-bill/1133.

[39] J. Silver-Greenberg and R. Gebeloff, 'Arbitration Everywhere, Stacking the Deck of Justice', *New York Times*, 1 November 2015; J. Silver-Greenberg and M. Corkery, 'A 'Privatization of the Justice System', *New York Times*, 2 November 2015; M. Corkery and J. Silver-Greenberg, 'When Scripture is the Rule of Law', *New York Times*, 3 November 2015; J. Silver-Greenberg and M. Corkery, 'Well-Financed Campaign Attacks Federal Efforts to Rein In Arbitration', *New York Times*, 16 November 2015; J. Silver-Greenberg and M. Corkery, 'Bill Would Help Troops to Avoid Arbitration', *New York Times*, 21 November 2015; J. Silver-Greenberg and

Regulatory Control: Consumer Arbitration under the EU's Unfair Terms Directive and ADR Directive

In contrast to the approach adopted in the United States, the European Union has taken a far more restrictive approach to consumer arbitration. Although specific rules on the admissibility of pre-dispute arbitration clauses in consumer contracts vary from one Member State to another, each State's rules are ultimately determined by the need to conform to the requirements of the EU's Unfair Terms Directive.[40]

The Unfair Terms Directive classifies as 'unfair' those contractual terms that 'exclude or hinder the consumer's right to take legal action . . . in particular by requiring the consumer to take disputes exclusively to arbitration not covered by legal provisions'.[41] It thus incorporates a presumption that any pre-dispute arbitration agreement entered into by a consumer is unfair, and thus invalid.[42]

As already noted, the specific implementation of this provision varies from one Member State to another. For instance, in Ireland, the Arbitration Act states that a consumer arbitration agreement will be unfair, and hence invalid, if each party is required to bear its own costs.[43] In England and Wales, Sections 89 and 91 of the 1996 Arbitration Act control the use of consumer arbitration agreements, differentiating between agreements above and below a certain amount, currently £5,000. Pre-dispute arbitration clauses in consumer contracts with a value under £5,000 are automatically invalid, while those in consumer contracts worth more than £5,000 are subject to a test with respect to their fairness.[44] Post-dispute arbitration

M. Corkery, 'Creditors Sue, Then Block Use of Courts to Fight Back', *New York Times*, 23 December 2015.

40 Council Directive 93/13/EC.

41 Annex I [q] Council Directive 93/13/EC. The phrase 'covered by legal provisions' refers to a statutory arbitration system. It is therefore possible to distinguish between private arbitration (which would be potentially unfair) and public or statutory arbitration (or processes akin to the small claims procedure or a statutory ombudsman process). *Landgericht Krefeld* Case 6 O 186/95. Judgment of 29 April 1996 [1997] ILPr 716; *Picardi* v. *Cuniberti* [2002] EWHC 2923 (QB), para 102; *Mylcrist Builders Ltd* v. *Mrs G Buck* [2008] EWHC 2172 (TCC), para 54.

42 It should be emphasised that the existence of this presumption does not mean that such agreements are automatically invalid. Rather, the presumption can be overridden if a business demonstrates that the arbitral procedure included in a pre-dispute arbitration agreement is not unfair to consumers, in accordance with standards adopted independently by each Member State.

43 Arbitration Act 2010, Article 21(6).

44 OFT's guidance on the Unfair Terms in Consumer Contracts Regulations, para. 17.2. See also the Unfair Arbitration Agreements (Specified Amounts) Order (SI 1999/2167) which

agreements containing clear and not misleading language 'are unlikely to encounter objections'.[45] In Sweden, Section 6 of the Swedish Arbitration Act entirely invalidates pre-dispute arbitration agreements regarding the sale of goods and services for private use.[46] In Germany, pre-dispute arbitration agreements in consumer contracts are enforceable if they are included in a separate document from the remainder of the agreement or in a fully notarized contract.[47]

In addition to the EU's legislative restrictions on the arbitration of consumer disputes and in sharp contrast to the decisions taken by the US Supreme Court, the Court of Justice of the European Union (CJEU) has adopted decisions protective of consumers who enter into arbitration agreements. In *Asturcom Telecomunicaciones* and in *Mostaza Claro*, for example, the Court suggested that consumer protection laws rank as an aspect of the public policy of the EU and thus trump the enforceability of arbitration agreements.[48] More specifically, in *Mostaza Claro*, the Court held that the Unfair Terms Directive requires that any national court seized of an action for annulment of an arbitration award must determine whether the arbitration agreement underlying the award is void under the Unfair Terms Directive. The award must be annulled if the arbitration agreement contains unfair terms, even if the consumer did not challenge the validity of the arbitration agreement during the arbitral proceedings.[49] In its subsequent *Asturcom Telecomunicaciones* ruling, the CJEU went even further, holding that if the law of a Member State

stipulates £5,000 as the sum below which an agreement is regarded as being unfair under section 91 of the Arbitration Act 1996. When the amount in dispute exceeds £5,000 the unfair terms' test will apply on a case-by-case basis, but some guidelines have already been developed by the English courts. For example, English courts have applied the fairness test in respect to arbitration clauses by finding an arbitration clause fair when the consumer has been professionally advised. *Allen Wilson* v. *Buckingham* (2005) EWHC 1165 (TCC) para 43; *Westminster Building Company* v. *Beckingham* (2004) BLR 508 (QB) para 45.

45 Ibid. at para. 17.3.

46 Swedish Arbitration Act (SFS 1999:116), Section 6.

47 S. Schiavetta, 'Does the Internet Occasion New Directions in Consumer Arbitration in the EU?' (2004) 3 *The Journal of Information Law and Technology* 1; see Chapter 7.

48 CJEU, 26 October 2006, case 168/05 *E.M.M. Claro* v. *Centro Movil Milenium* [2006] ECR I-10421 and CJEU, 6 October 2009, case 40/08 *Asturcom Telecomunicaciones* v. *Christina Rodrígues Noguera* [2009] ECR I-9579. For an analysis of these cases see generally M. Piers 'Consumer Arbitration in the EU: A Forced Marriage with Incompatible Expectations' (2011) 2(1) *Journal of International Dispute Settlement* 209–230. See also N. Reich 'Party Autonomy and Consumer Arbitration in Conflict: A "Trojan Horse" in the Access to Justice in the EU ADR Directive 2013/11?' (2015) 4(1) *Penn State Journal of Law and International Affairs* 290–232.

49 C-168/05 *Claro* para 39.

allows arbitral awards to be refused enforcement on public policy grounds, then any court of that State asked to enforce an award arising from a consumer arbitration must, on its own motion, evaluate whether the arbitration agreement underlying the arbitration is 'unfair' under the Unfair Terms Directive. If it finds that it is, it must refuse to enforce the award.

Nonetheless, while strongly protective of consumers, and willing to overrule arbitration agreements when necessary in the interests of consumer protection, the EU has nonetheless also passed legislation that encourages the use of high-quality consumer ADR/ODR schemes. According to the ADR Directive, all Member States must ensure the availability within their jurisdiction of ADR entities that comply with minimum legal standards when resolving disputes between traders and consumers.[50] Of specific relevance to this chapter, one of the requirements of the ADR Directive is that certified ADR entities, including arbitration providers, must be able to process consumer complaints online. While participation by businesses in ADR remains voluntary in most economic sectors, businesses are obligated to inform consumers about the availability of these certified ADR entities.

Fundamentally, the ADR Directive contains two principles with which certified arbitration bodies must comply. These are the principles of 'liberty' and 'legality' which were originally contained in the 1998 European Commission Recommendations.[51] According to the principle of liberty, consumers cannot be required to agree on a legally binding dispute resolution process before the dispute has materialised.[52] In addition, an arbitral procedure must comply with the requirements set in the Unfair Terms Directive, including that it cannot provide an advantage to the trader, such as by only allowing the trader to participate in the selection of the arbitrator(s).[53] The ADR Directive also requires consumers to be expressly informed about the binding nature of arbitration and to accept this expressly.[54] Reich observes that this information must be made

[50] Council Directive 2013/11/EU on Alternative Dispute Resolution for Consumer Disputes OJ 2013 No. L165/63.

[51] Commission Recommendation 98/257/EC of 30 March 1998 on the Principles Applicable to the Bodies Responsible for Out-of-Court Settlement of Consumer Disputes O.J. 1998 No. L 115.

[52] Article 10.

[53] Annex I [q] of Council Directive 93/13/EEC of 5 April 1993 on Unfair Terms OJ 1993 No. L 95/29. In this regard see also M. Piers 'Is Europe Skipping a Step? Exploring the Harmonisation of ADR Agreements' (2013) 20(4) *Maastricht Journal of European and Comparative Law* 506, 520.

[54] Article 10(2).

available in a durable medium and it would not be sufficient to include it through a hyperlink, in the general terms of the contract, or in a click-wrap clause.[55]

Conversely, according to the principle of legality, arbitral awards are not permitted to result in the consumer receiving a lower level of protection than the mandatory law of the Member State in which they habitually reside.[56] In domestic disputes, the settlement cannot deny consumers their statutory protections. In cross-border disputes, the Rome I Regulation will apply, under which the applicable law will often be the law of the consumers' habitual residence, particularly where the trader has actively targeted the consumer's jurisdiction by, for instance, offering goods online in the language and currency of the consumer.[57]

Finally, in addition to the previous, the ODR Regulation complements the ADR Directive and requires the European Commission to establish and maintain a pan-European ODR Platform to operate as a single point of entry for resolving consumer complaints (and traders' complaints when the consumers' national law allows it).[58] The platform, which started operating in February 2016, does not itself resolve consumer disputes, but links parties in a dispute to nationally certified ADR entities, enabling the online resolution of domestic and cross-border disputes that arise from e-commerce.

In contrast to the United States, then, which has applied the traditional light touch approach to arbitration in the context of consumer arbitration, the EU has combined legislative and case law-based restrictions intended to preclude unfair consumer arbitration processes while simultaneously encouraging and facilitating the use of certified high-quality arbitral procedures. Given this two-faceted approach, consciously designed to protect consumers while still encouraging high-quality consumer arbitration, it is perhaps unsurprising that consumer arbitration has not generated the same hostility in the EU that it has generated in the United States.

Combining Online Arbitration and Consumer Arbitration

The argument of this chapter has been that online consumer arbitration needs particular attention beyond the traditional regulation of

[55] See Reich, 'Party Autonomy and Consumer Arbitration in Conflict'. [56] Article 11.

[57] See Article 6(2) of the Rome I Regulation O.J. 2008, L 177/6, and *Peter Pammer* (C–585/08).

[58] Online Dispute Resolution for Consumer Disputes Regulation, Council Regulation 524/2013 on OJ 2013 No. L165/1.

arbitration because it combines two features, namely online technology and the involvement of consumers, each of which fundamentally transforms arbitration. Consequently, while online consumer arbitration is, of course, ultimately a form of arbitration, it must be the subject of specifically directed legislation if it is to operate fairly and effectively.

On one level, the combination of consumer arbitration and online technology seems a particularly appropriate fit. The parties in consumer arbitrations are rarely in any form of intimate or ongoing relationship; the dispute will often be factually simple and resemble many similar disputes; and the amounts at stake will rarely justify an arbitrator spending significant time resolving the dispute. Consequently, an online procedure that involves little investment of time or effort by the parties and is designed to be both fast and cheap appears ideal. It is precisely this perception that underlies the appeal of using online consumer arbitration for the resolution of consumer disputes.

The problem is that however desirable online consumer arbitration may be in its ideal form, in practice it must be evaluated in terms of how it operates within the regulatory system that is being used to ensure its fairness. As has been noted repeatedly throughout, however, the contemporary regulation of arbitration has been developed in a context dominated by commercial arbitration. It is thus designed to allow flexibility for and support to arbitrations entered into by reasonably sophisticated and reasonably equal parties, and directed by experienced and knowledgeable professionals.

Consumer arbitration, by contrast, meets neither of these criteria, and is instead a procedure dominated by one of the parties, often entered into unknowingly by the other, and usually involves arbitrators either with little expertise or with little time to apply the expertise they possess. In addition, the small amounts at stake in consumer arbitration mean that arbitrators involved in such cases are unlikely to have been freely agreed upon by both parties based upon a careful analysis of their credentials and their suitability for the case, as consumers lack both the incentive and the resources to undertake such an investigation. Moreover, the disparity between the one-time participation in arbitration of each consumer and the repeated involvement of businesses creates a risk that businesses will develop a working relationship with arbitration providers and with arbitrators while consumers cannot.[59]

[59] C. Menkel-Meadow 'Do the Haves Come out Ahead in Alternative Judicial Systems: Repeat Players in ADR' (1999) 15(1) *Ohio St. J. on Disp. Resol.* 19–62.

Online arbitration, in turn, when taken to its full potential, fundamentally abstracts the dispute resolution procedure from the parties who formally own the process, and from the traditional engagement of the arbitrator with the individualised resolution of the dispute at hand. The parties may never meet or interact directly, and neither party may ever meet or interact directly with the arbitrator. The arbitrator, in addition, while retaining the power to reach the final decision in the case, can be assisted by technology in ways that facilitate decision-making, but result in a decision that is no longer the individualised resolution of a dispute that arbitration has traditionally been emphasised to be.

Moreover, in fundamental ways the online context magnifies some of the most problematic aspects of consumer arbitration. One of the primary restraints on abusive consumer arbitration, for example, is the broader reputation of arbitral institutions as providers of fair and reliable services. It is no coincidence that in the United States the American Arbitration Association (AAA), the most important commercial arbitration institution, has led the way in developing procedures for fair and efficient consumer arbitrations, as exemplified by the AAA Consumer Arbitration Rules and the Consumer Arbitration Due Process Protocol.[60] The AAA stands to lose significantly across its range of services, including large-scale consumer arbitrations and international arbitrations administered through its offshoot the International Centre for Dispute Resolution (ICDR), if it develops a reputation for participating in biased or otherwise unfair arbitrations. Online arbitration, however, precisely because of its high-technology and significantly automated nature, is a procedure that can be operated by any entity calling itself an arbitral institution but with little more than a computer system to support its activities. As a result, without significant legislative control, consumer arbitration is particularly at risk of the kind of biasing of arbitral institutions, and hence of arbitral proceedings, that was allegedly seen in the case of the National Arbitration Forum in the United States.[61]

More broadly, the detachment of parties from the online arbitration process facilitates the disengagement of consumers from the arbitral process, encouraging them merely to submit their dispute to arbitration and await a decision. In a context in which the consumer is likely to have

[60] See AAA Consumer Arbitration Rules 2014. Available at www.tinyurl.com/hqj2b7h and Consumer Due Process Protocol. Available at www.tinyurl.com/h3qgtfp.

[61] See, e.g. K. Mirando 'National Arbitration Forum Class Action Settlement' Top Class Actions (25 May 2011). Available at www.topclassactions.com/lawsuit-settlements/lawsuit-news/1182-national-arbitration-forum-class-action-settlement.

entered into the arbitration agreement through an adhesion contract, however, and hence have had no role in selecting or designing the arbitral process, the active engagement of the consumer in the arbitral process is an essential means of ensuring the fairness of the arbitration. That online arbitration discourages such engagement raises further concerns about the likelihood that it will be operated fairly in the soft touch legislative environment that characterises contemporary arbitration.

Online consumer arbitration, then, unquestionably holds significant attractions as a method for the resolution of consumer disputes. It can be designed to operate quickly and cheaply, in reflection of the small monetary value of most consumer disputes, and requires little engagement from the consumer, in reflection of the unwillingness of most consumers to spend significant time and effort on what they ultimately see as relatively minor disputes. These same characteristics, however, create unique opportunities for those wishing to use the freedom inherent in arbitration to bias the arbitral process against the consumer. Moreover, the soft touch approach that characterises most contemporary arbitration legislation is poorly designed for controlling the previously mentioned unique difficulties that online consumer arbitration creates.

Alternatives to Online Consumer Arbitration

While consumer arbitration has already been widely adopted as a mechanism for the resolution of consumer disputes, it has, as discussed earlier, also proved highly problematic. Hence, it is unsurprising that in addition to the promotion by some legislative and judicial bodies of non-contentious methods for the resolution of consumer disputes, such as mediation, alternative adjudicative processes for the resolution of consumer disputes have also begun to appear. These alternatives are important to address here, as they form a background against which an evaluation of online consumer arbitration must be made. After all, an important factor in evaluating the desirability of online consumer arbitration is not only whether it can function adequately for the resolution of consumer disputes, but also whether it is superior to the alternatives. This section, therefore, examines three leading alternatives to online consumer arbitration: online courts, online adjudication and ombudsmen systems.

Online Courts: The Online Court of England and Wales

Undoubtedly the most high-profile and ambitious competitor to online consumer arbitration is the recent proposal by Lord Justice Briggs in the

July 2016 Final Report of the Civil Courts Structure Review for the Judiciary of England of Wales, for the creation of an 'Online Solutions Court', separate from the ordinary court of first instance and with mandatory jurisdiction within its scope.[62] The proposed scope covers civil and commercial monetary claims under £25,000,[63] a group of cases in which currently those with full legal representation can be expected to incur costs disproportionate to the amount in dispute.

Although the online court is envisaged to be accessible to litigants in person (i.e. those without legal representation), both claimants and defendants will be able to obtain legal advice before going to court, and to recover the costs of this advice on a fixed recoverable basis. This approach aims to promote the unbundling of legal services, ending the traditional solicitors' retainer 'from cradle to grave'. However, while these limits on the recovery of the costs of legal advice would certainly bring greater proportionality and fairness to the judicial process, the consequent reduction of expert guidance during the dispute resolution process will inevitably lead to higher costs in the process itself, which in turn risks excluding the great majority of law-value consumer disputes.

The proposed online court is an impressively ambitious amalgam of computer technology, mediation and the traditional court system, and represents well a larger group of similar initiatives established or considered in other jurisdictions, including the online Civil Resolution Tribunal in British Columbia[64] and the E-Courts in China.[65]

As currently proposed, the online court would involve a three-stage process. In Stage One, individuals bringing a claim that falls within the court's jurisdiction will use an online triage system to identify the legal basis of their claim and the information needed to substantiate it, as well as to upload supporting documents. In Stage Two, a case officer, who will be legally qualified and trained by judges, will work with the disputing parties, both online and by telephone, to attempt to either settle the dispute or to help them with the case management necessary if they are to be prepared for trial. Decisions from case officers will be reviewed by a judge

[62] See Lord Justice Briggs, Final Report, *Civil Courts Structure Review* (July 2016). See also Lord Justice Briggs, Interim Report, *Civil Courts Structure Review* (December 2015) and Civil Justice Council Online Dispute Resolution Advisory Group, 'Online Dispute Resolution for Low Value Claims' (February 2015). Available at www.judiciary.gov.uk/publications/civil-courts-structure-review-final-report.

[63] An initial pilot with a £10,000 limit commenced on 31 July 2017.

[64] Bill 44 – 2012 Civil Resolution Tribunal Act. See www.civilresolutionbc.ca.

[65] See China.org.cn, 'E-courts promise online justice for Chinese shoppers' (11 December 2015). Available at www.tinyurl.com/j9yxwkz.

when requested by either party. Thus, the case officer's main role will be to recommend to parties the best way to resolve their dispute. In addition to case management suggestions and 'simple telephone mediation' (to some degree replicating the role currently carried out by the small claims mediation service[66] and the National Mediation Helpline[67]), this may also include recommending the use of expert ADR providers, of online dispute resolution techniques without the intervention of a human third party, or of early neutral evaluation carried out by a specialised judge.[68] However, for this system to work well, parties will need strong incentives to settle before they resort to the next and final stage.[69] At Stage Three, the dispute will finally be brought before a judge, anticipated to be a District Judge, who will try the case, either based on the documents submitted, or where necessary through online, telephone, or exceptionally in-person hearings. These latter, however, need not correspond to a traditional trial process.

The online court is unquestionably an ambitious proposal, for which the UK government has already committed £736 million as part of an investment to revamp and digitalise the court system.[70] It will rely on a new set of procedural rules underpinned by primary legislation and designed for litigants in person. In doing so, it clearly departs from the adversarial approach in English courts, and moves instead towards the inquisitorial model that characterizes the civil law tradition. It retains, however, a defining common law feature, in the form of a preference for the settlement of private matters over judicial adjudication.

Some may be concerned that the court's design prioritises efficiency and the minimisation of cost over the individualised resolution of specific disputes that characterises justice, particularly as the English court system is expected ultimately to be self-funding, primarily through court fees. With respect to the focus of this chapter, the concern would be that, rather than improving upon online consumer arbitration, the court could instead resemble the worst aspects of consumer arbitration in the United States, as discussed previously, in which financial constraints encourage cases to be decided as quickly as possible, most likely through the categorisation of

[66] See Small Claims Mediation Service at www.smallclaimscourtgenie.co.uk/small-claims-mediation-service.

[67] See National Mediation Helpline at www.nationalmediationhelpline.co.uk.

[68] Briggs Final Report, at para. 6.112.

[69] P. Cortés 'Consumer justice in the dock as legal system juggles competing schemes' *The Conversation* (2 August 2016). Available at www.theconversation.com/consumer-justice-in-the-dock-as-legal-system-juggles-competing-schemes-62654.

[70] Briggs Final Report, at para. 4.2.

claims by decision makers, rather than through an individualised analysis of each case.

Thus, the challenge for case officers and the dispute system designers in charge of the development of the online court will be to deliver a proportionate and accessible online court process. Moreover, that system must integrate England and Wales' existing ODR/ADR structure, which already delivers bespoke and high-quality consumer redress through expert third-party neutrals. It must also be able to reliably identify those cases that need individualised attention by a judge. Finally, and as noted earlier, this must be done in a way that avoids the court becoming too expensive and even too formal for all consumer disputes but those with a value in the thousands of pounds.

If this goal is achieved, the online court would represent a significant advance in the structure of contemporary litigation, presenting an attractive alternative to online consumer arbitration. It would, as a result, create a strong incentive for providers of consumer arbitration to design a process that fairly exhibits the attractions of arbitration over litigation, delivering a system that consumers might freely elect to use instead of taking their disputes to court, as is currently the case in commercial arbitration.

Online Adjudication: The UDRP

A second alternative to online consumer arbitration is the use of online out-of-court adjudication. The most successful current example of such a system is the Uniform Dispute Resolution Policy (UDRP) Administrative Procedure, for disputes regarding Internet domain names.[71] While the UDRP Administrative Procedure is not itself directed at the resolution of consumer disputes, it provides an important model for how a system for the online adjudication of consumer disputes could operate.[72]

Under the Administrative Procedure, any individual or entity may file a complaint alleging the 'abusive registration and use' of a specific Internet domain name. For example, in a 2001 case Peter Billerbeck had registered the domain www.billerbeck.com for his personal use. A Swiss business, Billerbeck Schweiz AG, commenced proceedings under the UDRP Administrative Procedure requesting the transfer to it of the domain

[71] P. Cortés 'An Analysis of the UDRP Experience: Is it Time for Reform?' (2008) 24(4) *Computer Law and Security Report* 349–359 and 'The UDRP Reviewed: The Need for a "Uniform" Policy' (2008) 14(6) *Computer and Telecommunications Law Review* 133–139.

[72] See also Chapter 8.

name, alleging that the domain was being used to mislead Internet users into believing that the site they were accessing was in fact operated by Billerbeck Schweiz AG.[73] In this case the Panel found that Mr Billerbeck was not in breach, and so he was entitled to retain ownership of the domain.

For a fee of US $1,500 or more (depending on the number of adjudicators used and the number of domains included in the claim), a Panel will examine the claim and issue a decision. The Panel cannot order money damages be paid, but can order that ownership of a domain name be transferred, or that use of the domain name be terminated. Disputes brought to the Administrative Procedure are usually resolved within 60 days, and rarely involve significant expenses. The UDRP Administrative Procedure is currently under revision, but any possible changes are expected to take several years.[74]

In form, the UDRP Administrative Procedure strongly resembles a 'documents only' arbitration, in which the parties are permitted to provide documents supporting their case, but no in-person hearing is held. What sharply distinguishes the procedure from arbitration, however, is that decisions issued under the Administrative Procedure are not legally binding on the parties, and hence do not preclude a subsequent court case being brought on precisely the same facts and issue.[75]

Despite its non-binding nature, the Administrative Procedure has been effective because the decision issued by the Administrative Panel is binding on the domain name registrar, i.e. the entity that issued the domain name, as all domain name registrars accredited with ICANN, the body that administers the Procedure, have agreed to implement Panel decisions. Consequently, while the parties retain the right to pursue their dispute in court despite the decision of the Administrative Panel, that decision will nonetheless be implemented by the domain name registrar despite the pending/ongoing court case. In addition, the practical reality is that while parties formally retain the right to take their dispute to court, this is rarely done, as doing so would require parties to engage in expensive and slow cross-border litigation that would often not be justified by the value of the domain name in dispute.

[73] See *Billerbeck Schweiz AG* v. *Peter Billerbeck*, D2001–0825. WIPO Arbitration and Mediation Center.

[74] ICANN, Final Issue Report on a Policy Development Process to Review All Rights Protection Mechanisms in All Generic Top-Level Domains (11 January 2016), p. 35. Available at www.gnso.icann.org/en/issues/new-gtlds/rpm-final-issue-11jan16-en.pdf.

[75] T. Schultz 'Private Legal Systems: What Cyberspace Might Teach Legal Theorists' (2008) 10(1) *Yale Journal of Law and Technology* 153–193.

The UDRP Administrative Procedure provides a genuine alternative to arbitration and court litigation precisely because it does not attempt to replace these traditional processes. Rather, the Procedure merely provides an efficient 'place-holder', providing a quick resolution to a dispute that can nonetheless still be addressed more thoroughly in subsequent arbitration or litigation. In this way, a party complaining that it is being damaged by a bad faith domain name registration can obtain quick and cheap redress, and a party that has had a frivolous complaint brought against it can obtain a quick and cheap dismissal. However, in recognition of the limited nature of the review cases will receive under the Procedure, a losing party always has the right to proceed to further review in litigation (or in arbitration if both parties consent), if it decides that doing so would be worthwhile.

In terms of consumer disputes, then, an adjudication mechanism would provide consumers with a cheap and quick procedure for the resolution of their disputes – an essential need in the consumer context, as consumer disputes overwhelmingly involve claims of small value, and usually concern purchases or other transactions that the consumer will need to repeat if redress is not quickly provided. In turn, it would allow companies to avoid potentially expensive collective/class actions by securing a quick and effective resolution of individual claims.

Nonetheless, a significant problem remains with online adjudication, reflected precisely in the low rate of court litigation of disputes decided by the UDRP. As already noted, the practical reality is that even if parties are unhappy with the Administrative Panel's decision, it will rarely be economically justifiable to pursue court litigation, given the low financial value of most Internet domain names. This is precisely the situation faced by consumers involved in consumer disputes. As appealing as certain aspects of the online adjudication of consumer disputes might be, then, there is a very real danger that an uncertified system of online consumer adjudication would become a default mechanism for obtaining fast and cheap decisions, regardless of quality. Formally, it would be an improvement over poorly regulated consumer arbitration, as court litigation would not be precluded. In practice, however, the possibility of such litigation would arguably be illusory, leaving online adjudication subject to many of the same problems that currently exist for consumer arbitration.

Ombudsman Schemes

One final alternative to online consumer arbitration that has received significant support in many EU Member States are ombudsman schemes, which represent an alternative to the online resolution of disputes, rather than a version of it. Under a standard ombudsman scheme, consumers are initially required to raise their complaint with the trader that supplied the good or service in question. Only once the trader has had an opportunity to respond, and the consumer is dissatisfied with the trader's response, may the consumer make a complaint to the ombudsman service. If a complaint has been made, the ombudsman takes on a role as independent investigator of the dispute, calling for any evidence required to resolve the dispute properly, rather than merely making a decision based on the materials that the parties supply. Ombudsman schemes are standardly free or near-free for the consumer, with businesses covered by the scheme contributing an annual levy, increasingly complemented by per-case fees as well.

Unlike in arbitration, ombudsman procedures often start with an attempt first to find an acceptable settlement of the dispute, and settlement is indeed the most common outcome. Negotiations between traders and consumers are more successful when they are moderated by an authoritative third party or case handler with technical expertise in the economic sector in which the trader operates: a situation referred to in the literature as 'arm twisting'.[76] When a settlement cannot be found, a recommendation is issued by the case handler to the parties, allowing them to comment on it. Once the feedback has been considered, a final decision is issued by the case handler, which normally becomes legally binding on the trader if it is accepted by the consumer. However, traders can appeal the decision to a more senior 'case-handler' called the 'ombudsman'.[77] In most ombudsman processes consumers also have the option of rejecting the decision and taking the case to court. Nevertheless, feedback from established ombudsman schemes clearly suggests that consumers very rarely take court action.[78]

Because of the informal and investigative nature of an ombudsman scheme, and the involvement of a consistent body of dispute resolvers (rather than a constantly changing series of arbitrators), ombudsman schemes have been argued to provide significant benefits over consumer

[76] V. Bondy, M. Doyle and C. Hirst, *The Use of Informal Resolution Approaches by Ombudsmen in the UK and Ireland: A Mapping Study* (London: Hot Off the Press, 2014). Available at www.ombudsresearch.org.uk/2014/10.

[77] This is more likely to happen when new types of cases appear, as in such cases a 'precedent' from an experienced ombudsman is seen as desirable.

[78] Bondy et al., 'The Use of Informal Resolution Approaches by Ombudsmen in the UK and Ireland'.

arbitration. Arbitral procedures will, for example, often be more formalistic than the informal investigatory approach adopted by ombudsman schemes, and arbitrators will rarely be aware of how similar cases have been resolved in other arbitrated disputes, while the corporate nature of an ombudsman's office allows experience and information to be built up and shared between ombudsmen.

Hodges, for example, has called for the migration of consumer arbitration to ombudsman schemes,[79] arguing that ombudsman schemes are better placed to provide widespread advice (to individual consumers, regulators and enforcement bodies) and aggregate data of cases, creating useful feedback for traders and market regulators, and generating information useful for addressing market problems and for crafting effective regulatory responses.[80] In addition, information generated by an ombudsman service can help to identify an appropriate enforcement mechanism. In the UK, for example, the Financial Ombudsman Service noticed that one in six payday lending complaints were related to fraud, which led to these cases being dealt with by the Financial Conduct Authority.[81] The UK has indeed moved many consumer ADR schemes from arbitration to an ombudsman model, establishing entities such as the Financial Ombudsman Service.[82]

These points being acknowledged, it should nonetheless also be conceded that a similar role of market control can occur through the use of arbitration, particularly when arbitration is conducted through a publicly established body rather than through private providers. This, for example, is the case in Spain, where consumer arbitration is offered free of cost by the government. Under the relevant Spanish legislation, the arbitration must be carried out by a civil servant, who has the obligation to report to the public enforcement body (which is linked to the arbitration body) any systematic infringement of consumer law.[83] As a result, even though each individual arbitral procedure will be private and confidential, on aggregate they can nonetheless trigger public enforcement action.

[79] C. Hodges, N. Creutzfeldt and S. Macleod, 'Reforming the EU Consumer ADR Landscape: Implementation and its Issues' Third Oxford Consumer Conference Report (30–31 October 2014), p. 7.

[80] C. Hodges, 'Consumer Ombudsmen: Better Regulation and Dispute Resolution' 15 (2014) *ERA Forum* 593.

[81] Payday Lending: Pieces of the Picture, Financial Ombudsman Service Insight Report (August 2014).

[82] See Financial Ombudsman Service, available at www.financial-ombudsman.org.uk.

[83] See Real Decreto Legislativo 1/2007 Texto Refundido de la Ley General para la Defensa de los Consumidores y Usuarios.

An ombudsman scheme, then, provides a valuable mechanism for the resolution of consumer disputes, ensuring an individualised resolution of consumer disputes in a way that does not impose significant costs on the consumer. It is, arguably, an ideal mechanism for the resolution of consumer disputes.

The primary disadvantage of ombudsman schemes, of course, is their cost. As the consumer does not bear the cost of the procedure, this cost must be covered either by the trader, through general subscription or individual case fees, or by the government. In addition, the creation of an effective ombudsman service requires the ability to identify a discrete area of consumer transactions, in order to provide a specialised ombudsman service capable of delivering the benefits described earlier. Unavoidably, however, these requirements limit the usability of ombudsman schemes to certain prominent and discretely identifiable forms of consumer transactions. Governments are, after all, unlikely to be willing to fully fund ombudsman schemes for all of the extraordinarily broad range of consumer disputes, and although in some industries trade associations may be willing to establish private ombudsman schemes, many consumer transactions will unavoidably occur in unregulated industries or with companies not members of official trade bodies. Consequently, while ombudsman schemes offer a valuable form of consumer dispute resolution, they cannot be the only mechanism available.

Conclusion: Legislating on Online Consumer Arbitration

This chapter has focused on arguments intended to establish the need for specific legislation regarding online consumer arbitration if it is to operate in a fair and effective manner. But prior to turning to a discussion of legislative approaches, it is worth emphasising the particular importance of the effective regulation of consumer disputes, and why their regulation should be a priority for any government.

While consumer disputes are generally small, the frequency with which ordinary members of the public are likely to become involved in such disputes means that experience with the resolution of consumer disputes will unavoidably have a central role in determining the public perception of the quality of justice available in a jurisdiction. That is, no matter how effective high stakes commercial litigation and arbitration may be, if the ordinary citizen's experience of government-endorsed dispute resolution is that it is ineffective or biased, this will significantly colour public perception of the justice system as a whole. Guaranteeing the fair and efficient resolution of consumer disputes, then, despite their small size, is central to ensuring that the general public believes that the justice system genuinely delivers justice. For this reason, any approach to the regulation of consumer arbitration that does not ensure that participants in the process view it as fair and efficient risks undermining public confidence in the justice system far beyond consumer arbitration itself.

This chapter has argued that online consumer arbitration raises particular considerations that are not present in traditional commercial arbitration, and that as a result the contemporary approach to the regulation of arbitration is simply poorly designed for the regulation of online consumer arbitration. It has also considered three alternatives to online consumer arbitration in terms of their ability to function as adequate consumer dispute resolution mechanisms instead of consumer arbitration, and has concluded that none of these alternatives can serve as a complete replacement for online consumer arbitration. As a result, it has been argued, online consumer arbitration must be facilitated as an option for consumer dispute resolution, but legislation must be specifically developed to target the unique aspects of online consumer arbitration if it is to operate fairly and effectively. Two primary jurisdictions were considered in this context, with the United States providing an illustration of the consequences of failing to attend to the distinctiveness of consumer arbitration and the EU serving as an illustration of a more effective approach, in which both legislation and case law have attempted to ensure that consumer arbitration operates fairly.

However, neither of these jurisdictions has paid serious attention to the impact of the 'online' element of online consumer arbitration and how legislation must be fashioned to address it. In this respect, the most significant development has instead occurred at the international level, with UNCITRAL assigning Working Group III, from 2010 to 2016, the task of issuing recommendations on ODR for resolving e-commerce disputes, covering both consumer and commercial cases.[84] As has been noted elsewhere, UNCITRAL's goal in this work was to incentivise the use of ODR by providing a legal framework that would support the use of ODR for cross-border, small-value claims in particular.[85] Unfortunately, the opposing approaches to consumer arbitration in the United States and the EU,

[84] UNCITRAL Working Group III 2010–2016: Online Dispute Resolution. Available at www.uncitral.org/uncitral/commission/working_groups/3Online_Dispute_Resolution.html.

[85] UNCITRAL, 'Possible Future Work on Online Dispute Resolution in Cross-Border Electronic Commerce Transactions' 43rd Session, 21 June–9 July 2010, A/CNN.9/706. See also

especially concerning pre-dispute agreements to arbitrate, frustrated the Working Group's aim to create model rules for online arbitration. Instead, the Working Group has recently completed Technical Notes incorporate watered-down procedural rules, which in effect have excluded arbitration from its tiered online dispute resolution process.

The result of this situation is that if online consumer arbitration is to operate fairly, new legislation must be developed and passed. Legislating effectively on arbitration, however, is not only politically sensitive, as seen in the experience of UNCITRAL, but also extremely difficult as a formal matter. Arbitration works best when it is allowed to operate freely, and so too restrictive legislation unavoidably limits arbitration's effectiveness. Nonetheless, the freedom that is so essential to successful arbitration also creates significant opportunities for any party that is more interested in winning its dispute than in undergoing a fair dispute resolution procedure, opportunities for abuse that are intensified in the online context. Accordingly, the true challenge of legislating for online consumer arbitration is to create a legislative structure that allows online consumer arbitration to retain its procedural freedom, but ensures that arbitration only occurs when it can reasonably be expected to occur fairly.

To achieve this balance, we argue it is necessary to establish the following four safeguards in online consumer arbitration schemes. Firstly, there must be a total ban on pre-dispute contractual arbitration agreements. Secondly, consumers must be able to withdraw from arbitration at any time during the process, up until the delivery of the final award. Thirdly, only arbitral awards delivered through an online consumer arbitration administered by a certified arbitration provider should be enforceable in court. Fourthly, anonymised consumer arbitration awards must be publicly available, thus encouraging earlier settlements and ensuring increased consistency of the application of consumer law. The remainder of this chapter will elaborate the rationale behind these recommendations.

First and foremost, arbitration should never be a consumer's only available forum of redress.[86] Arbitration is in some respects an ideal dispute resolution mechanism for the consumer context, as its procedural flexibility entails that procedures can be adopted which ensure that disputes are

Cortés and Esteban de la Rosa; and P. Cortés 'A New Regulatory Framework for Extra-Judicial Consumer Redress: Where We Are and How to Move Forward' (2015) 35(1) *Legal Studies* 114–141.

86 This might be acceptable if the arbitral forum in question was provided by a public body that ensured the same procedural guarantees as a court or tribunal. However, in such a case arbitration's procedural freedom would be lost.

resolved fairly and efficiently. That same flexibility, however, also means that the asymmetry of power and sophistication of the parties in the dispute (i.e. the consumer and the business) creates significant opportunities for companies to design arbitral procedures biased in their favour. Because of this, consumer arbitration can only be acceptable when consumer consent to arbitrate is genuine and informed, and is not merely based on the existence of an arbitration clause in an agreement that the consumer has never read, or that the consumer was obligated to sign in order to conclude the transaction. Thus, this goal can only be achieved if legislation establishes clearly that pre-dispute arbitration clauses contained in consumer contracts are not binding on the consumer. Past attempts to merely limit the binding nature of such clauses have only created confusion and further avenues that less scrupulous businesses have used to continue to bring consumers into unbalanced arbitral proceedings. The rule in question, then, must be absolute: even when consumers have knowingly signed pre-dispute arbitration agreements, such agreements are not binding on them, and their right to use a dispute resolution mechanism other than arbitration (e.g. litigation or an ombudsman) remains.

Secondly, consumers must be able to withdraw from the online arbitration process at any time before the final award is delivered. Consumers should have the right to decide whether or not to use arbitration once they are clear what that decision entails. Precisely for this reason, it does not suffice merely to require that consumers be asked to make (or at least to ratify) their original arbitration agreement at some point after the dispute has arisen. After all, consumers may not understand the true nature of arbitral proceedings prior to experiencing the procedure for the first time. They may, for example, expect that arbitration necessarily involves a hearing, as would normally occur in court, or that the arbitrator will have certain formal qualifications, as is the case with a judge. In the online context, consumers may agree to arbitration but face great difficulties using the arbitration technology adequately.

However, where the withdrawal occurs after the commencement of proceedings, the consumer should be liable for the costs of the proceeding up until the time of withdrawal (excluding attorneys' fees) if the arbitration was being administered by a consumer arbitration provider certified by a publicly accountable accreditation body. Such a rule ensures that only consumers who have made an informed decision to arbitrate will be bound by an arbitral award, while also providing a disincentive for consumers to 'try their luck' in arbitration, withdrawing near the end of proceedings if they appear unlikely to win.

Thirdly, only arbitration providers that have been certified and monitored by a publicly accountable accreditation body should be able to issue awards that are enforceable in court. This is because the procedural freedom inherent to arbitration means that manipulation of the arbitral process for unfair benefits would still be possible, even given the preceding two rules. Consumers, for example, are likely to have little ability to play a meaningful role in the selection of either arbitration providers or arbitrators, or the ability to understand the impact that apparently minor procedural rules might have on the overall fairness of an arbitral proceeding. These are, though, not concerns that can be dealt with properly through legislation, as legislation in areas such as arbitrator selection and arbitral procedure would unavoidably inhibit the freedom of arbitration, and so limit the benefits that consumers can derive from the process.

An effective approach to this issue is the one adopted in the EU through the ADR Directive, which sets up a public certification process for ADR providers. However, to ensure that the certification process is run in a way that reflects an informed understanding of arbitration, leading commercial arbitration bodies, such as the AAA and ICC, or the Chartered Institute of Arbitrators, which would suffer broad reputational damage from being involved in unfair consumer arbitration procedures, should be engaged in the development and implementation of the certification process. Only awards delivered through arbitrations administered by a certified provider should be enforceable in court.

It should also be emphasised, though, that, while the EU accreditation process is a useful model, it does not, in our view, go far enough in guaranteeing fair online consumer arbitration, due to the flexibility that it allows to Member States regarding its implementation. Because of this flexibility, some EU Member States, such as Germany, have excluded arbitration providers altogether from their accreditation system, while others, such as Portugal, have limited accreditation to existing regional arbitration boards. Such rules prevent the effective development of consumer arbitration by precluding the entry of new competitor institutions. In addition, the EU's rules on the free movement of services mean that nothing stops businesses from signing up with consumer arbitration schemes that have obtained accreditation in a Member State with lax accreditation rules but sell their services in Member States whose accreditation standards they do not meet. Such a situation can lead to forum shopping and a race to the bottom, with arbitration providers adopting questionable procedural standards to attract new clients (i.e. businesses). Therefore, within the context of the EU's single market, only a uniform, EU-wide certification scheme can be effective.

Fourthly, certified online consumer arbitration providers must be required to make their decisions publicly available online, suitably redacted to protect identities and confidential information. This would ensure necessary transparency for a binding dispute resolution process in which the parties have a great asymmetry of power, allowing for proper monitoring by both accreditation agencies and the general public. In addition, it will encourage earlier confidential settlements by clarifying for both parties the likely outcome of the arbitral process. Publicly available awards would also lead to greater consistency between awards, ensuring the consistent application of consumer protection laws. Finally, it would provide regulators with essential information for targeting market problems.

It might be argued that constraints of the type proposed here will effectively eliminate online consumer arbitration, as businesses could not rely upon the existence within a contract of an agreement to arbitrate, and so would see no benefit in including such arbitration clauses. In reality, however, these constraints would merely ensure that online consumer arbitrations operated on a genuinely consensual basis. Companies focused on the legitimate resolution of consumer disputes will have no need to be concerned about consumer willingness to engage in arbitration, precisely because arbitration can indeed provide the benefits for consumer dispute resolution that it is often argued to provide. The restrictions proposed here, however, would ensure that less scrupulous businesses will recognise that online arbitration does not provide them with a mechanism for avoiding the proper application of consumer law.

10

Arbitrators and Their Online Identity

NIUSCHA BASSIRI

Summary: The issue of arbitrators and their online identity is one that is rather untapped. The use of new technologies, in particular, mobile devices in combination with new ways of communication via social media networks, has added another dimension to the everlasting hot topic of arbitrators' independence and impartiality. The arbitrators' online identity proliferates the transparency of arbitrators' performance, reputation and profile in general. With the rapidly growing virtual population and accessibilities of the biggest worldwide territory, the Internet, guidance concerning arbitrators' online behaviour is welcomed. The author puts forward that certain inspirations concerning arbitrators' online behaviour may be derived from their offline behaviour while applying a nuanced use of social media networks in order to protect arbitrators' online identity.

Introduction: General Features of Online Identities

According to Schmidt and Cohen, the Internet is one of the few things that humans have built and which they do not truly understand.[1] The Internet has the biggest worldwide territory within which hundreds of millions of people freely transmit information from one side of the globe to the other within seconds while simultaneously consuming an immense amount of digital content.[2]

According to sources from Silicon Valley, in the first decade of the twenty-first century, the number of people connected to the Internet increased from 350 million to more than two billion.[3] In the same period,

[1] Eric Schmidt and Jared Cohen, *The New Digital Age, Reshaping the Future of People*, National and Businesses, Knopf, Borzoi Books, 2013, p. 3.

[2] Ibid.

[3] Ibid., p. 4; see also Jeannie Pridmore and John Overocker, 'Privacy in Virtual Worlds: A US Perspective to a Global Concern' in Yesha Siva (ed), *Handbook on 3D3C Platforms* (Springer International Publishing, 2016), p. 161.

the number of mobile phone subscribers rose from 750 million to more than five billion. This creates a liquid fluid of gigantic volumes of accessible information. It is predicted that by 2025, the majority of the world's population will, in one generation, have gone from having virtually no access to unfiltered information, to accessing all of the world's information 'through a device that fits in the palm of the hand'.[4] If the current pace of technological innovation is maintained, most of the projected eight billion people on Earth will be online.[5] Furthermore, it is predicted that by the 2020s, the world's virtual population will outnumber the population of Earth as practically every person will be represented in multiple ways online.[6] In light of the uncontrollable flow of information, it is without doubt that every individual will easily be stripped of much of his or her control over his or her personal information in the virtual space.[7]

As of today, an individual's online identity rarely overshadows his or her physical person. In the future, however, an individual's identity will be defined more by his or her virtual activities and associations than ever before.[8] But what exactly does online identity mean? It is who you are and who you purport to be. At best, this would entail that individuals control their online appearance by building their online profile as well as maintaining their online historical data. This may be by way of social media networks as well as entries in online databases.

At worse, however, other individuals create a virtual identity of an individual or make personally or professionally detrimental statements on an individual's social media network account, with no knowledge and approval of the latter. Thus, a central question connected to an individual's online identity is how to verify the real – physical – person behind the online identity of an individual. This is a question that is closely linked to the question of how to protect and manage an individual's online identity.[9]

In this respect, a positive trend towards more conscious social media network behaviour is visible. Already in 2012, it became apparent that most social media network users restrict access to their respective social media network profiles.[10] This may be related to the fact that over the last

[4] Eric Schmidt and Jared Cohen, *The New Digital Age, Reshaping the Future of People*, National and Businesses, p. 4.

[5] Ibid. [6] Ibid. at 32. [7] Ibid. [8] Ibid.

[9] See Alexander Ljung and Eric Wahlforss, *People, Profiles and Trust: On Interpersonal Trust in Web-mediated Social Spaces*, Alexander Ljung & Eric Wahlforss. 2008, p. 128 (speaking about the dichotomy between an individual's real and virtual identities).

[10] Mary Madden, Pew Internet & American Life Project, Privacy management on social media sites, 24 February 2012, available at www.pewinternet.org/Reports/2012/Privacy-management-on-social-media.aspx, p. 2–3.

decade, a shift has taken place from virtual identity towards online identity of individuals. In this regard, it must be noted that the online space affords an individual the opportunity to create broadly two kinds of identities. The first kind constitutes the individual's virtual identities or avatars, which the individual may create as many as possible by using a variety of pseudonyms. This opportunity is often exercised by participants in virtual game worlds. Simultaneously, the second identity that an individual may create is his or her online identity, often referred to as the individual's 'inner identity', quintessentially through social media network profiles, which represents a person's sense of who he or she 'really is'.[11] While both identities have a potential of misutilization, in respect of the individual's online identity (which constitutes the focus of this chapter) it must be noted that the (mis)use of personal and professional data for purposes that are alien to the social media network's user's main and ultimate motivation have led many users of social media networks to limit access to their profiles.

In terms of social media networks, it comes as no surprise that there is not an end to the growth of the networks, both in terms of the number of users and in terms of the number and diversity of social media networks created.[12] A special social media network for arbitrators is the mailing list, also called listserv, OGELFORUM/OGEMID/YOUNG-OGEMID. It is described as 'a platform for discussion, sharing of insights and intelligence of relevant issues related in a significant way to international dispute management'.[13]

In light of the relevance of social media networks in our modern society, one would be ill-advised to ignore (i) social media networks, both in terms of their existence and their features; and (ii) the impact of the use of social media networks on arbitrators and their integrity – whether online or real. In what follows, the author will deal with two of the most critical aspects, i.e. the impact which the use of social media networks may have on the

[11] For a distinction between the virtual and online identities, see Harry Henderson, *Encyclopaedia of Computer Science and Technology*, Facts on File, Inc., 2009, p. 237.

[12] Statistics for 2015 show that Facebook reached 1.59 billion users, followed by WhatsApp with 900 million, Qzone (a major Chinese social media network) with 653 million, Instagram with 400 million, Twitter with 316 million, Tumbler with 230 million, and LinkedIn with 96 million users. In the fourth quarter of 2015, of the 1.59 billion Facebook users, 1.44 billion users are accessing Facebook on mobile devices, which is a significant increase of 21 per cent from the same year period in 2014 (see www.bbc.com/news/business-35425669). As a side note, the profits of Facebook for the fourth quarter of 2015 raised to US $1.56 billion, which basically results in nearly US $1 profit per active user!

[13] See www.transnational-dispute-management.com/ogemid.

independence and impartiality of arbitrators and the use of social media networks for the promotion of the professional services of the arbitrator. Based on this discussion, certain guidelines for social media behaviour of arbitrators will be suggested.

Independence and Impartiality Jeopardized Through Social Media Networks?

The Special Situation of the Arbitrator

Traditionally, law firms' websites disclosed a lawyer's affiliation with a specific law firm or a lawyer working also in the same law firm.[14] They now also feature speaking engagements and publications. Law firm websites are, however, slower in diffusing the information than social media networks, as the latter are updated instantly. This discord of information between the law firm and social media websites may lead to more instances where justifiable doubts as to an arbitrator's independence and impartiality may arise.

Interacting on social media networks also changes the visibility of arbitrators. The professional and personal connections, relationships and dealings of an arbitrator with other people are easily accessible and visible. They are permanent and public, no matter how the privacy settings of social media networks in general and the profile of the user in particular are featured. The arbitrator's profile may have the most restrictive privacy setting in place, but the arbitrator's connections on the social media network may not have such a privacy setting. Consequently, even if the arbitrator's information is inaccessible through his or her own profile due to the stringent privacy setting in place, the relaxed privacy settings of the arbitrator's connections enables that certain information about the arbitrator (more particularly, information pertaining to his or her online relationship with the connection) may still quite easily be obtained.

Obviously, one can have hundreds of friends, connections, or followers in the digital world to whom an individual can reach out in a matter of seconds. However, despite the features on Facebook to become 'friends', on LinkedIn to 'connect', or on Twitter to 'follow',[15] it is globally and

[14] See for example, Paris Court of Appeal, decision of 15 September 2015, *Société Monte Carlo Aviation Corporation* v. *S.A. Dassalult Aviation*; Brussels Court of Appeal, decision of 29 October 2007, *Poland* v. *Euroke & Stephen M. Schwebel*.

[15] These three platforms, namely LinkedIn, Facebook and Twitter, are known to be the most popular amongst law firms (In this regard, see Martindale-Hubbell, *Global Social Media*

commonly understood that these terms do not reflect more than a virtual connection. The few legal commentaries on this nascent issue of arbitrator conduct on social media also agree with the proposition that the nature of a relationship should matter more than its source;[16] its substance more than its form.[17] In particular, Facebook friendships and LinkedIn connections do not define the level and depth of closeness between two users. A Facebook friendship or LinkedIn connection may or may not be based on a personal friendship or close business connection. The social media network connection has been the subject of only a handful of court cases so far in the context of a judge's or an arbitrator's independence and impartiality, which will be analyzed later.

In this regard, some valuable light has recently been shed by scholarly writings on the question of how, when adjudging an arbitrator's impartiality or independence, social media proximities should be studied to prioritize the substance of the arbitrator's relationships over their form. One article argues that the question of the arbitrator's independence and impartiality (or of the duty to disclose) should not be determined in black-and-white terms of whether or not the arbitrator is connected on social media networks to one of the parties or the counsel, but instead should be contextualized in the broader setting of the type of social media network in question, the kind of relationship the social media network fosters, and the extent of the relationship.[18] Particularly, the article contemplated a classification of social media relationships into two categories, i.e. connection on exclusively professional social network sites, such as LinkedIn and connection on general social network sites, such as Facebook.[19] While the former, since it is not intended to be anything more than a professional gateway, should ideally not trigger any threat on an arbitrator's impartiality or independence, the latter in certain situations would be more likely to do so.[20]

Check Up: A Global Audit of Law Firm Engagement in Social Media Methods, LexisNexis, 2011, p. 3; Suar Sanubari, 'Arbitrator's Conduct on Social Media' (2017) *Journal of International Dispute Settlement*, available at www.doi.org/10.1093/jnlids/idw026, accessed 24 January 2017, p. 1, 5).

16 Hilary Heilbron QC in Kyriaki Karadelis, 'Boston: IBA Round-Up' (2013) 8 GAR, available at www.globalarbitrationreview.com/article/1032835/boston-iba-round-up, (accessed 24 January 2017).

17 Suar Sanubari, 'Arbitrator's Conduct on Social Media' (2017) *Journal of International Dispute Settlement*, available at www.doi.org/10.1093/jnlids/idw026 (accessed 24 January 2017), p. 1, 13; see also Julian DM Lew in 'The Procedure of International Arbitration: How Effective are the Tools?' (Alumni and Friends of the School of International Arbitration Conference, London, 22 April 2015).

18 Ibid. 19 Ibid., p. 12. 20 Ibid.

This distinction is premised on the notion that each social media network has a different functional purpose, or 'functional building blocks' as certain commentators call it,[21] and not all of them can be viewed in the same light. Whereas this distinction is necessary, it is certainly not adequate, as a social media connection can in no way operate as a conclusive proof of the extent and intensity of an arbitrator's relationship with any person. Thus, in and of itself, such a connection is indicative of very little. Commentators have suggested social media data mining as a tool to adjudge the intensity of relationships,[22] and have advocated its use in the assessment of arbitrator challenges.[23] However, the extraction of data from social media companies is bound to face many legal hurdles emanating from privacy laws or confidentiality embargoes in contracts, which make the practicability of social media mining questionable.

That aside, this topical discussion only fortifies the point made earlier, that an arbitrator's relationships on social media should ideally be assessed keeping in mind that at the end of the day they represent solely virtual connections, and are only in certain infrequent circumstances indicative of a real or substantive relationship – one which is challenge-worthy or even disclosure-worthy.

Social media connections, however, are not the only possible risk to an arbitrator's independence and impartiality: The use of social media networks by arbitrators in order to search and verify parties and counsel may also influence the arbitrator's impartiality. For instance, there are a number of social media networks, such as LinkedIn (especially if one is a Premium subscriber), that readily and immediately disclose information about who is viewing one's profile. Many others also have the option of disclosing this information, albeit not as a default setting, but subject to arranging the privacy settings accordingly. Such information, if made available to counter-parties in an arbitration either on disclosure or through other

[21] See J. H. Kietzmann et al., 'Social Media? Get Serious! Understanding the Functional Building Blocks of Social Media' (2011) 54 *Business Horizons* 241.

[22] 'Social media mining is the process of representing, analyzing, and extracting meaningful patterns from data in social media, resulting from social interactions' (See Reza Zafarani et al., *Social Media Mining: An Introduction*, Cambridge University Press, 2014, p. 21). In simpler terms, social media mining is a branch of the science of data mining, whereby the data of any person that is in the possession of social media companies, such as his or her messages on Facebook or his or her profile views on LinkedIn, is collated and studied to reflect certain trends. These trends in turn demonstrate the intensity of any relationship that exists in the virtual world of social media networks.

[23] Suar Sanubari, 'Arbitrator's Conduct on Social Media' (2017) *Journal of International Dispute Settlement*, available at www.doi.org/10.1093/jnlids/idw026 (accessed 24 January 2017), pp. 13–15.

means, may be used to challenge an arbitrator's independence and impartiality by highlighting the frequency or recurrence of profile viewership.

Justifiable doubts as to the arbitrator's independence and impartiality is aptly defined in the IBA Guidelines on Conflicts of Interest in International Arbitration 2014 (hereinafter IBA Guidelines),[24] in their General Standard 2(c): 'Doubts are justifiable if a reasonable and informed third party would reach the conclusion that there was a likelihood that the arbitrator may be influenced by factors other than the merits of the case as presented by the parties in reaching his or her decision.'[25] In more elaborate terms: 'If the doubt only arises in the mind of a party contesting the impartiality of an arbitrator, it is not 'justifiable'. Thus, the doubt must be justifiable from an objective point of view.[26] The party that is challenging the independence and impartiality has to furnish adequate and solid grounds for doubts and these must respond to reasonable criteria. The interested party needs to show that a reasonably well-informed person would believe that the perceived apprehension, the doubt, is justifiable. Only when the doubt is ascertainable by that reasonable and well-informed person, it can warrant the removal of the arbitrator.[27]

Such doubts as to the arbitrator's independence and impartiality may be exacerbated if the arbitrator is associated with confidential information and details concerning past or ongoing arbitration proceedings and counsel appearing before the arbitrator. The difficulty in maintaining the arbitrator's independence and impartiality on social media networks is connected to the lack of control in the interactions. While the arbitrator may avoid the appearance of bias by not making any comments that would cast justifiable doubts on his or her independence and impartiality, he or she has to make sure that others do not create the appearance of bias of the arbitrator by posting inappropriate comments on the arbitrator's profile.

In addition, the active use of social media networks by arbitrators potentially risks the prohibition of *ex parte* communication between the arbitrator and a counsel that may appear or is appearing in a pending case before the arbitrator. This can also occur by favouring one counsel over another by positively commending the former counsel on the social media

[24] International Bar Association, *IBA Guidelines on Conflicts of Interest in International Arbitration*, adopted by resolution of the IBA Council on Thursday 23 October 2014 (ISBN: 978-0-948711-36-7).

[25] Ibid. at 5. [26] Ibid. at 6, Explanation to General Standard 2.

[27] Challenge Decision of 11 January 1995, reprinted in (1997) XXII YBCA 227, at 234 (i.e. at (23)).

network (e.g. endorsements or expressions of professional expertise of a counsel by an arbitrator).

A Foray Through the World of Guidelines, Rules, Notes and Court Decisions

Unsurprisingly, the special situation of the arbitrator and his or her exposure to social media networks has already been addressed by a multitude of guidelines, rules and even court decisions. Some of them address the independence and impartiality of judges, but they can be used as a source of inspiration. In the following sections, the most pertinent rules will be discussed.

The IBA Guidelines and Their Relevance for Social Media Networks

According to the IBA Guidelines, an arbitrator's contact through a social media network with another arbitrator, counsel, and/or one of the parties does not amount to a fact that needs to be disclosed, as no appearance and no actual conflict of interest exist from an objective point of view. Articles 4.3.1 and 4.4.4 are the relevant provisions in the IBA Guidelines that relate to the social media network connection of an arbitrator vis-à-vis a counsel and, respectively, of an arbitrator vis-à-vis a party. Both articles feature in the Green List.

Article 4.3.1 of the IBA Guidelines includes in the Green List the situation where 'the arbitrator has a relationship with another arbitrator, or with the counsel for one of the parties through membership in the same professional association, or social or charitable organisation, or through a social media network.'[28] Similarly, Article 4.4.4 describes contacts between the arbitrator and one of the parties on social media networks, which do not call for disclosure, as follows: 'The arbitrator has a relationship with one of the parties or its affiliates through a social media network.'[29]

A glimpse into the IBA Panel discussion preceding the adoption of the Guidelines is indicative of the drafter's understanding of social media connections, which led to their inclusion in the Green List. This understanding aligns itself with the discussion in the preceding section of

[28] International Bar Association, *IBA Guidelines on Conflicts of Interest in International Arbitration*, adopted by resolution of the IBA Council on Thursday 23 October 2014 (ISBN: 978-0-948711-36-7), p. 26.

[29] Ibid., p. 7.

this chapter, as is exemplified in Laurence Schaner's statement that 'having a "friend" or "connection" online does not necessarily mean there is a relationship that might give rise to justifiable doubts about an arbitrator's impartiality and independence. In many cases, these connections mean nothing at all except that an arbitrator accepted a request to be their "friend"'.[30]

Indeed, there is little room to differentiate social media networks from memberships in professional associations or social and charitable organisations, specifically, when it relates to the connection of profiles on LinkedIn, which is a 100 per cent professional social media network.[31] This is more so for social media networks targeted at professionals, which may be considered as a virtual networking event, during which individuals exchange business cards, information about the profession, and pleasantries,[32] or as 'modern address books'.[33]

However, some believe that this hypothesis may not hold true for networks such as Facebook, wherein a connection is more likely to have a friendlier undertone, or even Twitter, which gives two members direct access to each other if they follow one another. Accordingly, the IBA Guidelines have recently been criticized for their restricted view of social media networks, as they have considered all social media networks as homogenous entities, all of which are sufficiently harmless to be categorized in the Green List. Such criticism has also warranted a suggestion of elevating Facebook connections to the Orange List.[34]

Further, the IBA Guidelines refer only to the limited activity of being connected on social media networks. Just as during half-leisurely, half-professional conversations between colleagues, confidential information

[30] Lawrence Schaner in Kyriaki Karadelis, 'Boston: IBA Round-Up' (2013) 8 *GAR*, available at www.globalarbitrationreview.com/article/1032835/boston-iba-round-up (accessed 24 January 2017).

[31] In fact, LinkedIn describes itself as a social networking platform. See www.linkedin.com/topic/social-networking#definition (last accessed on 9 September 2016).

[32] See example mentioned by Hilary Heilbron QC in Kyriaki Karadelis, 'Boston: IBA Round-Up' (2013) 8 *GAR*, available at www.globalarbitrationreview.com/article/1032835/boston-iba-round-up, (accessed 24 January 2017)

[33] Christine Heeg in Kyriaki Karadelis, 'Boston: IBA Round-Up' (2013) 8 GAR, available at www.globalarbitrationreview.com/article/1032835/boston-iba-round-up (accessed 24 January 2017).

[34] Suar Sanubari, 'Arbitrator's Conduct on Social Media' (2017) *Journal of International Dispute Settlement*, available at www.doi.org/10.1093/jnlids/idw026 (accessed 24 January 2017).

might be disclosed which would trigger justifiable doubts as to an arbitrator's independence and impartiality, the same is true for comments, contents and posts put on social media networks. If confidential information is disclosed or a statement expressed that would cast justifiable doubt as to the independence or impartiality of an arbitrator, the arbitrator may face challenge proceedings and the award may be sought to be annulled. For instance, an arbitrator's comment or post pertaining to an impending or ongoing arbitration proceeding he or she is involved in, which has the effect of disclosing certain information obtained during the proceeding, or of revealing the very existence of the particular proceedings – or even evaluating the proceedings, pleadings or performance of counsel – may threaten his or her impartiality or independence, not to mention the ethical conflicts triggered by such unwarranted public disclosures. In fact, the comment or post need not even pertain to strictly confidential information regarding the particular arbitration proceedings. Legal professionals, including arbitrators, often use social media networks to engage in a discussion or to articulate their opinion on certain events that may incidentally be connected to one of the parties in an arbitration, albeit completely unrelated to the arbitration under progress. Illustrations include high-profile takeover or acquisition deals that a corporation is involved in, or a long-drawn negotiation of an Investment Treaty that a State party is involved in. Such discussions are indicative of the affiliations and inclinations of an arbitrator and may therefore emanate justifiable doubts regarding his or her impartiality, even if not independence. In addition, the non-disclosure of close relationships between an arbitrator and counsel or party in real life may be enhanced through the use of social media networks potentially leading to challenge proceedings both of the arbitrator in question and the award.

The Guidance Note: Arbitration and Social Media

In 2015, the College of Commercial Arbitrators, together with other international arbitration stakeholders, published a paper that incorporates arbitration institutions and practitioners' concerns in relation to the use of social media networks by arbitrators. The resulting paper, A Guidance Note: Arbitration and Social Media (hereinafter 'Guidance Note') highlights the impact that the arbitrators' use of social media networks may have on their duty (i) to maintain impartiality and independence; (ii) to refrain from *ex parte* communications; (iii) to maintain confidentiality of the proceedings; (iv) to act in accordance with applicable law and ethical canons specific to arbitration; and (v) to avoid activities that impair confidence in the integrity of arbitration.[35] The Guidance Note rightly points out that whatever the conditions of posting or the privacy settings of an account may be, information posted on social media networks or communicated among users cannot be assumed to be or remain confidential.[36]

Indeed, while posts remain the ownership of posters on social media networks, users of social media networks consent that the content and information posted on social media networks is used, shared, collected and distributed by the social media network provider as it sees fit.[37] Accordingly, irrespective of the privacy settings, posts and comments on Facebook and LinkedIn, for example, are not private. Moreover, information and communication posted by arbitrators on social media networks may risk violating the obligation of the arbitrator to maintain the confidentiality of the proceedings. It is foreseeable that such information and communication may be asserted in post-award proceedings as evidence of earlier bias or lack of independence, jeopardizing the existence of the award.[38] This would in particular be the case where the arbitrator would post information about an ongoing arbitration.

Moreover, the Guidance Note helpfully sets out the risks inherent to advertisement and solicitation by arbitrators on social media networks, in particular in breach of ethical obligations of arbitrators, as it may (i) constitute improper advertising or solicitation of business if it is a posting by the arbitrator that may be viewed by third parties; (ii) be a prohibited recommendation of the arbitrator; (iii) constitute the unauthorized practice of law if it may be construed as legal advice communicated by the arbitrator in response to an inquiry by a third party.[39] Overall, and despite being rather general, the Guidance Note captures in a sensible way the major risks and challenges that arbitrators face when using social media networks.

[35] www.thecca.net/sites/default/files/Social_Media_Guidance_Note.pdf, Chapter II(A)-(E), pp. 3–10.

[36] www.thecca.net/sites/default/files/Social_Media_Guidance_Note.pdf, Chapter II(C), p. 4.

[37] See Facebook Terms of Service, para. 2(4) and 18, available at www.facebook.com/terms; see LinkedIn Publishing Platform Guidelines available at www.linkedin.com/help/linkedin/topics/6198/6207/47545.

[38] See www.thecca.net/sites/default/files/Social_Media_Guidance_Note.pdf, Chapter II(C), p. 4.

[39] See www.thecca.net/sites/default/files/Social_Media_Guidance_Note.pdf, Chapter II(D), p. 4.

Ethical Rules

Generally speaking, there are no mandatory rules of professional conduct or ethics applicable specifically to international commercial arbitrators across the board. However, arbitral institutions, such as the American Arbitration Association,[40] the CIETAC[41] and the International Institute for Conflict Prevention and Resolution,[42] and other training and networking institutes such as the Chartered Institute of Arbitrators,[43] do contain codes of ethics that apply to arbitrations conducted under them. However, none of these codes address the issue of the social media responsibility that an arbitrator must exercise.

Rules pertaining to this issue have been created for lawyers by certain national and international bar associations and arbitrators may often be bound to adhere to these rules, depending on where they are admitted to the bar. On the international level, the IBA has formulated the International Principles on Social Media Conduct for the Legal Profession[44] which require legal professionals to 'maintain the highest standards of integrity in all dealings, including those conducted over social media'[45] and to ensure, inter alia, that (i) they understand the use of social media, specifically its privacy settings; (ii) they clarify their statements on social media which may often be misconstrued as unsolicited legal advice; (iii) they adhere to practice promotion, advertising and solicitation rules in their respective national bar's codes of conduct; and (iv) they maintain confidentiality with respect to client data.

Similarly, on the national level, a number of American bar associations, including the American Bar Association (hereinafter ABA) have created guidelines regulating attorney's social media presence. Interestingly, the

40 AAA, Code of Ethics for Arbitrators in Commercial Disputes 2004, available at www.adr.org/aaa/ShowProperty?nodeId=%2FUCM%2FADRSTG_003867&revision=latestreleased.

41 CIETAC, Code of Conduct for Arbitrators 1994, available at www.cietac.org/index.php?m=Page&a=index&id=113&l=en.

42 CPR, Code of Ethics for Arbitrators in Commercial Disputes 2005, available at www.cpradr.org/RulesCaseServices/CPRRules/CodeofEthicsforArbitratorsinCommercialDisputes.aspx.

43 The Chartered Institute of Arbitrators Code of Professional and Ethical Conduct for Members, 2009, available at www.ciarb.org/docs/default-source/ciarbdocuments/guidance-and-ethics/practice-guidelines-protocols-and-rules/code-of-professional-and-ethical-conduct-october-2009.pdf?sfvrsn=2.

44 IBA International Principles on Social Media Conduct for the Legal Profession 2014, available at file:///C:/Users/xyz/Downloads/IBA%20International%20Principles%20on%20Social%20Media%20Conduct.pdf.

45 Ibid., see 'principle 2'.

ABA Guidelines by the Standing Committee on Ethics and Professional Responsibility,[46] are designed to address the issue of prohibition of *ex parte* communications between judges/jurors/arbitrators[47] and attorneys via social media networks. Specifically, according to the ABA Guidelines, a passive review of an arbitrator's website or profile is not per se prohibited by these Guidelines, as long as it is made without making an access or a friend request. The moment an access request is sent, the same amounts to a type of *ex parte* communication prohibited between the attorney and the arbitrators.[48]

A more expansive set of guidelines has been created by the New York State Bar Association,[49] which are reminiscent of the Guidance Note discussed in the previous section, since they contain regulations on not only the aspect of reviewability of a judge's or arbitrator's profile on the social media network, but also more general norms of social media behaviour, such as advertising and solicitation rules, monitoring social media content, prohibition of certain kind of attorney endorsements, and prohibition of public solicitation of advice, amongst others.

Arbitrators that are qualified as lawyers are bound by these social media guidelines and have a duty to ensure that they do not overstep their permissible lines of interactions on social media. While, currently, such guidelines exist primarily in American bar associations, associations across the world will be well-advised to seek inspiration from these guidelines and incorporate them in their respective code of ethics in order to encourage propriety over social media networks.

Inspiration from Guidelines for Judges on Social Media Networks

One may derive some inspiration as to arbitrators' online behaviour on social media networks from existing guidelines for judges. For example, in Belgium, specific guidelines for judges take account of social media

[46] American Bar Association, Formal Opinion No. 466, Lawyer Review of Jurors' Presence, 2014 available at www.americanbar.org/content/dam/aba/administrative/professional_responsibility/formal_opinion_466_final_04_23_14.authcheckdam.pdf.

[47] Model Rule 3.5, ABA Model Rules of Professional Conduct, 1983 contains this prohibition. Notably, while 'arbitrators' are not mentioned in the Rule, they are likely to be covered under the category of 'or other official' mentioned therein along with jurors and judges. Available at www.americanbar.org/groups/professional_responsibility/publications/model_rules_of_professional_conduct.html.

[48] American Bar Association, Formal Opinion No. 466, Lawyer Review of Jurors' Presence, 2014, p. 4.

[49] New York State Bar Association, Social Media Ethics Guidelines, 2015, available at www.nysba.org/socialmediaguidelines.

networks. While the guidelines provide that the use of social media networks is a personal choice, caution is recommended in order to avoid compromising the independence, impartiality and integrity of judges.[50] In addition, the judges' right that their private life be respected is equally enshrined in the Belgian guidelines for judges. However, Belgian judges are reminded to behave discretely and cautiously when using social media networks in order not to impair the dignity of their functions or their capacity to exercise them.[51] As general as they may be, the Belgian guidelines for judges strike a sensible balance between a judge's private life and a professional life. As they give little room for criticism, they should be considered by international arbitrators too.

Another example stems from the United States, where a number of States, notably Arizona,[52] Florida[53] and New York[54] have adopted guidelines on the permissible use of social media by judges. Of particular significance is the work of the Judicial Ethics Committee of the California Judges Association (the 'Judicial Ethics Committee'), the State in which the most popular of all social media networks, Facebook, was first developed that has provided a rather extensive and determinative opinion on social media networks. It sets out in clear terms what is and is not permissible in terms of the judges' use of social media networks.[55] The Judicial Ethics Committee focuses in its opinion on the interaction

50 'Guide pour les Magistrats – principes, valeurs et qualités/Gids voor de magistraten – principes, warden en kwaliteiten', Principe 3. 'Dignité': 'La participation aux réseaux sociaux informatisés relève d'un choix personnel, mais demande une grande prudence pour éviter la mise en cause de l'indépendance, de l'impartialité et de l'intégrité du magistrat', available at www.csj.be/fr/content/guide-pour-magistrats.

51 'Guide pour les Magistrats – principes, valeurs et qualités/Gids voor de magistraten – principes, warden en kwaliteiten', Principe 4. 'Réserve et discretion': 'Comme toute personne, le magistrat a droit au respect de sa vie *privée. Son devoir de reserve ne s'oppose pas à ce qu'il mène une vie sociale normale: il lui suffit de se comporter avec discernement et precaution poru éviter de porter atteinte à la dignité de ses fonctions ou à sa capacité de les exercer*', available at www.csj.be/fr/content/guide-pour-magistrats.

52 Use of Social and Electronic Media by Judges and Judicial Employees, Advisory Opinion 14–01, Arizona Supreme Court Judicial Ethics Advisory Committee (5 May 2014), available at www.azcourts.gov/LinkClick.aspx?fileticket=zNRP1_l8sck%3D&portalid=137.

53 Opinion Number: 2009–20, Florida Supreme Court, Ethics Advisory Committee (November 2009), available at www.jud6.org/LegalCommunity/LegalPractice/opinions/jeacopinions/2009/2009–20.html.

54 Advisory Opinion 08–176. Advisory Committee on Judicial Ethics (29 January 2009), Advisory Committee on Judicial Ethics (29 January 2009), available at www.nycourts.gov/ip/judicialethics/opinions/08–176.htm.

55 California Judges Association, Judicial Ethics Committee, Opinion 66, Online Social Networking available at www.caljudges.org/docs/Ethics%20Opinions/Op%2066%20Final.pdf.

between judges and attorneys, and highlights that this interaction should be assessed on the basis of the nature of the interaction, not the medium.[56] As such, the opinion rightly considers that form should not prevail over content.

The opinion of the Judicial Ethics Committee distinguishes between the interactions of judges with attorneys who may appear before the judge and who are appearing before the judge. It sets forth the realities of today's life by not per se prohibiting interactions between judges and attorneys who may appear before the judge,[57] whereas barring communications between judges and attorneys in matters pending before the judge.[58] In the latter case, the Judicial Ethics Committee recommends that the judge should cease any interaction with the attorney in question and disclose that this was done.[59] Similarly, transposing this interaction to the one between the arbitrator and counsel, it would be going too far to prohibit communications based on any hypothetical concerns relating to the arbitrator's independence and impartiality if a case is not even pending and counsel has not yet appeared before the arbitrator.

From an arbitrator's point of view, the tipping point would be the level of interaction between the arbitrator and the counsel of a party in an ongoing arbitration. It is argued here that it would not be necessary for the arbitrator to disconnect the counsel in question on social media networks. Rather, if a connection is already existent, the arbitrator should refrain from interacting with any counsel (or party, for that matter) involved in the arbitration. In the event that a counsel would ask to be connected with the arbitrator pending the arbitration, the same applies, i.e. the arbitrator should refrain from accepting the invitation to be connected.

One may further consider, as is recommended by the Judicial Ethics Committee of the California Judges Association, to disclose the fact that the arbitrator has ceased any interaction on social media networks with a counsel who is connected with the arbitrator on the networks.[60] However, there is no real urgency and need to do so, as one would also not disclose the fact that any interaction is ceased with the counsel beyond social media

[56] California Judges Association, Judicial Ethics Committee, Opinion 66, Online Social Networking available at www.caljudges.org/docs/Ethics%20Opinions/Op%2066%20Final .pdf, Chapter IV, p. 11.

[57] Ibid., p. 7. [58] Ibid., p. 10.

[59] California Judges Association, Judicial Ethics Committee, Opinion 66, Online Social Networking available at www.caljudges.org/docs/Ethics%20Opinions/Op%2066%20Final .pdf, Chapter III(D), pp. 10–11.

[60] Ibid., p. 10–11.

networks. In this respect, the opinion of the Judicial Ethics Committee contains an overly cautious approach.

Furthermore, as a general obligation endorsed by the Judicial Ethics Committee, the judges are asked to familiarize themselves with the social media network's privacy settings and with how to modify those.[61] While it is questionable whether this should be an obligation, it is indeed highly recommended for any arbitrator and counsel to become knowledgeable about social media networks in general and their setting features in particular. They may no longer be ignored as a justification for jeopardizing the arbitrator's independence and impartiality. The guidelines and obligations suggested in the opinion of the Judicial Ethics Committee of the California Judges Association are rather concrete and more restrictive in comparison with those set out for Belgian judges. They are forward-thinking in their scope and may be used as inspiration for arbitrators, although, as mentioned earlier, they would go beyond what would be necessary in relation to the disclosure requirement.

Analysis of Case Law

There are currently only a handful of relevant cases available that specifically deal with arbitrators and their online identity. As the following analysis will show, however, we can also learn from decisions that deal with a judge's independence and impartiality in light of his or her online behaviour on social media networks. Specifically, this section will discuss French, Danish and German court decisions where an arbitrator's or a judge's impartiality and independence has been called into question due to his online activities.

French Court Decision on Arbitrators' Independence and Impartiality when Using Social Media Networks With respect to potential repercussions on the arbitrator's impartiality or appearance of impartiality, the French Lyon Court of Appeal's decision of 11 March 2014 is of interest. Although the case may not be considered ground-breaking, it highlights the matters that may arise in relation to an arbitrator's Facebook friendship with a counsel appearing before that arbitrator in an arbitration matter.

The facts of the case are rather brief. On 4 June 2009, an arbitral tribunal composed of three arbitrators with seat in Paris rendered an award.

[61] California Judges Association, Judicial Ethics Committee, Opinion 66, Online Social Networking available at www.caljudges.org/docs/Ethics%20Opinions/Op%2066%20Final.pdf, Chapter IV, p. 11.

Unsatisfied with the award, one party sought to annul the award before the Paris Court of Appeal, submitting that the arbitral tribunal had been irregularly constituted. One of the reasons presented in relation to the irregular constitution argument was that, allegedly, the opposing party's counsel was a Facebook friend with the presiding arbitrator and that she supported his candidacy for the election to the Paris Bar by 'liking' his Facebook status. The Paris Court of Appeal accepted the moving parties' arguments and annulled the award.[62]

Subsequently, the opposing party appealed to the French Supreme Court, which held that the Paris Court of Appeal had not explained the reasons why the submitted facts could create justifiable doubts as to the arbitrator's independence and impartiality in the parties' minds. Eventually, the French Supreme Court reversed the decision of the Paris Court of Appeal and remanded the case to the Lyon Court of Appeal.[63] Unlike the Paris Court of Appeal, the Lyon Court of Appeal did not set aside the award. The Lyon Court of Appeal concluded that the alleged Facebook friend argument was irrelevant as the counsel in question supported the president's candidacy after the award was issued.[64]

The Lyon Court of Appeal fell short of mentioning the relevance of the Facebook friendship between the arbitrator and counsel as such. Whereas one commentator has considered that this silence may possibly signify that the Facebook friendship could have created justified reasonable doubts as to the presiding arbitrator's independence and impartiality if the friendship had existed from before the award was rendered, or if the relationship did not arise as a result of professional circumstances, such as the president's candidacy for the Paris Bar elections.[65] However, as regrettable as the Court's silence on this issue may be, it may also be interpreted as implying that the Court did not consider a simple Facebook friendship between a counsel and an arbitrator as significant in itself, without the existence of other compelling circumstances to cast justifiable doubts as to the arbitrator's independence and impartiality.

[62] Paris Court of Appeal, 10 March 2011, n°09/28537.

[63] Cass. civ. 1e, 10 October 2012, n°11–20299, FS-P+B+I* (*decision published in the Report of the Civil Chamber of the Supreme Court, in the Information Report of the Supreme Court and on its website).

[64] Lyon Court of Appeal, 11 March 2014, n°13/00447.

[65] Suar Sanubari, 'Arbitrator's Conduct on Social Media' (2017) Journal of International Dispute Settlement, available at www.doi.org/10.1093/jnlids/idw026 (accessed 24 January 2017), p. 4.

Furthermore, one searches in vain for a hint whether the Lyon Court of Appeal also considered the IBA Guidelines. However, it is to be assumed that if and when the court would have taken into account the IBA Guidelines, the result would have been the same in light of Article 4.3.1 of the IBA Guidelines. Such relationship in itself does not need to be disclosed.

This case highlights the delicate situation of arbitrators being connected with the counsel appearing before them. It is not only up to the arbitrator to cease the interaction between him or her and the counsel, but also for the counsel to refrain from any interaction if they do not wish the arbitrator or the award to be tarnished and made susceptible for challenge proceedings. This case is also a reminder to users of social media networks that the online identity of an arbitrator is not fully controllable by the arbitrator, but that it can be influenced by third parties as well. This is all the reason more to restrict access and interaction on social media networks.

Danish Court Decision on Judge's Independence and Impartiality when Using Social Media Networks In a Danish court decision, the issue of a judge's independence and impartiality was at stake in connection with the use of social media networks, more specifically Facebook. The issue that the Danish Supreme Court ruled upon on 11 September 2011 concerned the Facebook friendship between a lay judge and a crime victim. Ultimately, just like the Lyon Court of Appeal case in relation to the independence and impartiality of arbitrators, the Danish Supreme Court did not consider that the facts supported the position that the judge lacked independence and impartiality.[66]

In the case at hand, the defendant had been convicted by the District Court of Copenhagen for violating the Danish Criminal Code for assaulting the victim. Having discovered that the lay judge was a Facebook friend of the victim, the defendant appealed the District Court's decision by arguing that the lay judge was not able to make a completely impartial judgement and that therefore the decision of the District Court should be annulled. More specifically, the defendant contended that the lay judge had on two occasions written positive comments on the victim's Facebook wall. In addition, he had made a supportive statement toward the victim in a campaign that was critical of the victim's political views.

[66] Peter F. Thommesen, *The Prosecution of Denmark* v. *'T'* (anonymous), Supreme Court of Denmark, Case No 100/2015, 11 September 2015, A contribution by the ITA Board of Reporters, Kluwer Law International.

It is a fact that the lay judge and the victim did not know each other personally and had never met before. The lay judge's comments on Facebook were in no relation to the criminal case for which the defendant was convicted. Thus, the appeal was not successful. The High Court of Eastern Denmark rejected the request for annulment.

The Danish Supreme Court considered whether the fact of the case could give rise to doubts as to the complete impartiality of the lay judge provided for in Article 61 of the Danish Administration of Justice Act, which reads as follows: 'No one may act as judge in a case when there are other circumstances present that can cause doubt as to the judge's complete impartiality.' On the basis of the facts, i.e. the Facebook friendship between the lay judge and the victim as well as the interaction of the lay judge on the victim's Facebook page, the Danish Supreme Court ruled that there was no doubt as to the complete impartiality of the lay judge in the present case. The lay judge was competent to rule in the criminal case.

The decision of the Danish Supreme Court is to be commended, as it cautiously analyzes the online activity of the judge and level of intimacy between the judge and the crime victim in order to determine whether these elements had an impact on the judge's independence and impartiality. Considering that both the nature of the online activity by the judge and the level of intimacy between the judge and the victim were too far removed to have any impact, the Danish Supreme Court rightly held that the judge in question was independent and impartial to decide the case.

German Court Decision on Judge's Independence and Impartiality when Using Social Media Networks The German Supreme Court[67] also had to consider whether a judge's online profile and statement concerning his attitude on his social media network page – Facebook –cast doubt as to his independence and impartiality in a criminal case. The German Supreme Court was called upon to consider, inter alia, whether the conviction of two suspects was overshadowed by doubts as to the independence and impartiality of the presiding judge at the Criminal Court of the Regional Court of Rostock that convicted the two suspects.

The case is based on the following facts. Before a scheduled hearing, counsel for one of the suspects reviewed the Facebook page of the presiding judge of the Criminal Court of the Regional Court of Rostock. The counsel discovered that the presiding judge's profile picture depicted him wearing a t-shirt with the statement 'We will provide you a home: Prison'.

[67] BGH, Jan. 12, 2016, docket no. 3 StR 482/15, 12 January 2016 (Federal Court of Justice).

On his profile page, it was mentioned that the judge works at the Criminal Court of the Regional Court of Rostock since 1996 to date. Furthermore, on the profile page, a comment was made by the judge concerning his picture, stating that: '[t]his is my "when you get out, I'll be in retirement" look', to which he added the 'Like' button. At the preceding hearing, counsel for the first suspect objected to the presiding judge for lack of independence and impartiality and challenged him. The second suspect joined the challenge of the presiding judge.

In his reply to the challenge, the presiding judge only mentioned that he would abstain from making any comments about the circumstances of his private life. Ultimately, the Criminal Court of the Regional Court of Rostock rejected the challenge of the presiding judge by reasoning that the presiding judge's online behaviour affected exclusively his private sphere and was, obviously, meant to be humoristic. However, the German Supreme Court did not follow this reasoning. It granted the challenge of the presiding judge of the Criminal Court of the Regional Court of Rostock pursuant to Article 24(2) of the German Criminal Procedure Code. Article 24 of the German Criminal Procedure Code provides that:[68]

(1) The challenge on grounds of fear of bias of an adjudicating judge shall be admissible prior to commencement of examination of the first defendant as to the defendant's personal circumstances or, during the main hearing on the appeal on fact and law or the appeal on law, prior to commencement of the rapporteur's statement. All reasons for the challenge shall be stated at the same time.
(2) Thereafter a judge may be challenged only if
    1. the circumstances on which the challenge is based occurred later or became known to the person entitled to challenge at a later date and
    2. the right of challenge is asserted without delay.

After the defendant's last word a challenge shall no longer be admissible.

[68] Article 25 of the German Criminal Procedure Code provides in original: (1) Die Ablehnung eines erkennenden Richters wegen Besorgnis der Befangenheit ist bis zum Beginn der Vernehmung des ersten Angeklagten über seine persönlichen Verhältnisse, in der Hauptverhandlung über die Berufung oder die Revision bis zum Beginn des Vortrags des Berichterstatters, zulässig. Alle Ablehnungsgründe sind gleichzeitig vorzubringen. (2) Nach diesem Zeitpunkt darf ein Richter nur abgelehnt werden, wenn 1. die Umstände auf denen die Ablehnung gestützt wird, erst später eingetreten oder dem zur Ablehnung Berechtigten erst später bekannt geworden sind und 2. die Ablehnung unverzüglich geltend gemacht wird. Nach dem letzten Wort des Angeklagten ist die Ablehnung nicht mehr zulässig.

The German Supreme Court held that the content of the public Facebook page of the presiding judge shows the attitude of the presiding judge, which objectively fuels the concern that he does not consider the criminal proceedings he is dealing with objectivity, but rather has fun in condemning suspects with hefty convictions in addition to ridiculing suspects.

Furthermore, the Supreme Court pointed out that the Facebook page contains clear references to the professional activities of the presiding judge and is therefore not limited to his private sphere. According to the Supreme Court, under the circumstances, there is no need for a closer connection to the concrete criminal proceedings that affect the suspects in order for them to have the justified concern that the presiding judge lacks the required neutrality. The Supreme Court found that, in general, the online behaviour of the presiding judge is not compatible with the required attitude of a judge practicing in criminal cases to have no prejudices.

With a specific view on German criminal cases, the German Supreme Court considered that a challenge of a judge based on Article 24(2) of the German Criminal Procedure Code is justified if in light of comprehensive consideration of the known facts, the appearance exists that the judge has an attitude that could detrimentally influence the required impartiality and lack of prejudice. According to the German Supreme Court, the requisite standard is the consideration of these requirements by a reasonable and considered accused.[69]

As a consequence of the successful challenge of the presiding judge of the Criminal Court of the Reginal Court of Rostock, the Supreme Court ordered that the case be remitted to another Criminal Court of another Regional Court in the same German State.

The German Supreme Court case can be seen as a landmark case for various reasons. First, this is the only known case that granted the challenge of a judge, in particular, a presiding judge, on the basis of inappropriate statements on social media networks. Second, the German Supreme Court clarified that a distinction between a judge's private sphere and professional conduct does not exist where a judge's private comments on social media networks concern his profession. Third, the German Supreme Court considered that a judge's online behaviour on social media networks does not require a close and concrete connection to a challenge, where his behaviour concerns his attitude towards his profession in

[69] German Supreme Court, decision of 12 January 2016 – 3 StR 482/15.

general. Fourth, the German Supreme Court considered the lack of independence and impartiality so severe that neutrality towards the challenging parties can only be fully achieved by deciding on the criminal proceedings by another court. The alternative would have been for another chamber of the same Criminal Court to decide the criminal court matter.

The ruling of the German Supreme Court is a loud reminder that decision-makers, whether judges or arbitrators, should limit their online behaviour for the benefit of the integrity of the judiciary and arbitration process and should refrain from engaging in certain online activities even in their private sphere.

Promotion of Arbitrators' Use of Online Sources

The other side of the arbitrator's online identity is the promotional effect that the use of online sources may have on the appointment as an arbitrator. While unrelated to arbitration, but equally telling in terms of the use of online sources when profiling an arbitrator, a survey of more than 400 human resources staff in companies with more than 50 employees in Germany showed that half of the human resources staff conduct a background check on applicants via social media networks.[70]

Besides the marketing efforts undertaken by arbitrators on social media networks, such as LinkedIn, and dedicated websites provide information on case law, commentaries, and legal news that may also be of assistance in promoting arbitrators.[71] Furthermore, a number of law firms notify their clients and colleagues with targeted 'client alters', 'law firm advertisement', or 'notifications' in order to promote their own expertise in the field of arbitration. As previously mentioned, individual arbitrators may also make use of listservs such as OGELFORUM/OGEMID/YOUNG-OGEMID and similar mailing lists that allow arbitrators to share information on relevant topics. Arbitrators' profiling by parties for selection purposes may also be influenced by an individual's public statement made on these listservs and mailing lists.

The previously mentioned online sources are excellent means for the younger generation of arbitration practitioners or practitioners who wish

70 See www.bitkom.org/Presse/Presseinformation/Jedes-zweite-Unternehmen-ueberprueft-Bewerber-in-Sozialen-Netzwerken.html.

71 P. Pinsolle, 'Arbitration and New Technologies' in A. J. van den Berg (ed), *International Arbitration: The Coming of a New Age?*, ICCA Congress Series, Volume 17 (Kluwer Law International, 2013), p. 646.

to be more involved in arbitration to enter the pool of established arbitrators. The exposure that one can achieve with one mouse click is unsurpassed by any other means of communication.

Moreover, other means of promoting the online presence of arbitrators stem from the initiatives of institutions and organizations to provide a service for evaluating arbitrators, which evaluations are made available online and ensure greater transparency concerning arbitrators' availability and performance, by pushing the 'black box' open. Thus, in 2015, the Hong Kong International Arbitration Centre (the 'HKIAC') launched a system to evaluate, amongst others, the performance of arbitrators that have acted in HKIAC cases.[72] Similarly, in February 2016, the International Court of Arbitration of the International Chamber of Commerce (the 'ICC') published the 'Note to Parties and Arbitral Tribunals on the Conduct of the Arbitration under the ICC Rules of Arbitration', which provides, amongst other things, for the publication of information concerning appointed arbitrators in each case, including the arbitrators' names and nationalities and whether the arbitration is pending or closed.[73] Other arbitral institutions have followed suit to publish arbitrators' names on their websites, such as the Vienna International Arbitration Centre (the 'VIAC').[74]

The information that the HKIAC, the International Court of Arbitration of the ICC and the VIAC publish on their respective websites is of particular interest to parties involved in commercial cases. This is because stakeholders in international commercial arbitrations are usually deprived for reasons of confidentiality to obtain any information about the arbitrators' performance in other cases. They are not even privy to the quality of the awards drafted because the awards are mostly confidential. These online publications of arbitrator performance by arbitral institutions help transmitting this otherwise confidential information to these stakeholders and help them make a more informed choice about choosing their arbitrators. Needless to say, confidentiality is less of a hindrance in investment arbitration, since stakeholders have access to orders, decisions and awards rendered by tribunals, including the names of the individual arbitrators; all of which information is available on the institutions' websites, such as that of the International Centre for the Settlement of Investment Dispute and the Permanent Court of Arbitration. Furthermore, dedicated websites act as depositories and databases (for example, IA Reporter and TDM).

[72] See www.hkiac.net/en/arbtration/fees/9-arbitration.

[73] See https://iccwbo.org/publication/note-parties-arbitral-tribunals-conduct-arbitration.

[74] http://www.viac.eu/images/Arbitral_Tribunals_2017_f%C3%BCr_Web.pdf.

Other Internet databases are the Arbitrator Intelligence website[75] and the Global Arbitration Review's Arbitrator Research Tool ('ART').[76] The aim of these websites is to promote transparency and diversity in the selection of arbitrators. In order to achieve that, the websites collect quantitative feedback from users and counsel about key features of arbitrator decision-making. Information is collected through surveys that allow users to provide feedback on specific questions on case management, evidence taking and award rendering. It is to be expected that both projects will prove to be a valuable source for counsel to conduct research on arbitrators. Thus, they will be further tools for individuals to boost their online identity.

Tools like this will surely help in fostering the careers of younger arbitrators who can make their presence felt in the arbitration community through these publically available quality assessments over the Internet. The expanse of the Internet will prove to be instrumental in loosening the currently closely knit community of arbitrators, which would consequently be compelled to welcome a new generation of arbitrators into their prestigious club.

Recommendations and Guidelines for Arbitrators' Social Media Behaviour

Arbitrators are increasingly active on social media. A substantial amount of today's communication is filtered through social media networks. An arbitrator, in particular, should be allowed to make use of social media networks. However, it is advisable to separate the use and accessibility of the social media profiles between professional and private social media networks (for example, LinkedIn for exclusive professional use and Facebook for exclusive private use). Furthermore, as the Internet has an eternal memory, arbitrators should be cautious in restricting access to their profiles by making requisite changes to the privacy settings, limiting their online identity to only recognized known individuals. Thus, for example, on LinkedIn, an arbitrator may opt for connecting only to arbitration practitioners the arbitrator personally knows or knows of.

In terms of the number of connections through social media networks, arbitrators are advised to refrain from making a selection of professional arbitration-related connections. Rather, they may wish to make a conscious decision to connect to as many arbitration practitioners as possible

[75] See www.arbitratorintelligence.org.

[76] http://globalarbitrationreview.com/arbitrator-research-tool.

in order to balance any inadvertently created relationship with one arbitration practitioner over another through social media networks. It would reduce the appearance of bias if the arbitrator is connected on social media networks to not only a one-off arbitration lawyer, who happens to be representing one of the parties in the arbitration, but to a number of lawyers across the community, increasing the chance that the arbitrator is connected with counsel from both sides in a future arbitration. This would mirror the physical appearance and behaviour of an arbitrator at the many international conferences the arbitrator would attend.

Pending arbitration, the arbitrator shall refrain from any activity on social media networks that could – even remotely – be put in connection with a counsel or fellow arbitrator involved in a specific arbitration matter.

In creating a profile, an arbitrator should not be tempted to make more available than what is visible on his or her publicly available *curriculum vitae*, mostly uploaded on the website of the arbitrator's law firm and databases of arbitration institutions. The same advice applies to speaking engagements and publications, which are very often featured on the website of the arbitrator's law firm, provided that they do not contain confidential information or violate in any way the arbitrator's duty of independence and impartiality.

Social media networks and online sources may be equally beneficial for the promotion of arbitrators while jeopardizing arbitrators' independence and impartiality and, in some instances, also the integrity and confidentiality of the arbitration. It is often a thin line to walk, which requires careful judgment. A moderate use of social media networks and online sources enables the online identity of arbitrators to reflect the physical self without it being hijacked by the uncertainties and uncontrollable features that the Internet brings along.

Conclusion

The advance of social media networks can no longer be called a revolution. Instead, it can safely be said that social media networks are now here to stay for long and are a fact of life. A transition from being a revolution to being a part of everyday mundane reality is simultaneously marked by a transition from times of warm-blooded excitement about a novel phenomenon to times where everyone realizes that the phenomenon, like any other, has a good and a bad side in equal doses. This chapter was intended to bring to the fore the good and the bad of arbitrators' social media network presence.

The good comes in the form of using social media networks as a promotional tool, where arbitrators, especially the younger aspirational ones, find a platform to interact with the rest of the arbitration community, and to make their presence felt. Not to mention, the online publication of quality assessments is also a helpful tool for stakeholders to get familiarized with good arbitrators and in the process explore the possibility of appointing some new faces, other than the usual appointees, who also promise integrity and quality.

On the other hand, the banes of social media networks are exemplified by the instances discussed earlier where certain activities on social media networks may result in creating justifiable doubts on the arbitrator's independence and impartiality. Except for a few cases, such activities are not usually driven by irresponsible online behaviour by arbitrators and are mostly a by-product of the respective arbitrator's lack of understanding of the scope and expanse of social media.

This issue of a lack of understanding calls for a solution at both the institutional and the individual level. At the institutional level, the arbitration community will benefit from a set of guidelines regulating social media network behaviour and defining the permissible limits with precision. Of course, until the same is done, inspiration may be drawn from the Guidance Note, or rules of ethics that exist for judges and for lawyers enrolled in bars.

On the other hand, at the individual level, arbitrators must monitor their online identity to ensure that they do not engage in irresponsible conduct or in any activity that may give rise to justifiable doubts on their impartiality or independence. At the end of the day, the Internet is defined by how we use it and what we make of it. While it is impossible for any individual to understand the entirety of the Internet,[77] a genuine attempt must be made to delimit and comprehend its boundaries for the limited purpose of one's own use.

[77] 'The Internet is the first thing that humanity has built that humanity doesn't understand . . . ' – Eric Schmidt, 1997, see Peter Singer and Allan Friedman, *Cybersecurity: What Everyone Needs to Know* (Oxford University Press, 2014), p. 26.

11

How Online Sources Affect Counsel Strategies and Behavior in Arbitration

MARC D. VEIT

Summary: Information is key in international arbitration and dispute resolution in general. This chapter describes how advocates can either obtain or create information through the use of online resources. In addition to traditional web searches, advocates can often find invaluable information in the so-called deep web, i.e. the part of the Internet that is not indexed by common search engines. Obtaining information through social media may create ethical issues advocates need to be aware of. Similarly, counsel play a role in advising their clients in creating appropriate online information before or during a dispute. The chapter finishes with an outlook on the Internet of Things and how this infrastructure of the information society is going to change the way disputes are being resolved.

Introduction

Although the Internet and IT are prevalent in today's business as well as in dispute resolution in general, there is a remarkable lack of legal writing as to how online sources and IT affect counsel strategies and behavior in international arbitration or dispute resolution in general. Perhaps the reason for this general lack of writing in the field is that, as Pinsolle puts it, "it seems that the technological revolution in international [arbitration] has been somehow overstated."[1]

The role of counsel in international arbitration is to represent the interest of its client and to present the client's case in a way that the arbitral tribunal decides the dispute in the counsel's client's favour. While a

[1] P. Pinsolle, 'Arbitration and New Technologies' in A. J. van den Berg (ed), *International Arbitration: The Coming of a New Age?*, ICCA Congress Series, Volume 17 (Kluwer Law International, 2013), at 651.

thorough understanding of technology cannot replace the classical skills of good lawyers, such as analytical skills, drafting skills and advocacy skills, a good arbitration lawyer has to be able to understand and use technology to achieve the best result possible for his or her client. An increasingly important feature of advocacy that is largely overlooked in today's common law writing on advocacy is the sources of persuasive legal and factual argument. Or put differently: where do advocates find their arguments?[2]

This chapter attempts to shed light on how counsel can use online sources in their strategic case management and advocacy. The paradigm used here is that counsel in international arbitration are both users and producers of (online) information. The possibilities for counsel in these two roles are explored next.

Legal Counsel as Users and Producers of (Online) Information

Information is key in international arbitration as in all other forms of dispute resolution. Advocates present information and arguments to the arbitral tribunal with the aim of obtaining a favorable award. In that process, the advocate is both the user and producer of information.

In the context of online sources, legal counsel have traditionally been seen as users of information: advocates use general purpose search engines such as Google to find information about a certain incident, opposing parties, witnesses, and so on. Commercial providers such as Kluwer, LexisNexis, or Westlaw cater the needs of litigators with comprehensive online databases on legal authorities, case law, and the like. In addition to these traditional online sources, advocates can and should make use of information that is available through social media or other private sources of information, subject to requirements by the applicable law or ethical obligations.

Additionally, advocates participate at least indirectly in the production of online information. Lawyers are not only involved in advising clients on traditional public communication in events of dispute or crisis, but also advise clients on how to reply in emails or letters to the counter-party. However, advocates should think further than the public communiqués or drafting letters or emails for their clients; clients should also be advised on how to use social media and other online sources in order to shape public

[2] Cairns 2006, available at www.transnational-dispute-management.com (last visited 2 September 2016).

or the decision makers' perception in a way that is most favorable to the clients' position in arbitration. Again, this is subject to the legal requirements and ethical obligations of the lawyers involved.

Using Online Sources to Obtain Information about Witnesses and Counter-Parties

Conventional Web Searches

It is common practice for advocates in international arbitration to use search engines such as Google and Yahoo to obtain information about counter-parties, witnesses and even their own clients. The amount of information available is often astonishing and thus it is well worth continuing the research during the arbitration and in particular during the hearing. Often, the information found is included in written submissions or used during cross-examination of witnesses.

However, the content accessible through search engines, the so-called surface web or visible web is only a small fraction of the total content available sub-surface on the Internet. The deep web,[3] i.e. the part of the Internet that cannot be accessed by search engines, is several orders of magnitude larger than the surface web. There are a number of reasons as to why the content in the deep web is not accessible by conventional search engines.[4] For instance, because the content varies depending on the context in which it is accessed (e.g. ranges of client IP addresses, previous navigation); because the content is created dynamically or by scripts in response to a certain query; because it is deliberately kept away from conventional search engines through technical means; because the site requires registration and log-in credentials; because the content is not linked to by other pages, which may prevent web crawling programs from accessing the content; because the content is intentionally hidden in the so-called dark net.[5]

3 The term 'deep web' is credited to the computer scientist Michael Bergman who used the analogy of dragging a net across the surface of the ocean: a great deal may be caught in the net, but there is a wealth of information that is deep and therefore missed, see Bergman 2001, available at www.quod.lib.umich.edu/j/jep/3336451.0007.1*?rgn=full+text (last visited 2 September 2016).

4 See also deep web, www.en.wikipedia.org/w/index.php?title=Deep_web&oldid=733527825 (last visited 12 August 2016).

5 The deep web is often confused with the so-called 'dark web', the content that exists on darknets, overlay networks that use the public Internet but which require specific software, configurations or authorization to access, such as Tor, I2P, or other darknet software. These systems encrypt web traffic in layers and bounce it through randomly chosen computers around the world, each of which removes a single layer of encryption before passing the

Leaving aside the dark net, paid cloud-based databases, such as Kluwerarbitration, LexisNexis or Westlaw[6] and web-based email servers, the part of the deep web that is most interesting for counsel in international arbitration are the following:

- Non-indexed and potentially password-protected sites of local courts, census records, government archives, etc.;
- Web-archives; and
- Social media sites that are typically password-protected.

Non-Indexed Government/Court Sites

A large number of government-related sites that can provide a wealth of information for arbitration counsel are not indexed by standard search engines. Many court sites, census data records, government archives and commercial registers are not indexed as they are either password-protected (e.g. because they charge a nominal access fee) or as they generate content dynamically that escapes the indexing process by normal search engines. However, all these sites provide an internal search engine with which the content can be searched for.

The way to approach these databases is to use normal search engines to find the relevant databases, rather than the information one is interested in. For example, in almost every jurisdiction it is rather easy to find court databases or commercial registers using Google; these databases and registers can then be searched using the databases' search tools. However, it is almost impossible to use Google or similar search engines to search court databases directly. Thus, a two-step approach is often the most promising: First search for the database that is of interest using conventional search tools and then search within the database using the tools provided by the database.

Internet Archives

The Internet Archive to some extent resembles a backup of the Internet. It was founded in 1996 as a non-profit organization with the aim of building an Internet library.[7] It provides free access to collections of

data on to its next hop in the network. This should prevent any spy from matching the traffic's origin with its destination. The dark web forms a small part of the deep web. See Greenberg 2014, www.wired.com/2014/11/hacker-lexicon-whats-dark-web (last visited 12 August 2016).

[6] As for the creation of arbitration related databases, see also Chapter 2, p. 35.

[7] See www.archive.org.

archived websites, software, games, music, images and public domain books. The most popular part of the Internet Archive is the Wayback Machine service, which allows users to insert a web address and discover if the Internet Archive contains earlier versions of that webpage. There are currently more than 445 billion webpage captures in the archive.

Lawyers have made use of the Internet Archive in interesting ways. It is a very useful method of proving how a website appeared on a certain date. While evidentiary rules in domestic litigation can lead to academically fruitful battles centred upon hearsay objections, proper authentication and the 'best evidence' rule[8], these formalistic hurdles fortunately do not apply in international arbitration. The author is aware of several international arbitration cases where printouts of the Wayback Machine have successfully been used as evidence.

Social Media

Social media in international arbitration has so far been analyzed under the aspect of whether its use may jeopardize the independence and impartiality of arbitrators for an actual or prospective case[9]. Social media, however, is highly relevant for counsel work and has been an important topic for US litigators for quite a while. It has been said that "lawyers who elect not to participate in social media may be in for a rude awakening,"[10] meaning that the failure to consider social media in a case may at best result in ineffective advocacy and at worst in disciplinary proceedings or even in a malpractice claim. The areas of discussion have included topics such as whether there is a duty to preserve and collect social media evidence, whether social media data are discoverable, and whether jurors or witnesses should be investigated through social media.[11]

Indeed, social media has become a real treasure trove[12] for litigators and there is no reason counsel in international arbitration should not take

[8] See, e.g. D. R. Eltgroth, 'Best Evidence and the Wayback Machine Toward a Workable Authentication Standard for Archived Internet Evidence', (2009) 28(1) *Fordham Law Review*, 181–215, at 181.

[9] See in detail Chapter 10, p. 249.

[10] See Jan L. Jacobowitz & Danielle Singe, 'The Social Media Frontier: Exploring a New Mandate for Competence in the Practice of Law', 2014, *University of Miami Law School Institutional Repository*, 445–484, at 447.

[11] See, e.g. Simon/Ettari 2014, at 34–44; Monnat/Nichols 2015, at 8–11; Wicks et al., 2015, available at www.nysba.org/socialmediaguidelines (last visited 16 August 2016); Hoffmeister 2012, at 611–648.

[12] Jacobowitz/Singer 2014, p. 456.

advantage of its benefits. While the discussion in US domestic litigation practice has no direct impact on international arbitration, it nevertheless is useful to identify the issues that are relevant in international arbitration, in particular ethical issues.

Indeed, counsel are using social media to investigate counter-parties and prospective witnesses. When doing so, they should be mindful of ethical limitations that may apply, depending on the jurisdiction. However, it is acceptable for a lawyer to research a witness' public social media profile and posts that are readily accessible.[13] This includes information that is available to any member of the social media network without the need for permission from the person whose account is being viewed. While reviewing publicly available information may not give rise to ethical concerns, it should be noted that some social media networks automatically notify members when someone else is viewing their accounts.[14] Even if such unintentional communication is generally not critical from an ethics point of view, counsel for obvious reasons prefer that the witnesses remain unaware of the fact that they are being researched. It is therefore highly advisable to turn off the auto-notify functionality, as is possible in most social networks.

The extent to which counsel can "friend" a witness or counter-party on social media platforms to obtain restricted information is a bit more delicate. The IBA Guidelines on Party Representation ('IBA Guidelines') provide in Guidelines 18 and 19 that:

> 18. Before seeking any information from a potential Witness or Expert, a Party Representative should identify himself or herself, as well as the Party he or she represents, and the reason for which the information is sought.
>
> 19. A Party Representative should make any potential Witness aware that he or she has the right to inform or instruct his or her own counsel about the contact and to discontinue the communication with the Party Representative.

While the IBA Guidelines neither apply automatically in international arbitration nor represent a set of best practices,[15] they do represent the views of the eminent members of the drafting committee as to how the integrity and fairness of arbitral proceedings can be maintained. Applying

[13] Monnat/Nichols 2015, at 10.

[14] In particular, the popular LinkedIn platform regularly sends such automatic messages.

[15] According to Guideline 1, the Guidelines shall apply where and to the extent that the Parties have so agreed, or the Arbitral Tribunal, after consultation with the Parties, wishes to rely upon them after having determined that it has the authority to rule on matters of Party representation to ensure the integrity and fairness of the arbitral proceedings.

Guidelines 18 and 19 literally, one could argue that a counsel who intends to "friend" a witness on Facebook or considers inviting her or him to join the counsel's LinkedIn network to obtain information would have to state that she or he is approaching the witness on behalf of party X and that (s)he would like to review her Facebook posts or LinkedIn profile to see if there is anything that could be used against him or her in cross-examination. Most likely a quixotic endeavour, in particular, as the IBA Guidelines seem to impose a higher standard than even some US state courts in domestic litigation.[16]

In any event, it is often unnecessary for a lawyer to "friend" an opposing witness or counter-party to obtain information available through the witnesses' social media account. Often the witnesses in the arbitration have worked together on the project that eventually turned into an arbitration during quite some time. Therefore, it is highly likely with today's proliferation of social media networks that the witnesses are already connected on various social media networks, so that there is no need for a lawyer to connect with an opposing witness during an arbitration. While the ethical constraints that would prevent counsel from contacting, i.e. "friending," an opposing witness in an arbitration would almost always apply to the counsel's agent, such as a lawyer's investigator, legal assistant, secretary and arguably also to the client (or its employees), the lawyer's client (or an employee of the client) should be able to use any information in arbitration to which it already has access. Thus, if the client or an employee of the client already has access to the opposing witnesses' social media accounts, nothing will prevent them from handing over that information to their lawyer for use in the arbitration.

The Counsel's Role in Creating Online Information

Counsel in international arbitration often advise their clients on communication matters during an arbitration. This not only includes drafting letters and emails for the client, but also advice on public communication matters. Similar to advising clients on how to reply in emails or letters, counsel should advise their clients as to how to use the Internet and in

[16] E.g. the New York City Bar Association has opined that a lawyer shall not 'friend' an unrepresented individual using 'deception'. There is no 'deception' when a lawyer utilizes her 'real name and profile' to send a 'friend' request to obtain information from an unrepresented person's social media account. The lawyer is not required to disclose the reasons for making the 'friend' request. NYCBA, Formal Op. 2010–2 (2010). See also Wicks et al., 2015, available at www.nysba.org/socialmediaguidelines (last visited 16 August 2016).

particular social media before, during and after an arbitration with the aim to shape the public or the decision makers' perception in a way that is most favourable to the clients' position in the dispute. To properly advise their clients, arbitration lawyers first will need to have a thorough understanding of how social media networks function. Second, there may be legal and ethical intricacies that have to be considered.

The first issue in this context is to what extent counsel can advise a client or witness to add new social media content. An answer can be found neither in the most common arbitration rules nor in the IBA Guidelines. The limits of advising a client with regard to posting new content on a website or in social media networks will often be governed by the local bar or ethics rules at the place where the lawyer is practicing. However, a lawyer will be able to advise and guide a client with regard to posting new content, as long as the proposed content is not known to be false or misleading by the lawyer. In particular, a lawyer will be able to advise a client to refrain from or limit social media postings during the course of the arbitration.[17]

The more difficult question may be to what extent counsel can advise a client to restrict access to or remove social media content. Again, arbitration rules are typically silent on this issue. Guideline 12 attempts to introduce a litigation hold by proposing that when the arbitral proceedings involve or are likely to involve document production, a party representative should inform the client of the need to preserve, so far as reasonably possible, documents, including electronic documents that would otherwise be deleted in accordance with a document retention policy or in the ordinary course of business. The IBA Guidelines have been heavily criticized for this attempt[18] and given the absence of an international consensus on the point, the effort to introduce a litigation hold in international arbitration has been characterized as more of a "desire by the drafters to influence counsel practice over time (. . .) rather than a duty of all counsel in international arbitration."[19]

In any event, even if a litigation hold as envisaged by IBA Guideline 12 were to apply in international arbitration – and it is the author's firm view that it does not unless there is mandatory law applicable providing the

[17] Wicks et al., 2015, p. 20, available at www.nysba.org/socialmediaguidelines (last visited 16 August 2016).

[18] See Michael E. Schneider, 'President's Message: Yet another Opportunity to Waste Time and Money on Procedural Skirmishes: The IBA Guidelines on Party Representation', (2013) 31 *ASA Bull.* at 497.

[19] See Jean-Christophe Honlet, 'The IBA Guidelines on Party Representation in International Arbitration' (2013) 30(6) *Journal of International Arbitration*, 701–709, at 706.

contrary – counsel can always advise clients to change the privacy settings or access to social media content so that it is no longer visible as long as the content is not destroyed.[20] The argument is that restricting access to certain content does not delete the content and therefore no destruction or spoliation of evidence can occur.

Internet of Things: A Game-Changer for International Commercial Arbitration in the Near Future?

The Internet of Things (IoT) has quickly ascended to be the new frontier in technology. The IoT is the network of physical devices, vehicles, buildings and other items embedded with electronics, software, sensors, actuators and network connectivity that enable these objects to collect and exchange data.[21] In 2013, the Global Standards Initiative on Internet of Things (IoT-GSI) defined the IoT as "the infrastructure of the information society."[22]

Simply put, the IoT is the concept of connecting any device with an on/off switch to the Internet (and/or to each other). This not only includes the technology industry or consumer devices such computers, cell phones, refrigerators, lamps, wearable devices and cars, but also devices in every major industry, such as utilities, warehouses, manufacturing, energy, mining, agriculture, insurance, healthcare and transports.[23] Essentially, in a few years, the IoT will include a large majority of devices or machines that are currently traded through contracts providing for arbitration as the dispute resolution mechanism. According to Cisco, the number of Internet-connected devices by 2020 will be in the magnitude of 50 billion.[24] The crucial element of the IoT is that the devices are able to communicate autonomously, i.e. without the intervention of humans. This autonomous communication will also considerably increase the data volume generated, which may be stored temporarily on the device or a local gateway but then transmitted to cloud computing platforms for further analysis and storage.

[20] This seems to be the prevailing position in domestic US litigation as long the social media content is not destroyed, see Wicks et al., 2015, p. 19, available at www.nysba.org/socialmediaguidelines (last visited 16 August 2016); Berman 2015, www.newyorklegalethics.com/counseling-a-client-to-change-herprivacy-settings-on-her-social-media-account (last visited 16 August 2016).

[21] Internet of things, www.en.wikipedia.org/w/index.php?title=Internet_of_things&oldid=734906455 (last visited 16 August 2016).

[22] Internet of Things Global Standards Initiative, ITU, available at www.itu.int/en/ITU-T/gsi/iot/Pages/default.aspx (last visited 16 August 2016).

[23] Morgan Stanley Blue Paper 2014, at 4.

[24] See www.blogs.cisco.com/news/cisco-connections-counter (last visited 16 August 2016).

It does not take a lot of imagination to predict the impact of the IoT on dispute resolution in many industries: the key issue in thousands of commercial arbitrations every year is whether a certain product is defective and, if so, who is responsible for the defect. The buyer typically alleges that the product was defective from the beginning or not fit for purpose, while the manufacturer regularly claims that the machine was not installed, used, or maintained properly, and that the alleged defect was, in any event, not timely notified. Typically, in arbitrations, much of the evidence adduced by the parties is indirect evidence, i.e. email correspondence, meeting minutes, witness testimony, and so on. In a world where the devices continuously communicate autonomously about their current status, use, maintenance, generate error logs and so forth, the evidence to be adduced in arbitrations will change radically. It will become a simple task for the party in possession of the data generated to prove whether a certain device has been used according to specification or whether it has been maintained as proscribed by the manufacturer.[25] Equally, it will become difficult for a manufacturer to claim that it was not aware of a certain defect. One can also imagine situations in which a buyer that wants to prove a systemic defect in a certain device or gross negligence would like to obtain access to all data generated by devices sold to other customers to find failure patterns.

Access to the data generated will become key in this scenario. Typically, the devices that generate data will have limited storage capacity and the data centres with which the devices communicate may or may not store the data long term. The matter becomes more complicated in this instance, as much of the data generated will not be "human-readable" and will thus require specific software tools to be read and expert advice to be analyzed.

However, these issues already exist in modern arbitration in the context of document production. Whether or not the scope of document production is going to expand remains to be seen. While one can imagine that there will be attempts by counsel to add data generated by the IoT to the traditional document requests, one can only hope that robust tribunals will preserve the efficiency of the process and be able to limit document production to the data generated by the IoT. This is because the data will often be readily available and – depending on the allegations – the most relevant and material to the outcome of the dispute. This shift from indirect and difficult to obtain evidence to readily available direct

25 Already today, car manufactures such as Tesla are in a position to download and analyze the complete vehicle logs from the car in case of a crash or an allegation of a defect.

evidence will result in significantly lower cost of arbitration. The lower transaction costs will result in more disputes being able to be resolved through arbitration that would otherwise simply have been settled (or not been pursued at all). It is thus to be expected that the total number of arbitrations is going to increase with the advent of the IoT while the costs of arbitrating these disputes is going to decrease.

Conclusion

Through traditional web searches alone, advocates can often find invaluable information for their case preparation. However, the most valuable information for counsel is often to be found in the so-called deep web, i.e. the part of the Internet that is not indexed by common search engines. This includes, among other sources, social media content. Obtaining information through social media may create ethical issues, which advocates have to be aware of, but most often these concerns can be taken care of with some careful planning. In particular, there is often no need for counsel (or their clients) to create new connections (i.e. to "friend") with (adverse) witnesses, but very often the client itself or employees of the client are already connected with witnesses through social media and can therefore provide access to information available.

Counsel often also play a role in advising their clients in creating appropriate online information before or during a dispute. In particular, a lawyer will often be able to advise a client to refrain from or to limit social media postings during the course of the arbitration. Also, counsel can always advise clients to change the privacy settings or access to social media content so that it is no longer visible as long as the content is not destroyed.

The IoT is to be considered as a game-changer in the not-so distant future of international arbitration. The IoT will shift the focus from indirect evidence such as email correspondence, meeting minutes and witness statements to more direct evidence or data collected by the devices or machines itself. This readily available evidence will reduce the transaction costs of arbitrating disputes, which will result in more disputes being resolved through arbitration. In this context, access to the data generated by the devices will become key. Those counsel who understand how to deal with and interpret these data will have a competitive edge over the others.

12

Conclusion

MAUD PIERS AND CHRISTIAN ASCHAUER

> The future is here, it's just not evenly distributed yet.
>
> W. Gibson

The authors in this book explored how and under which conditions technology can, could or should be used to enhance and ultimately transform arbitration. They identified the issues that arbitration practitioners will encounter during the various stages of digitalization. It is self-evident that the pace with which digitalization sets in and the nature of the ICTs employed may differ contingent on the commercial context concerned. This is also clear from how this topic has been covered by legal scholarship to a varying degree depending on the parties involved. In fact, until quite recently, the focus of legal research on the interface between arbitration and technology was on the different forms of so-called Online Arbitration or OArb. OArb is a term used to describe arbitral proceedings that are, to a more or lesser extent, conducted online.[1] The context

[1] E. Katsh, 'Online Dispute Resolution: The Next Phase', (2002) 7(2) *Lex Electronica*; H. Yu & M. Nasir, 'Can Online Arbitration Exist within the Traditional Arbitration Framework?', (2003) 20 *Journal of International Arbitration*; G. Kaufmann-Kohler & T. Schulz, *Online Dispute Resolution: Challenges for Contemporary Justice* (Kluwer Law International, 2004); S. Kallel, 'Online Arbitration', (2008) 25 *Journal of International Arbitration*, 345–353; C. Rule, 'Making Peace on eBay: Resolving Disputes in the World's Largest Marketplace', (2008) *Conflict Resolution Quarterly*, Association for Conflict Resolution 1–10; P. Stylianou, 'Online Dispute Resolution: The Case for a Treaty Between the United States and the European Union in Resolving Cross-Border E-Commerce Disputes' (2008) 36 *Syracuse Journal of International Law and Communication* 117; J. Hörnle, 'Encouraging Online Alternative Dispute Resolution in the EU and Beyond', (2013) 38 *European Law Review* 187–208; Hörnle, Cross-border Internet Dispute Resolution, (2009) 4 *Web Journal of Current Legal Issues*; U. Kacker & T. Saluja, 'Online Arbitration for Resolving E-Commerce Disputes: Gateway to the Future', (2014) *International Journal of Arbitration Law* 31–44; G. Brian Hutchinson, 'Ten things you wanted to know about the European ODR Regulation (but were too afraid to ask)', (2015) *Journal of Technology in International Arbitration*.

of these studies was mostly that of business-to-consumer (B2C) disputes. Some interesting and important questions arose here that go to the very core of arbitration. These questions are dealt with by the authors Schmitz, Cortés and Cole throughout their discussion on OArb in the United States and Europe, respectively. These authors demonstrate how B2C dispute resolution continues to lead the way with its innovating tools (e.g. automated decision-making) and more advanced legal framework. Evidently, some useful lessons can be drawn that are relevant for arbitration in general, as well as the business-to-business (B2B) context in particular. Our research shows, however, that the B2B arbitration community has been rather hesitant in welcoming the trend of digitalization. Nevertheless, the growing presence of e-arbitration, which is a general term used to loosely indicate that arbitration is colliding with the digital world, can no longer be ignored. E-arbitration is a development that takes a slow but definite course with every new technological tool that the arbitration community embraces.

Thus, we do see a measured but steady change in the recent years. When setting up this book project in 2015, we were convinced that it was time to have a forward look at the use of technology in arbitration. Today, two years down the road, we realize that some of the concerns that lay at the origin of this book project have become, although not yet quite mainstream, clearly subjects of today's broader legal discourse.

One of these concerns was the fact that, in spite of the growing digitalization of dispute resolution, ICTs have not yet had a revolutionary impact on the quality of arbitration. While the overwhelming majority of arbitration practitioners use ICTs on a day-to-day basis, this is still limited to a functional integration of the most common means of technology, such as email, phone/video conferencing, e-filing, live transcription of hearings, and so on. As indicated by Nappert and Cohen, these technological advances undoubtedly facilitate the immediacy of communication and access to information. However, they do not go as far as to assist a tribunal's capacity to sift through information, digest it, and use it to inform its decision-making. As shown by various authors in this book, although there are many ICTs that could be useful to upgrade the arbitration procedure, today, they are not applied to their full extent. Meanwhile, the time and costs of arbitral proceedings are on the rise. For the 'customers' of the arbitration industry, namely the parties, this is all the more disappointing, as they expect a dispute resolution mechanism that lives up to the standards of virtual mobility and connectivity that they are used to in their day-to-day dealings. The liquid expectations paradigm, described by Wahab and Katsh, certainly plays here as well. In addition, one of the biggest challenges in (traditional commercial) arbitration is the fact that arbitrators often have to process a vast trove of written and oral data within a reasonable amount of time in order to come to a legitimate decision. Arbitration laws certainly build in mechanisms that deal with an arbitrator's shortcomings when processing this information, such as his or her fallibility in recollection (e.g. by requiring arbitrators to answer all issues submitted) or a potential cognitive bias (e.g. by requiring arbitrators to be impartial and independent). However, we believed it worth to explore whether these human shortcomings could perhaps be more efficiently dealt with by technology.

A second concern that inspired this book was the realization that awareness should be raised amongst arbitration practitioners regarding the risks and the potential of a virtually connected (legal) community as well as an increasingly digitalized arbitration procedure and legal practice. Many is the arbitration practitioner that is welded to his or her smartphone and is prominently present on social media, but that does not have even the slightest clue of the extent of security issues involved in the day-to-day (and even private) use of these acquired technological applications. Schaumann and Burger-Scheidlin point out a number of security issues and only confirm how important it is that bridges are built between the worlds of arbitration and information technologies. Veit demonstrates how counsel in arbitration should not only be made aware of the risks, but also be taught about the growing opportunities of technology for counsel strategies. Caution is, however, urged when 'treasure diving' the Internet, deep web or the Internet of Things. A number of (oftentimes ethical) boundaries should not be crossed. Bassiri explains this very well when discussing the novel dimension of social media that evokes the need for new standards on the arbitrators' and parties' online behaviour. These issues also illustrate how the law keeps lagging behind technology.

This brings us to a third important reason behind this book. It is evident that many questions (will) arise when the framework of arbitration, which is designed for offline arbitration and human arbitrators, is applied to a digitalized arbitration procedure and – when taking it a step further, artificial intelligence (AI) or robot arbitration. With a few exceptions, such as the ones pointed out by Van Hooft and Kroes, even the most modern arbitration laws did not feel the need to regulate the digitalization of arbitration, let alone reckon with the advent of an AI arbitrator. However, in light of the dramatic advances in technology and AI, we can no longer afford to ignore the fact that we must be prepared to set up a regulatory framework that deals with this revolutionary form of dispute resolution. It has been forecasted that, perhaps at this stage still premature, laws that regulate AI arbitration would be necessary to 'minimise the hazards that tend to accompany consequential change'.[2] Moreover, the absence of adequate laws may slow down the trend of digitalization, as was illustrated by Wolff with regard to digital arbitral awards and to a lesser extent digital arbitration agreements. This issue also begs the question of who should regulate and what the role should be of the arbitration institutions in supporting and regulating the use of technology in arbitration. Schaefer critically examines the role that arbitration institutions currently play or should take up in the future. In spite of the clear expertise present in these institutions, he calls for caution (cobbler, stick to your last!) and indicates that an arbitration institution should not offer technology unless there is a clear demand from the parties (who, in the end, are the ones paying the bills).

Despite the hesitance toward applying or developing ICTs, we believe that parties and their counsel will be the most important drivers for development and change. Their hesitance may, to a certain extent, have been justified. Moving arbitration online certainly affects the essence of arbitration as a dispute resolution mechanism and the role of the (human) counsel and arbitrator. What should be maintained, though, is that justice is served: procedural due process should be guaranteed and the result should be a legitimate arbitral award. Yet, the question no longer is whether the wave of digitalization will hit the arbitration community, as this seems inevitable, but rather when it will start showing effect, what its intensity will be, and how the arbitration community should deal with it in order to benefit. This all leads us to conclude that there is an urgent need to explore the opportunities and challenges of the use of technology in arbitration and to stimulate debate amongst practitioners on this topic. If we want to stay ahead of the game, now is the time to analyze the status quo and to embark on an informed speculation as to what the future may bring.

There are clearly different perspectives to the study of how technology could be used as a means to optimize efficiency in the arbitration procedure. First of all, there is the perspective of parties and their counsel. The emphasis here lies on the question how technology can be used to improve the efficiency of and strategies adopted in an arbitration without jeopardizing the legitimacy and quality of the process and the parties' right of due process? The technological tools that have, so far, had a great impact mainly facilitate communication as well as the retrieval and

[2] See www.youngicca-blog.com/machine-arbitration-and-machine-arbitrators.

exchange of information. Secondly, there is the perspective of the arbitrator. This perspective entails a challenge to think out of the box and to examine whether and under what conditions a technology-assisted or even technology-based arbitration could be more effective than the traditional human driven equivalent. AI is key and could have a truly transformative impact on decision-making. A third perspective is a legal theory perspective and pertains to the question that inevitably overarches these two main issues, namely how do the use of technology and the fundamental principles underlying arbitration coincide? This perspective calls for an evaluation of the fundamentals of arbitration.

In this book, the authors assessed and predicted a number of transformations that highlight these three perspectives. In what follows, we will draw on the authors' analyses of these developments to formulate a number of conclusions. The three perspectives will guide us in illustrating the slowly moving trend toward the digitalization of arbitration and in identifying certain legal and operational concerns that go along with this trend.

Arbitration 2.0: Upgrading the Arbitration Procedure

The authors of this book have given a critical assessment of the trend of digitalization of the arbitration procedure. They provided us with relevant data on the current and potential degree of utilization of modern technological tools and software applications. Moreover, they gave a highly insightful perspective on the legal context within which a technology-driven arbitration procedure could move forward. In what follows, we will highlight some of these developments, balance, once again, the human factor and the electronic element in the arbitration process, and place a number of warning signs along this road to virtualization.

Communication is front and centre for each court and arbitration procedure. Therefore, communication technology is the obvious starting point. It is therefore obvious that a change of communication technologies will also have a huge impact on the organization and conduct of these proceedings. The book has at various occasions indicated how written electronic communication oozed its way into the daily legal and arbitration practice without causing any noteworthy revolution. Conversely, a technology that has a greater transformative impact on the arbitral process is video-conferencing. Our Survey showed that the use of video-conferencing has become quite a prominently used means of communication in arbitration. This calls for a reflection on the bearing hereof on the arbitration actors' sense of participation, on the parties' rights of defence, and on the accuracy of the arbitrators' assessment of the presented information. The newest generation of high-definition video-conferencing tools provides as clear a picture of a participant on the screen as we would get if we were sitting right next to him or her in the hearing room. In the view of Nappert and Cohen, it is, therefore, no longer tenable to object that one cannot process a witness's non-verbal and subliminal cues. In addition, the use of video-conferencing may greatly reduce the costs of the proceedings and thus increase the opportunity for parties to participate. This is said to be the upside of the use of other technologies as well, such as modern translation devices that may also help to overcome language barriers.

Can we therefore go so far as to expect that video-conferences will gradually replace in-person meetings, including hearings for the taking of evidence? And will the consequence of these developments amount to arbitration being more readily available for new categories of customers, and thus, at increasing access to justice? Or, will a required high level of sophistication (think of the more sophisticated option of virtual reality) come at too high a cost and therewith rather exclude a class of parties? One should, in this context, be vigilant to the requirements of due process that call for equality of the parties and a sufficient opportunity to present their case. One could also wonder whether the right to a hearing is not considered to be an important aspect of due process. A hearing that is conducted in virtual reality could call into question whether this right has been respected. Waiver of this right must generally be made in an unequivocal manner and not run counter to any important public interest.[3] One could wonder whether a mere reference to arbitration rules that provide for virtual arbitration is sufficient to waive this right.

Another dimension of communication is the Internet and social media. In recent years, the way in which the protagonists of arbitral proceedings get to know each other has reached a whole new level. Many professionals are on LinkedIn and other social media. It is only natural that these sources are effectively used to acquaint oneself with parties, counsel and possible arbitrators. To deal with this new situation in an adequate way, Bassiri recommends certain common-sense guidelines. First of all, they should separate the use and accessibility of the social media profiles between professional and private social media networks (e.g. LinkedIn for exclusive professional use and Facebook for exclusive private use). In addition, they

[3] *Håkansson and Sturesson* v. *Sweden* 15/1988/159/215, A171-A, European Court of Human Rights 1990, para. 66.

should restrict access to their private profile by making requisite changes to the privacy settings, limiting their online identity to only recognized known individuals. Moreover, arbitrators should refrain from making a selection of professional arbitration-related connections and be as open as possible. It speaks for itself that, pending an arbitration, the arbitrator should refrain from any activity on social media networks that could be put in connection with a counsel or fellow arbitrator involved in a specific arbitration matter. In creating a profile, an arbitrator should not be tempted to make more available than what is visible on his or her publicly available *curriculum vitae*, mostly uploaded on the website of the arbitrator's law firm and databases of arbitration institutions. The same advice applies to speaking engagements and publications.

Furthermore, the Internet, if it is used wisely, is also a treasure trove of factual information. It is therefore not surprising that counsel are routinely researching the Internet. This can be done with more or less expertise, leading to a huge difference for the client. As Veit has demonstrated, research over the Internet is a new field not only of activity, but also of responsibility. In this regards, the so-called surface web or visible web is only a small fraction of the total content available on the Internet. The deep web – the part of the Internet that cannot be accessed by search engines – is several orders of magnitude larger than the surface web. However, it is the advent of the Internet of Things that will effectively transform dispute resolution as a whole, including arbitration. According to Cisco, the number of Internet-connected devices by 2020 will be in the magnitude of 50 billion. In a world where devices communicate autonomously about their current status, use, maintenance, generate error logs and so on, we will have a clear record about historic facts. It will become a simple task for the party in possession of the data to prove whether a certain device has been used according to specification or whether it has been maintained as proscribed by the manufacturer, among others. This may lead to displacement or minimal use of oral evidence. On the one hand, this may also narrow down the scope of legal controversies, because the historic facts are all on record and undisputable. On the other hand, we may expect more disputes as to who has access to the data generated by the Internet of Things and who is responsible for storage (or lack of storage).

Finally, the analysis put forward by Wolff shows how the issuance of electronic awards is an aspect of arbitration where clarity and even some level of international regulation is desired. Many law systems already make it possible to sign and notify awards electronically in a legally valid way. More problematic is what happens on an international level, namely at the state courts of the country where the award will have to be enforced. Even if the *lex arbitri* makes it possible to issue electronic awards, it is by no means certain that the state court of the country where the debtor has assets will acknowledge electronic documents. Therefore, it may remain the practice for arbitration institutions and arbitral tribunals to issue hard copies of the award that are undersigned by the members of the arbitral tribunal (with authenticated signatures), and subsequently notified by postal services. Thus, the award will remain a piece of hard copy for some time to come.

Nevertheless, one should evaluate the value of current formal enforcement mechanisms in light of the growing number of alternative mechanisms that ensure compliance with awards. The B2B arbitration community could learn from the example of B2C arbitration where accreditation (trustmark) systems are used. Another interesting technique is used in sports arbitration, where non-compliance with awards can be sanctioned through penalties or even the relegation to a lower league. These private enforcement mechanisms are tested on a broader level as well. Certain arbitral institutions (the Centre of Arbitration and Mediation of the Chamber of Commerce Brazil-Canada) disclose the names of parties that do not comply with their awards. This is a private enforcement mechanism that we also encounter in other sector arbitrations. The downside of all these private enforcement mechanisms is, of course, that they are not directly subject to the control of state courts. In other words, they may compel a party to comply with an award that would not deserve recognition and enforcement by state courts. Even though the enforcement of awards primarily remains the prerogative of state courts, research into this development is becoming imperative.

Artificial Intelligence: Upgrading the Arbitrator

One of the most prominent issues of the immediate future will be whether ICTs will also transform the process of decision-making, the deliberation process that is at the heart of the mission of the arbitrators. While it is almost common ground that deliberations can be done by videoconferences, the real issue that we see coming is if, and to what extent, the arbitral tribunal may use AI for decision-making.

AI is the theory and development of computer systems that learn how to competently perform cognitive functions that we intuitively associate with human minds, such as decision-making, speech recognition and visual perception.[4] The functionality of AI thus even goes beyond that of algorithms. Algorithms operate much like decision trees set up by humans, wherein the resolution to a problem can be broken down to a string of binary choices requiring consideration of variables.[5] AI is said to be self-learning because by performing pre-programmed tasks, an AI improves its own performance without human intervention. As has been pointed out by Nappert and Cohen, AI could be used in arbitration to sift through the applicable law more thoroughly, assess the credibility of witness evidence more accurately and generate, in record time, a reasoned (and possibly more objective) decision that takes into account and cross-references all data pertaining to the dispute. An AI arbitrator thus has the potential to directly and significantly improve the quality of decision-making, time and cost efficiency, as well as throw a new light on this frequently debated issue.[6] Nappert and Cohen, Wahab and Katsh, as well as Schmitz have sufficiently shown that AI in arbitration is no longer an imaginary tale.

Much to the contrary, on the current trajectory, it is conceivable that an AI may function as an arbitrator within the next decade. AI has already begun to do the jobs of white-collar professionals, for instance in the medical sector. Nappert and Cohen referred to IBM's Dr Watson. More recently, AI also clearly caught the attention of the legal sector. In 2016, tens of

[4] See 38th International Conference on Data Protection and Privacy Commissioners, 2016, pg. 18–19; C. Steiner, *Automate This: How Algorithms Came to Rule our World* (Penguin Books, 2012).

[5] Steiner, Ibid.

[6] M. E. Schneider, 'Lean Arbitration: Cost Control and Efficiency through Progressive Identification of Issues and Separate Pricing of Arbitration Services', (1994) 10(2) *Arbitration International* 119–140; M. Gaudet, *Improving International Arbitration: The Need for Speed, Liber Amicorum* (ICC Publishing, 1998); P. Berger, 'The Need for Speed in International Arbitration', (2008) 5(25) *Journal of International Arbitration*; D. J. A. Cairns, 'Oral Advocacy and Time Control in International Arbitration', in *Arbitration Advocacy in Changing Times* (Kluwer Law International, 2011); I. Welser, 'Efficiency – Today's Challenge in Arbitration Proceedings,' (2014) *Austrian Yearbook on International Arbitration*, 151–166; J. Graves, 'Essay: Leveraging Technology for more Cost-Effective Arbitration of Cross-Border Commercial Disputes: An Introduction to the Range of Possibilities with a Focus on MSMEs', (2015) 35 *Journal of Technology In International Arbitration*; D. E. Gonzalez and M. C. Carmona, e.a., 'Controlling the Rising Costs in Arbitration: Where Technology Can Help (and Where It Can't)', (2015) 1 *Journal of Technology In International Arbitration*; J. Kirby, 'Efficiency in International Arbitration: Whose Duty Is It?', (2015) Journal of International Arbitration; A. V. Schläpfer & M. Paralika, 'Striking the Right Balance: The Roles of Arbitral Institutions, Parties and Tribunals in Achieving Efficiency in International Arbitration', (2015) 2(2) *BCDR International Arbitration Review*; M. Dunmore, 'Increased Efficiency and Lower Cost in Arbitration: Sole Member Tribunals', (2015) 4(1) *Indian Journal of Arbitration Law*, 27–33.

global law firms announced their use of AI to increase the efficiency of legal tasks.[7] AI is quicker and more thorough than lawyers at contract review,[8] legal research,[9] drafting legal documents[10] and 'e-discovery'[11] An example of such an AI paralegal is ROSS,[12] built on IBM's Watson computer. A related AI application is one within the judicial profession. In 2014, an AI system was designed that predicted verdicts of the individual justices of the US Supreme Court across 7,700 cases with 70.9 per cent accuracy, compared to leading academics' accuracy rate of 59 per cent.[13] Likewise in October 2016, an AI was developed that predicted verdicts of the European Court of Human Rights with 79 per cent accuracy.[14] The system of having AI rather than an attorney or judge wade through thousands of papers has also been explored and made operational in other areas of the law, such as in the context of investment investigations and more particularly merger and acquisition due diligence.[15] Of particular interest here is also the current application of AI in online dispute resolution (ODR). Schmitz brought up a foremost example in this regard, namely Modria. Modria is an ODR provider that handles cases including B2C e-commerce, divorce and landlord-tenant disputes. It offers several ODR processes, including online arbitration.

In spite of these promising developments, there is a foreseeable resistance against AI from the arbitration community. Undoubtedly, where the interest in, resistance against and use for AI in arbitration is concerned, there is an obvious distinction between B2C and B2B. Whilst in limited types of small-value cases, automated decision-making is already functional, as was shown by Schmitz, the B2B camp expresses particular concern and even shows resistance to the idea of giving up human

[7] See www.ft.com/content/5d96dd72–83eb-11e6–8897–2359a58ac7a5.

[8] See beagle.ai. [9] See www.casetext.com.

[10] See www.allenovery.com/news/en-gb/articles/Pages/AllenOvery-and-Deloitte-tackle-OTC-derivatives-market-challenge.aspx.

[11] See www.zylab.com/blog/id/294/how-artificial-intelligence-can-optimize-your-ediscovery-process#.

[12] See www.rossintelligence.com.

[13] D. M. Katz, M. J. Bommarito II & J. Blackman, *Predicting the Behaviour of the Supreme Court of the United States: A General Approach*, 2014.

[14] N. Aletras, D. Tsarapatsanis, D. Preoţiuc-Pietro & V. Lampos, 'Predicting Judicial Decisions of the European Court of Human Rights: A Natural Language Processing Perspective', (2016) 2:e93 *Peer J Computer Science*.

[15] See www.canadianbusiness.com/investing/artificial-intelligence-due-diligence-risk-management; www.kirasystems.com/how-it-works/due-diligence; www.ravn.co.uk/products/extract/legal-automated-due-diligence; www.umiacs.umd.edu/˜oard/desi5/additional/Klaber.pdf; www.mergertechnology.com/security/artificial-intelligence-merger-acquisition-due-diligence-3662.

decision-making.[16] It is all the more relevant to address this resistance, especially because, as we already pointed out on several occasions, the arbitration practitioners are the crucial drivers of innovation and change. We believe the resistance may have to do with a number of factors.

First, there is the nature of the dispute resolution business. Unlike in B2C e-commerce disputes, B2B disputes are often of high value and more money is at stake for the parties. Arbitrators may resist embracing technology that could replace the role of human arbitrators, as it could put them out of their jobs. There might also be opposition from arbitration institutions that are set up to administer proceedings with human arbitrators. Secondly, and alongside this perceived threat, parties in B2B disputes traditionally rely on legal representatives that are often more acutely aware of essential due process norms, which, if breached, may provide grounds for annulment or non-enforcement of an award. Indeed, a number of concerns with regard to due process may arise in the event that an AI arbitrator operates under today's legal arbitration framework. These concerns have never been effectively addressed (neither in the B2C context). This may explain the 'justifiable' distrust. Thirdly, and further to this fear of the later annulment or non-enforcement of awards in processes led by technology, there is simply the fact of unfamiliarity. This factor is confirmed by the survey results, where there appeared to be no indication whatsoever that the survey participants had an awareness of AI software that could take over any part of the argumentation or decision-making process. A basic lack of knowledge and comfort with innovation and an insufficient awareness of the risks and possibilities involved thus lie at the basis of this resistance. This all shows that if the concept of AI arbitration is to gain momentum in the wider field of arbitration, meticulous prior legal evaluation and proper guidance is essential.

We see a large number of issues that would need to be addressed and that will have a great effect on the current legal framework within which arbitration functions. A first set of issues relate to the role, identity of and the requirements imposed on an AI arbitrator. These issues all stem from the fact that the current arbitration laws depart from the assumption that an arbitrator is a human being with a unique identity, a nationality, a number of qualifications, and a potential risk of predisposition toward a case or a party. The IBA Guidelines on Conflict of Interests cast doubt on the impartiality of an arbitrator, for instance, when there are more than two

[16] R. H. Smit, 'The Future of Science and Technology in International Arbitration: The Next Thirty Years', in S. Brekoulakis, J. Lew and L. Mistells eds. *Evolution and Future of International Arbitration* (Kluwer Law International, 2016).

previous appointments of that arbitrator by the same party or its affiliates in the past three years. This may be problematic where an AI arbitrator could (and to be economically viable should be able to) replace human arbitrators in a multitude of cases that may concern the same party or parties. How can we exclude that the self-learning functions of AI form a hidden predisposition? Question marks could also be placed next to the current 'intuitu personae' appointment of an arbitrator, which entails that arbitrators must fulfil their mandate personally without delegation to a third party. One could wonder whether a tribunal's use of an AI constitutes an acceptable delegation of its functions. Underlying these issues is of course the central question on the extent to which technology can replace human decision-making in arbitration. Could an AI be a final decision-maker or do the aforementioned considerations lead to the conclusion that, if anything, an AI ought to be an assistant to a human tribunal?

The advent of a non-human AI arbitrator will evidently also have a major effect on the arbitration procedure and more particularly the decision-making process itself. The AI arbitrator comes to its decision as a result of a deliberate 'thinking process'. The fact that an algorithm must be programmed to factor in a number of considerations that lie at the basis of a legitimate arbitral award calls for decisive action in response to a second set of legal questions. This will, for instance, resuscitate the interesting discussion on the sources of law (and/or equity) that an arbitrator should rely on and on the *iura novit curia* theorem.

Thirdly, there is a group of issues concerning the role of human intervention in an AI arbitration. The fact that arbitration is conducted under the direction of an AI does not necessarily mean that any human intervention, for instance, by a human arbitrator, the courts or an arbitration institution, should be ruled out. This raises questions on the specific role of these interveners as well as on the legal relationships in an AI arbitration. In a traditional institutional arbitration procedure, there are five relationships present, namely, party-arbitrator, arbitrator-arbitrator (if more than one arbitrator has been appointed), arbitrator-institution, parties-institution and party-party. It will be important to establish how these relationships (and the respective parties' liability) will transfer when working with an AI in arbitration, since the parties and the institution would have a relationship with the legal entity that represents the AI and (probably) not with the AI arbitrator.[17] Research on these issues should lead to

[17] B. Warwas, *The Liability of Arbitral Institutions: Legitimacy Challenges and Functional Responses*, (T.M.C. Asser Press, 2016).

suggestions on adapting the law or proposing rules in order to get ahead of the potential problems that may arise and to allow the arbitration process to optimally benefit from technological progress.

Rethinking the Fundamentals of Arbitration

It is time to accept that we are slowly arriving at a defining point where technology in arbitration may go from merely utilitarian to truly transformative. This development could lead to a dramatically reshaped arbitration landscape where the role and reach, and even the current business model of many arbitration protagonists will need to be reconsidered. This is certainly true for the arbitration institutions. Will they go through the same development that is presently affecting banks, where day-to-day businesses have moved online and electronic banking has become the norm? Schaefer points out that arbitral institutions will in that case presumably become Internet Service Providers with all the special statutory duties in regard to personal data and intellectual property, as well as the contractual duties toward parties regarding 24/7 system availability, data integrity and data authenticity.

We believe, as has been indicated by the participants in the survey, that arbitral institutions could be truly instrumental for the promotion of the use of ICTs. They have the necessary expertise to, at least, give input in the development of supplementary technologies that can be used to conduct arbitration online. These technologies should include professional videoconferencing, secure and data-integrity-preserving communications, and the basic know-how required for so-called e-briefs. This might not only make arbitration more cost-efficient, and thus be in the interest of all, but also allow the arbitration institutions to tap into a new arbitration market. The administration of (tens of thousands of) small claims can be an attractive new field of activity, especially if this is combined with new procedures that make it possible to deal with uncontested claims in an expedited way. This is all the more so in those jurisdictions where the state court system is too slow or too expensive. Finally, and quite importantly for the development of the law, these developments might perhaps lead to a new wave of transparency. This can already be felt inasmuch as the ICC Court of Arbitration, the Chamber of Arbitration of Milan and VIAC have begun to publish the names of arbitrators. Awards and procedural orders that are already published in redacted versions can be made accessible in electronic format. This will help to establish practices and to promote uniform standards and the predictability of decisions. The interest in our work demonstrated by CEPANI and VIAC and their support prove that arbitral institutions are starting to become aware of the challenges and chances which lie ahead.

Technological developments also increase the pressure on counsel and arbitrators to upgrade their practices. Attorneys feel the pressure of competition most directly and have the closest contact with clients. Therefore, they have always had quite an incentive to look for the most cost- and time-efficient solutions, and have, comparatively speaking, always appeared the most technology ready. They have been the first to take full advantage of modern presentation techniques, and to make extensive use of databases and the Internet to increase the quality (and sometimes also the volume) of legal submissions. With these opportunities come responsibilities. New areas of responsibility emerge as counsel will have to advise their clients as to how to use the Internet, and in particular social media, before, during and after an arbitration. Furthermore, law firms will have to expect a profound impact on the level of remuneration if considerable parts of the work can or must be left to computers. The traditional business model of firms, where associates and younger partners produce huge numbers of billable hours by conducting legal research, document inspection, translations and so on, will not be accepted by clients who are themselves in the process of implementing AI in their working processes.[18]

For the arbitrators, technological development will add an extra layer of responsibility. In addition to their traditional roles as legal experts, communicators and wise people, they will become dispute resolution engineers who work with different technological tools for different cases. In the end, however, they will always have to guarantee the fairness and integrity of the process. As such, they may also have to protect the parties from new technologies that are not compatible with due process.

Finally, the role and position of the courts should be reassessed. One could expect that the courts would at a certain point need technical schooling to understand how an arbitration procedure came about and to assess whether it complies with the standard of a fair and equitable process. Moreover, one could wonder whether the courts will be expected to do the same kind of judicial review of the award when rendered by an AI rather than a human arbitrator.

Evidently, the assessed and predicted transformations, and especially the revolutionary advent of the AI arbitrator, might go to the very core of arbitration. That is why we believe that a positive law approach in which

[18] R. Susskind, *Tomorrow's Lawyers* (Oxford University Press, 2013).

we merely rethink some of the rules does not go far enough. We should also embark on a theory of arbitration approach[19] and dare to rethink some of the fundamentals of arbitration. One such a fundamental feature of arbitration is the traditional divide between ad hoc and institutional arbitration. This binary arbitration landscape might have to be rethought when introducing online tools and even more so with the advent of the AI arbitrator as a new player. It is for instance not yet certain who will and should operate the AI arbitrator. Will law firms/software companies operate the AI arbitrator themselves and in essence replace the traditional arbitration institutions? A contrasting view that was hinted at by Wahab and Katsh is that the introduction of AI into arbitration would mean the end of ad hoc arbitration, since arguably, an online arbitration cannot be ad hoc as it requires a central administrator to enable use of technology. In his foreword to this book, Dirk De Meulemeester indicates that it is not unthinkable that in the foreseeable future one no longer speaks of institutional versus ad hoc arbitration, but rather distinguishes human and AI arbitration.

Note that it will not be sufficient to rethink the fundamental principles that underpin the arbitration procedure. It is also important to reevaluate and redefine a number of terms and phrases that are now currently used in the arbitration context and in the law. An already well-established example is the word document. As Van Hooft and Kroes indicated, laws are gradually modifying their arbitration laws to include a wider range of data carriers in this concept. A further digitalization of the arbitration procedure will call for the same exercise with a number of other terms, such as seat of arbitration, meeting, tribunal, and so on.

This reevaluation exercise should be done with the necessary caution and consideration. When questioning the pertinence and durability of certain laws, principles, as well as legal terms and concepts in view of (potential) technological and other evolutions, one should strive for a framework within which a digitalized arbitration procedure can be facilitated without compromising due process.

* * *

Some Final Thoughts . . .

There is no longer doubt that the time is ripe for a marriage between arbitration and technology. Clearly, this would not be based on love at first

[19] As some notable scholars have done before us, see for example E. Gaillard, *Legal Theory of International Arbitration* (Martinus Nijhoff Publishers, 2010).

sight. However, a rational marriage could work very well, provided that such an arrangement is made keeping in mind the very specific goal that it serves. This goal is, of course, improving the quality of the decision-making process as well as providing better access to justice to the parties involved. Out of its nature, arbitration is marked by a number of qualities that fill in a specific need, but that are at the same time, arbitration's Achilles' heel and may thus undermine its effectiveness. For instance, an arbitration procedure's flexibility and private character could lead to unpredictability. Furthermore, the freedom of parties to appoint expert arbitrators and to set up a tailor-made procedure, which takes place in a neutral forum and outside the (state-sponsored) court system, may come at a high cost. There is thus still some room for improvement. Both the tech enthusiasts and sceptics cannot but agree that technology could play a much bigger role in arbitration than it has so far and that one at least should explore its potential of increasing cost-efficiency, predictability and speed.

Arbitration has been courted by technology long enough to be given a fair shot at making this partnership work. However, some clear parameters should be set to make this partnership work. We already mentioned due process, but also party autonomy should be guaranteed. Arbitration is at its best when allowed to operate freely. This could have some unforeseen consequences when technology takes up a more prominent role. Although the advent of technology will cater to various needs in the dispute resolution business, it could also result in a fragmentation of the (domestic and international) arbitration landscape. We might see a proliferation of arbitration variants. On one end of the spectrum, there will be the traditional arbitration procedure, conducted face to face and entirely under the control of human minds. On the other end, we will find totally automated processes. This broad range of options may lead to an extraordinarily intriguing paradox: arbitration might no longer be needed as a dispute resolution mechanism when parties become aware of the potential of AI and automated processes, for instance, to predict the outcome and duration of a procedure with a very reasonable degree of likelihood. We already see that such algorithms (like Legalist) are applied by insurers and third-party financers to decide whether a case should go to the arbitral tribunal or to the state court (predictive justice). If these devices become more popular, we may expect rising settlement rates and a decreasing caseload.

The advance of technology may thus bring about quite a change. Part of our legal work may become redundant. However, intelligence has many facets and thus human arbitrators and arbitration practitioners will have to distinguish themselves from robots. This is a trend that is predicted, not only for arbitration, but for the legal profession as such. Although, this should lead to improvement and solve many defined problems, it is certain that technology will open up a whole new area of ethical and regulatory challenges. Evidently, the future belongs to those who embrace these challenges with human intelligence.

INDEX

www.ingramcontent.com/pod-product-compliance
Lightning Source LLC
LaVergne TN
LVHW011527200926
848484LV00001B/172
9781108417907